Kaplan Publishing are constantly finding new ways to make a difference to your studies and our exciting online resources really do offer something different to students looking for exam success.

This book comes with free MyKaplan online resources so that you can study anytime, anywhere. **This free online resource is not sold separately and is included in the price of the book.**

Having purchased this book, you have access to the following online study materials:

CONTENT	ACCA (including FBT, FMA, FFA)		FIA (excluding FBT, FMA, FFA)	
	Text	Kit	Text	Kit
Electronic version of the book	✓	✓	✓	✓
Knowledge checks with instant answers	✓		✓	
Material updates	✓	✓	✓	✓
Latest official ACCA exam questions*		✓		
Pocket Notes (digital copy)	✓		✓	
Study Planner	✓			
Progress Test including questions and answers	✓		✓	
Syllabus recap Videos		✓		✓
Revision Planner		✓		✓
Question Debrief and Walkthrough Videos		✓		
Mock Exam including questions and answers		✓		

* Excludes BT, MA, FA, FBT, FMA, FFA; for all other papers includes a selection of questions, as released by ACCA

How to access your online resources

Received this book as part of your Kaplan course?
If you have a MyKaplan account, your full online resources will be added automatically, in line with the information in your course confirmation email. If you've not used MyKaplan before, you'll be sent an activation email once your resources are ready.

Bought your book from Kaplan?
We'll automatically add your online resources to your MyKaplan account. If you've not used MyKaplan before, you'll be sent an activation email.

Bought your book from elsewhere?
Go to **www.mykaplan.co.uk/add-online-resources**
Enter the ISBN number found on the title page and back cover of this book.
Add the unique pass key number contained in the scratch panel below.
You may be required to enter additional information during this process to set up or confirm your account details.

This code can only be used once for the registration of this book online. This registration and your online content will expire when the examinations covered by this book have taken place. Please allow one hour from the time you submit your book details for us to process your request.

Please scratch the film to access your unique code.

Please be aware that this code is case-sensitive and you will need to include the dashes within the passcode, but not when entering the ISBN.

AF891377

ACCA

Applied Skills

Performance Management (PM)

EXAM KIT

KAPLAN
PUBLISHING

British Library Cataloguing-in-Publication Data

A catalogue record for this book is available from the British Library.

Published by:
Kaplan Publishing UK
179 - 191 Borough High Street,
London,
SE1 1HR

ISBN: 978-1-83735-280-7

The text in this material and any others made available by any Kaplan Group company does not amount to advice on a particular matter and should not be taken as such. No reliance should be placed on the content as the basis for any investment or other decision or in connection with any advice given to third parties. Please consult your appropriate professional adviser as necessary. Kaplan Publishing Limited and all other Kaplan group companies expressly disclaim all liability to any person in respect of any losses or other claims, whether direct, indirect, incidental, consequential or otherwise arising in relation to the use of such materials.

Printed and bound in Great Britain

Acknowledgements

The past ACCA examination questions are the copyright of the Association of Chartered Certified Accountants. The original answers to the questions from June 1994 onwards were produced by the examiners themselves and have been adapted by Kaplan Publishing.

We are grateful to the Chartered Institute of Management Accountants and the Institute of Chartered Accountants in England and Wales for permission to reproduce past examination questions. The answers have been prepared by Kaplan Publishing.

CONTENTS

Section

Key features in this edition

In addition to providing a wide ranging bank of practice questions, we have also included in this edition:

- An analysis of all of the recent examinations.
- Exam-specific information and advice on exam technique.
- Our recommended approach to make your revision for this particular subject as effective as possible.
- This includes step by step guidance on how best to use our Kaplan material (Study text, pocket notes and exam kit) at this stage in your studies.
- Enhanced tutorial answers packed with specific key answer tips, technical tutorial notes and exam technique tips from our experienced tutors.
- Complementary online resources including full tutor debriefs to point you in the right direction when you get stuck.

You will find a wealth of other resources to help you with your studies on the following sites:

www.MyKaplan.co.uk

www.accaglobal.com

Quality and accuracy are of the utmost importance to us so if you spot an error in any of our products, please send an email to mykaplanreporting@kaplan.com with full details.

Our Quality Co-ordinator will work with our technical team to verify the error and take action to ensure it is corrected in future editions.

INDEX TO QUESTIONS AND ANSWERS

INTRODUCTION

Following the introduction of the revised exam format, all previous ACCA constructed response (long) exam questions within this kit have been adapted.

The specimen exam is included at the end of the kit.

KEY TO THE INDEX

EXAM ENHANCEMENTS

We have added the following enhancements to the answers in this exam kit:

Key answer tips

All answers include key answer tips to help your understanding of each question.

Tutorial note

Many answers include more tutorial notes to explain some of the technical points in more detail.

Top tutor tips

For selected questions, we 'walk through the answer' giving guidance on how to approach the questions with helpful 'tips from a top tutor', together with technical tutor notes.

These answers are indicated with the 'footsteps' icon in the index.

Within the questions in the exam kit you will see the following icons, shown in the question requirements:

= word processing

= spreadsheet

The icons highlighting the constructed response workspace tool alongside some of the questions are for guidance only – it is important to recognise that each question is different and that the answer space provided by ACCA in the exam is determined by both the technical content of the question as well as the quality assurance processes ACCA undertakes to ensure the student is provided with the most appropriate type of workspace.

ONLINE ENHANCEMENTS

Answer debrief

For selected questions, we recommend that they are to be completed in full exam conditions (i.e. properly timed in a closed book environment).

In addition to the examining team's technical answer, enhanced with key answer tips and tutorial notes in this exam kit, online you can find an answer debrief by a top tutor that:

- works through the question in full
- explains key elements of the answer
- ensures that the easy marks are obtained as quickly as possible.

These questions are indicated with the 'video' icon in the index.

Answer debriefs will be available on MyKaplan at:

www.mykaplan.co.uk

SECTION A – OBJECTIVE TEST QUESTIONS

Questions with online debriefs in section A are Qs 18 – 22

SECTION B – OBJECTIVE TEST CASE STUDY QUESTIONS

SECTION C – CONSTRUCTED RESPONSE QUESTIONS

ANALYSIS OF PAST EXAMS

The table below summarises the key topics that have been tested within sections B & C in the examinations. A much wider range of topics will now be examined following the introduction of objective test questions.

	M21/ J21	S21/ D21	M22/ J22	S22/ D22	M23/ J23	S23/ D23	M24/ J24	S24/ D24	M25/ J25	S25/ D25
Specialist cost and management accounting techniques										
ABC						✓				
Target costing		✓								✓
Lifecycle costing										
Throughput accounting								✓		
Decision making techniques										
CVP					✓					✓
Key factor analysis	✓	✓	✓							
Linear programming		✓								
Pricing				✓			✓			
Relevant costing						✓		✓	✓	
Uncertainty and risk				✓						
Budgeting										
Budgeting			✓						✓	
Forecasting and regression analysis							✓			
Learning curves										
Standard costing and variance analysis										
Standard costing										
Mix & Yield variances										
Planning and operational variances	✓				✓					
Performance measurement and control										
Performance measurement	✓	✓			✓	✓				✓
ROI/RI			✓					✓		
Transfer pricing							✓			
Not for profit organisations				✓					✓	

EXAM TECHNIQUE

GENERAL COMMENTS

- Read the examination questions carefully.
- **Divide the time** you spend on questions in proportion to the marks on offer:
  - one suggestion for this examination is to allocate 1.8 minutes to each mark available, so a 20 mark question should be completed in approximately 36 minutes.
  - within that, try to allow time at the end of each question to review your answer and address any obvious issues.

  Whatever happens, always keep your eye on the clock and **do not over run on any part of any question!**
- If you **get completely stuck** with a question:
  - flag the question and
  - **return to it later**.
- Stick to the question and **tailor your answer** to what you are asked.
  - Pay particular attention to the verbs in the question.
  - Try to apply your comments to the scenario where possible.
- If you do not understand what a question is asking, **state your assumptions**.

  Even if you do not answer in precisely the way the examiner hoped, you should be given some credit, if your assumptions are reasonable.
- You should do everything you can to make things easy for the marker.

  The marker will find it easier to identify the points you have made if your **answers are labelled and workings are well referenced**.

OBJECTIVE TEST QUESTIONS

- Decide whether you want to attempt these at the start of the exam or at the end.
- No credit for workings will be given in these questions, the answers will either be correct (2 marks) or incorrect (0 marks).
- Read the question carefully, as any alternative answer choices will be given based on common mistakes that could be made in attempting the question.
- If a question looks particularly difficult or time consuming, then miss it out first time through (make sure you flag it) and come back to it later.

CONSTRUCTED RESPONSE (LONG) QUESTIONS

- **Written elements:**

  Your answer should have:

  - a clear structure
  - short paragraphs containing short, succinct sentences.
  - heading and sub-headings (where possible).

  Be concise.

  Cover a range of points but make sure you can provide evidence and justification from the scenario.

  Where possible, try to relate comments to the specific context given rather than your answer looking like it was simply copied out of the textbook.

- **Computations:**

  It is essential to include all your workings in your answers.

COMPUTER-BASED EXAMS – ADDITIONAL TIPS

- Do not attempt a CBE until you have **completed all study material** relating to it.
- On the ACCA website there is a CBE demonstration. It is **ESSENTIAL** that you attempt this before your real CBE. You will become familiar with how to move around the CBE screens and the way that questions are formatted, increasing your confidence and speed in the actual exam.
- Be sure you understand how to use the **software** before you start the exam. If in doubt, ask the assessment centre staff to explain it to you.
- Questions are **displayed on the screen** and answers are entered using keyboard and mouse.
- In addition to the traditional multiple choice question type, CBEs will also contain other types of questions, such as number entry questions, multiple correct answers (select two or more), matching labels to targets, stem questions with multiple parts and written questions requiring text entry.
- You need to be sure you **know how to answer questions** of these types before you sit the exam, through practice.

EXAM SPECIFIC INFORMATION

THE EXAM

FORMAT OF THE EXAM

The exam will be in **THREE sections**, and will be a mix of narrative and computational answers.

All questions are compulsory.

		Number of marks
Section A:	Fifteen objective test questions of 2 marks each	30
Section B:	Three objective test case studies	
	– five questions per case study of 2 marks each	30
Section C:	Two constructed response (long) questions	
	Question 1	20
	Question 2	20
		100

Total time allowed: 3 hours. Prior to the exam, candidates are given an extra 10 minutes to read the exam instructions.

Note that:

- the Performance Management exam will have both a discursive and computational element. The objective test questions and the objective test case study questions will therefore include a mix of calculation-based and explanation-based questions.
- there is likely to be a discussion element included in the constructed response questions in Section C.
- Section C questions only come from syllabus areas C, D and E (with potentially a bit of syllabus area A), but not from syllabus area B. At least one of the section C questions in each exam will come from syllabus area E.

PASS MARK

The pass mark for all ACCA Qualification examinations is 50%.

SECTION A QUESTIONS

The computer-based exam will include different question styles, as described in the previous section on exam technique.

A mixture of these question types is included within this exam kit.

APPROACH TO THIS EXAM

Performance Management is divided into three different sections, requiring the application of different skills to be successful.

Section A

Stick to the timing principle of 1.8 minutes per mark. This means that the 15 OT questions in Section A (30 marks) should take 54 minutes.

Work steadily. Rushing leads to careless mistakes and the OT questions are designed to include answers which result from careless mistakes.

If you don't know the answer, eliminate those options you know are incorrect and see if the answer becomes more obvious.

Remember that there is no negative marking for an incorrect answer. After you have eliminated the options that you know to be wrong, if you are still unsure, guess.

Section B

There is likely to be a significant amount of information to read through for each case. You should begin by reading the OT questions that relate to the case, so that when you read through the information for the first time, you know what it is that you are required to do.

Each OT question is worth two marks. Therefore, you have 18 minutes (1.8 minutes per mark) to answer the five OT questions relating to each case. It is likely that all of the cases will take the same length of time to answer, although some of the OT questions within a case may be quicker than other OT questions within that same case.

Once you have read through the information, you should first answer any of the OT questions that do not require workings and can be quickly answered. You should then attempt the OT questions that require workings utilising the remaining time for that case.

All of the tips for Section A are equally applicable to each Section B question.

Section C

The constructed response questions in Section C will require a written response rather than being OT questions. Therefore, different techniques need to be used to score well.

Unless you know exactly how to answer the question, spend some time planning your answer. Stick to the question and tailor your answer to what you are asked. Pay particular attention to the verbs in the question e.g. 'Calculate', 'State', 'Explain', 'Discuss'.

As stated earlier, if you **get completely stuck** with a question, move on and return to it later.

If you do not understand what a question is asking, state your assumptions. Even if you do not answer in precisely the way the examining team hoped, you should be given some credit, provided that your assumptions are reasonable.

You should do everything you can to make things easy for the marker. The marker will find it easier to identify the points you have made if your answers are well structured and well referenced.

Computations: It is essential to include all your workings in your answers. Many computational questions require the use of a standard format. Be sure you know these formats thoroughly before the examination and use the layouts that you see in the answers given in this book and in model answers.

Remember you can use the spreadsheet function to help you with the layout and calculation of your answers. Markers are able to see the formula you are using.

Adopt a logical approach and cross reference workings to the main computation to keep your answers tidy.

All sections

Don't skip any parts of the syllabus. The PM exam has 32 different questions so the examination can cover a very broad selection of the syllabus each sitting.

Spend time learning the rules and definitions.

Practice plenty of questions to improve your ability to apply the techniques and perform the calculations.

Spend the last five minutes reading through your answers and making any additions or corrections.

Always keep your eye on the clock and do not over run on any part of any question!

DETAILED SYLLABUS, STUDY GUIDE AND CBE SPECIMEN EXAM

The detailed syllabus and study guide written by the ACCA, along with the specimen exam, can be found at:

https://www.accaglobal.com/gb/en/student/exam-support-resources/fundamentals-exams-study-resources/f5.html

KAPLAN'S RECOMMENDED REVISION APPROACH

QUESTION PRACTICE IS THE KEY TO SUCCESS

Success in professional examinations relies upon you acquiring a firm grasp of the required knowledge at the tuition phase. In order to be able to do the questions, knowledge is essential.

However, the difference between success and failure often hinges on your exam technique on the day and making the most of the revision phase of your studies.

The **Kaplan study text** is the starting point, designed to provide the underpinning knowledge to tackle all questions. However, in the revision phase, poring over text books is not the answer.

Kaplan Online fixed tests help you consolidate your knowledge and understanding and are a useful tool to check whether you can remember key topic areas.

Kaplan pocket notes are designed to help you quickly revise a topic area, however you then need to practice questions. There is a need to progress to full exam standard questions as soon as possible, and to tie your exam technique and technical knowledge together.

The importance of question practice cannot be over-emphasised.

The recommended approach below is designed by expert tutors in the field, in conjunction with their knowledge of the examiner and their recent real exams.

The approach taken for the fundamental exams is to revise by topic area. However, with the professional stage exams, a multi topic approach is required to answer the scenario based questions.

You need to practice as many questions as possible in the time you have left.

OUR AIM

Our aim is to get you to the stage where you can attempt exam standard questions confidently, to time, in a closed book environment, with no supplementary help (i.e. to simulate the real examination experience).

Practising your exam technique on real past examination questions, in timed conditions, is also vitally important for you to assess your progress and identify areas of weakness that may need more attention in the final run up to the examination.

In order to achieve this we recognise that initially you may feel the need to practice some questions with open book help and exceed the required time.

The approach below shows you which questions you should use to build up to coping with exam standard question practice, and references to the sources of information available should you need to revisit a topic area in more detail.

Remember that in the real examination, all you have to do is:

- attempt all questions required by the exam
- only spend the allotted time on each question, and
- get them at least 50% right!

Try and practice this approach on every question you attempt from now to the real exam.

EXAMINER COMMENTS

We have included the examiners comments to the specific new syllabus examination questions in this kit for you to see the main pitfalls that students fall into with regard to technical content.

However, too many times in the general section of the report, the examiner comments that students had failed due to:

- "not answering the question"
- "a poor understanding of why something is done, not just how it is done"
- "simply writing out numbers from the question. Candidates must understand what the numbers tell them about business performance"
- "a lack of common business sense" and
- "ignoring clues in the question".

Good exam technique is vital.

ACCA SUPPORT

For additional support with your studies please also refer to the ACCA Global website.

THE KAPLAN PERFORMANCE MANAGEMENT (PM) EXAMINATION REVISION PLAN

Stage 1: Assess areas of strengths and weaknesses

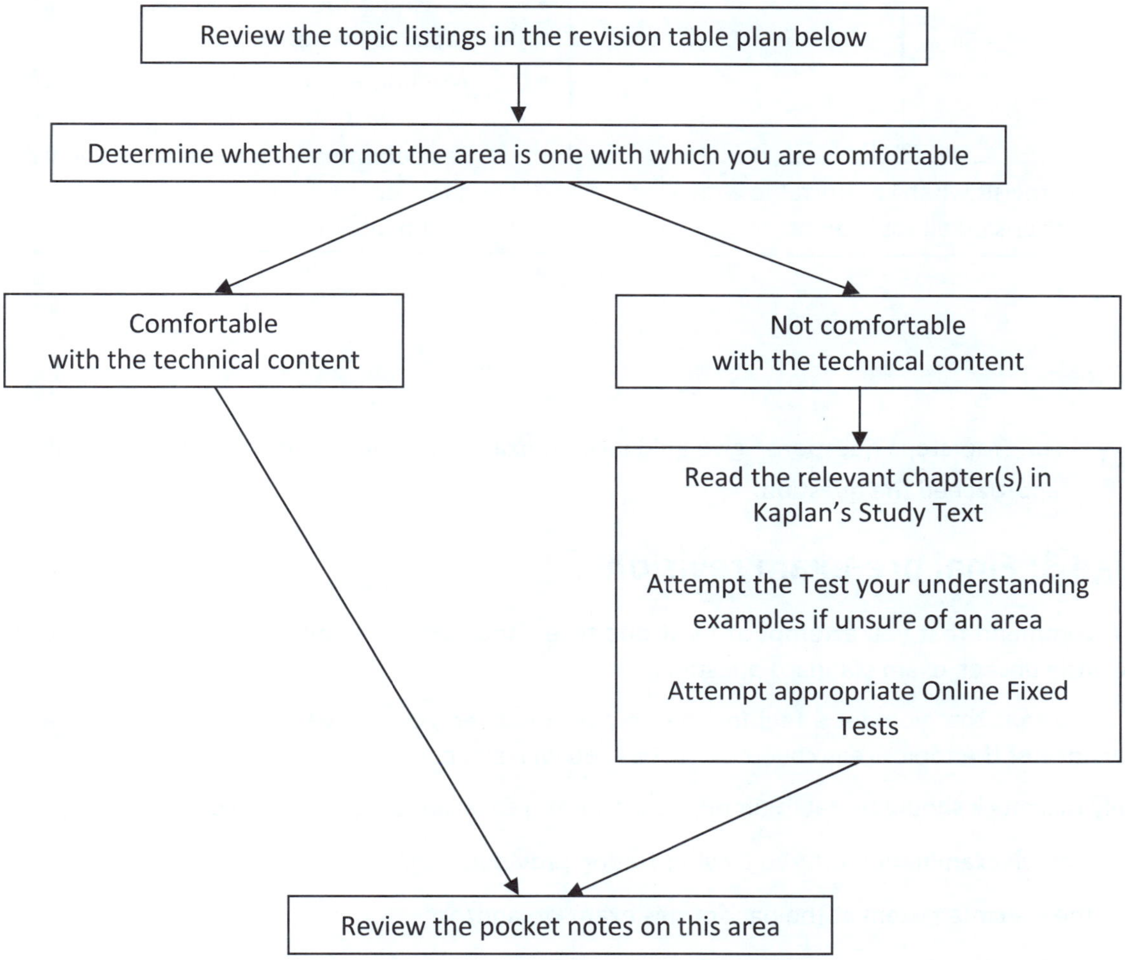

Stage 2: Practice questions

Follow the order of revision of topics as recommended in the revision table plan below and attempt the questions in the order suggested.

Try to avoid referring to text books and notes and the model answer until you have completed your attempt.

Try to answer the question in the allotted time.

Review your attempt with the model answer and assess how much of the answer you achieved in the allocated exam time.

Fill in the self-assessment box below and decide on your best course of action.

Comfortable with question attempt

↓

Only revisit when comfortable with questions on all topic areas

Not comfortable with question attempts

↓

Focus on these areas by:

- Reworking test your understanding examples in Kaplan's Study Text
- Revisiting the technical content from Kaplan's pocket notes
- Working any remaining questions on that area in the exam kit
- Reattempting an exam standard question in that area, on a timed, closed book basis

Note that:

The "footsteps questions" give guidance on exam techniques and how you should have approached the question.

Stage 3: Final pre-exam revision

We recommend that you **attempt at least one three hour mock examination** containing a set of previously unseen exam standard questions.

It is important that you get a feel for the breadth of coverage of a real exam without advanced knowledge of the topic areas covered – just as you will expect to see on the real exam day.

Ideally this mock should be sat in timed, closed book, real exam conditions and could be:

- a mock examination offered by your tuition provider, and/or
- the specimen exam at the back of this exam kit, and/or
- the latest released examination Constructed Response (section C) questions. Ensure that you use the ACCA practice platform to attempt these.

KAPLAN'S DETAILED REVISION PLAN

Topic	Study Text Chapter	Pocket note Chapter	Questions to attempt	Tutor guidance	Date attempted	Self assessment
Information, technologies and systems for organisational performance						
– Management information systems	2,3	2,3	Questions 1 to 6 and 16 to 22 in Section A.	Questions on systems and information will serve as excellent preparation for any exam question on this area, which has become all-important in this exam. This syllabus area will be tested in section A of the exam, and potentially part of a section B or C question.		
– Uses and control of information			Questions 6 to 11 in Section A.			
– Big data and data analytics			Questions 23 to 28 in Section A.			
Specialist cost and management accounting techniques						
– ABC	4	4	Questions 29 to 40 inclusive in Section A. Question 231 to 235 in Section B.	Activity-based Costing (ABC) is a key costing technique. In many questions, you will be asked to calculate the cost per unit using both full absorption costing, and an ABC approach. Be ready to explain the reasons for the development of ABC, its pros and cons and its implications.		

Topic	Study Text Chapter	Pocket note Chapter	Questions to attempt	Tutor guidance	Date attempted	Self assessment
– Target costing	4	4	Questions 41 to 46 inclusive in Section A. Question 237 Helot Co in Section B.	Calculations for target costing are key, but they're not everything: Exam questions may ask for a discussion of the implications of target costing or of the use of target costing in the service industry.		
– Life-cycle costing	4	4	Questions 47 to 53 inclusive in Section A. Question 240 Volt Co in Section B.	This is a relatively straightforward technique but it is still important to practice at the very least one long question to ensure you have the required knowledge.		
– Accounting for environmental and sustainability factors	4	4	Questions 60 to 69 in Section A.	It is important that you can explain what is meant by EMA and that you understand how it should be used.		
– Throughput accounting	4	4	Questions 53 to 58 inclusive in Section A. Question 242 in Section B.	Section B question ('Sweet treats bakery') covers the different calculations that could be examined on throughput accounting. This is a more difficult costing technique and it is therefore important to complete these questions before the exam.		

Topic	Study Text Chapter	Pocket note Chapter	Questions to attempt	Tutor guidance	Date attempted	Self assessment
Decision making techniques						
– Cost volume profit analysis	5	5	Questions 78 to 92 inclusive in Section A. Question 247 Racquetz in Section B. Question 267 Health Nuts in Section C.	A good recent question is 'Health Nuts' covering CVP. Remember, you are not going to be requested to draw a graph in the exam, but may be required to interpret one.		
– Linear programming	6	6	Questions 93 to 103 inclusive in Section A. Question 250 Home Electrics Co in Section B. Question 269 Cut and Stitch in Section C.	'Home Electrics Co' is an excellent question on linear programming testing the use of simultaneous equations. The examiner is likely to examine some peripheral areas such as shadow prices, slack or linear programming assumptions.		

Topic	Study Text Chapter	Pocket note Chapter	Questions to attempt	Tutor guidance	Date attempted	Self assessment
– Pricing	7	7	Questions 104 to 113 inclusive in Section A. Question 252 Skulpt in Section B. Question 275 TR Co in Section C.	The Section C question, 'TR Co', is a good practice question testing both pricing and learning curves. It also mixes calculations with written parts. An excellent question to practice as part of your revision programme.		
– Relevant costing	8	8	Questions 70 to 77, 114 to 117 in Section A. Question 245 Sip in Section B. Question 278 Belton Park Resort in Section C.	This is a tricky area but a methodical approach to answering questions should help. If you are not sure about a particular number, take a guess and move on. The aim is not to get the question 100% correct but to get through the question in time and to score a pass in the question.		
– Dealing with risk and uncertainty	9	9	Questions 118 to 131 inclusive in Section A. Question 255 Mylo in Section B. Question 274 Keytone in Section C.	Whilst the calculations are important, you must also be prepared to discuss the various methods of managing risk. Some of the terms, e.g. minimax regret, make this area appear difficult but the underlying concepts are relatively straightforward.		

Topic	Study Text Chapter	Pocket note Chapter	Questions to attempt	Tutor guidance	Date attempted	Self assessment
Budgeting and control						
– Budgeting systems and types of budget	10	10	Questions 132 to 147 inclusive in Section A. Question 258 LRA in Section B. Question 281 Yumi in Section C.	Do not overlook this area. Knowledge of the written areas of budgeting can help you to score relatively easy marks in the exam, like most well-prepared candidates do when narrative questions are set. 'Static Co' is a good example when it comes to testing the topic of rolling budgets.		
– Quantitative techniques	11	11	Questions 148 to 163 inclusive in Section A. Question 259 Bokco in Section B. Question 284 Venhosp in Section C.	'Venhosp' on regression analysis and 'Henry Company' on learning curves are excellent practice questions in this area. Be prepared to discuss the reservations with the learning curve. Forecasting techniques –such as linear regression, correlation are expected to be regularly examined.		
– Mix and yield/quantity variances	12	12	Questions 170 to 187 inclusive in Section A. Question 262 in Section B. Question 287 Clear Co in Section C.	These require a calculation of mix and yield variances and are good preparation for the exam. Kappa Co, for example, is a very good one to practice and also a recent exam question (Sept 2018). Sales mix and quantity variances should not be omitted either.		

Topic	Study Text Chapter	Pocket note Chapter	Questions to attempt	Tutor guidance	Date attempted	Self assessment
– Planning and operational variances	12	12	Questions 188 to 194 inclusive in Section A. Question 264 Greyshott in Section B. Question 286 Medical Temp Co in Section C.	This is representative of the type of question that may come up on this area. 'Medical Temp Co' is a must-practice question on revision.		
Performance measurement and control						
– ROI/RI	14	14	Questions 209, and 211 to 215 inclusive in Section A. Question 293 Yetgo Co in Section C.	It is important that you can calculate the ROI and RI but you must also be able to discuss the pros and cons of each of these methods. Some of these questions are challenging but necessary, testing your knowledge of how ROI and RI are affected by different transactions which may take place.		
– Transfer pricing	14	14	Questions 208, 210, and 216 to 218 inclusive in Section A. Question 302 Caroline Co in Section C.	For all questions on transfer pricing, you will require an in-depth understanding of the information contained in the scenario.		

Topic	Study Text Chapter	Pocket note Chapter	Questions to attempt	Tutor guidance	Date attempted	Self assessment
– Performance analysis in not-for-profit organisations and the public sector	15	15	Questions 219 to 224 inclusive in Section A. Question 304 Tonford School in Section C.	Questions on not-for-profit organisations will serve as excellent preparation for any exam question on this area. You should focus on understanding and applying the 'Value For Money' (or 3Es) framework.		

Note that not all of the questions are referred to in the programme above. We have recommended a large number of exam standard questions and successful completion of these should reassure you that you have a good grounding of all of the key topics and are well prepared for the exam.

The remaining questions are available in the kit for extra practice for those who require more questions and focus on some areas.

FORMULAE

Performance Management (PM)
Formulae sheet

Regression analysis

$$y = a + bx$$

$$a = \frac{\sum y}{n} - \frac{b\sum x}{n}$$

$$b = \frac{n\sum xy - \sum x \sum y}{n\sum x^2 - (\sum x)^2}$$

$$r = \frac{n\sum xy - \sum x \sum y}{\sqrt{(n\sum x^2 - (\sum x)^2)(n\sum y^2 - (\sum y)^2)}}$$

Learning curve

$$Y = ax^b$$

Where Y = cumulative average time per unit to produce x units

a = the time taken for the first unit of output

x = the cumulative number of units produced

b = the index of learning (log LR/log2)

LR = the learning rate as a decimal

Demand curve

$$P = a - bQ$$

$$b = \frac{\text{change in price}}{\text{change in quantity}}$$

a = price when Q = 0

MR = a – 2bQ

Section 1

OBJECTIVE TEST QUESTIONS – SECTION A

MANAGEMENT INFORMATION SYSTEMS AND DATA ANALYTICS

MANAGEMENT INFORMATION SYSTEMS

1 **Which TWO of the following are typical advantages of investing in a new information system?**

- Enhanced compatibility with other systems
- Enhanced information processing capacity
- Enhanced information processing efficiency
- Enhanced staff training needs

2 An airline wants to provide access to a select group of travel agents to real time information held by the airline regarding flights which may have the potential for passenger seat upgrades.

Which of the following is likely to be used to achieve this?

A Intranet

B Extranet

C Internet

D Email

3 A government department generates information which should not be disclosed to anyone who works outside of the department. There are many other government departments working within the same building.

Which of the following would NOT be an effective control procedure for the generation and distribution of the information within the government department?

A If working from home, departmental employees must use a memory stick to transfer data, as laptop computers are not allowed to leave the department.

B All departmental employees must enter non-disclosed and regularly updated passwords to access their computers.

C All authorised employees must swipe an officially issued, personal identity card at the entrance to the department before they can gain access.

D All hard copies of confidential information must be shredded at the end of each day or locked overnight in a safe if needed again.

4 A small doctors' surgery is considering providing a wireless network for use by nurses to access patient data in real time.

Which of the following is a DISADVANTAGE of using a wireless network in this way?

A Access to the network cannot be limited

B The network cannot match the coverage of a wired network

C The network will be less stable than a wired network

D It will be necessary to buy lots of new user devices

5 **Which of the following methods would be LEAST effective in ensuring the security of confidential information?**

A Monitoring emails

B Encryption of files

C Training staff on GDPR requirements

D Universal passwords

6 **Which of the following statements regarding technologies and systems are correct?**

(1) Networked computers can save costs by sharing hardware, software and data.

(2) An intranet provides quick, effective communication with suppliers.

(3) Wireless networks allow businesses to expand with less disruption than wired networks.

(4) The internet can be used to monitor and measure customer interest.

A (2), (3) and (4)

B (1) and (2)

C (1), (3) and (4)

D (1) and (4) only

7 Which ONE of the following is NOT a benefit of effective data visualisation?

A Reports can be more user friendly

B Improves the accuracy of the data being analysed

C The use of dashboards can highlight and summarise key information

D Allows for headline figures to be presented with an option to drill down into the detail

8 Which TWO of the following are characteristics of effective data visualisation?

A Presented only on screen

B Real time information

C High level only

D Presents all data obtained

E User friendly

F Guarantees good management decisions

9 Which of the following statements about data visualisation is true?

A The most common use of data visualisation is the creation of a dashboard displaying real time KPIs

B Data is always displayed in standardised formats to ensure consistency

C Data visualisation refers to data that is mainly analysed and presented using basic spreadsheet software

D Increased use of data visualisation within organisations increases the need for more IT experts

10 A company's board of directors were recently embarrassed when a very unhappy junior human resources employee emailed details of their salaries to the entire company.

An investigation revealed that the human resources director had lent his username and password to the junior employee so that routine maintenance of the human resources database could be conducted whilst the director was on vacation. During the director's vacation, the junior employee had used the director's username and password to access the board's salary records.

Which of the following controls could have helped to prevent this breach of confidential information?

A Monitoring the database system logs on a regular basis to see what information is being accessed

B Building levels of access into the database so that only senior staff have access to board records

C Keeping all the human resource records for salaries on a separate server

D Having a policy of regularly updating the passwords required to access the system

11 Bazile Co uses the services of a number of market research consultants based in the different geographical regions in which it operates. These consultants are provided with hard copies of designs for new products, sent in sealed packages via a courier service due to their commercially sensitive nature.

To further ensure that details of new products are not leaked, the consultants are required to work using non-networked computers, and to save all market research findings on a password protected hard drive that is again sent by courier.

Which TWO of the following controls are likely to be of use to this company?

A An anti-spyware software program

B A lockable cabinet or safe

C A firewall

D A confidentiality contract

12 **Which of the following is a disadvantage of cloud computing?**

A Reduced flexibility around working arrangements

B More reliance on third party suppliers

C Higher maintenance costs

D Harder to integrate systems

13 The qualities of good information contained in reports are more easily remembered using the mnemonic ACCURATE.

Which one of the following is NOT normally associated with a quality of good information?

A Adaptable to the needs of the user

B Acceptable to the user

C Accurate

D Understandable by the user

14 An accountant wants to determine the increase in average usage of paper per employee from printing out of emails. She is concerned that paper usage in her business has risen by 10% in the last year to $40,400.

She has estimated that it will take 4 weeks of her time to prepare the report. As well as other incremental costs she has estimated that the total cost of preparing the report will be $28,000.

This report is an example of bad information. Which one of the principles of good information does it breach?

A Relevant

B Complete

C Cost beneficial

D Understandable

15 Local managers within organisations often use operational reports.

Which of the following features of reports would be most true of an operational report?

A Summarised information

B Mainly external information on local competition

C Accurate information on current position

D Infrequent

USES AND CONTROL OF INFORMATION

16 Strategic reports have many features, which of the following is the most likely feature of a strategic report?

A Prepared regularly

B Total accuracy of past and forecast data

C Highly summarised showing overall trends

D Demonstrates only the company's current position

17 Long-term sales forecasts are an example of accounting information used at which level of control in an organisation?

A Strategic planning

B Management control

C Tactical control

D Operational control

18 Information systems described below may or may not be suited to all levels of management.

Identify by placing a tick in the relevant boxes in the table below, the suitability of the systems for all levels of management.

	Suited to all levels of management	**Not suited to all levels of management**
A Management Information System producing management accounts showing margins for individual customers		
A Customer Relationship Management system tracking the acquisition, retention and extension of all customers		
An Executive Information System giving access to internal and external information in summarised form, with the option to drill down to a greater level of activity		

19 A manufacturer and retailer of kitchens introduces an enterprise resource planning system.

Which of the following is NOT likely to be a potential benefit of introducing this system?

A Schedules of labour are prepared for manufacturing

B Inventory records are updated automatically

C Sales are recorded into the financial ledgers

D Critical strategic information can be summarised

20 **Which of the following is an example of an Executive Information System (EIS)?**

A Software to identify customer trends and marketing opportunities

B A database management system

C A system summarising sales to assist in identifying trends and hiring new workers

D A system providing internal and external information to help senior managers monitor the performance of the entire organisation

21 You have been presented with a summary report of sales in the last month, with a breakdown of totals per product, and with variances from the corresponding monthly sales plan.

Which of the following systems would generate such a report?

A A transaction processing system

B A management information system

C An executive Information system

D None of the above

22 **Which of the following could be described as an Enterprise Resource Planning system (EPRS)?**

A A system that identifies trends and patterns in large sets of data

B A system integrating data from all operations within the organisation

C A marketing database holding records of past advertising campaigns and the sales generated by those campaigns

D A system that captures, processes, and stores low level transaction data

BIG DATA AND DATA ANALYTICS

23 **Which of the following is NOT normally considered to be a feature of big data?**

A Volume

B Velocity

C Variety

D Vicinity

24 Which TWO of the following statements regarding big data are true?

- It is more reliable than other sources of data
- It can change very quickly
- It can take multiple forms
- It involves dealing with large financial numbers

25 Which of the following statements regarding big data is true?

A It is only useful for big organisations

B It is all contained on the internet

C It is all generated external to the organisation

D It can lead to a competitive advantage

26 It is often said that big data enhances business decisions.

Which of the following statements regarding big data and decision making is/are true?

(i) Decisions which include big data analytics can lead to a competitive edge over rivals.

(ii) Big data analytics cannot account for competitors' expected actions.

A Statement (i) only

B Statement (ii) only

C Both statements

D Neither statement

27 Which TWO of the following statements are thought to be benefits when using big data to enhance business decisions?

- There is no need to have a deep understanding of the industry in order to interpret the data
- Customer relationship management can be improved resulting in better repeat business and customer loyalty
- Business performance can be better tracked and analysed against a wider set of criteria
- All available big data will create value for an organisation when analysed

28 Which of the following is NOT considered a risk when using big data to enhance business decision making?

A The veracity of the data is difficult to assess

B Traditional sources of data are ignored

C The data may be distorted by data outliers

D The benefits may be outweighed by the financial costs

SPECIALIST COST AND MANAGEMENT ACCOUNTING TECHNIQUES

ACTIVITY-BASED COSTING

29 A company produces a range of products and uses an absorption costing system. Which two of the following are UNLIKELY to be a consequence of the company switching to an activity based costing (ABC) system?

- Indirect overheads will be shared between products on fairer bases
- Product pricing decisions will be improved
- The prime production cost of each product will fall
- Cost control on indirect overheads will be harder to achieve
- Total production cost of each product will change

30 A company which makes two products, Alpha and Zeta, uses activity-based costing to absorb its overheads. It has recently identified a new overhead cost pool for inspection costs and has decided that the cost driver is the number of inspections.

The following information has been provided:

Total inspection costs	$250,000	
	Alpha	**Zeta**
Production volume (units)	2,500	8,000
Machine hours per unit	1	1.5
Units per batch	500	1,000
Inspections per batch	4	1

What is the inspection cost per unit of product Alpha? Select from the list below.

List options are as follows:

- $23.81
- $17.24
- $71.43
- $80.00

31 Which of the following statements are true regarding activity-based costing (ABC) and cost drivers?

(1) A cost driver is any factor that causes a change in the cost of an activity.

(2) For long-term variable overhead costs, the cost driver will be the volume of activity.

(3) Traditional absorption costing tends to under-allocate overhead costs to low-volume products.

A (1) and (3) only

B (2) and (3) only

C (1) and (2) only

D (1), (2) and (3)

32 A company makes products A and B. It is experimenting with activity-based costing. Production set-up costs are $12,000; total production will be 20,000 units of each of products A and B. Each run is 1,000 units of A or 5,000 units of B.

Using activity-based costing, what is the set-up cost per unit of A? (Give your answer to the nearest cent.)

$ [ ]

33 **Which of the following statement(s) is/are true regarding activity-based costing?**

(1) A cost pool is an activity which consumes resources and for which overhead costs are identified and allocated.

(2) An activity-based costing overhead absorption rate (OAR) is calculated in the same way as an absorption costing OAR, and will result in the same OAR being calculated for each cost pool.

A (1) only

B (2) only

C Neither (1) nor (2)

D Both (1) and (2)

34 A company uses activity-based costing to calculate the unit cost of its products. The figures for Period 3 are as follows: production set-up costs are $84,000. Total production is 40,000 units of each of products A and B, and each run is 2,000 units of A or 5,000 units of B.

What is the set-up cost per unit of B (to 2 decimal places)?

$ [ ]

35 The ABC Company manufactures two products, product Alpha and Product Beta. Both are produced in a very labour-intensive environment and use similar processes. Alpha and Beta differ by volume. Beta is a high-volume product, while Alpha is a low-volume product. Details of product inputs, outputs and the costs of activities are as follows:

	Direct labour hours/unit	**Annual output (units)**	**Number of purchase orders**	**Number of set-ups**
Alpha	5	1,200	75	40
Beta	5	12,000	85	60
			160	**100**

Fixed overhead costs amount to a total of $420,000 and have been analysed as follows:

	$
Volume-related	100,000
Purchasing related	145,000
Set-up related	175,000

Using a traditional method of overhead absorption based on labour hours, what is the overhead cost per unit for each unit of product Alpha (to two decimal places)?

$ [ ]

36 The ABC Company manufactures two products, product Alpha and Product Beta. Both are produced in a very labour-intensive environment and use similar processes. Alpha and Beta differ by volume. Beta is a high-volume product, while Alpha is a low-volume product. Details of product inputs, outputs and the costs of activities are as follows:

	Direct labour hours/unit	**Annual output (units)**	**Number of purchase orders**	**Number of set-ups**
Alpha	5	1,200	75	40
Beta	5	12,000	85	60
			160	**100**

Fixed overhead costs amount to a total of $420,000 and have been analysed as follows:

	$
Volume-related	100,000
Purchasing related	145,000
Set-up related	175,000

Using a traditional method of overhead absorption based on labour hours, what is the overhead cost per unit for each unit of product Beta (to two decimal places)?

A $6.36

B $22.75

C $31.82

D $122.55

37 The ABC Company manufactures two products, Product Alpha and Product Beta. Both are produced in a very labour-intensive environment and use similar processes. Alpha and Beta differ by volume. Beta is a high-volume product, while Alpha is a low-volume product. Details of product inputs, outputs and the costs of activities are as follows:

	Direct labour hours/unit	**Annual output (units)**	**Number of purchase orders**	**Number of set-ups**
Alpha	5	1,200	75	40
Beta	5	12,000	85	60
			160	**100**

Fixed overhead costs amount to a total of $420,000 and have been analysed as follows:

	$
Volume-related	100,000
Purchasing related	145,000
Set-up related	175,000

Using Activity-based costing as the method of overhead absorption, what is the overhead cost per unit for each unit of product Alpha (to two decimal places)?

A $6.36

B $22.75

C $122.55

D Cannot be determined without more information

38 A company makes two products using the same type of materials and skilled workers. The following information is available:

	Product A	**Product B**
Budgeted volume (units)	1,000	2,000
Material per unit ($)	10	20
Labour per unit ($)	5	20

Fixed costs relating to material handling amount to $100,000. The cost driver for these costs is the volume of material purchased.

General fixed costs, absorbed on the basis of labour hours, amount to $180,000.

Using activity-based costing, what is the total fixed overhead amount to be absorbed into each unit of product B (to the nearest whole $)?

A $113

B $120

C $40

D $105

39 A company is changing its costing system from traditional absorption costing based on labour hours to activity-based costing. It has overheads of $156,000 which are related to taking material deliveries.

The delivery information about each product is below.

Product:	**X**	**Y**	**Z**
Total units required	1,000	2,000	3,000
Delivery size	200	400	1,000

Total labour costs are $360,000 for 45,000 hours. Each unit of each product takes the same number of direct hours.

Assuming that the company uses the number of deliveries as its cost driver, what will be the effect on the costs per unit following the change from absorption costing to activity-based costing?' Place a tick in the boxes in the table below where appropriate.

	Increase	**Decrease**
Product X		
Product Y		
Product Z		

40 DRP Ltd has recently introduced an activity-based costing (ABC) system. It manufactures three products, details of which are set out below:

Product:	**D**	**R**	**P**
Budgeted annual production (units)	100,000	100,000	50,000
Batch size (units)	100	50	25
Machine set-ups per batch	3	4	6
Purchase orders per batch	2	1	1
Processing time per unit (minutes)	2	3	3

Three cost pools have been identified. Their budgeted costs for the year ending 30 June 20X3 are as follows:

Machine set-up costs	$150,000
Purchasing of materials	$70,000
Processing	$80,000

What is the budgeted machine set-up cost per unit of product R?

A $6.52

B $0.52

C $18.75

D $1.82

TARGET COSTING

41 **In target costing, which ONE of the following would be an appropriate strategy to reduce a cost gap for a product that existed in a competitive industry with demanding shareholders?**

A Increase the selling price

B Reduce the expectation gap by reducing the selling price

C Reducing the desired margin on the product

D Mechanising production in order to reduce average production cost

42 The predicted selling price for a product has been set at $56 per unit. The desired mark-up on cost is 25% and the material cost for the product is estimated to be $16 before allowing for additional materials to allow for shrinkage of 20% (for every 10 kg of material going in only 8 kg comes out).

If labour is the only other cost and 2 hours are needed what is the most the business can pay per hour if a cost gap is to be avoided?

The maximum rate per hour is (2 d.p) $

43 **Which of the following techniques is NOT relevant to target costing?**

A Value analysis

B Variance analysis

C Functional analysis

D Activity analysis

44 The selling price of product Zigma is set to be $250 for each unit and sales for the coming year are expected to be 500 units. The company requires a return of 15% in the coming year on its investment of $250,000 in product Zigma.

What is the target cost for each unit of Zigma for the coming year? Select from the list as appropriate.

List options are as follows:

- $145
- $155
- $165
- $175

45 VC Co is a company of opticians. It provides a range of services to the public, such as eye tests and contact lens consultations, and has a separate dispensary selling glasses and contact lenses. Patients book appointments with an optician in advance.

A standard appointment is 30 minutes long, during which an optician will assess the patient's specific requirements and provide them with the eye care services they need. After the appointment, patients are offered the chance to buy contact lenses or glasses from the dispensary.

Which of the following describes a characteristic of the services provided by an optician at VC Co during a standard appointment?

A Tangible

B Homogeneous

C Non-perishable

D Simultaneous

46 **Match the stages required to the correct step number to describe the sequence used when operating target costing.**

Stages required
Cost the product
Determine the profit margin
Set the selling price
Use functional and value analysis
Identify the cost gap
Develop the product concept

Order of steps
Step 1
Step 2
Step 3
Step 4
Step 5
Step 6

LIFE-CYCLE COSTING

47 A company has produced the following information for a product it is about to launch. The product is expected to have a life of three years.

Year	1	2	3
Expected sales units	2,000	5,000	7,000
Variable production cost per unit	$2.30	$1.80	$1.20
Fixed production costs	$3,000	$3,500	$4,000
Variable selling cost per unit	$0.50	$0.40	$0.40
Fixed selling costs	$1,500	$1,600	$1,600
Administrative costs	$700	$700	$700

What is the life-cycle cost per unit?

A $2.81

B $2.32

C $3.22

D $3.07

48 A manufacturing company which produces a range of products has developed a budget for the life-cycle of a new product, P. The information in the following table relates exclusively to product P:

	Lifetime total	Per unit
Design costs	$800,000	
Direct manufacturing costs		$20
Depreciation costs	$500,000	
Decommissioning costs	$20,000	
Machine hours		4
Production and sales units	300,000	

The company's total fixed production overheads are budgeted to be $72 million each year and total machine hours are budgeted to be 96 million hours. The company absorbs overheads on a machine hour basis.

What is the budgeted life-cycle cost per unit for product P?

A $24.40

B $25.73

C $27.40

D $22.73

49 SNT is a Japanese electronics giant specialising in the production of game consoles. SNT is planning to introduce the latest 'next-generation' console and range of games in the summer of 20X0. Development of the new console is due to commence on January 1st, 20X0 and SNT is currently working out at what price the new console should be sold then.

The new console is expected to incur the following costs in the four years it will be developed and commercialised:

	20X0	**20X1**	**20X2**	**20X3**
Consoles manufactured and sold	10,000	12,000	11,100	3,000
R&D costs	$950,000	$0	$0	$0
Marketing costs	$230,000	$120,000	$20,000	$5,000
Production cost per console	$450	$430	$290	$290
Warranty costs per console	$30	$30	$40	$45
End of life costs	$0	$0	$0	$125,000

Market research has indicated that customers will be prepared to pay an average price of $420 per console, but SNT's Chief Executive believes this will not be sufficient to make production worthwhile.

Which of the following statements, made by the Chief Executive, are true regarding the costs of the console?

(1) The cost per console, calculated using life-cycle costing principles, is higher than the price customers are prepared to pay.

(2) More attention to R&D costs in 20X0 could reduce warranty costs in later years.

A (1) only

B (2) only

C Neither (1) nor (2)

D Both (1) and (2)

50 While a drag and drop style question is impossible to fully replicate within a paper based medium, some questions of this style have been included for completeness.

Which FOUR of the following are said to be benefits of life-cycle costing?

- It provides the true financial cost of a product
- The length of the life-cycle can be shortened
- Expensive errors can be avoided in that potentially failing products can be avoided
- Lower costs can be achieved earlier by designing out costs
- Better selling prices can be set
- Decline stages of the life-cycle can be avoided

Drag the items selected into the box below:

51 Which of the following statements are true regarding the justification of the use of life cycle costing?

(1) Product life cycles are becoming increasingly short. This means that the initial costs are an increasingly important component in the product's overall costs.

(2) Product costs are increasingly weighted to the start of a product's life cycle, and to properly understand the profitability of a product these costs must be matched to the ultimate revenues.

(3) The high costs of (for example) research, design and marketing in the early stages in a product's life cycle necessitate a high initial selling price.

(4) Traditional capital budgeting techniques do not attempt to minimise the costs or maximise the revenues over the product life cycle.

A (1), (2) and (4) only

B (2) and (3) only

C (1) and (3) only

D (1), (2), (3) and (4)

52 Which of the following statement(s) is/are true regarding life-cycle costing?

(1) Life cycle costing takes into account all costs incurred in a product life cycle with exception of sunk costs incurred on research and development.

(2) Life cycle costing ensures a profit is generated over the life of the product.

(3) Life cycle costing is most useful for products with an even weighting of costs over their life.

A (1) and (3) only

B (2) only

C (2) and (3) only

D (1), (2) and (3)

53 Company B is about to start developing a new product for launch in its existing market. They have forecast sales of 20,000 units and the marketing department suggest a selling price of $43/unit. The company seeks to make a mark-up of 40% product cost. It is estimated that the lifetime costs of the product will be as follows:

(1) Design and development costs $43,000.

(2) Manufacturing costs $15/unit.

(3) Plant decommissioning costs $30,000.

What is the life cycle cost per unit of the new product?

A $18.65

B $22

C $22.87

D $24

THROUGHPUT ACCOUNTING

54 When demand exceeds supply, which one of the following situations would increase the throughput accounting ratio?

A An increase in the speed of the fastest machine in the production process

B An unexpected increase in the factory rent

C A 5% wage increase linked to an 8% improvement in productivity

D A 10% sales discount to stimulate demand by 20%

55 A manufacturing company decides which of three mutually exclusive products to make in its factory on the basis of maximising the company's throughput accounting ratio.

Current data for the three products is shown in the following table:

	Product X	Product Y	Product Z
Selling price per unit	$60	$40	$20
Direct material cost per unit	$40	$10	$16
Machine hours per unit	10	20	2.5

Total factory costs (excluding direct materials) are $150,000. The company cannot make enough of any of the products to satisfy external demand entirely as machine hours are restricted.

What would be the effect of the following actions on the company's throughput accounting ratio (TPAR)?' Place a tick in the appropriate boxes in the table below.

	Would improve the company's existing TPAR	Would NOT improve the company's existing TPAR
Increase the selling price of product Z by 10%		
Increase the selling price of product Y by 10%		
Reduce the material cost of product Z by 5%		
Reduce the material cost of product Y by 5%		

56 Skye Limited operates in an environment where products go through two processes and details of their capacity are below:

Process P

There are 8 machines operating at 90% capacity. Each machine produces 6 units per hour.

Process Q

There are 6 machines operating at 85% capacity. Each machine produces 9 units per hour.

Skye Limited produces the 'Cloud' which is not a popular product. The marketing manager has therefore decided to apply a price discount of 15% on the selling price of $20 per unit.

The material cost per unit is $5 and the direct labour cost per unit is twice that of the material costs for the 'Cloud'. It currently takes 0.2 hours and 0.3 hours to make a unit of the 'Cloud' on the machines in process P and process Q respectively.

What is the Cloud's throughput per hour of the bottleneck resource (to two decimal places)?

$ [ ]

57 A manufacturing company uses machine C, which is operational for five hours a day to manufacture four products: W, X, Y and Z. Factory costs are $150,000 per day. The company uses throughput accounting and its objective is to maximise profits.

Information relating to these products is as follows:

Product	Production rate per machine hour (units)	Selling price per unit ($)	Material cost per unit ($)	Conversion cost per unit ($)
W	200	350	120	40
X	500	190	95	25
Y	400	270	160	20
Z	350	215	75	35

If the company is not able to increase the availability of machine C's operational hours, what is the production ranking of product Y?

A First

B Second

C Third

D Fourth

58 A manufacturing company uses three processes to make its two products, X and Y. The time available on the three processes is reduced because of the need for preventative maintenance and rest breaks.

The table below details the process times per product and daily time available:

Process	Hours available per day	Hours required to make one unit of product X	Hours required to make one unit of product Y
1	22	1.00	0.75
2	22	0.75	1.00
3	18	1.00	0.50

Daily demand for product X and product Y is 10 units and 16 units respectively.

Which of the following will improve throughput?

A Increasing the efficiency of the maintenance routine for Process 2

B Increasing the demand for both products

C Reducing the time taken for rest breaks on Process 3

D Reducing the time product X requires for Process 1

59 Which ONE of the below statements is NOT true of throughput accounting?

A Throughput accounting considers that the only variable costs in the short run are materials and components.

B Throughput accounting considers that time at a bottleneck resource has value, not elsewhere.

C Throughput accounting views stock building as a non-value-adding activity, and therefore discourages it.

D Throughput accounting was designed as a decision-making tool for situations where there is a bottleneck in the production process.

ENVIRONMENTAL ACCOUNTING

60 Which TWO of the following activities are environmental INTERNAL failure costs?

A Quality control inspections to monitor pollution levels in water leaving a production process

B Water purification treatment to clean waste water before it leaves the factory

C Fitting of carbon filters to machine processes to reduce carbon emissions

D Power usage measuring system to monitor energy consumption within the factory

E Payment of fines for breaching environmental regulations in the industry

F Insulation of heating pipes in the factory to reduce heat loss

G Public relations costs to remedy reputational damage caused by accidental river pollution

H Capturing and recycling of waste exhaust gases to generate energy

61 The monthly budget for process X shows the following input/output analysis:

INPUTS

Description	**Comment**	**Weight (kg)**	**$**
Materials		1,000	(50,000)
System costs	Labour, utilities and other overheads	–	(30,000)
Total		1,000	(80,000)

OUTPUTS

Description	**Comment**	**Weight (kg)**	**$**
Good output	Expected good output is 70% of input and can be sold for $120 per kg	700	84,000
Waste	Expected waste is 10% of input and must be scrapped at a cost of $10 per kg	100	(1,000)
Scrap	Expected scrap is 20% of input and can be sold for $15 per kg	200	3,000
Total		1,000	86,000

Monthly profit is thus expected to be $6,000.

The company is looking at introducing new quality systems that will increase system costs by $5,000 per month but will reduce waste from 10% to 4% of input. Scrap is expected to stay at 20% of input.

What would be the impact on monthly profit of implementing the proposal?

A $4,400 reduction in profit

B $200 increase in profit

C $2,200 increase in profit

D $2,800 increase in profit

62 Different management accounting techniques can be used to account for environmental costs.

One of these techniques involves analysing costs under three distinct categories: material, system, and delivery and disposal.

What is this technique known as?

A Activity-based costing

B Life-cycle costing

C Input-output analysis

D Flow cost accounting

63 **Which TWO of the following statements about the advantages of using Activity-based costing for Environmental Management Accounting are correct?**

- Higher environmental costs can be reflected in higher prices
- Cost savings achieved through environmental policies can be measured
- It is simple to determine the environmental costs and cost drivers
- It considers all environmental effects of the company's actions

64 The monthly budget for process X shows the following input/output analysis:

INPUTS

Description	**Comment**	**Weight (kg)**	**$**
Materials		1,000	(50,000)
System costs	Labour, utilities and other overheads	–	(30,000)
Total		1,000	(80,000)

OUTPUTS

Description	**Comment**	**Weight (kg)**	**$**
Good output	Expected good output is 70% of input and can be sold for $120 per kg	700	84,000
Waste	Expected waste is 10% of input and must be scrapped at a cost of $10 per kg	100	(1,000)
Scrap	Expected scrap is 20% of input and can be sold for $15 per kg	200	3,000
Total		1,000	86,000

The company is looking at adopting environmental flow cost accounting, in which all material and system costs will be apportioned on the basis of weight.

Calculate the total net cost of waste and scrap using flow cost accounting. Give you answer to the nearest $.

$ ____________

65 **Which TWO of the following statements about flow cost accounting are correct?**

- Manufacturing costs are categorised into material costs, system costs and delivery and disposal costs
- Flow cost accounting records material inflows and balances this with outflows both in terms of physical quantities and, at the end of the process, in monetary terms too, so that businesses are forced to focus on environmental costs
- In flow cost accounting, output costs are allocated between positive and negative product costs
- The aim of flow cost accounting is to increase the quantity of materials which, as well as having a positive effect on the environment, should have a positive effect on a company's total costs in the long run

66 Which of the following statements is/are true regarding the issues faced by businesses in the management of their environmental costs?

(1) The costs involved are difficult to define.

(2) Environmental costs can be categorised as quality related costs.

(3) Cost control can be an issue, in particular if costs have been identified incorrectly in the first place.

A (1) only

B (2) and (3) only

C None of them

D All of them

67 Flow cost accounting is a technique which can be used to account for environmental costs. Inputs and outputs are measured through each individual process of production.

Which of the following is NOT a category used within flow cost accounting?

A Material flows

B System flows

C Delivery and disposal flows

D Waste flows

68 Accountants usually find it difficult to deal with environmental costs.

Which of the following is NOT a reason for this?

A Costs are often hidden

B Costs are mostly minor

C Costs are often very long term

D Accounting systems rarely split off these costs automatically

69 Which of the following statements are true regarding Triple Bottom Line (TBL) reporting as part of accounting for sustainability factors?

(1) Triple bottom line reporting would involve measuring the organisation's profit, as well as the impact on people and the planet.

(2) Measuring the impact on people, planet, and profit is very straightforward for most businesses.

(3) It could be a useful way for an organisation to encourage staff to make efficiency cost savings and could even help them attract ethically aware staff and customers.

A (1) and (2) only

B (2) and (3) only

C (1) and (3) only

D (1), (2) and (3)

DECISION-MAKING TECHNIQUES

RELEVANT COST ANALYSIS

70 UU Company has been asked to quote for a special contract. The following information about the material needed has been given:

Material X:

Original cost	Scrap value	Replacement cost
$5.00 per kg	$0.50 per kg	$5.50 per kg

The contract requires 10 kgs of Material X. There are 250 kgs of this material in inventory which was purchased in error over two years ago. If Material X is modified, at a cost of $2 per kg, it could then be used as a substitute for material Y which is in regular use and currently costs $6 per kg.

What is the relevant cost of the materials for the special contract?

A $5

B $40

C $50

D $55

71 VV Company has been asked to quote for a special contract. The contract requires 100 hours of labour. However, the labourers, who are each paid $15 per hour, are working at full capacity.

There is a shortage of labour in the market. The labour required to undertake this special contract would have to be taken from another contract, Z, which currently utilises 500 hours of labour and generates $5,000 worth of contribution.

If the labour was taken from contract Z, then the whole of contract Z would have to be delayed, and such delay would invoke a penalty fee of $1,000.

What is the relevant cost of the labour for the special contract?

A $1,000

B $1,500

C $2,500

D $7,500

72 In order to utilise some spare capacity, K is preparing a quotation for a special order which requires 2,000 kgs of material J.

K has 800 kgs of material J in inventory (original cost $7.00 per kg). Material J is used in the company's main product L. Each unit of L uses 5 kgs of material J and, based on an input value of $7.00 per kg of J, each unit of L yields a contribution of $10.00.

The resale value of material J is $5.50 per kg. The present replacement price of material J is $8.00 per kg. Material J is readily available in the market.

What is the relevant cost of the 2,000 kgs of material J to be included in the quotation?

A $11,000

B $14,000

C $16,000

D $18,000

73 A company is calculating the relevant cost of the material to be used on a particular contract. The contract requires 4,200 kgs of material H and this can be bought for $6.30 per kg. The company bought 10,000 kgs of material H some time ago when it paid $4.50 per kg. Currently 3,700 kgs of this remains in inventory. The inventory of material H could be sold for $3.20 per kg.

The company has no other use for material H other than on this contract, but it could be modified it at a cost of $3.70 per kg and use it as a substitute for material J. Material J is regularly used by the company and can be bought for $7.50 per kg.

What is the relevant cost of the material for the contract?

A $17,210

B $19,800

C $26,460

D $30,900

74 Ace Limited is considering a new project that will require the use of a currently idle machine. The machine has a current book value of $12,000 and a potential disposal value of $10,500 (before $200 disposal costs) and hence has been under depreciated by $1,500 over its life to date. If the machine is to be fit for purpose on the new project it will have to be relocated at a cost of $500 and refitted at a further cost of $800.

What is the relevant cost of using the machine on the new project?

A $9,000

B $10,300

C $11,600

D $13,300

75 Blunt is considering a new project but is unsure how much overhead to include in the calculations to help him decide whether or not to proceed. Existing fixed overheads are absorbed at the rate of $8 per hour worked. Blunt is certain that the project will involve an incremental 500 labour hours.

The project will involve extra machine running costs and these variable overheads cost him $4 per hour. The number of extra machine hours is expected to be 450 hours. The difference between this figure and the 500 labour hours above is expected idle time.

The project will require a little more temporary space that can be rented at a fixed cost of $1,200 for the period of hire. This overhead is not included in the fixed overhead absorption rate above.

What is the overhead to be charged to the project?

A $3,000

B $3,200

C $7,000

D $7,200

76 Cleverclogs is short of labour for a new one-off project needing 600 hours of labour and has choices as to where to source this. They could hire new people temporarily from an agency at a cost of $9 per hour. Alternatively, they could recruit new temporary staff at a fixed cost of advertising of $1,200 but then only pay $6 per hour for the time. They could also redirect some staff from existing work who are currently paid $7 per hour and who make sandals that generate a contribution of $3 per hour after all variable costs. Sandals are a good selling product and Cleverclogs will lose the production and the related sales whilst staff is working on the new one-off project.

What is the relevant cash flow?

A $1,800

B $3,600

C $4,200

D $4,800

77 X plc intends to use relevant costs as the basis of the selling price for a special order: the printing of a brochure. The brochure requires a particular type of paper that is not regularly used by X plc although a limited amount is in X plc's inventory which was left over from a previous job. The cost when X plc bought this paper last year was $15 per ream and there are 100 reams in inventory. The brochure requires 250 reams. The current market price of the paper is $26 per ream, and the resale value of the paper in inventory is $10 per ream.

What is the relevant cost of the paper to be used in printing the brochure?

A $2,500

B $4,900

C $5,400

D $6,500

COST VOLUME PROFIT ANALYSIS

78 A company makes and sells product X and product Y. Twice as many units of product Y are made and sold as that of product X. Each unit of product X makes a contribution of $10 and each unit of product Y makes a contribution of $4. Fixed costs are $90,000.

What is the total number of units which must be made and sold to make a profit of $45,000?

A 7,500

B 22,500

C 15,000

D 16,875

79 Betis Limited is considering changing the way it is structured by asking its employed staff to become freelance. Employees are currently paid a fixed salary of $240,000 per annum, but would instead be paid $200 per working day. On a typical working day, staff can produce 40 units. Other fixed costs are $400,000 per annum.

The selling price of a unit is $60 and material costs are $20 per unit.

What will be the effect of the change on the breakeven point of the business and the level of operating risk?

A The breakeven point reduces by 6,000 units and the operating gearing goes down

B The breakeven point reduces by 4,571 units and the operating gearing goes down

C The breakeven point reduces by 4,571 units and the operating gearing goes up

D The breakeven point reduces by 6,000 units and the operating gearing goes up

80 P Co makes two products – P1 and P2 – budgeted details of which are as follows:

	P1	**P2**
	$	$
Selling price	10.00	8.00
Cost per unit:		
Direct materials	3.50	4.00
Direct labour	1.50	1.00
Variable overhead	0.60	0.40
Fixed overhead	1.20	1.00
Profit per unit	**3.20**	**1.60**

Budgeted production and sales for the year ended 30 November 20X5 are:

Product P1	10,000 units
Product P2	12,500 units

The fixed overhead costs included in P1 relate to apportionment of general overhead costs only. However P2 also includes specific fixed overheads totalling $2,500.

If only product P1 were to be made, how many units (to the nearest unit) would need to be sold in order to achieve a profit of $60,000 each year?

81 An organisation manufactures and sells a single product, the G. It has produced the following budget for the coming year:

	$000	$000
Sales revenue (20,000 units)		5,000
Manufacturing costs		
Fixed	1,600	
Variable	1,400	
Selling costs		
Fixed	1,200	
Variable	400	
Cost of sales		(4,600)
Profit		400

If inventory levels are negligible, what is the breakeven point in units?

A 13,634

B 13,750

C 17,500

D 28,000

82 A company manufactures and sells a single product with a variable cost per unit of $36. It has a contribution to sales ratio (C/S ratio) of 25%. The company has weekly fixed costs of $18,000.

Which of the following is the weekly breakeven point in units? Pick from list

List options are as follows:

- 1,500
- 1,600
- 1,800
- 2,000

83 A company makes a single product with the following data:

	$	$
Selling price		25
Material	5	
Labour	7	
Variable overhead	3	
Fixed overhead	4	
		(19)
Profit per unit		6

Budgeted output is 30,000 units.

In relation to this data, which ONE of the following statements is correct?

A The margin of safety is 40%

B The contribution to sales ratio is 24%

C The volume of sales needed to make a profit of $270,000 is 45,000 units

D If budgeted sales increase to 40,000 units, budgeted profit will increase by $100,000

84 The management accountant of Caroline plc has calculated the firm's breakeven point from the following data:

Selling price per unit	$20
Variable costs per unit	$8
Fixed overheads for next year	$79,104

It is now expected that the product's selling price and variable cost will increase by 8% and 5.2% respectively.

By how much will Caroline's breakeven point for next year change by as a result of these changes?

A Rise by 9.0%

B Rise by 2.8%

C Fall by 2.8%

D Fall by 9%

85 Edwards sells two products with selling prices and contributions as follows:

	Product F	Product G
Selling price per unit	$40	$20
Contribution per unit	$10	$4
Budgeted sales units	150,000	100,000

Edwards' fixed costs are $1,400,000 per year.

What is Edwards' current breakeven revenue (to the nearest $)?

A $100,000

B $200,000

C $5,600,000

D $5,894,737

86 Edwards sells two products with selling prices and contributions as follows:

	Product F	**Product G**
Selling price	\$40	\$20
Contribution	\$10	\$4
Budgeted sales units	150,000	100,000

Edwards' fixed costs are \$1,400,000 per year.

Edwards now anticipates that more customers will buy the cheaper product G and that budgeted sales will be 150,000 units for each product.

What would be the impact on the break-even revenue if the sales volume of G increases?

A Increase by the extra revenue from G of 50,000 × \$20 per unit, or \$1,000,000

B Decrease by the extra revenue from G of 50,000 × \$20 per unit, or \$1,000,000

C Increase by a different amount

D Decrease by a different amount

87

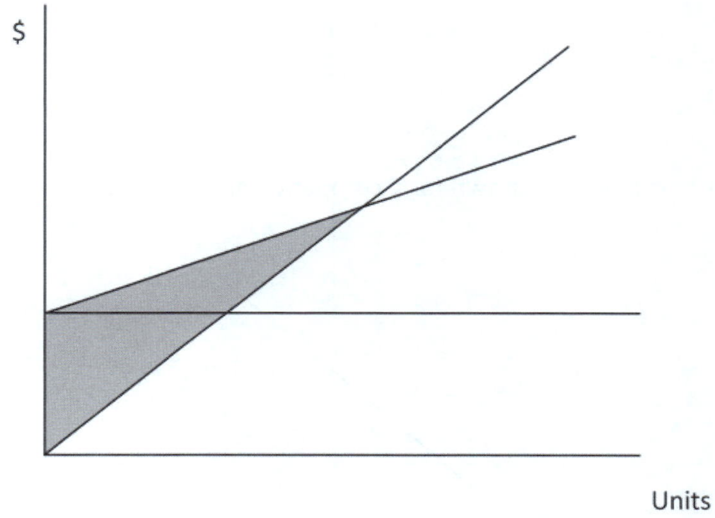

What does the shaded area on the breakeven chart above represent?

A Loss

B Fixed cost

C Variable cost

D Profit

88 A company has produced the following Profit/Volume (P/V) chart for its sole product:

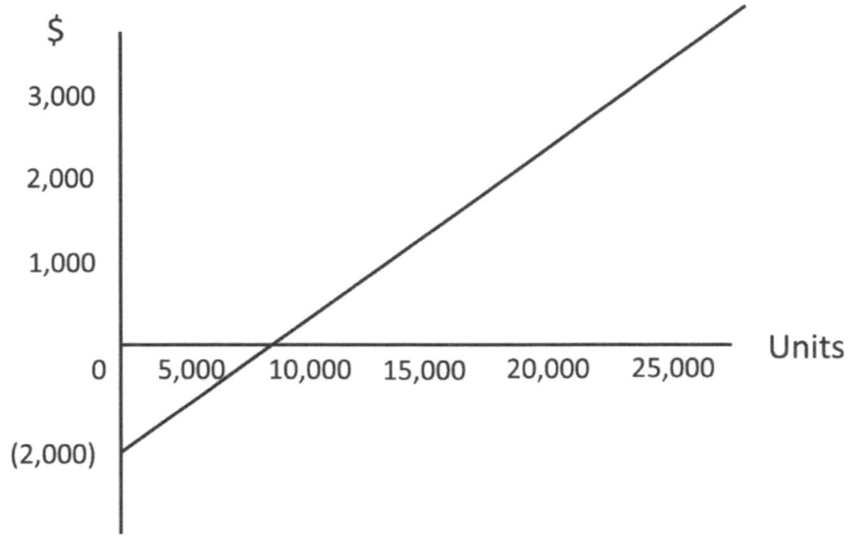

What are the total fixed costs for the product?

A $0

B $2,000

C $8,000

D $10,000

89 The following breakeven chart has been drawn for a company's single product:

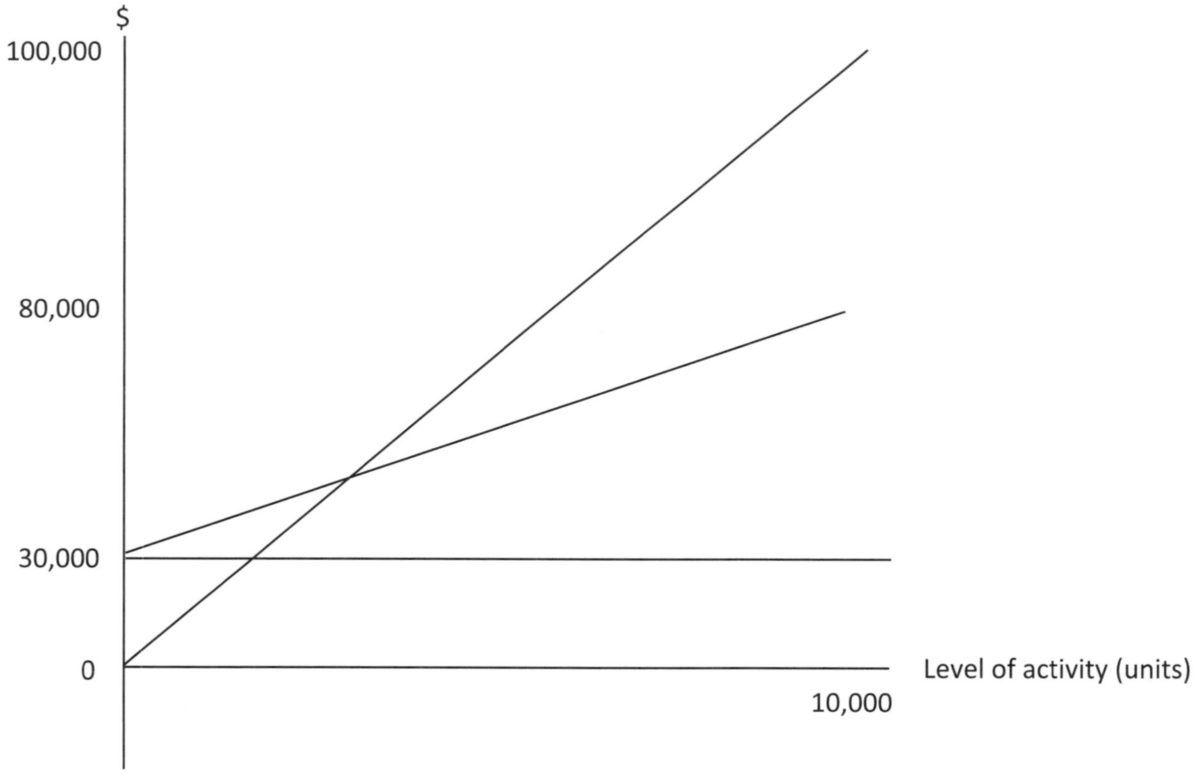

Which of the following statements about the product are correct?

(1) The product's selling price is $10 per unit.

(2) The product's variable cost is $8 per unit.

(3) The product incurs fixed costs of $30,000 per period.

(4) The product earns a profit of $70,000 at a level of activity of 10,000 units.

A (2) and (3)

B (1) and (3)

C (1) and (4) only

D (1), (2) and (4)

90 Hubbard Ltd manufactures and sells a single product that has the following cost and selling price structure:

	$/unit
Selling price	199
Direct material	54
Direct labour	50
Variable overhead	20
Fixed overhead	22
	53

The fixed overhead absorption rate is based on the normal budgeted capacity of 6,200 units per month. The same amount is spent each month on fixed overheads.

Which TWO of the following statements about the performance of Hubbard Ltd next month are correct?

- 1,921 units are required to breakeven next month
- 3,152 units of sales are required to achieve a profit of $100,000 next month
- Monthly fixed costs amount to $136,400
- The margin of safety next month is 75%

91 The following profit-volume chart for three products, has been prepared:

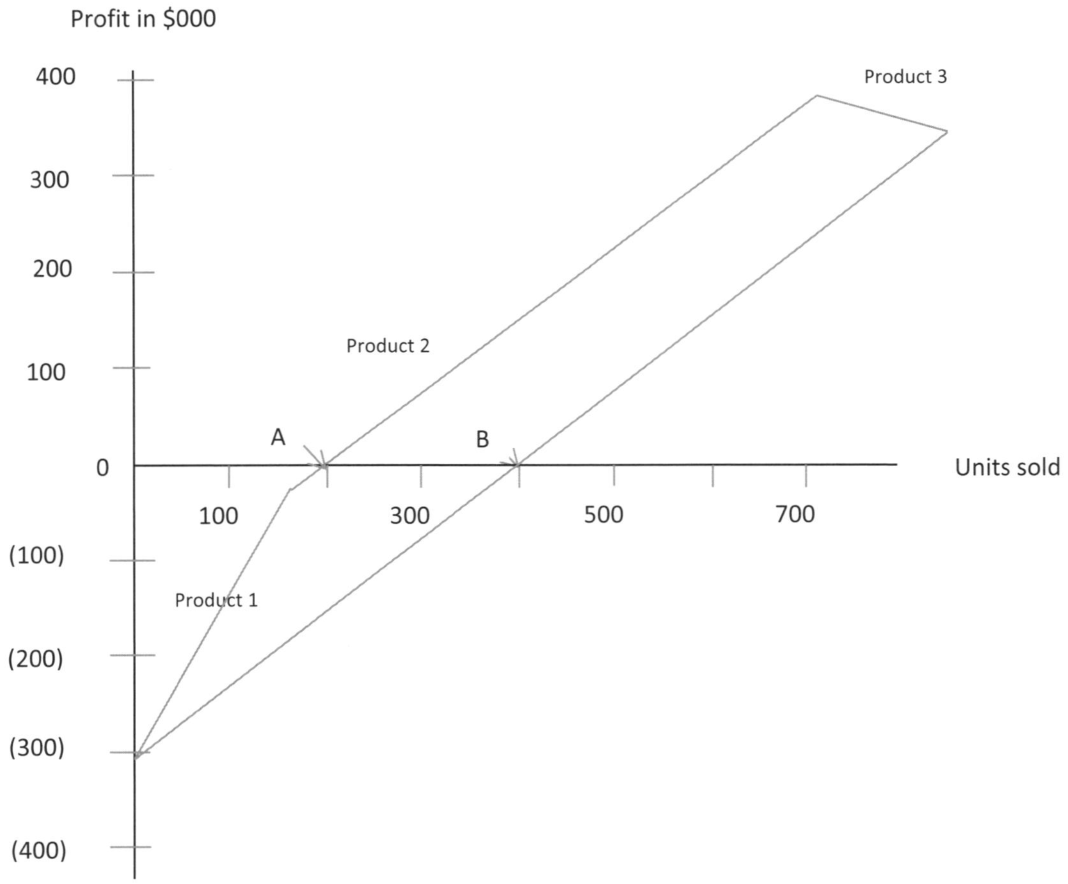

Which TWO of the following statements about the above chart are correct?

- Point A is the breakeven point if the company's products are sold in order of their C/S ratio
- Point B is the breakeven point if the company's products are sold in the budgeted sales mix
- Changing the product mix in favour of Product 3 would improve the overall c/s ratio
- If all three products are produced, then the company can expect sales revenues of $350,000

92 The contribution to sales (C/S) ratio for a business is 0.4 and its fixed costs are $1,600,000. Budget revenue has been set at 6 times the amount of the fixed costs.

What is the margin of safety % measured in revenue (to 1 decimal place)?

[ ] %

LIMITING FACTORS

93 A company has the following production planned for the next four weeks. The figures reflect the full capacity level of operations. Planned output is equal to the maximum demand per product.

	Product A	**Product B**	**Product C**	**Product D**
	$/unit	$/unit	$/unit	$/unit
Selling price	160	214	100	140
Raw material cost	24	56	22	40
Direct labour cost	66	88	33	22
Variable overhead cost	24	18	24	18
Fixed overhead cost	16	10	8	12
Profit	30	42	13	48
Planned output	300	125	240	400
Direct labour hours per unit	6	8	3	2

The direct labour force is threatening to go on strike for two weeks out of the coming four. This means that only 2,160 hours will be available for production, rather than the usual 4,320 hours.

If the strike goes ahead, which product or products should be produced if profits are to be maximised? Place a tick in the boxes in the table below as appropriate.

	Should be produced	**Should not be produced**
Product A		
Product B		
Product C		
Product D		

94 An organisation has the following contribution function:

Contribution = 5X + 10Y

where

X = the number of units of product X produced, and

Y = the number of units of product Y produced.

A graph has identified that the optimal production plan exists at the point where the following two constraints cross:

Skilled labour: $6X + 4Y \leq 62{,}000$

Unskilled labour: $2X + 5Y \leq 50{,}000$

There is a maximum demand of 12,000 units of each product.

What is the number of units of Product Y produced in order to maximise contribution (to the nearest whole unit)?

95 A jewellery company makes rings (R) and necklaces (N).

The resources available to the company have been analysed and two constraints have been identified:

Labour time $3R + 2N \leq 2{,}400$ hours Machine time $0.5R + 0.4N \leq 410$ hours

The management accountant has used linear programming to determine that R = 500 and N = 400.

Which of the following is/are slack resources?

(1) Labour time available

(2) Machine time available

A (1) only

B (2) only

C Both (1) and (2)

D Neither (1) nor (2)

96 Q plc makes two products – Quone and Qutwo – from the same raw material. The selling price and cost details of these products are as shown below:

	Quone	**Qutwo**
	$	$
Selling price	20.00	18.00
Direct material ($2.00 per kg)	6.00	5.00
Direct labour	4.00	3.00
Variable overhead	2.00	1.50
	12.00	9.50
Contribution per unit	8.00	8.50

The maximum demand for these products is 500 units per week for Quone, and an unlimited number of units per week for Qutwo.

What is the shadow price of these materials, if material were limited to 2,000 kgs per week? Pick from list

List options are:

- $nil
- $2.00 per kg
- $2.66 per kg
- $3.40 per kg

97 The shadow price of skilled labour for CBV is currently $8 per hour. What does this mean?

A The cost of obtaining additional skilled labour resources is $8 per hour

B There is a hidden cost of $8 for each hour of skilled labour actively worked

C Contribution will be increased by $8 per hour for each extra hour of skilled labour that can be obtained

D Total costs will be reduced by $8 for each additional hour of skilled labour that can be obtained

98 The following details relate to three services provided by RST Company:

	Service R	Service S	Service T
	$	$	$
Fee charged to customers	100	150	160
Unit service costs:			
Direct materials	15	30	25
Direct labour	20	35	30
Variable overhead	15	20	22
Fixed overhead	25	50	50

All three services use the same type of direct labour which is paid $25 per hour.

The fixed overheads are general fixed overheads that have been absorbed on the basis of machine hours.

What are the most and least profitable uses of direct labour, a scarce resource?

	Most profitable	Least profitable
A	S	R
B	S	T
C	T	R
D	T	S

99 A linear programming model has been formulated for two products, X and Y. The objective function is depicted by the formula C = 5X + 6Y, where C = contribution, X = the number of product X to be produced and Y = the number of product Y to be produced.

Each unit of X uses 2 kg of material Z and each unit of Y uses 3 kg of material Z. The standard cost of material Z is $2 per kg.

The shadow price for material Z has been worked out and found to be $2.80 per kg.

If an extra 20 kg of material Z becomes available at $2 per kg, what will the maximum increase in contribution be?

A Increase of $96

B Increase of $56

C Increase of $16

D No change

100 An organisation is experiencing a shortage of resources and has graphed a potential linear programming solution which shows its first product, televisions, on the horizontal axis and its other product, tablet computers, on the vertical axis.

The iso-contribution line to solve the linear programme is very flat and downward sloping.

Which of the following statements is likely to be true for the company?

A The contribution per unit for tablet computers must be higher than that for televisions

B The contribution per unit for televisions must be higher than that for tablet computers

C The contribution per unit for each type of product is very similar

D The contribution per unit for one of the products must be negative

101 A linear programming model has been formulated for two products, A and B, manufactured by J Co.

Which TWO of the following statements about linear programming are true?

- J Co can use linear programming if it starts to manufacture another product, C.
- J Co would not need to use linear programming if there was not a demand constraint.
- J Co should ignore fixed costs when making decisions about how to utilise production capacity in the short run, using linear programming.
- Linear programming models can be used when there is an experience curve, once the steady state has been reached.

102 An organisation has the following contribution function:

Contribution = 12A + 8B, where

A = the number of units of product A produced, and

B = the number of units of product B produced.

A graph has identified that the optimal production plan exists at the point where the following two constraints cross:

Material X: A + 2B ≤ 8,000

Material Y: 2A + B ≤ 13,000

There is a maximum demand of 10,000 units of each product.

How many units of Product A are produced in order to maximise contribution?

A 0

B 1,000

C 6,000

D 10,000

103 An organisation has created the following linear programming solution to represent the position it faces currently in the presence of short term scarce resources:

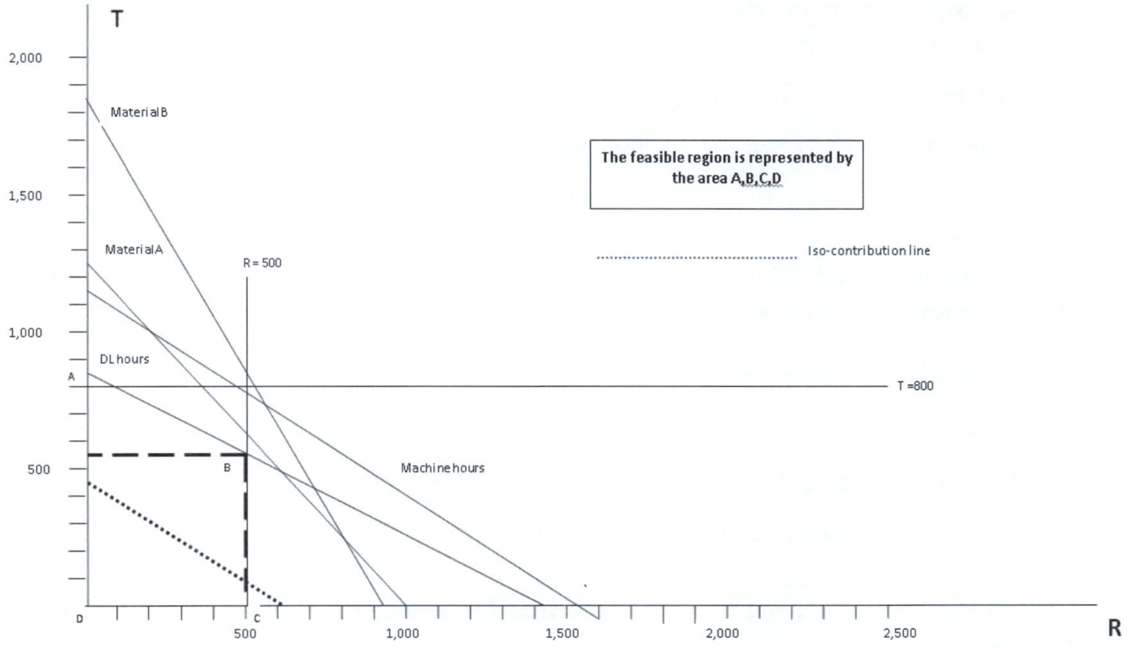

Note: DL = Direct labour hours

The point marked B has been determined to be the point which provides the optimal production plan.

Which of the following resources will have a shadow price greater than 0? (select all that apply)

- Direct labour hours
- Material A
- Material B
- Machine hours

PRICING DECISIONS

104 Which of the following statements regarding market penetration as a pricing strategy is/are correct?

(1) It is useful if significant economies of scale can be achieved.

(2) It is useful if demand for a product is highly elastic.

A (1) only

B (2) only

C Neither (1) nor (2)

D Both (1) and (2)

105 Which of the following conditions would need to be true for a price skimming strategy to be effective?

A An existing product where the owners have decided to increase prices to move the product up market

B Where the product has a long life-cycle

C Where the product has a short life-cycle

D Where only modest development costs had been incurred

106 Which TWO of the following circumstances (in relation to the launch of a new product) favour a penetration pricing strategy?

- Demand is relatively inelastic
- There are significant economies of scale
- The firm wishes to discourage new entrants to the market
- The product life cycle is particularly short

107 Which of the following conditions must be true for a price discrimination strategy to be effective?

A Buying power of customers must be similar in both market segments

B Goods must not be able to move freely between market segments

C Goods must be able to move freely between market segments

D The demand curves in each market must be the same

108 The demand for product S is 50,000 units at the current price of $1,000. Market research has determined that there is a linear relationship between price and demand that can be calculated using the following function:

$P = 1{,}500 - 0.01Q$

The variable cost per unit of producing product S is $200, and fixed costs are $20 million.

What is the maximum total profit for product S?

A $13,000,000

B $22,250,000

C $42,250,000

D $55,250,000

109 A product has a prime cost of $12, variable overheads of $3 per unit and fixed overheads of $6 per unit.

Which pricing policy gives the highest price?

A Prime cost + 80%

B Marginal cost + 60%

C Total absorption cost + 20%

D Net margin of 14% on selling price

110 The demand for a product is 5,000 units when the price is $400 and 6,000 units when price is $380. The variable cost of the product is $200.

What is the optimum price to be charged in order to maximise profit?

A $150

B $200

C $350

D $700

111 A brand new game is about to be launched. The game is unique and can only be played on the Star2000 gaming console, another one of the businesses products. Students are entitled to a small discount.

Which THREE of the following pricing strategies could be used to price the game?

- Penetration pricing
- Price skimming
- Complimentary product pricing
- Product line pricing
- Price discrimination
- Variable production cost + %

112 The following price and demand combinations have been given:

P1 = $400, Q1 = 5,000 units

P2 = $380, Q2 = 5,500 units

The variable cost is a constant at $80 per unit and fixed costs are $600,000 per annum.

What is the demand function?

A P = 200 – 0.04Q

B P = 600 – 0.04Q

C P = 600 + 0.04Q

D P = 200 – 20Q

113 The following price and demand combinations have been given:

P1 = $400, Q1 = 5,000 units

P2 = $380, Q2 = 5,500 units

The variable cost is a constant at $80 per unit and fixed costs are $600,000 per annum.

The optimal price is (to the nearest $):

$ ______

MAKE-OR-BUY AND OTHER SHORT TERM DECISIONS

114 Which FOUR of the following are to be correctly included in the considerations in a make or buy decision?

(i) The amount of re-allocated rent costs caused by using the production space differently.

(ii) The variable costs of purchase from the new supplier.

(iii) The level of discount available from the new supplier.

(iv) The redundancy payments to the supervisor of the product in question.

(v) The saved labour costs of the production staff re-directed to other work.

(vi) The materials no longer bought to manufacture the product.

115 While a drag and drop style question is impossible to fully replicate within a paper based medium, some questions of this style have been included for completeness.

Ace Limited is considering whether or not to cease production of leather-bound diaries.

Which TWO of the following items are valid factors to consider in this decision?

- The diaries made a loss in the year just passed
- The diaries made a positive contribution in the year just passed
- The market outlook in the long term looks very poor
- The budget for next year shows a loss
- The business also sells pens and many diary buyers will often also buy a pen
- The business was founded to produce and sell diaries

Drag and drop the correct factors in the box below:

116 Jorioz Co makes joint products X and Y. $120,000 joint processing costs are incurred.

At the split-off point, 10,000 units of X and 9,000 units of Y are produced, with selling prices of $1.20 for X and $1.50 for Y.

The units of X could be processed further to make 8,000 units of product Z. The extra costs incurred in this process would be fixed costs of $1,600 and variable costs of $0.50 per unit of input.

The selling price of Z would be $2.25.

What profit or loss will arise if product X is further processed? Pick from

List options are

- $600 loss
- $400 gain
- $3,900 gain
- $1,600 loss

117 P is considering whether to continue making a component or to buy it from an outside supplier. It uses 12,000 of the components each year.

The internal manufacturing cost comprises:

	$/unit
Direct materials	3.00
Direct labour	4.00
Variable overhead	1.00
Specific fixed cost	2.50
Other fixed costs	2.00
	12.50

If the direct labour were not used to manufacture the component, it would be used to increase the production of another item for which there is unlimited demand. This other item has a contribution of $10.00 per unit but requires $8.00 of labour per unit.

What is the maximum price per component, at which buying is preferable to internal manufacture?

A $8.00

B $10.50

C $12.50

D $15.50

DEALING WITH RISK AND UNCERTAINTY IN DECISION-MAKING

118 Shuffles Co uses fork-lift trucks in its warehouses. The management accountant is deciding which grade of trucks to buy based on the company's risk appetite. There are three grades of truck, the A series, B series and the C series. The decision for the truck is dependent on Shuffles Co's growth in its online market which could be at 15%, 30% or 40% for the next period.

The management accountant has correctly produced a pay-off table showing the daily contribution earned for each of the outcomes.

Pay-off table		**Type of truck**		
		A series	**B series**	**C series**
Growth rate	15%	$2,400	$1,800	$3,600
	30%	$1,400	$1,900	$4,500
	40%	$4,900	$2,800	$3,900

If Shuffles Co is risk averse, which grade of truck will it purchase?' Enter the letter only.

[ ] **series**

119 Shuffles Co uses fork-lift trucks in its warehouses. The management accountant is deciding which grade of trucks to buy based on the company's risk appetite. There are three grades of truck, the A series, B series and the C series. The decision for the truck is dependent on Shuffles Co's growth in its online market which could be at 15%, 30% or 40% for the next period.

The management accountant has correctly produced a pay-off table showing the daily contribution earned for each of the outcomes.

Pay-off table		**Type of truck**		
		A series	**B series**	**C series**
Growth rate	15%	$2,400	$1,800	$3,600
	30%	$1,400	$1,900	$4,500
	40%	$4,900	$2,800	$3,900

If Shuffles Co is risk seeking, which grade of truck will it purchase?' Enter the letter only.

[ ] **series**

120 Shuffles Co uses fork-lift trucks in its warehouses. The management accountant is deciding which grade of trucks to buy based on the company's risk appetite. There are three grades of truck, the A series, B series and the C series. The decision for the truck is dependent on Shuffles Co's growth in its online market which could be at 15%, 30% or 40% for the next period.

The management accountant has correctly produced a pay-off table showing the daily contribution earned for each of the outcomes.

Pay-off table		**Type of truck**		
		A series	**B series**	**C series**
Growth rate	15%	$2,400	$1,800	$3,600
	30%	$1,400	$1,900	$4,500
	40%	$4,900	$2,800	$3,900

If Shuffles Co adopt the minimax regret approach to decision-making, which grade of truck will it purchase? Enter the letter only.

	series

121 Shuffles Co uses fork-lift trucks in its warehouses. The management accountant is deciding which grade of trucks to buy based on the company's risk appetite. There are three grades of truck, the A series, B series and the C series. The decision for the truck is dependent on Shuffles Co's growth in its online market which could be at 15%, 30% or 40% for the next period.

The management accountant has correctly produced a pay-off table showing the daily contribution earned for each of the outcomes.

Pay-off table		**Type of truck**		
		A series	**B series**	**C series**
Growth rate	15%	$2,400	$1,800	$3,600
	30%	$1,400	$1,900	$4,500
	40%	$4,900	$2,800	$3,900

Based upon the scenario information, if the probabilities of the given growth rates are 15%: 0.4, 30%: 0.25 and 40%: 0.35, and Shuffles Co is risk neutral, which grade of truck will it purchase? Enter the letter only.

	series

122 Which TWO of the following statements about sensitivity analysis are correct?

(1) Sensitivity analysis can be used to gain insight into which assumptions or variables in a situation are critical.

(2) Sensitivity analysis provides information on the basis of which decisions can be made but it does not point to the correct decision directly.

(3) As well as identifying how far a variable needs to change, sensitivity analysis looks at the probability of such a change.

(4) Sensitivity analysis not only assumes that variables can change independently, it also allows to change more than one variable at a time.

A (1) and (2) only

B (2) and (3) only

C (1) and (4) only

D (2) and (4) only

123 Indicate, by clicking in the relevant boxes, whether the following statements about simulation are true or not true:

	True	Not true
Simulation models the behaviour of a system.		
Simulation models can be used to study alternative solutions to a problem.		
The equations describing the operating characteristics of the system are known.		
A simulation model cannot prescribe what should be done about a problem.		

124 A company has used expected values to evaluate a one-off project. The expected value calculation assumed two possible profit outcomes which were assigned probabilities of 0.4 and 0.6.

Which TWO of the following statements about this approach are correct?

- The expected value profit is the profit with the highest probability of being achieved
- The expected value gives no indication of the dispersion of the possible outcomes
- Expected values are relatively insensitive to assumptions about probability
- The expected value may not correspond to any of the actual possible outcomes

125 Tree Co is considering employing a sales manager. Market research has shown that a good sales manager can increase profit by 30%, an average one by 20% and a poor one by 10%. Experience has shown that the company has attracted a good sales manager 35% of the time, an average one 45% of the time and a poor one 20% of the time. The company's normal profits are $180,000 per annum and the sales manager's salary would be $40,000 per annum.

Based on the expected value criterion, which of the following represents the correct advice which Tree Co should be given?

A Do not employ a sales manager as profits would be expected to fall by $1,300

B Employ a sales manager as profits will increase by $38,700

C Employ a sales manager as profits are expected to increase by $100

D Do not employ a sales manager as profits are expected to fall by $39,900

126 Which of the following is the correct definition of IMPERFECT information?

A Information which costs more to collect than its value to the business

B Information which is available only after preliminary decisions on a business venture have been taken

C Information which does not take into account all factors affecting a business

D Information which may contain inaccurate predictions

127 A company is considering the development and marketing of a new product. Development costs will be $2m and are not accounted for in the profit figures below. There is a 75% probability that the development effort will be successful, and a 25% probability that it will be unsuccessful. If development **is** successful and the product **is** marketed, it is estimated that:

	Profit	**Probability**
Product very successful	$6.0m	0.4
Product moderately successful	$1.8m	0.4
Product unsuccessful	($5.0m)	0.2

What is the expected value of profit for the new product?

A ($0.41m)

B $2.12m

C $1.59m

D $0.41m

128 A company can make either of two new products, X and Y, but not both. The profitability of each product depends on the state of the market, as follows:

Market state	**Profit from product**		**Probability of market state**
	X $	Y $	
Good	20,000	17,000	0.2
Fair	15,000	16,000	0.5
Poor	6,000	7,000	0.3

What is the expected value of perfect information as to the state of the market?

$ ________

129 A business is considering investing in a project which is very dependent on whether a government grant is received.

Details on the project are as follows:

	Grant received	**Grant not received**	**Overall expected value**
Probability	30%	70%	
Expected profits/(loss)	$200,000	($80,000)	$4,000

It is now concerned that the expected loss when the grant is not received has been underestimated.

What would the expected loss when the grant is not received have to increase to in order to no longer make the project worthwhile?

A $84,000

B $85,714

C $114,286

D $200,000

130 An organisation is considering launching a new product, X. If the product is successful in its first month there will be an opportunity to either make a further investment or to outsource all future development to another company. The decision for the company is illustrated by the following decision tree:

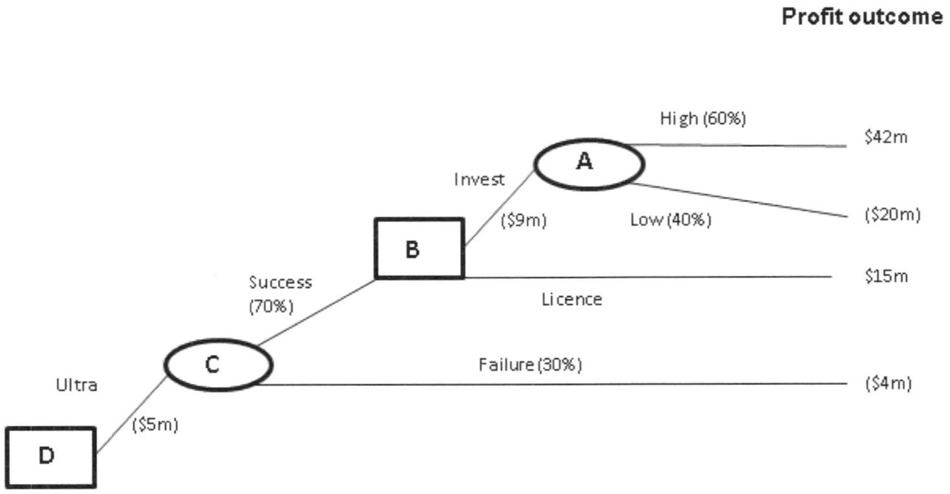

The profit outcomes do not include the cost of any investments made.

What is the expected value from investing in product X (i.e. at point D)?

A $0

B $4.3m

C $6.2m

D $6.5m

131 Which of the following is considered to be a form of secondary research?

A Desk research

B Motivational research

C Measurement research

D Field research

BUDGETING AND CONTROL

BUDGETARY SYSTEMS AND TYPES OF BUDGET

132 Which of the following statements are true regarding activity-based budgeting (ABB)?

(1) The costs determined using activity-based costing (ABC) are used as a basis for preparing budgets.

(2) The aim of ABB is to control the number of units output rather than the costs themselves.

A (1) only

B (2) only

C Neither (1) nor (2)

D Both (1) and (2)

133 Which of the following statement(s) is/are true regarding budgetary systems in the performance hierarchy?

(1) Developing new products in response the changes in technology is a budgeting activity that would fall within operational planning and control.

(2) Budgetary systems at strategic planning levels look at the business as a whole and define resource requirements.

A (1) only

B (2) only

C Neither (1) nor (2)

D Both (1) and (2)

134 What is the purpose of a flexible budget?

A To allow budgets to be produced for virtually any level of production

B To reduce the total time in preparing the annual budget

C To allow management some latitude in meeting goals

D To eliminate cyclical fluctuations in production reports by ignoring variable costs

135 **Which of the following statement(s) is/are true regarding feed-forward control budgetary systems?**

(1) Feed-forward control systems have an advantage over other types of control in that it establishes how effective planning was.

(2) Feed-forward control can start as soon as actual results become available.

A (1) only

B (2) only

C Neither (1) nor (2)

D Both (1) and (2)

136 Incremental budgeting can sometimes be an appropriate methodology for setting budgets.

Which THREE of the following statements are true?

Incremental budgets could be appropriate when:

- The business is growing rapidly
- Applied to total sales in an international seasonal business
- Applied to stationary costs
- Applied to production costs
- The business is stable
- For administration costs when the experience of the managers is limited

Drag the correct answers in to the box:

137 Which of the following best describes an incremental budgeting system?

A a system that budgets only for the extra costs associated with a particular plan

B a system that budgets for the variable manufacturing costs only

C a system that prepares budgets only after the manager responsible has justified the continuation of the relevant activity

D a system that prepares budgets by adjusting the previous year's values by expected changes in volumes of activity and price/inflation effects

138 Which of the following is an advantage of non-participative budgeting as compared to participative budgeting?

A It increases motivation

B It is less time consuming

C It increases acceptance

D The budgets produced are more attainable

139 Which of the following is a common feature of a beyond budgeting approach?

A A greater use of rolling budgets

B A greater use of top-down budgets

C A greater emphasis on financial targets

D A greater focus on standardisation

140 EFG uses an activity-based budgeting system. It manufactures three products, budgeted details of which are set out below:

	Product E	**Product F**	**Product G**
Budgeted annual production (units)	75,000	120,000	60,000
Batch size (units)	200	60	30
Machine set-ups per batch	5	3	9
Purchase orders per batch	4	2	2
Processing time per unit (minutes)	3	4	4

Three cost pools have been identified. Their budgeted costs for the year ending 30 September 20X3 are as follows:

Machine set-up costs	$180,000
Purchasing of materials	$95,000
Processing	$110,000

Which of the following is the budgeted machine set-up cost per unit of product F? Pick from list

List options are:

- $0.1739
- $0.35
- $6.96
- Cannot be determined without any more information

141 Which of the following best describes a master budget?

A Budgeted Statement of profit or loss and budgeted cash flow only

B Budgeted Statement of profit or loss and budgeted Statement of financial position only

C Budgeted Statement of profit or loss and budgeted capital expenditure

D Budgeted Statement of profit or loss, budgeted Statement of financial position and budgeted cash flow

142 Which TWO of the following are expected benefits from a beyond budgeting approach?

- Coordination between activities becomes easier
- It is cheap and easy to introduce
- Innovation and continuous improvement become more likely
- The organisation becomes more customer focused

143 X Co uses rolling budgeting, updating its budgets on a quarterly basis. After carrying out the last quarter's update to the cash budget, it projected a forecast cash deficit of $400,000 at the end of the year. Consequently, the planned purchase of new capital equipment has been postponed.

Which of the following types of control is the sales manager's actions an example of?

A Feedforward control

B Negative feedback control

C Positive feedback control

D Double loop feedback control

144 Which of the following statement(s) is/are true regarding different types of budget?

(1) A flexible budget can be used to control operational efficiency.

(2) Incremental budgeting can be defined as a system of budgetary planning and control that measures the additional costs that are incurred when there are unplanned extra units of activity.

(3) Rolling budgets review and, if necessary, revise the budget for the next quarter to ensure that budgets remain relevant for the remainder of the accounting period.

A (1) and (3)

B (2) and (3)

C (3) only

D (1) only

145 A definition of zero-based budgeting is set out below, with two blank sections.

"Zero-based budgeting: a method of budgeting which requires each cost element __________, as though the activities to which the budget relates ______________."

Which combination of two phrases correctly completes the definition?

	Blank 1	Blank 2
A	to be specifically justified	could be out-sourced to an external supplier
B	to be set at zero	could be out-sourced to an external supplier
C	to be specifically justified	were being undertaken for the first time
D	to be set at zero	were being undertaken for the first time

146 Which TWO of the following statements regarding zero-based budgeting are correct?

- It is best applied to support expenses rather than to direct costs
- It can link strategic goals to specific functional areas
- It carries forward inefficiencies from previous budget periods
- It is consistent with a top-down budgeting approach

147 Which of the following statement(s) regarding the drawbacks of activity-based budgeting (ABB) is/are true?

(1) It is not always useful or applicable, as in the short term many overhead costs are not controllable and do not vary directly with changes in the volume of activity for the cost driver.

(2) ABB will not be able to provide useful information for a total quality management programme (TQM).

A (1) only

B (2) only

C Neither (1) nor (2)

D Both (1) and (2)

QUANTITATIVE TECHNIQUES

148 The following table shows the number of clients who attended a particular accountancy practice over the last four weeks and the total costs incurred during each of the weeks:

Week	Number of clients	Total cost ($)
1	400	36,880
2	440	39,840
3	420	36,800
4	460	40,000

Applying the high low method to the above information, which of the following could be used to forecast total cost ($) from the number of clients expected to attend (where x = the expected number of clients)?

A 7,280 + 74x

B 16,080 + 52x

C 3,200 + 80x

D 40,000/x

149 PT has discovered that, when it employs a new test engineer, there is a learning curve with a 75% rate of learning that exists for the first 12 customer assignments. A new test engineer completed their first customer assignment in 6 hours.

Note: The index for a 75% learning curve is –0.415.

Calculate the time that the new test engineer should take for their 7th assignment to the nearest 0.01 hours.

A 1.52 hours

B 1.62 hours

C 2.68 hours

D 18.73 hours

150 The first unit of product A takes 50 hours to produce. The learning rate is 85%, meaning b is –0.234.

What is the total time taken to produce 17 units (to the nearest 0.01 hours)?

A 19.88 hours

B 25.77 hours

C 418.14 hours

D 438.02 hours

151 The time taken to produce the first batch of 50 units was 500 hours. The total time for the first 16 batches of 50 units was 5,731 hours.

What is the learning rate (to the nearest %)?

[ ] %

152 The budgeted electricity cost for a business is $30,000 based upon production of 1,000 units. However, if 1,400 units were to be produced, the budgeted cost would rise to $31,600.

Using the high/low approach what would be the budgeted electricity cost if 2,100 units were to be produced (to the nearest $)?

$ [ ]

153 The time taken to produce the first unit produced was 100 hours. The time for the second unit was 90 hours.

What is the learning rate (to the nearest %)?

[ ] %

154 The time taken to produce the first batch of 50 units was 400 hours but the labour budget is subject to a learning effect where the learning rate is 90%. The rate of pay for labour is $12 per hour.

The business had received and satisfied an order for 600 units but it has now received a second order for another 800 units.

The value of b is = –0.152

What will be the labour cost for the second order? (to the nearest $))

$ [ ]

155 The times taken to produce each of the first four batches of a new product were as follows:

Batch number	**Time taken**
1	100 minutes
2	70 minutes
3	59 minutes
4	55 minutes

What was the rate of learning closest to? (1 d.p)

[ ] %

156 Kim Co has recently developed a new product. The nature of Kim Co's work is repetitive, and it is usual for there to be an 80% learning effect when a new product is developed. The time taken for the first unit was 22 minutes.

Note: For this question, use a value for b of –0.3219

How long would it take to make the fourth unit? Select from the list below.

List options are as follows:
17.6 minutes
14.08 minutes
15.45 minutes
9.98 minutes

157 Z plc has found that it can estimate future sales using time series analysis and regression techniques. The following trend equation has been derived:

$$y = 25{,}000 + 6{,}500x$$

where 'y' is the total sales units per quarter and 'x' is the time period reference number.

Z has also derived the following set of seasonal variation index values for each quarter using a multiplicative (proportional) model:

Quarter 1	70%
Quarter 2	90%
Quarter 3	150%
Quarter 4	90%

Assuming that the first quarter of year 1 is time period reference number 1, what would be the forecast sales units for the third quarter of year 7?

A 174,500 units

B 200,500 units

C 261,750 units

D 300,750 units

158 Hi-Tech plc is a mobile phone repair shop. The director is interested in the relationship between the amount that is spent on advertising and the sales revenue that is achieved. They have established that the regression equation y = 150 + 7x can be used, where y is the total sales revenue and x is the advertising spend (in $000s).

Which ONE of the following statements is a correct interpretation of the relationship?

A If $7,000 is spent on advertising, then sales revenue would be $150,000

B If no money is spent on advertising, then sales revenue would be $7,000

C If $150,000 is spent on advertising, then $7,000 sales revenue per month will be generated

D If no money is spent on advertising, then sales revenue would be $150,000

159 Production overhead costs at company MZ Ltd are assumed to vary in line with the number of labour hours worked. The following data has been collected:

Year	Total production overheads $	Number of labour hours	Cost index
20X4	205,000	4,200	189
20X5	226,180	4,700	205

If the line of best fit, based on current (20X5) prices is calculated as y = 127,000 + 18.6x, calculate the total expected overhead costs in 20X6 if expected production activity is 4,600 labour hours and the expected cost index is 225.

A $193,666

B $212,560

C $233,298

D $253,048

160 The overhead costs of RP have been found to be accurately represented by the formula:

y = $10,000 + $0.25x

where y is the monthly cost and x represents the activity level measured as the number of orders.

Monthly activity levels of orders may be estimated using a combined regression analysis and time series model:

a = 100,000 + 30b

where a represents the de-seasonalised monthly activity level and b represents the month number.

In month 240, the seasonal index value is 108.

The overhead cost for RP for month 240 is $_______ (round to the nearest $1,000)

161 Cosy Co is utilising time series analysis to forecast sales volume. An additive model has been developed:

- Trend is T = 1,800 + 4x where x is the quarter number (x = 1 for quarter 1 20X1)
- Average seasonal variations are:

	Quarter 1	Quarter 2	Quarter 3	Quarter 4
Average seasonal variation (units)	+1,450	?	-1,000	+800

Indicate, by selecting the relevant boxes in the table below, the quarter 2 average seasonal variation and the seasonally adjusted forecast sales units for quarter 2 20X2.

Quarter 2 average seasonal variation	**+1,250**	**-1,250**	**1.25**
Quarter 2 20X2 seasonally adjusted forecast sales units	**3,074**	**1,824**	**574**

162 A company has calculated that the coefficient of determination between output and production costs over a number of months is 89%.

Which TWO of the following comments can you deduce to be correct, based ONLY on the information provided?

	Correct?
89% of the variation in production costs from one month to the next can be explained by corresponding variation in output.	
Costs increase as output increases.	
The linear relationship between output and costs is very strong.	
An increase of 100% in output is associated with an increase of 89% in costs.	
An increase of 89% in output is associated with an increase of 100% in costs.	

163 Which TWO of the following statements about forecasting based on simple linear regression are correct?

A It can account for the effect of multiple independent variables

B It assumes that historical data is a reliable guide to the future

C It is not suitable when the variables show strong negative correlation

D Cost forecasts using extrapolation are less accurate than those using interpolation

STANDARD COSTING

164 Which of the following best describes a 'basic standard' within the context of budgeting?

A A standard which is kept unchanged over a period of time

B A standard which is based on current price levels

C A standard set at an ideal level, which makes no allowance for normal losses, waste and machine downtime

D A standard which assumes an efficient level of operation, but which includes allowances for factors such as normal loss, waste and machine downtime

165 Which TWO of the following statements about budgets and standards are true?

- Budgets can be used in situations where output cannot be measured, but standards cannot be used in such situations
- Budgets can include allowances for inefficiencies in operations, but standards use performance targets which are attainable under the most favourable conditions
- Budgets are used for planning purposes, standards are used only for control purposes
- Standards which remain unaltered for long periods of time are referred to as basic standards

166 Which one of the following best defines standard costing in a system of budgeting?

A all activities are examined without reference to history each year

B output level and costs are predetermined, actual results then compared with these predetermined costs and variances analysed

C actual costs are compared with predetermined costs for the level of activity

D costs are assigned to a manager in order that controllable and non-controllable costs are accounted for

167 When considering setting standards for costing, which of the following would NOT be appropriate?

A The normal level of activity should always be used for absorbing overheads

B Average prices for materials should be used, encompassing any discounts that are regularly available

C The labour rate used will be the rate at which the labour is paid

D Average material usage should be established based on generally-accepted working practices

168 Which of the following statements is/are true regarding standard costing and total quality management (TQM)?

(1) They focus on assigning responsibility solely to senior managers.

(2) They work well in rapidly changing environments.

A (1) only

B (2) only

C Neither (1) nor (2)

D Both (1) and (2)

169 While a drag and drop style question is impossible to fully replicate within a paper based medium, some questions of this style have been included for completeness.

A business is expanding rapidly and buying its material in a variety of countries in a variety of currencies. It has an exclusive supply delivery contract whereby the same logistics expert makes all deliveries in to its warehouses on a cost plus basis. It pays all delivery charges on a per unit basis.

Which THREE of the following are valid explanations of an adverse material price variance measured to include delivery costs as part of the cost per kg delivered?

Drag the correct items into the box below:

- Exchange rate movements
- Extra discounts agreed
- Increased world-wide demand for the material
- Extra supply of the material becoming available from new suppliers
- World oil price rises
- Increases in the dividends paid by the delivery business

MIX AND YIELD VARIANCES

170 While a drag and drop style question is impossible to fully replicate within a paper based medium, some questions of this style have been included for completeness.

The following are potential causes of a material usage variance; drag the TWO reasons that could properly explain an adverse usage variance and at the same time indicate poor performance of the production manager into the box below.

The business has separate managers for production, material purchase and machine maintenance.

- Selection of a new supplier offering similar quality for lower prices
- Inadequate training of newly recruited staff in the production department
- Movements in the exchange rates causing more expensive materials
- Machine breakdown due to delays in the annual maintenance schedule
- Reduced quality materials bought
- Change in the production process causing extra losses of materials

171 **Which of the following statements is/are true regarding the material mix variance?**

(1) A favourable total mix variance would suggest that a higher proportion of a cheaper material is being used instead of a more expensive one.

(2) A favourable total mix variance will usually result in a favourable material yield variance.

A (1) only

B Both (1) and (2)

C (2) only

D Neither (1) nor (2)

172 Which of the following concerning a labour planning variance is true?

A A labour planning variance will always be adverse if actual labour rates increase

B A labour planning variance will be caused by a manager changing the labour mix during the year

C A labour planning variance will be caused by an unexpected government policy to increase labour rates

D A labour planning variance will always lead to a variable overhead planning variance

173 Which of the following statements is/are true regarding the materials yield variance?

(1) An adverse total yield variance would suggest that less output has been achieved for a given input, i.e. that the total input in volume is more than expected for the output achieved.

(2) A favourable total mix variance will usually result in an adverse material yield variance.

A (1) only

B Both (1) and (2)

C (2) only

D Neither (1) nor (2)

174 A business advisor had planned to use 3 hours of labour on 700 client services in June. Labour is paid $40 per hour.

In June there were actually 900 services provided. Total labour hours were 3,240 and the actual labour rate was $42 per hour.

The advisor has since discovered that, due to a change in legislation that meant extra client responsibilities, the budget should have provided for 3 ½ hours of labour per service.

What is the adverse planning labour efficiency variance for June (to the nearest $000)?

$ ______

175 Product GX consists of a mix of three materials, J, K and L. The standard material cost of a unit of GX is as follows:

		$
Material J	5 kg at $4 per kg	20
Material K	2 kg at $12 per kg	24
Material L	3 kg at $8 per kg	24

During March, 3,000 units of GX were produced, and actual usage was:

Material J	13,200 kg
Material K	6,500 kg
Material L	9,300 kg

What was the materials yield variance for March?

A $6,800 favourable

B $6,800 adverse

C $1,000 favourable

D $1,000 adverse

176 An organisation has recorded a favourable labour rate planning variance for the year of $40,000.

On investigation it has discovered that, whilst actual labour rates were $60 per hour, a revised standard rate for labour should have been $70 per hour for the actual hours worked of 20,000.

What was the original planned labour rate per hour for the year (to the nearest $)?

$ ________

177 JC Ltd mixes three materials to produce a chemical SGR. The following extract from a standard cost card shows the materials to be used in producing 100 kg of chemical SGR:

	kg		$
Material A	50	$10 per kg	500
Material B	40	$5 per kg	200
Material C	20	$9 per kg	180
	110		880

During October, 23,180 kg of SGR were produced using the following materials:

	kg
Material A	13,200
Material B	7,600
Material C	5,600
	26,400

What is the total material mix variance?

A $1,984 adverse

B $7,216 adverse

C $9,200 adverse

D $16,416 adverse

178 Mr. Green makes salads. The standard plate of salad has 30 g of lettuce (L), 50 g of peppers (P) and 80 g of beetroot (B). The standard prices of the three ingredients are $0.2/kg, 0.4/kg and 0.8/kg respectively. The actual prices were $0.22/kg, $0.38/kg and $0.82/kg.

Mr. Green has been experimenting and so in July he changed the mix of vegetables on the plate thus: 1,500 plates contained 62,000 grams of lettuce, 81,000 grams of peppers and 102,000 grams of beetroot.

What is the value of the total favourable material mix variance (to the nearest cent)?

$ ________

179 Mr. Green makes salads. The standard plate of salad has 30 g of lettuce (L), 50 g of peppers (P) and 80 g of beetroot (B). The standard prices of the three ingredients are $0.2/kg, 0.4/kg and 0.8/kg respectively.

Mr. Green has been experimenting and so in July he changed the mix of vegetables on the plate thus: 1,500 plates contained 62,000 grams of lettuce, 81,000 grams of peppers and 102,000 grams of beetroot.

What is the total material yield variance?

A $2.8125 favourable

B $2.8125 adverse

C $2,812.5 favourable

D $2,812.5 adverse

180 A company has a process in which the standard mix for producing 9 litres of output is as follows:

	$
4.0 litres of D at $9 per litre	36.00
3.5 litres of E at $5 per litre	17.50
2.5 litres of F at $2 per litre	5.00
Total	58.50

A standard loss of 10% of inputs is expected to occur. The actual inputs for the latest period were:

	$
4,300 litres of D at $9.00 per litre	38,700
3,600 litres of E at $5.50 per litre	19,800
2,100 litres of F at $2.20 per litre	4,620
Total	63,120

Actual output for this period was 9,100 litres.

What is the total material mix variance?

A $2,400 adverse

B $2,400 favourable

C $3,970 adverse

D $3,970 favourable

181 Operation B, in a factory, has a standard time of 15 minutes. The standard rate of pay for operatives is $10 per hour. The budget for a period was based on carrying out the operation 350 times. It was subsequently realised that the standard time for Operation B included in the budget did not incorporate expected time savings from the use of new machinery from the start of the period. The standard time should have been reduced to 12 minutes.

Operation B was actually carried out 370 times in the period in a total of 80 hours. The operatives were paid $850.

The operational labour efficiency variance was:

A $60 adverse

B $75 favourable

C $100 adverse

D $125 adverse

SALES MIX AND QUANTITY VARIANCES

182 Bloom Limited was the subject of the following press story:

"Bloom is proud to announce that it has managed to maintain its market share despite an overall increase in the market size by 10%." However, the sales director when challenged, by this journalist recently admitted having been forced to reduce prices by $1.50 per bunch on average on a budget volume of 12,000 bunches. All is not as rosy as it seems in Bloom's garden!" If the standard variable cost of a bloom bunch of flowers is $20 and the standard contribution gained is $5.

What is the adverse sales price variance (to the nearest $)?

$ [ ]

183 Bloom Limited was the subject of the following press story:

"Bloom is proud to announce that it has managed to maintain its market share despite an overall increase in the market size by 10%." However, the sales director when challenged, by this journalist recently admitted having been forced to reduce prices by $1.50 per bunch on average on a budget volume of 12,000 bunches. All is not as rosy as it seems in Bloom's garden!" If the standard variable cost of a bloom bunch of flowers is $20 and the standard contribution gained is $5.

What is the favourable sales volume variance (to the nearest $)?

$ [ ]

184 Yellow sells two types of squash balls: the type A and the type B. The standard contribution from these balls is $4 and $5 respectively and the standard profit per ball is $1.50 and $2.40 respectively. The budget was to sell 5 type A balls for every 3 type B balls.

Actual sales were 240,000 balls which is 20,000 balls higher than budgeted. The actual sales included 200,000 of the type A balls. Yellow values its stock of balls at standard marginal cost.

What is the value of the adverse sales mix variance (to the nearest $)?

$ [ ]

185 Yellow sells two types of squash ball, the type A and the type B. The standard contribution from these balls is $4 and $5 respectively and the standard profit per ball is $1.50 and $2.40 respectively. The budget was to sell 5 type A balls for every 3 type B balls.

Actual sales were 240,000 balls which is 20,000 balls higher than budgeted. The actual sales included 200,000 of the type A balls. Yellow values its stock of balls at standard marginal cost.

What is the value of the favourable sales quantity variance (to the nearest $)?

$ [ ]

186 Jones' monthly absorption costing variance analysis report includes a sales mix variance, which indicates the effect on profit of actual sales mix differing from the budgeted sales mix. The following data are available.

	Product X		**Product Y**	
	$	$	$	$
Selling price		12		11
Less Variable cost	6		2	
Fixed cost	2		3	
	—	(8)	—	(5)
Standard net profit per unit		4		6
July sales (units)				
Budget		3,000		6,000
Actual		2,000		8,000

Which one of the following best gives the favourable sales mix variance in July? Pick from list

List options include:

- $8,000
- $5,333
- $4,000
- $2,667

187 You have been provided with the following information relating to three products:

	Product X	Product Y	Product Z
Demand (units)	1,000	2,000	3,000
Selling price	$15	$20	$30
Profit per unit	$2	$5	$2

Actual sales for the year showed the following results.

	Product X	Product Y	Product Z
Units sold	1,100	2,050	2,800
Sales value	$17,050	$38,950	$86,800
Profit	$3,080	$10,455	$6,160

What is the sales quantity variance?

A $150 adverse

B $50 favourable

C $1,208 adverse

D $1,695 favourable

PLANNING AND OPERATIONAL VARIANCES

188 Which of the following statements are true regarding material price planning variances?

(1) The publication of material price planning variances should always lead to automatic updates of standard costs.

(2) The causes of material price planning variances do not need to be investigated by managers at any level in the organisation.

A (1) only

B (2) only

C Neither (1) nor (2)

D Both (1) and (2)

189 Leaf Limited has had a mixed year. Its market share has improved 2% to 20% but the overall market had contracted by 5% in the same period. The budgeted sales were 504,000 units and standard contribution was $12 per unit.

What is the level of actual sales?

A Two percentage points up on budget at 510,080 units

B Three percent down overall on budget at 488,880 units

C Three percent up on budget at 519,120 units

D Up by 5.55% to 532,000 units

190 Leaf Limited has had a mixed year. Its market share has improved 2% to 20% but the overall market had contracted by 5% in the same period. The budgeted sales were 504,000 units and standard contribution was $12 per unit.

The sales market size variance is:

A $1,680,000 favourable

B $1,680,000 adverse

C $302,400 adverse

D $302,400 favourable

191 A company manufactures a specific clinical machine used in hospitals. The company holds a 2% share of the market and the total market demand has been constant at 250,000 machines for the last few years. The budgeted selling price for each machine is $10,000 and standard contribution is equivalent to 10% of the budgeted selling price.

An initial performance review of the company's actual results showed a sales volume of 5,600 machines had been achieved. The total market demand for the machines, though, had risen to 300,000 units.

What is the market share variance for the clinical machines?

A $200,000 favourable

B $400,000 adverse

C $600,000 favourable

D $1,000,000 adverse

192 PlasBas Co uses recycled plastic to manufacture shopping baskets for local retailers. The standard price of the recycled plastic is $0.50 per kg and standard usage of recycled plastic is 0.2 kg for each basket. The budgeted production was 80,000 baskets.

Due to recent government incentives to encourage recycling, the standard price of recycled plastic was expected to reduce to $0.40 per kg. The actual price paid by the company was $0.42 per kg and 100,000 baskets were manufactured using 20,000 kg of recycled plastic.

What is the materials operational price variance?

A $2,000 favourable

B $1,600 favourable

C $400 adverse

D $320 adverse

193 A profit centre manager claims that the poor performance of her division is entirely due to factors outside her control. She has submitted the following table along with notes from a market expert, which she believes explains the cause of the poor performance:

Category	**Budget this year**	**Actual this year**	**Actual last year**	**Market expert notes**
Sales volume (units)	500	300	400	The entire market has decreased by 25% compared to last year. The product will be obsolete in four years
Sales revenue	$50,000	$28,500	$40,000	Rivalry in the market saw selling prices fall by 10%
Total material cost	$10,000	$6,500	$8,000	As demand for the raw materials is decreasing, suppliers lowered their prices by 5%

After adjusting for the external factors outside the manager's control, in which category/ categories is/are there evidence of poor performance?

A Material cost only

B Sales volume and sales price

C Sales price and material cost

D Sales price only

194 Which of the following statement(s) is/are true regarding planning and operational variances?

(1) Planning and operational variances are calculated when it is necessary to assess a manager on results that are within his/her control.

(2) Revised standards are required because variances may arise partly due to an unrealistic budget, and not solely due to operational factors.

A (1) only

B (2) only

C Neither (1) nor (2)

D Both (1) and (2)

PERFORMANCE ANALYSIS

195 The finance director of Paint Mixers Ltd has produced the table below showing the variance results for the first three months of the year:

	January	February	March
Material price variance	$3,000 adverse	$2,000 adverse	$1,000 adverse
Material mix variance	$2,000 adverse	$750 adverse	$100 favourable
Material yield variance	$4,000 adverse	$2,000 adverse	$50 favourable

Which of the following interpretations of the variances analysis exercise above is NOT correct?

A The purchasing manager should be able to threaten to switch suppliers to get better deals and address the adverse material price variance

B The materials mix variance is entirely under the control of the production manager

C The favourable yield variance in March could be the result of operational efficiency

D The responsibility for the initial poor performance must be borne by both the purchasing manager and the production manager

196 Which of the following statement(s) regarding the use of standard costs in rapidly changing environments is/are true?

(1) Variance analysis results will take into account important criteria such as customer satisfaction or quality of production.

(2) Achieving standards is suitable in most modern manufacturing environments.

A (1) only

B (2) only

C Neither (1) nor (2)

D Both (1) and (2)

PERFORMANCE MEASUREMENT AND CONTROL

PERFORMANCE ANALYSIS IN PRIVATE SECTOR, PUBLIC SECTOR AND NOT-FOR-PROFIT ORGANISATIONS

197 Why would a company want to encourage the use of non-financial performance indicators?

A To encourage short-termism

B To look at the fuller picture of the business

C To enable results to be easily manipulated to the benefit of the manager

D To prevent goal congruence

198 Quotations have been sent to clients either late or containing errors. The department concerned has responded that it is understaffed, and a high proportion of current staff has recently joined the firm. The performance of this department is to be carefully monitored.

Which ONE of the following non-financial performance indicators would NOT be an appropriate measure to monitor and improve the department's performance?

A Percentage of quotations found to contain errors when checked

B Percentage of quotations not issued within company policy of three working days

C Percentage of department's quota of staff actually employed

D Percentage of budgeted number of quotations actually issued

199 Which TWO of the following key performance indicators would be appropriate to assess the customer perspective within a traditional balanced scorecard?

- Customer profitability analysis
- Customer retention rates
- Customer satisfaction ratings
- Customer ordering processing times

200 HH plc monitors the percentage of total sales that derives from products developed in the last year.

How would this be classified in the balanced scorecard? Pick from list

List options are as follows:

- Financial perspective
- Customer perspective
- Internal business process perspective
- Innovation and learning perspective

201 Which of the following is the best measure of quality to be included within a building block model in a rapidly growing clothing business?

A Number of returns in the month

B Number of faulty goods returned as a percentage of number of orders received in the month

C Average customer satisfaction rating where customers were asked a range of questions including quality, delivery and customer service

D Number of faulty goods returned as a percentage of deliveries made in the month

202 While a drag and drop style question is impossible to fully replicate within a paper based medium, some questions of this style have been included for completeness.

Drag the six dimensions of performance contained within the building block model into the box below:

- Customers
- Competitive Performance
- Learning
- Innovation
- Financial Performance
- Resource utilisation
- Flexibility
- Equity
- Controllability
- Quality of Service

203 The following extracts relate to Company X and Company Y for 20X1:

	Company X	**Company Y**
	$000	$000
Revenue	20,000	26,000
Cost of sales	(15,400)	(21,050)
Gross profit	4,600	4,950
Expenses	(2,460)	(2,770)
Operating profit	2,140	2,180

What is the operating profit margin for both companies for 20X1?

	Company X	**Company Y**
A	10.7%	8.38%
B	8.38%	10.7%
C	23%	19%
D	12%	10%

204 Companies A and B are both involved in retailing. Relevant information for the year ended 30 September 20X1 was as follows:

	A	B
	$000	$000
Sales revenue	50,000	200,000
Profit	10,000	10,000
Capital employed	50,000	50,000

Which of the following statements is true?

A The profit margin of both companies is the same

B Company B is generating more profit from every $1 of asset employed than Company A

C Company B is using its assets more efficiently

D Company B is controlling its costs better than Company A

205 The trading account of Calypso for the year ended 30 June 20X0 is set out below:

	$	$
		430,000
Sales		
Opening inventories	50,000	
Purchases	312,500	
Closing inventories	(38,000)	
Cost of sales		(324,500)
Gross profit		105,500

The following amounts have been extracted from the company's statement of financial position at 30 June 20X0.

	$
Trade receivables	60,000
Prepayments	4,000
Cash in hand	6,000
Bank overdraft	8,000
Trade payables	40,000
Accruals	3,000
Declared dividends	5,000

Which one of the following correctly gives the inventories holding period (using average inventories) and the current ratio for Calypso Ltd for the period?

	Inventory days	**Current ratio**
A	33 days	1.25:1
B	49 days	1.25:1
C	49 days	1.93:1
D	33 days	1.93:1

206 In an investment centre, a divisional manager has autonomy over negotiating all selling prices, has local functions set up for payables, inventory and cash management, and uses a full debt factoring service.

Which of the following should the divisional manager be held accountable for? Place a tick in the boxes in the table below as appropriate.

	Accountable	**Not accountable**
The generation of revenues		
Transfer prices		
Management of working capital		
Apportioned head office costs		

207 Binny Co has annual sales of $960,000 and a current ratio of 3.2:1. All of its sales are for cash and are priced at a mark-up on cost of 50%. The average cash balance is $40,000 and the inventory holding period is 90 days.

Assuming 360 days in a year, what is Binny Co's quick ratio (acid test ratio)?

A 0.64

B 0.53

C 0.80

D 1.56

DIVISIONAL PERFORMANCE AND TRANSFER PRICING

208 Oxco has two divisions, A and B. Division A makes a component for air conditioning units which it can only sell to Division B. It has no other outlet for sales.

Current information relating to Division A is as follows:

Marginal cost per unit	$100
Transfer price of the component	$165
Total production and sales of the component each year	2,200 units
Specific fixed costs of Division A per year	$10,000

Cold Co has offered to sell the component to Division B for $140 per unit. If Division B accepts this offer, Division A will be shut down.

If Division B accepts Cold Co's offer, what will be the impact on profits per year for the group as a whole?

A Increase of $65,000

B Decrease of $78,000

C Decrease of $88,000

D Increase of $55,000

209 Dust Co has two divisions, A and B. Each division is currently considering the following separate projects:

	Division A	Division B
Capital required for the project	$32.6 million	$22.2 million
Sales generated by the project	$14.4 million	$8.8 million
Operating profit margin	30%	24%
Cost of capital	10%	10%
Current return on investment of division	15%	9%

If residual income is used as the basis for the investment decision, what decision is each division likely to make? Place a tick in the boxes in the table below as appropriate.

	Would choose to invest in the project	Would choose not to invest in the project
Division A		
Division B		

210 JB Ltd is a divisionalised organisation comprising a number of divisions, including divisions A and B. Division A makes a single product, which it sells on the external market at a price of $12 per unit. The variable cost of the product is $8 per unit and the fixed cost is $3 per unit. Market demand for the product considerably exceeds Division A's maximum production capacity of 10,000 units per month.

Division B would like to obtain 500 units of the product from Division A. If Division A does transfer some of its production internally rather than sell externally, then the saving in packaging costs would be $1.50 per unit.

What is the minimum price per unit that Division A would accept?

$ ______

211 Pro is a division of Mo and is an investment centre. The head office controls finance, HR and IT expenditure but all other decisions are devolved to the local centres.

The statement of financial position for Pro shows net value of all assets and liabilities to be $4,500m. It carries no debt itself although the group has debt liabilities.

The management accounts include the following:

	$m
Revenue	3,500
Cost of sales	1,800
Local administration	250
IT costs	50
Distribution	80
Central administration	30
Interest charges	90
Net profit	1,200

Ignore taxation.

If the cost of capital is 12%, what is the division's residual income (to the nearest $m)?

$ ______

212 Summary financial statements are given below for a division of a divisionalised company:

Statement of financial position		**Statement of profit or loss**	
	$000		$000
Non-current assets	2,400	Revenue	7,300
Current assets	1,000	Operating costs	(6,800)
Total assets	3,400	Operating profit	500
		Interest paid	(320)
Divisional equity	1,500	Profit before tax	180
Long-term borrowings	900		
Current liabilities	1,000		
Total equity and liabilities	3,400		

The cost of capital for the division is estimated at 11% each year. The annual rate of interest on the long-term loans is 9%. All decisions concerning the division's capital structure are taken by central management.

What is the divisional return on capital employed (ROCE) for the year ended 31 December (to 1 decimal place)?

[ ] %

213 Summary financial statements are given below for a division of a divisionalised company:

Statement of financial position		**Statement of profit or loss**	
	$000		$000
Non-current assets	2,400	Revenue	7,300
Current assets	1,000	Operating costs	(6,800)
Total assets	3,400	Operating profit	500
		Interest paid	(320)
Divisional equity	1,500	Profit before tax	180
Long-term borrowings	900		
Current liabilities	1,000		
Total equity and liabilities	3,400		

The cost of capital for the division is estimated at 11% each year. The annual rate of interest on the long-term loans is 9%. All decisions concerning the division's capital structure are taken by central management.

What is the divisional residual income (RI) for the year ended 31 December?

A –$84,000

B $180,000

C $236,000

D $284,000

214 Pro is a division of Mo and is an investment centre. The head office controls finance, HR and IT expenditure but all other decisions are devolved to the local centres.

The statement of financial position for Pro shows net value of all assets and liabilities to be $4,500m at the start of the year and $4,890m at the end. It carries no debt itself although the group has debt liabilities.

The management accounts include the following:

	$m
Revenue	3,500
Cost of sales	1,800
Local administration	250
IT costs	50
Distribution	80
Central administration	30
Interest charges	90
Net profit	1,200

Ignore taxation.

What is the divisional ROI (1 d.p)? (The closing Capital Employed should be used to calculate the ROI).

[ ] %

215 At the end of 20X1, an investment centre has net assets of $1m and annual operating profits of $190,000. However, the bookkeeper forgot to account for the following:

A machine with a carrying value of $40,000 was sold at the start of the year for $50,000, and replaced with a machine costing $250,000. Both the purchase and sale are cash transactions. No depreciation is charged in the year of purchase or disposal. The investment centre calculates return on investment (ROI) based on closing net assets.

Assuming no other changes to profit or net assets, what is the return on investment (ROI) for the year (to 1 decimal place)?

[ ] %

216 Division B of a company makes units which are then transferred to other divisions. The division has no spare capacity, and sells units externally as well as internally.

Which of the following statement(s) regarding the minimum transfer price that will encourage the divisional manager of B to transfer units to other divisions is/are true?

(1) Any price above variable cost will generate a positive contribution, and will therefore be accepted.

(2) The division will need to give up a unit sold externally in order to make a transfer; this is only worthwhile if the income of a transfer is greater than the net income of an external sale.

A (1) only

B (2) only

C Neither (1) nor (2)

D Both (1) and (2)

217 Perrin Co has two divisions, A and B.

Division A has limited skilled labour and is operating at full capacity making product Y. It has been asked to supply a different product, X, to division B. Division B currently sources this product externally for $700 per unit.

The same grade of materials and labour is used in both products. The cost cards for each product are shown below:

Product	**Y**	**X**
	($)/unit	($)/unit
Selling price	600	–
Direct materials ($50 per kg)	200	150
Direct labour ($20 per hour)	80	120
Apportioned fixed overheads ($15 per hour)	60	90

Using an opportunity cost approach to transfer pricing, what is the minimum transfer price?

A $270

B $750

C $590

D $840

218 TM plc makes components which it sells internally to its subsidiary RM Ltd, as well as to its own external market.

The external market price is $24.00 per unit, which yields a contribution of 40% of sales. For external sales, variable costs include $1.50 per unit for distribution costs, which are not incurred on internal sales.

TM plc has sufficient capacity to meet all of the internal and external sales. The objective is to maximise group profit.

At what unit price should the component be transferred to RM Ltd (to 2 decimal places)?

$ [ ]

PERFORMANCE ANALYSIS ISSUES IN NOT-FOR-PROFIT ORGANISATIONS AND THE PUBLIC SECTOR

219 Which of the following statements regarding measurement of performance in not-for-profit organisations is/are true?

(1) Output does not usually have a market value, and it is therefore more difficult to measure effectiveness.

(2) Control over the performance can only be satisfactorily achieved by assessments of 'value for money'.

A (1) only

B (2) only

C Neither (1) nor (2)

D Both (1) and (2)

220 Def Co provides accounting services to government. On average, each staff member works six chargeable hours per day, with the rest of their working day being spent on non-chargeable administrative work. One of the company's main objectives is to produce a high level of quality and customer satisfaction.

Def Co has set its targets for the next year as follows:

(1) Cutting departmental expenditure by 5%.

(2) Increasing the number of chargeable hours handled by advisers to 6.2 per day.

(3) Obtaining a score of 4.7 or above on customer satisfaction surveys.

Which of the above targets assesses economy, efficiency and effectiveness at Def Co? Place a tick in the boxes in the table below as appropriate.

	Economy	Efficiency	Effectiveness
Target (1)			
Target (2)			
Target (3)			

221 A government is looking at assessing hospitals by reference to a range of both financial and non-financial factors, one of which is survival rates for heart by-pass operations and another is 'cost per successfully treated patient'.

Which of the three E's in the 'Value For Money' framework is NOT measured here?

A Economy

B Effectiveness

C Efficiency

D Externality

222 Which of the following statements, regarding the existence of multiple objectives in not-for-profit organisations, is/are correct?

(1) They ensure goal congruence between stakeholders.

(2) Compromise between objectives can be problematic.

A (1) only

B (2) only

C Both (1) and (2)

D Neither (1) nor (2)

223 A government is trying to assess schools by using a range of financial and non-financial factors. One of the chosen methods is the percentage of students passing five exams or more.

Which of the three Es in the value for money framework is being measured here?

A Economy

B Efficiency

C Effectiveness

D Expertise

224 Which of the following statement(s) about measuring effectiveness in not-for-profit organisations is/are true?

(1) Effectiveness targets cannot usually be expressed financially, and therefore non-financial targets must be used.

(2) The effective level of achievement could be measured by comparing actual performance against target.

A (1) only

B (2) only

C Neither (1) nor (2)

D Both (1) and (2)

225 Core Care Trust is a public sector 'health and care' home providing care for the elderly. Income is received on a contract basis from the local government authority. Care workers are mainly full-time staff but occasionally temporary staff from a local employment agency must be brought in, at great expense, to fill staff rota gaps.

There is a regulatory body monitoring the work done by care homes known as CHQC which sets targets for the standard of care expected.

It is generally regarded that residents spend a much happier time whilst in a care home if they are able to establish long-lasting relationships with care home staff providing their direct care.

The six performance measures below are used by the management of Core Care Trust to monitor performance as part of the value for money framework.

Match the performance measures to the elements of the value for money framework which they are measuring.

Measures
Direct staff cost as a percentage of contract income
Temporary staff usage (hours) as a percentage of total staff hours
Food cost per meal served to residents
Achieving the CHQC's designated standard of care for the elderly
Number of voids (the number of empty beds as a percentage of total
Staff turnover

Economy
Efficiency
Effectiveness

EXTERNAL CONSIDERATIONS AND THE IMPACT ON PERFORMANCE

226 Which of the following statements regarding standard setting is correct?

A Imposed standards are more likely to be achieved

B Managers across the organisation should be targeted using the same standards

C Standards should be set at an ideal level with no built in stretch

D Participation in standard setting is more motivating than where standards are imposed

227 When setting performance measures, external factors should be taken into account.

Which THREE of the following statements regarding external factors is/are true?

A Stakeholders will have different objectives and companies may deal with this by having a range of performance measures to assess the achievement of these objectives

B A downturn in the industry or in the economy as a whole could have a negative impact on performance

C It is only important for companies to take account of internal stakeholders when setting performance targets

D Company performance could be affected if a competitor reduces its prices or launches a successful advertising campaign

E Changes to government policy are irrelevant to measuring internal company performance, as they are an external factor

228 When setting performance measurement targets it should be considered that there is the possibility that managers will take a short-term view of the company and may even be tempted to manipulate results in order to achieve their targets.

Which of the following would assist in overcoming the problems of short-termism and manipulation of results?

A Rewards should be linked to a wider variety of performance measures including some non-financial measures

B Managers should only be rewarded for the results achieved in their own departments

C Any capital investment decision should be judged using the payback method of investment appraisal

D Setting targets involving the overall performance of the company will be more motivating for managers

229 Stakeholders will have different objectives and companies may deal with this by having a range of performance measures to assess the achievement of these objectives.

Which of the following statements is true in relation to stakeholders?

A The aim of all performance measures should be to increase short term profit

B The only interest of the government is that companies pay their taxes

C Shareholders will be looking for increasing dividends and increased share price

D Only internal stakeholders need to be considered by companies

Section 2

OBJECTIVE TEST CASE STUDY QUESTIONS – SECTION B

SPECIALIST COST AND MANAGEMENT ACCOUNTING TECHNIQUES

230 MIDHURST CO (SEPTEMBER/DECEMBER 2020)

Midhurst Co manufactures air conditioning units and is considering an investment in a new unit that will be used in modern office buildings. Advances in technology mean that this unit is more sensitive to changes and variations in temperature and therefore it can regulate airflow and heating more efficiently. Midhurst Co's competitors currently do not have an equivalent product that can offer these features.

Midhurst Co expects to sell 10,000 units over the predicted five-year life cycle of the unit. The finance director has just prepared the initial costings for the unit as follows:

	$000s
Research and development costs	6,200
Design costs	33,450
Marketing costs	177,685
Variable production cost per unit	42
Fixed production cost	98,470
Variable distribution cost per unit	9
Fixed distribution cost	10,300
Variable selling cost per unit	4
Fixed selling cost	7,790
Administration cost	23,450

The finance director plans to use life-cycle costing to measure the profitability of the new product. The chief executive has asked for more information about life-cycle costing, as they are not sure whether it is the right method to use.

The production director has reviewed the costings in detail and suggested a couple of changes. They are enthusiastic about the product and believes that modifications could be made to prolong the product's life but wonders when the best time would be to make changes to the product.

1 **According to the life-cycle costing method, which TWO of the following statements regarding the stages of the life-cycle are true?**

A At the introduction stage, further capital expenditure will be needed as production capacity will need to increase to meet demand

B The maturity stage occurs when the market has reached 'saturation point' and bought enough of the product

C The majority of a product's life-cycle costs are determined by decisions which are made at the design and development stage

D The growth stage, when sales will have reached their peak and become stable, will be the most profitable stage

2 **What is the cost per unit for the new air conditioning unit using life-cycle costing (to the nearest $)?**

A $35,740

B $51,847

C $88,390

D $90,735

3 The production director has suggested the following change for the costing of the new unit:

Currently material costs are 20% of the variable production costs per unit. One of the materials used is stainless steel which is budgeted at $2,000 per unit but an alternative corrosion-resistant metal costing 25% less can be used. The production director believes a 15% discount can be negotiated for the remainder of the materials.

What would be the revised material cost per unit (to the nearest whole $)?

$ ____________

4 The production director has also asked about the implications for production planning if the company wishes to extend the product's life-cycle.

At what stage of the life-cycle is the new unit most likely to undergo product development?

A Introduction

B Growth

C Maturity

D Decline

5 The chief executive wants to be briefed on the advantages of using life-cycle costing.

Which of the following statements relating to the advantages of life-cycle costing are correct?

(1) It draws management's attention to all costs related to a product which other costing methods usually treat as period costs.

(2) It focuses on measuring a product's costs from concept to withdrawal rather than reviewing costs on a period by period basis.

(3) It focuses on what consumers are prepared to pay for a product and establishes cost budgets based on an expected selling price.

(4) It aids understanding of the relationship between decisions at the design stage and the cost of other functions, such as marketing.

A (2), (3) and (4) only

B (1), (2) and (4) only

C (1) and (3) only

D (1), (2), (3) and (4)

231 DUFF CO (JUNE 2014, ADAPTED)

Duff Co manufactures three products, X, Y and Z and uses cost-plus pricing. Each product uses the same materials and the same type of direct labour, but in different quantities. For many years, the company has been using full absorption costing and absorbing overheads on the basis of direct labour hours. Budgeted production and sales volumes for X, Y and Z for the next year are 20,000 units, 16,000 units and 22,000 units respectively.

The budgeted direct costs of the three products are:

	X	**Y**	**Z**
	$ per unit	$ per unit	$ per unit
Direct materials	25	22	28
Direct labour ($12 per hour)	30	36	24
Batch size (units per set-up)	500	800	400
Number of batches	40	20	55
Number of purchase orders per batch	4	5	4
Total machine hours	30,000	20,000	30,800

In the next year, Duff Co also expects to incur indirect production costs of $1,377,400, and the company has calculated the Overhead Absorption Rate (OAR) to be $9.70 per direct labour hour.

The indirect production costs of $1,377,400 are analysed as follows:

Cost pools	**$**	**Cost drivers**
Machine set up costs	280,000	Number of batches
Material ordering costs	316,000	Number of purchase orders
Machine running costs	420,000	Number of machine hours
General facility costs	361,400	Number of machine hours

1 **What is the full production cost per unit of product Z, using Duff's Co current method of absorption costing?**

A $71.40 per unit

B $79.25 per unit

C $93.10 per unit

D Cannot be determined without more information

2 **What is the overhead cost per unit for product X, using activity-based costing?**

A $19.25 per unit

B $24.64 per unit

C $26.21 per unit

D $72.21 per unit

3 **Using activity-based costing, total overheads allocated to Product Z amount to $576,583. What is the budgeted full cost production per unit using activity-based costing, for Product Z?**

A $65.40 per unit

B $78.21 per unit

C $79.64 per unit

D $83.20 per unit

4 **Which of the following statements about activity-based costing (ABC) in Duff Co are correct?**

(1) ABC can be applied to all overhead costs, not just production overheads.

(2) ABC provides a more accurate cost per unit of X, Y or Z, and as a result pricing should be improved.

(3) ABC recognises that overhead costs are not all related to production and sales volume of X, Y and Z.

(4) ABC will be of limited benefit if Duff Co's overhead costs are primarily volume related, or if the overheads represent a small proportion of the overall cost.

A (1) and (2) only

B (2) and (4) only

C (1) and (3) only

D (1), (2), (3) and (4)

5 Using activity-based costing (ABC), the production cost of product X is very similar to the cost calculated using traditional absorption costing, but the cost for product Y is almost $10 less.

Demand for products X and Y is relatively elastic.

Which statements regarding products X and Y are true?

(1) If the company decides to adopt ABC, the price of product X will change.

(2) If the company decides to adopt ABC, sales volumes of X are likely to remain unchanged.

(3) If the company decides to adopt ABC, the price of product Y will go down.

(4) A reduced selling price is unlikely to give rise to increased sales volumes.

A (1) and (2) only

B (2) and (3) only

C (1) and (4) only

D (1), (2), (3) and (4)

232 BECKLEY HILL (JUNE 2015, ADAPTED)

Beckley Hill (BH) is a private hospital carrying out two types of procedures on patients. Each type of procedure incurs the following direct costs:

	Procedure A	**Procedure B**
Surgical time and materials	$1,200	$2,640
Anaesthesia time and materials	$800	$1,620

BH currently calculates the overhead cost per procedure by taking the total overhead cost and simply dividing it by the number of procedures, then rounding the cost to the nearest 2 decimal places. Using this method, the total cost is $2,475.85 for Procedure A and $4,735.85 for Procedure B.

Recently, another local hospital has implemented activity-based costing (ABC). This has led the finance director at BH to consider whether this alternative costing technique would bring any benefits to BH. They have obtained an analysis of BH's total overheads for the last year and some additional data, all of which is shown below:

Cost	**Cost driver**	**Costs in $**
Administrative costs	Administrative time per procedure	1,870,160
Nursing costs	Length of patient stay	6,215,616
Catering costs	Number of meals	966,976
General facility costs	Length of patient stay	8,553,600
Total overhead costs		**17,606,352**

	Procedure A	**Procedure B**
Number of procedures	14,600	22,400
Administrative time per procedure (hours)	1	1.5
Length of patient stay per procedure (hours)	24	48
Average no. of meals required per patient	1	4

1 Using the traditional costing system, what is the overhead cost per procedure?

A $237.93 per procedure

B $713.78 per procedure

C $475.85 per procedure

D $951.70 per procedure

2 Under activity-based costing (ABC), what is the administration cost per hour?

A $38.80 per hour

B $50.54 per hour

C $58.20 per hour

D $77.60 per hour

3 Under activity-based costing (ABC), what is the nursing cost per hour?

A $4.30 per admin hour

B $4.30 per patient hour

C $4.36 per admin hour

D $4.36 per patient hour

4 When using activity-based costing (ABC), the full cost for Procedure A is approximately $2,297 and $4,853 for Procedure B.

Which of the following statements is/are true?

(1) Using ABC, the allocation of overhead costs would more fairly represent the use of resources driving the overheads.

(2) The cost of Procedure A goes up using ABC and the cost of Procedure B goes down because the largest proportion of the overhead costs is the nursing and general facility costs.

A (1) only

B (2) only

C Both (1) and (2)

D Neither (1) nor (2)

5 BH has decided that an activity-based costing (ABC) system is too time consuming and costly to implement.

Which of the following statements is/are true?

(1) Whilst the comparative costs of Procedures A and B are different under ABC, they are not different enough to justify the implementation of an ABC system.

(2) A similar allocation of overheads can be achieved simply by using 'patient hours' as a basis to absorb the costs.

A (1) only

B (2) only

C Both (1) and (2)

D Neither (1) nor (2)

233 ABKABER PLC

Abkaber plc assembles three types of motorcycle at the same factory: the 50cc Sunshine; the 250cc Roadster and the 1000cc Fireball.

Historically, the company has allocated all overhead costs using total direct labour hours, but is now considering introducing Activity Based Costing (ABC). Abkaber plc's accountant has produced the following analysis.

	Annual output (units)	**Annual direct labour hours**	**Selling price ($ per unit)**	**Raw material cost ($ per unit)**
Sunshine	2,000	200,000	4,000	400
Roadster	1,600	220,000	6,000	600
Fireball	400	80,000	8,000	900

The three cost drivers that generate overheads are:

- Deliveries to retailers – the number of deliveries of motorcycles to retail showrooms.
- Set-ups – the number of times the assembly line process is re-set to accommodate a production run of a different type of motorcycle.
- Purchase orders – the number of purchase orders.

The annual cost driver volumes relating to each activity and for each type of motorcycle are as follows:

	Number of deliveries to retailers	**Number of set-ups**	**Number of purchase orders**
Sunshine	100	35	400
Roadster	80	40	300
Fireball	70	25	100

The annual overhead costs relating to these activities are as follows:

	$
Deliveries to retailers	2,400,000
Set-up costs	6,000,000
Purchase orders	3,600,000
	12,000,000

All direct labour is paid at $5 per hour. The company holds no inventories.

At a board meeting there was some concern over the introduction of activity based costing.

The finance director argued: 'I very much doubt whether selling the Fireball is viable but I am not convinced that activity based costing would tell us any more than the use of labour hours in assessing the viability of each product.'

The marketing director argued: 'I am in the process of negotiating a major new contract with a motorcycle rental company for the Sunshine model. For such a big order they will not pay our normal prices but we need to at least cover our incremental costs. I am not convinced that activity based costing would achieve this as it merely averages costs for our entire production'.

The managing director argued: 'I believe that activity based costing would be an improvement but it still has its problems. For instance, if we carry out an activity many times surely we get better at it and costs fall rather than remain constant. Similarly, some costs are fixed and do not vary either with labour hours or any other cost driver.'

The chairman argued: 'I cannot see the problem. The overall profit for the company is the same no matter which method of allocating overheads we use. It seems to make no difference to me.'

1 **What is the split of annual overhead costs for each product using the existing method of labour hours to attribute overheads?**

	Sunshine	Roadster	Fireball
A	6,000,000	4,800,000	1,200,000
B	4,800,000	5,280,000	1,920,000
C	4,860,000	4,518,000	2,622,000
D	2,666,667	4,000,000	5,333,333

2 **What level of overheads would be attributed to the Fireball product if Abkaber plc introduced activity based costing?**

A 1,200,000

B 1,920,000

C 2,622,000

D 5,333,333

3 Which ONE of the following statements is TRUE about the difference in overhead attribution for the Fireball product (when comparing the existing and new methods) and how it may affect management decisions about this product?

A Both methods are acceptable so management shouldn't be concerned if overhead costs are higher for this product using ABC.

B ABC seems to be a more useful method for understanding the costs related to the Fireball, as the low volumes of Fireball sales cause a relatively high amount of set-ups, deliveries and purchase processes.

C Using ABC is likely to result in a higher profit being recognised for the Fireball product.

D The best way to improve the overhead costs for the fireball is to find efficiencies that reduce labour hours on this product.

4 Which of the following statements are true?

(1) The finance director is correct – ABC will not provide any further information in assessing how viable the Fireball product is, as it's just a different approach to allocating costs.

(2) The marketing director is correct – ABC can't help with improving our understanding of the incremental costs of a product, as it just averages costs for the entire production.

(3) The managing director is correct – ABC normally assumes that the cost per activity is constant as the number of times the activity is repeated increases. In practice there may be a learning curve, such that costs per activity are non-linear. As a result, the marginal cost of increasing the number of activities is not the same as the average.

A (1) and (2)

B (1) and (3)

C (2) and (3)

D (3) only

5 The chairman has stated that it is irrelevant which costing method is used as overall company profit will be unchanged. Which of the following is an advantage of using ABC despite it having no impact on overall company profits?

A It can allocate costs to specific activities with complete accuracy

B It is quick and cheap to introduce

C It is most useful in situations when the overheads are a small proportion of overall costs

D It provides a more accurate cost per unit, which helps with management decisions about specific products

234 RAASAY (SEPTEMBER/DECEMBER 2023)

Raasay Co manufactures three types of guitars in one of its divisions: the Jazz, the Rock, and the Classic.

Raasay Co currently operates a costing system which uses a single overhead rate, based on revenue, to charge overhead costs to the guitars. The finance director has suggested a change to an activity-based costing (ABC) system.

The following information has been collected about the manufacture of the components:

Component information	**Jazz**	**Rock**	**Classic**
Selling price	$620	$700	$450
Prime cost	$370	$400	$180
Number of components produced and sold	5,000	6,000	3,000
Production batch size (units)	100	150	200
Mahine set-ups per batch	3	5	4
Processing time per unit (hours)	4	5	3
Quality inspections per batch	4	6	8

Further details on the overheads incurred have also been ascertained:

Activity	**Cost driver**	**Production overhead cost ($)**
Quality inspection	Number of quality inspections	40,810
Machine set-up	Number of machine set ups	120,540
Component processing	Processing time (hours)	643,100

1 **What is the profit per unit of a Jazz guitar using the current basis for charging overhead costs (to two decimal places)?**

A $192.34

B $250.00

C $312.34

D $57.66

2 **Using activity-based costing, what is the machine set-up cost for a Rock guitar (to two decimal places)?**

$____________

3 **Using activity-based costing, what is the cost of component processing for a Classic guitar (to two decimal places)?**

A $32.70

B $3.00

C $7.01

D $95.26

4 Which of the following statements concerning the advantages of activity-based-costing (ABC), as opposed to a traditional absorption costing system, is correct?

A All overhead costs will be accurately linked with a measurable cost driver, which will facilitate the control of all overhead costs

B Costing will be more accurate when overheads are a small proportion of total costs

C Short-term decision-making will be more meaningful because all fixed production overheads are included in the calculations

D Costing will be more accurate as it recognises that activities are consumed at different rates by different products

5 The finance director is pleased with the results of the ABC analysis of the guitars and is keen to extend the use of ABC to other divisions in the company.

One such division, which manufactures electronic keyboards, has begun to introduce ABC and has identified some relevant activities and cost drivers.

Match the most appropriate cost driver to the activities identified.

Cost Driver
Number of service requests
Number of material movements
Number of purchase orders
Number of machine hours
Number of warranties handled

Activity
Material Handling
Customer Service
IT support
Procurement
Maintenance

235 GADGET CO (DECEMBER 2010 ADAPTED)

The Gadget Co produces three products, A, B and C, all made from the same material. Until now, it has used traditional absorption costing to allocate overheads to its products. The company is now considering an activity based costing system in the hope that it will improve profitability. Information for the three products for the last year is as follows:

	A	B	C
Production and sales volumes (units)	15,000	12,000	18,000
Selling price per unit	$7.50	$12	$13
Raw material cost per unit	$2.40	$3.60	$4.80
Direct labour hours per unit	0.1	0.15	0.2
Machine hours per unit	0.5	0.7	0.9
Number of production runs per annum	16	12	8
Number of purchase orders per annum	24	28	42
Number of deliveries to retailers per annum	48	30	62

The direct labour cost for the whole workforce was $14.80 per hour.

The annual overhead costs were as follows:

	$
Machine set up costs	26,550
Machine running costs	66,400
Procurement costs	48,000
Delivery costs	54,320

1 Which of the following statements are true for Gadget Co?

(i) Under traditional absorption costing, and using production volumes as a basis of apportionment, the overhead absorption rate is $4.34 per unit.

(ii) Under activity based costing, Product C would have $2.07 of machine running costs apportioned to each unit.

A (i) and (ii)

B (i) only

C (ii) only

D Neither (i) nor (ii)

2 What is the full cost per unit for product A under traditional absorption costing, using direct labour hours as the basis for apportionment.

A $3.88

B $6.71

C $8.22

D $23.80

3 Calculate the overhead cost per unit of product B using activity based costing.

A $3.88

B $4.00

C $4.35

D $4.72

4 The full cost per unit of product C is $13.42 under traditional absorption costing (using direct labour hours as the basis of apportionment), and $12.48 under ABC.

Which of the following statements about product C are true?

(i) Product C should not be produced, as it makes a loss per unit.

(ii) One of the reasons for the cheaper unit cost under ABC is the lower number of production runs needed for product C.

(iii) Switching to ABC is unlikely to change Gadget Co's decisions about product C, as the unit cost change is only 7.5%.

A (i) and (ii)

B (i) and (iii)

C (ii) and (iii)

D (ii) only

5 Which of the following statements concerning ABC are true?

(i) ABC always makes a big difference to overhead allocations.

(ii) Identifying the drivers of cost does not change the fact that fixed costs cannot be controlled, so real savings cannot be made.

A Both are true

B Both are false

C Only statement (i) is true

D Only statement (ii) is true

236 DARASK CO (SEPTEMBER/DECEMBER 2021)

Darask Co is a global consumer electronics manufacturer. It sells its own brand of smartphones, computers and personal entertainment devices. It uses target costing.

D-Paad – Feasibility study results

The board of Darask Co has conducted a feasibility study in order to decide whether or not to launch a new device, the D-Paad, in 20X9. The D-Paad will have a three-year life cycle, over which a total of 80 million units will be sold.

The variable manufacturing and selling cost of the D-Paad is currently estimated at $123 per unit. The total fixed product cost, including investment and overheads, is budgeted to be $3,360m over the whole life cycle.

The initial estimate of the selling price included in the feasibility study for the D-Paad was calculated to ensure a profit mark-up of 60%.

D-Paad – Market research analysis

The board decided to commission some market research to determine the price customers would be willing to pay for the D-Paad. Sales volumes and sales prices were estimated for the various stages of the D-Paad's product life cycle as follows:

	Sales volume (millions)	**Sales price ($/unit)**
Introduction	8	425
Growth	14	300
Maturity	56	220
Decline	2	120

Based on the market analysis, the board has approved the development of the D-Paad as long as the total product cost, including manufacturing, investment and overheads, does not exceed $13,000m.

Retail outlets

The board of Darask Co is also considering the opening of some retail outlets which will be located in major cities around the world. The outlets, as well as selling Darask Co's products, will also hold free-of-charge surgeries where the product users can seek help on how to use their devices and have their devices repaired.

The board has been discussing whether it is possible to use target costing in relation to the retail outlets. The following statements have been made:

Director X	Target costing cannot be used because it is difficult to estimate target selling prices for services.
Director Y	Target costing is most useful when what is being developed has a high degree of variability such as developing new services.
Director Z	Target costing when developing new services is difficult because services are intangible and measuring a unit of service is not always possible.

1 **Which of the following statements about the use of target costing at Darask Co is/are correct?**

(1) It relies on just-in-time processes in order to work.

(2) It can be used alongside life cycle costing and planning.

A (1) only

B (2) only

C Both (1) and (2)

D Neither (1) nor (2)

2 **What was the initial selling price of the D-Paad from the feasibility study results (to the nearest whole $)?**

$__________

3 **Based on the market research analysis, what is the total cost gap of the D-Paad, if Darask Co wants to achieve a target profit margin of 45%?**

A $3,928m

B $1,912m

C $9,072m

D $11,088m

4 The following proposals have been made in order to close the cost gap of the D-Paad:

(1) Introduce 24-hour working in the factories where the D-Paad is made in order to increase production and build inventory.

(2) Incorporate quality assurance inspections into the manufacturing processes to reduce faulty units.

(3) Increase the sales and marketing spend in order to boost the sales volumes of the D-Paad.

Which of these proposals is/are likely to reduce the cost gap?

A (1) and (2)

B (2) and (3)

C (2) only

D (1) and (3)

5 **In relation to the use of target costing for the retail outlets, which of the directors' statements is/are correct?**

A X, Y and Z

B Y and Z only

C X and Y only

D Z only

237 HELOT CO (SEPTEMBER 2016)

Helot Co develops and sells computer games. It is well known for launching innovative and interactive role-playing games and its new releases are always eagerly anticipated by the gaming community. Customers value the technical excellence of the games and the durability of the product and packaging.

Helot Co has previously used a traditional absorption costing system and full cost plus pricing to cost and price its products. It has recently recruited a new finance director who believes the company would benefit from using target costing. They are keen to try this method on a new game concept called Spartan, which has been recently approved.

After discussion with the board, the finance director undertook some market research to find out customers' opinions on the new game concept and to assess potential new games offered by competitors. The results were used to establish a target selling price of $45 for Spartan and an estimated total sales volume of 350,000 units. Helot Co wants to achieve a target profit margin of 35%.

The finance director has also begun collecting cost data for the new game and has projected the following:

Production costs per unit	$
Direct material	3.00
Direct labour	2.50
Direct machining	5.05
Set-up	0.45
Inspection and testing	4.30
Total non-production costs	$000
Design (salaries and technology)	2,500
Marketing consultants (external)	1,700
Distribution	1,400

1 **Which of the following statements would the finance director have used to explain to Helot Co's board what the benefits were of adopting a target costing approach so early in the game's life-cycle?**

(1) Costs will be split into material, system, and delivery and disposal categories for improved cost reduction analysis.

(2) Customer requirements for quality, cost and timescales are more likely to be included in decisions on product development.

(3) Its key concept is based on how to turn material into sales as quickly as possible in order to maximise net cash.

(4) The company will focus on designing out costs prior to production, rather than cost control during live production.

A (1), (2) and (4)

B (2), (3) and (4)

C (1) and (3)

D (2) and (4) only

2 **What is the forecast cost gap for the new game?**

A $2.05

B $0.00

C $13.70

D $29.25

3 The board of Helot Co has asked the finance director to explain what activities can be undertaken to close a cost gap on its computer games.

Which of the following would be appropriate ways for Helot Co to close a cost gap? Place a tick in the boxes in the table below as appropriate.

	Appropriate ways to close a cost gap	**Not an appropriate ways to close a cost gap**
Buy cheaper, lower grade plastic for the game discs and cases.		
Using standard components wherever possible in production.		
Employ more trainee game designers on lower salaries.		
Use the company's own online gaming websites for marketing.		

4 The direct labour cost per unit has been based on an expected learning rate of 90% but now the finance director has realised that a 95% learning rate should be applied.

Which of the following statements is true?

A The target cost will decrease and the cost gap will increase

B The target cost will increase and the cost gap will decrease

C The target cost will remain the same and the cost gap will increase

D The target cost will remain the same and the cost gap will decrease

5 Helot Co is thinking about expanding its business and introducing a new computer repair service for customers. The board has asked if target costing could be applied to this service.

Which of the following statements regarding services and the use of target costing within the service sector is true?

A The purchase of a service transfers ownership to the customer

B Labour resource usage is high in services relative to material requirements

C A standard service cannot be produced and so target costing cannot be used

D Service characteristics include uniformity, perishability and intangibility

238 CHEMICAL FREE CLEAN CO (DECEMBER 2015, ADAPTED)

The Chemical Free Clean Co (C Co) provides a range of environmentally-friendly cleaning services to business customers, often providing a specific service to meet a client's needs. Its customers range from large offices and factories to specialist care wards at hospitals, where specialist cleaning equipment must be used and regulations adhered to.

C Co offers both regular cleaning contracts and contracts for one-off jobs. For example, its latest client was a chain of restaurants which employed them to provide an extensive clean of all their business premises after an outbreak of food poisoning.

The cleaning market is very competitive, although there are only a small number of companies providing a chemical free service. C Co had previously charged $20 per hour, in line with their closest competitors. C Co has always used cost-plus pricing to determine the prices which it charges to its customers but recently, the cost of the cleaning products C Co uses has increased. This has meant that C Co has had to increase its prices to $23 per hour, resulting in the loss of several regular customers to competing service providers.

The finance director at C Co has heard about target costing and is considering whether it could be useful at C Co. The FD has budgeted that C Co will deliver 462,000 hours of cleaning this year, and an operating profit of $2.5m is needed to provide the shareholders with their required return.

The budget costs incurred for each labour hour of cleaning are:

	$
Labour cost	10.00
Average cleaning product cost per labour hour	4.42

Fixed operating costs are budgeted to be $1,635,480.

1 What would be, in the right sequence, the main steps involved in deriving a target cost for C Co?

A Define the service, set a target price, derive the operating profit and calculate a target cost.

B Set a target price, derive the total operating profit, calculate a target cost per hour and define the service.

C Define the service, derive the operating profit, set a target price and calculate a target cost.

D Define the service, derive a target price, calculate a target cost and set the operating profit.

2 Which TWO of the following statements correctly explain the difficulties faced if target costing is used in a service industry?

- The service can be defined too easily and lacks the necessary complexity.
- The service is used at the same time it is produced.
- The service is standardised too easily.
- Unused labour capacity cannot be stored for use the next day.

3 What is the current cost gap based on the FD's figures for this year?

A $0.17

B $0.37

C $3.37

D $5.41

4 Which TWO of the following statements are true?

- Target costing is useful in competitive markets where a company is dominant in their market, like C Co is.
- Target costing is useful in C Co's competitive market in which price increases does lead to loss of customers.
- C Co can ignore the market price for cleaning services and simply pass on cost increases as it has done.
- Target costing would help C Co to focus on the market price of similar services provided by competitors, where this information is available.

5 **Which of the following statement(s) is/are true?**

(1) If after calculating a target cost C Co finds that a cost gap exists, it will then be forced to examine its internal processes and costs more closely.

(2) If C Co cannot achieve any reduction in the cost of the cleaning products it uses, it should consider whether it can source cheaper non-chemical products from alternative suppliers.

A (1) only

B (2) only

C Both (1) and (2)

D Neither (1) nor (2)

239 PRINTER UNIVERSE CO (SEPTEMBER/DECEMBER 2025)

Printer Universe (PU) Co is launching a new printer called Zone. It has invested $300,000 for the development and launch of Zone. The expected demand is 500 units in the current year at a selling price of $500 per unit. The target profit is the higher of 25% profit mark-up and 20% of investment per unit.

The following production information relates to the Zone printer:

Production resource	**Amount required per unit**	**Cost**
Glass	1kg	$50 per kg
Metal	1kg	$30 per kg
Plastic (see note)	2kg	$40 per kg
Machining	2 hours	$20 per machine hour
Skilled labour	2 hours	$40 per labour hour

Note: The amount of plastic required for each Zone is before allowing for a normal loss of 20% on the plastic used.

Z1 cartridge

PU Co has also developed a new printer cartridge called the Z1 which will be compatible with the Zone printer. PU Co wishes to make a profit margin of 25% on the Z1 which has a selling price of $110 per cartridge. PU Co is known for the durability of its printer cartridges and wants to ensure the Z1 is also long-lasting.

The following production information relates to the Z1:

Production resource	**Amount required per unit**	**Cost**
Casing	1 casing	$10
Printhead	1 printhead	$16
Ink	0.5 grams	$64 per gram
Machining	1.5 hours	$20 per machine hour

After sales service

Following feedback from customers, PU Co is planning to start a dedicated department to provide after sales service to its customers. It plans to use target costing for the setting up of this department.

1 Which of the following types of control is target costing an example of?

A Positive feedback control

B Negative feedback control

C Double-loop feedback control

D Feed-forward control

2 What is the target cost per Zone printer in the current year (to the nearest whole $)?

$ ____________

3 What is the maximum rate per gram of ink which PU Co can pay to avoid a cost gap for the Z1 cartridge?

A $53.00

B $24.50

C $58.50

D $37.50

4 Which TWO of the following activities should PU Co undertake to close the cost gap on the Z1 cartridge?

A Increase the selling price of the cartridge in the market

B Reduce the amount of ink supplied in the cartridge

C Negotiate a bulk purchase discount with the casings' supplier

D Accept a lower profit margin being achieved on the cartridge

5 Which of the following is NOT a characteristic of a service and therefore a reason why PU Co may find it difficult to apply target costing to its after-sales service department?

A The intangibility of the service makes it difficult to define

B The production and consumption of service occurs simultaneously

C The quality and consistency of the service is homogeneous

D The service provided cannot be stored and used at a later date

240 VOLT CO (MARCH 2019)

Volt Co generates and sells electricity. It operates two types of power station: nuclear and wind. The costs and output of the two types of power station are detailed below:

Nuclear station

A nuclear station can generate 9,000 gigawatts of electricity in each of its 40 years of useful life. Operating costs are $486m per year. Operating costs include a provision for depreciation of $175m per year to recover the $7,000m cost of building the power station.

Each nuclear station has an estimated decommissioning cost of $12,000m at the end of its life. The decommissioning cost relates to the cost of safely disposing of spent nuclear fuel.

Wind station

A wind station can generate 1,750 gigawatts of electricity per year. It has a life cycle cost of $55,000 per gigawatt and an average operating cost of $40,000 per gigawatt over its 20-year life.

1 What is the life-cycle cost per gigawatt of the nuclear station (to the nearest $000)?

A $54,000

B $73,000

C $87,000

D $107,000

2 Which of the following will decrease the total life cycle cost of a nuclear station?

(1) Increasing the useful life of the station.

(2) Reducing the decommissioning cost.

A (1) only

B (2) only

C Both (1) and (2)

D Neither (1) nor (2)

3 How would the disposal cost of spent nuclear fuel be categorised in environmental management accounting (EMA)?

A A prevention cost

B A detection cost

C An internal failure cost

D An external failure cost

4 **If Volt Co sets a price to earn an operating margin of 40% over the life of a wind station, what will be the total lifetime profit per station (to the nearest $m)?**

A $35m

B $408m

C $560m

D $933m

5 **Which of the following are benefits of life cycle costing for Volt Co?**

(1) It facilitates the designing out of costs at the product development stage.

(2) It can encourage better control of operating costs over the life cycle.

(3) It gives a better understanding of the causes of overhead costs.

(4) It provides useful data for short-term decision-making.

A (1), (2) and (3)

B (1) and (2) only

C (1) and (4)

D (2), (3) and (4)

241 SHOE CO (JUNE 2016, ADAPTED)

Shoe Co, a shoe manufacturer, has developed a new product called the 'Smart Shoe' for children, which has a built-in tracking device. The shoes are expected to have a life cycle of two years, at which point Shoe Co hopes to introduce a new type of Smart Shoe with even more advanced technology. Shoe Co plans to use life cycle costing to work out the total production cost of the Smart Shoe and the total estimated profit for the two-year period. Shoe Co has spent $5.6m developing the Smart Shoe.

The time spent on this development meant that the company missed out on the opportunity of earning an estimated $800,000 contribution from the sale of another product.

The company has applied for and been granted a ten-year patent for the technology, although it must be renewed each year at a cost of $200,000. The costs of the patent application were $500,000, which included $20,000 for the salary costs of Shoe Co's lawyer, who is a permanent employee of the company and was responsible for preparing the application.

The following information relating to the Smart Shoe is also available for the next two years:

Total 'Smart Shoe' Revenue $34.3m

	Year 1	**Year 2**
Sales volumes (units)	280,000	420,000
Material costs per unit	$16	$14
Labour costs per unit	$8	$7
Total fixed production overheads	$3.8 m	
Selling and distribution costs	$1.5m	

Shoe Co is negotiating with marketing companies with regard to its advertising campaign on another product, 'Smart Boots'. Shoe Co is uncertain as to what the total marketing costs will be each year. However, the following information is available as regards the probabilities of the range of costs which are likely to be incurred:

Year 1		**Year 2**	
Expected cost ($m)	Probability	Expected cost ($m)	Probability
2.2	0.2	1.8	0.3
2.6	0.5	2.1	0.4
2.9	0.3	2.3	0.3

1 **Which TWO of the following statements about lifecycle costing are true?**

- Lifecycle costing should not be used by Shoe Co, because the material costs per unit differ between the two years of the life of the product.
- Lifecycle costing should not be used by Shoe Co, because the lifecycle of the 'Smart Shoe' is short and the development costs too high.
- Lifecycle costing should be used by Shoe Co because it will provide the true financial cost of producing the shoes.
- A higher price should be charged by Shoe Co from the start, as the product will be unique.

2 **What is the total expected profit for Shoe Co on the 'Smart Shoe' for the two-year period?** **$________**

3 Further research has shown that there will be environmental costs at the end of production of $250,000. Shoe Co is considering how to account for these costs.

Which TWO of the following statements about Environmental Management Accounting are true?

- Cost savings in environmental costs are easily identified.
- Environmental management accounting considers financial costs only.
- Activity-based costing (ABC) can be used to analyse environmental costs.
- Flow cost accounting is a recognised method of accounting for environmental costs.

4 **What is the total expected value of the marketing cost for the two years on the 'Smart Boots' range?**

A $2.61 m

B $2.07 m

C $4.68 m

D $5.21m

5 **Which ONE of the following statements is true, if a decision is made using expected values?**

A The risk is minimised for a set level of return

B The risk is minimised irrespective of the level of return

C The return is maximised for a given level of risk

D The return is maximised irrespective of the level of risk

242 SWEET TREATS BAKERY (DECEMBER 2016)

Sweet Treats Bakery makes three types of cake: brownies, muffins and cupcakes. The costs, revenues and demand for each of the three cakes are as follows:

	Brownies	**Muffins**	**Cupcakes**
Batch size (units)	40	30	20
Selling price ($ per unit)	1.50	1.40	2.00
Material cost ($ per unit)	0.25	0.15	0.25
Labour cost ($ per unit)	0.40	0.45	0.50
Overheads ($ per unit)	0.15	0.20	0.30
Minimum daily demand (units)	30	20	10
Maximum daily demand (units)	140	90	100

The minimum daily demand is required for a long-term contract with a local café and must be met.

The cakes are made in batches using three sequential processes: weighing, mixing and baking. The products must be produced in their batch sizes but are sold as individual units. Each batch of cakes requires the following amount of time for each process:

	Brownies	**Muffins**	**Cupcakes**
Weighing (minutes)	15	15	20
Mixing (minutes)	20	16	12
Baking (minutes)	120	110	120

The baking stage of the process is done in three ovens which can each be used for eight hours a day, a total of 1,440 available minutes. Ovens have a capacity of one batch per bake, regardless of product type.

Sweet Treats Bakery uses throughput accounting and considers all costs, other than material, to be 'factory costs' which do not vary with production.

1 On Monday, in addition to the baking ovens, Sweet Treats Bakery has the following process resources available:

Process	**Minutes available**
Weighing	240
Mixing	180

Which of the three processes, if any, is a bottleneck activity?

A Weighing

B Mixing

C Baking

D There is no bottleneck

2 On Wednesday, the mixing process is identified as the bottleneck process. On this day, only 120 minutes in the mixing process are available.

Assuming that Sweet Treats Bakery wants to maximise profit, what is the optimal production plan for Wednesday?

A 80 brownies, 30 muffins and 100 cupcakes

B 0 brownies, 90 muffins and 100 cupcakes

C 120 brownies, 0 muffins and 100 cupcakes

D 40 brownies, 60 muffins and 100 cupcakes

3 Sweet Treats Bakery has done a detailed review of its products, costs and processes and has identified potential actions to improve its throughput accounting ratio (TPAR).

Which of the following statements will improve the throughput accounting ratio (TPAR)? Place a tick in the boxes in the table below as appropriate.

	Will improve the TPAR	**Will not improve the TPAR**
The café customer will be given a loyalty discount.		
A bulk discount on flour and sugar is available from suppliers.		
There is additional demand for the cupcakes in the market.		
The rent of the premises has been reduced for the next year.		

4 On Friday, due to a local food festival at the weekend, Sweet Treats Bakery is considering increasing its production of cupcakes. These cupcakes can be sold at the festival at the existing selling price.

The company has unlimited capacity for weighing and mixing on Friday but its existing three ovens are already fully utilised. Therefore in order to supply cupcakes to the festival, Sweet Treats Bakery will need to hire another identical oven at a cost of $45 for the day.

How much will profit increase by if the company hires the new oven and produces as many cupcakes as possible?

A $55.00

B $140.00

C $95.00

D $31.00

5 In a previous week, the weighing process was the bottleneck and the resulting throughput accounting ratio (TPAR) for the bakery was 1.45.

Which of the following statements about the TPAR for the previous week is/are true?

(1) The bakery's operating costs exceeded the total throughput contribution generated from its three products.

(2) Less idle time in the mixing department would have improved the TPAR.

(3) Improved efficiency during the weighing process would have improved the TPAR.

A (3) only

B (2) only

C (1) and (2)

D (1) and (3)

243 BRICK BY BRICK (JUNE 2010, ADAPTED)

Brick by Brick (BBB) is a building business that provides a range of building services to the public. Recently they have been asked to quote for garage conversions (GC) and extensions to properties (EX) and have found that they are winning fewer GC contracts than expected.

BBB has a policy to price all jobs at budgeted total cost plus 50%. Overheads are currently absorbed on a labour hour basis. BBB thinks that a switch to activity based costing (ABC) to absorb overheads would reduce the cost associated to GC and hence make them more competitive.

You are provided with the following data:

Overhead category	**Annual overheads** $	**Activity driver**	**Total number of activities per year**
Supervisors	90,000	Site visits	500
Planners	70,000	Planning documents	250
Property related	240,000	Labour hours	40,000
Total	400,000		

A typical GC costs $3,500 in materials and takes 300 labour hours to complete. A GC requires only one site visit by a supervisor and needs only one planning document to be raised. The typical EX costs $8,000 in materials and takes 500 hours to complete. An EX requires six site visits and five planning documents. In all cases labour is paid $15 per hour.

1 **Calculate the quoted price of a GC using labour hours to absorb the overheads.**

A $10,260

B $11,000

C $15,390

D $16,500

2 Calculate the total cost of an EX using ABC to absorb the overheads.

A $20,500

B $20,980

C $30,750

D $31,470

3 Assume that the cost of a GC falls by nearly 7% and the price of an EX rises by about 2% as a result of the change from traditional absorption costing to ABC.

Which ONE of the following statements is TRUE?

A BBB can maintain total profits from EX at their current level by increasing the quoted price by 2% in line with costs.

B BBB can only improve overhead costs on the EX by reducing labour hours.

C The new overhead allocation is a fairer representation of the EX and GC use of resources driving the overheads.

D Maintaining existing mark ups should make both the EX and the GC more competitive.

4 One BBB manager has suggested that only marginal cost should be included in budget cost calculations as this would avoid the need for arbitrary overhead allocations to products.

Which of the following statements is/are true?

(1) The switch to marginal costing would avoid the problem of the uncertainty of budget volume. Budget volume is needed in order to calculate the fixed cost absorption rate.

(2) If BBB uses marginal costing, there is a risk that managers will not generate sufficient contribution to cover fixed costs.

A (1) only

B (2) only

C Both (1) and (2)

D Neither (1) nor (2)

5 Which THREE of the following statements about ABC and traditional costing systems (absorption costing and marginal costing) are correct?

A No over-absorption or under-absorption of overheads can occur under ABC.

B ABC is useful for businesses like BBB which have high overheads in their cost structure.

C ABC is not suitable for use in businesses like BBB that provide services.

D Marginal costing understates the true cost of a product when compared to ABC.

E ABC is better than absorption costing in understanding what causes overhead costs to be incurred.

F Both ABC and marginal costing treat all fixed costs as product costs.

244 GOODTYME CO (SEPTEMBER/DECEMBER 2024)

Answer debrief

Goodtyme Co produces clocks and watches. It manufactures a single model of clock and three models of watches: the GL, the RT and the SM. The clock is manufactured in a separate factory from the watches.

The main constraint Goodtyme Co faces for all its products is assembly machine hours available. The time available is reduced by temporary breakdowns of the assembly machinery and the need for maintenance.

The finance director of Goodtyme Co has decided to introduce throughput accounting in order to provide better information.

The following information relates to the products which Goodtyme Co manufactures:

	Clock	**Watches**		
		GL	**RT**	**SM**
	$/unit	**$/unit**	**$/unit**	**$/unit**
Sales price	40.00	36.00	26.00	22.00
Materials	15.50	14.70	10.30	8.80
Labour	6.60	5.80	4.20	2.80
Variable overheads	3.00	2.60	2.20	1.70
Contribution	**14.90**	**12.90**	**9.30**	**8.70**
Fixed overheads	2.40	2.50	1.40	1.20
Profit	**12.50**	**10.40**	**7.90**	**7.50**
Assembly machine time (minutes)	20	24	18	15

Goodtyme Co is also developing a new stopwatch for competitive watersports and is forecasting the product to have a throughput accounting ratio of 1.75. The company has budgeted to spend $50,000 on advertising when the product is launched.

1 **Which of the following statements about throughput accounting and the theory of constraints is/are true?**

(1) The theory of constraints suggests that when one bottleneck is overcome, another bottleneck will arise

(2) Throughput accounting aims to maximise the amount of non-bottleneck resources used

(3) In throughput accounting work in progress should be valued at the cost of materials only

A (1) only

B (2) and (3) only

C (1) and (3) only

D (1), (2) and (3)

2 What is the throughput accounting ratio for the clock (to two decimal places)?

A 1.45

B 2.04

C 2.55

D 3.31

3 For each of the following proposed actions, identify the impact on the throughput accounting ratio (TPAR) of the clock.

	Increase	**Decrease**
Improving the effectiveness and efficiency of the maintenance process to increase available machine hours		
Payment of overtime at time and a third to increase the number of labour hours available		
Negotiating a contract to buy materials at a lower price from a new supplier		
Changing electricity suppliers to one charging a lower standing charge per day for factory power		

4 What should be the production ranking for the watches in order to maximise throughput?

	1st	**2nd**	**3rd**
A	GL	RT	SM
B	SM	RT	GL
C	SM	GL	RT
D	GL	SM	RT

5 Which of the following statements, if any, about the throughput accounting ratio (TPAR) for the new stopwatch is/are true?

(1) The operating costs of the stopwatch are expected to exceed the total throughput contribution to be earned

(2) The cost per hour used in the TPAR calculation included the advertising costs for the stopwatch

A (1) only

B (2) only

C Both (1) and (2)

D Neither (1) nor (2)

DECISION-MAKING TECHNIQUES

245 SIP CO

Sip Co specialises in refurbishing the inside of yachts and has been asked to quote, on a relevant cost basis, for the refurbishment of a yacht called Bow. The refurbishment will start in one week's time. Sip Co has spent $100 obtaining the following information about the refurbishment:

Materials

The material required will be:

- 20 m^2 of upholstery fabric
- 10 m^2 of teak wood for the flooring.

The cheapest source for the upholstery fabric would be from an overseas supplier at a cost of $85/$m^2$. Sip Co buys most of its fabric from overseas and pays $400 per month to a shipping company as a retainer and then $7.50/$m^2$ for each metre transported.

Sip Co has 5m^2 of teak wood in inventory which cost $100/$m^2$ and could be sold at a 5% discount on original cost. This teak is left from a previous job and is stained dark mahogany. The colour of the stain required for Bow, tan, is lighter and the costs of sanding and staining the teak are:

- sanding $14/$m^2$
- staining $4.50/$m^2$
- reset of staining machine, arising after each staining job is completed $80.

To ensure the colour of the teak is consistent, all the teak for one job is stained at the same time, and the staining cost is the same irrespective of the age of the teak. The cost of purchasing new teak is $110/$m^2$. New teak can be stained the correct colour for Bow with no preparation.

Non-current assets

A new kitchen will be required. This can be purchased for $4,500 and the fitting costs will be $2,000. Alternatively, the existing kitchen can be refurbished. The materials for refurbishment will cost $4,000, and 40 hours of semi-skilled labour will be employed specifically for the refurbishment at a cost of $15/hour. The fitting costs of the refurbished kitchen will be 10% less than a new kitchen.

Labour

100 hours of skilled and 56 hours of unskilled labour will be required for the upholstery and flooring work. Skilled labour is paid the market rate of $25/hour and is currently fully employed on another job, where they earn a contribution of $6/hour. Alternatively new skilled labour could be employed, but the new workers will require training at a cost of $14/hour for the first 10 hours they are working.

Unskilled workers are currently paid $12/hour and each of the 5 workers is guaranteed a minimum wage of $420 per week. Each unskilled employee has enough work allocated to them for the next three weeks to earn $372 per week. The work to be done by the unskilled labour on Bow must be completed within the first week of the project starting and overtime is paid at time and half.

Other costs

It is factory policy to add $2,200 per week to a project, for the duration of the project. This is to cover:

Factory rates	$500
Plant and equipment depreciation	$700
Interest on long term loan to purchase plant and equipment	$400
Profit element	$600

1 **What are the costs to be included in the quote for the upholstery fabric and kitchen?**

$_______ upholstery fabric

$_______ kitchen

2 **What cost should be included in the quote for the teak wood?**

A $1,220

B $1,140

C $1,225

D $1,145

3 **What cost should be included in the quote for the skilled and unskilled labour?**

$_______ skilled labour **$_______ unskilled labour**

4 **Which option correctly classifies these costs? Place a tick in the boxes in the table below as appropriate.**

	Committed	**Notional**
Factory rates		
Depreciation		
Interest		

5 **Which TWO of the following statements are true?**

- The $100 spent obtaining the cost information should be included in the quote.
- Sip Co should consider the effect of the refurbishment on the tax the company will pay, and include the tax effect in the quote as a relevant cost.
- Opportunity costs arise when a scarce resource, which has an alternative use in the business, is used in a project.
- Relevant costing techniques should be used in cost volume profit analysis.

246 HARE EVENTS (DECEMBER 2016)

Hare Events is a company which specialises in organising sporting events in major cities across Teeland. It has approached the local council of Edglas, a large city in the north of Teeland, to request permission to host a running festival which will include both a full marathon and a half marathon race.

Based on the prices it charges for entry to similar events in other locations, Hare Events has decided on an entry fee of $55 for the full marathon and $30 for the half marathon. It expects that the maximum entries will be 20,000 for the full marathon and 14,000 for the half marathon.

Hare Events has done a full assessment of the likely costs involved. Each runner will receive a race pack on completion of the race which will include a medal, t-shirt, water and chocolate. Water stations will need to be available at every five kilometre (km) point along the race route, stocked with sufficient supplies of water, sports drinks and gels. These costs are considered to be variable as they depend on the number of race entries.

Hare Events will also incur the following fixed costs. It will need to pay a fixed fee to the Edglas council for permits, road closures and support from the local police and medical services. A full risk assessment needs to be undertaken for insurance purposes. A marketing campaign is planned via advertising on running websites, in fitness magazines and at other events Hare Events is organising in Teeland, and the company which Hare Events usually employs to do the race photography has been approached.

The details of these costs are shown below:

	Full marathon	**Half marathon**
	$	$
Race packs	15.80	10.80
Water stations	2.40	1.20
		$
Council fees		300,000
Risk assessment and insurance		50,000
Marketing		30,000
Photography		5,000

1 **If Hare Events decides to host only the full marathon race, what is the margin of safety?**

A 35.0%

B 47.7%

C 52.3%

D 65.0%

2 **Assuming that the race entries are sold in a constant sales mix based on the expected race entry numbers, what is the sales revenue Hare Events needs to achieve in order to break even (to the nearest $000)?**

A $385,000

B $575,000

C $593,000

D $597,000

3 Hare Events wishes to achieve a minimum total profit of $500,000 from the running festival.

What are the number of entries Hare Events will have to sell for each race in order to achieve this level of profit, assuming a constant sales mix based on the expected race entry numbers applies?

Work to the nearest whole number.

A Full marathon: 17,915 entries and half marathon: 12,540 entries

B Full marathon: 14,562 entries and half marathon: 18,688 entries

C Full marathon: 20,000 entries and half marathon: 8,278 entries

D Full marathon: 9,500 entries and half marathon: 6,650 entries

4 Hare Events is also considering including a 10 km race during the running festival. It expects the race will have an entry fee of $20 per competitor and variable costs of $8 per competitor. Fixed costs associated with this race will be $48,000.

If the selling price per competitor, the variable cost per competitor and the total fixed costs for this 10 km race all increase by 10%, what will happen to the breakeven volume and the breakeven revenue? Place a tick in the boxes in the table below as appropriate.

	Will change	**Will not change**
Breakeven volume		
Breakeven revenue		

5 Which of the following statements relating to cost volume profit analysis are true?

(1) Production levels and sales levels are assumed to be the same so there is no inventory movement.

(2) The contribution to sales ratio (C/S ratio) can be used to indicate the relative profitability of different products.

(3) CVP analysis assumes that fixed costs will change if output either falls or increases significantly.

(4) Sales prices are recognised to vary at different levels of activity especially if higher volume of sales is needed.

A (1), (2) and (3)

B (2), (3) and (4)

C (1) and (2) only

D (3) and (4) only

247 RACQUETZ CO (MARCH/JUNE 2023)

Racquetz Co is based in the country of Eastland and currently makes and sells racquets for children for three different sports: badminton, tennis and squash. The company has recently been trying to forecast expected sales and costs for the next three years.

20X1

Sales demand for 20X1 is expected to be in the ratio 4:2:1 for badminton, tennis and squash racquets respectively.

The following budgeted information is available:

	Badminton	**Tennis**	**Squash**
	$/racquet	$/racquet	$/racquet
Sales price	21	30	24
Variable costs	11	15	16

At the end of 20X1, Racquetz Co will stop making squash racquets.

20X2

The Tennis Association Foundation, funded partly by the government, is planning an investment in the sport in order to encourage more children to take up tennis. This funding will lead to an increased number of children's tennis facilities being available in 20X2 and a corresponding rise in the sale of tennis racquets. The sales volume ratio for the year is expected to be 3:5 for badminton and tennis racquets respectively, with a weighted average contribution to sales (C/S) ratio of 52.21%.

Racquetz Co has budgeted to sell badminton racquets for $22 per unit and tennis racquets for $32 per unit. Fixed costs are expected to be $604,750 for the year.

20X3

The Badminton World Championships are held every two years in a different country. In 20X3, they will be held in Eastland and Racquetz Co will be selling its badminton racquets at the event. This means that the proportion of badminton racquet sales is expected to be higher than usual in 20X3. A profit volume graph for 20X3 has been drawn as follows:

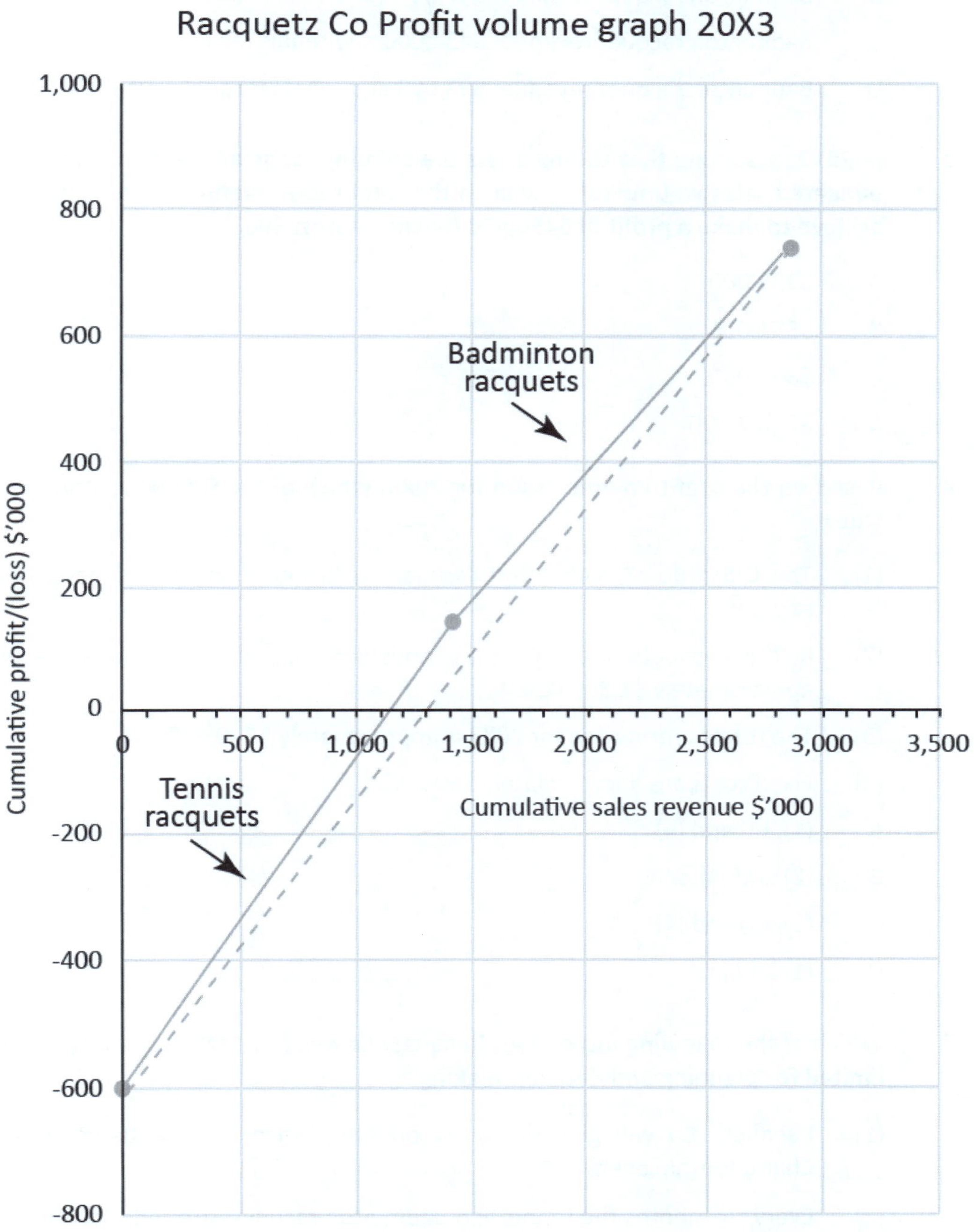

1 **For 20X1, calculate the forecast weighted average contribution to sales (C/S) ratio for Racquetz Co.**

A 53.6%

B 44.0%

C 56.0%

D 46.4%

2 **In 20X2, assuming that the racquets are sold in a constant sales mix based on the budgeted sales volume ratio, what is the sales revenue Racquetz Co needs to achieve in order to break even (to the nearest $000)?**

A Badminton racquet revenue: $338,000 and tennis racquet revenue: $820,000

B Badminton racquet revenue: $472,000 and tennis racquet revenue: $686,000

C Badminton racquet revenue: $434,000 and tennis racquet revenue: $724,000

D Badminton racquet revenue: $92,000 and tennis racquet revenue: $224,000

3 **In 20X2, assuming that the racquets are sold in a constant sales mix based on the budgeted sales volume ratio, what is the total sales revenue Racquetz Co needs to achieve to make a profit of $450,800 (to the nearest $000)?**

A $295,000

B $551,000

C $863,000

D $2,022,000

4 **Based on the profit volume graph for 20X3, which of the following statements are true?**

(1) The C/S ratio of badminton racquets is higher than the C/S ratio of tennis racquets.

(2) If the racquets are sold in a constant mix, the break-even revenue is approximately $1,300,000.

(3) The total contribution for 20X3 is approximately $740,000.

(4) Fixed costs are approximately $600,000.

A (1), (2) and (4)

B (2) and (4) only

C (2), (3) and (4)

D (1) and (3)

5 **Which of the following facts about Racquetz Co mean that the use of CVP analysis is limited for planning and decision-making?**

(1) Racquetz Co will give discounts on sales prices at the Badminton World Championship event.

(2) Every six months the tennis and badminton racquets are redesigned and given a new model name.

(3) All of Racquetz Co's costs are either fixed costs or variable costs and there are no semi-variable costs.

A (1), (2) and (3)

B (1) only

C (1) and (2) only

D (2) and (3) only

248 CARDIO CO (DECEMBER 2015, ADAPTED)

Cardio Co manufactures four types of fitness equipment: elliptical trainers (E), treadmills (T), cross trainers (C) and rowing machines (R). Cardio Co is considering ceasing to produce elliptical trainers at the end of 20X5.

The budgeted sales prices and volumes for the next year (20X6) are as follows:

	T	C	R	
Selling price	$1,600	$1,800	$1,400	
Units	420	400	380	
Total sales revenue	$672,000	$720,000	$532,000	**$1,924,000**

The standard cost card for each product is shown below:

	T	C	R
Material	$430	$500	$360
Labour	$220	$240	$190
Variable overheads	$110	$120	$95

Labour costs are 60% fixed and 40% variable. General fixed overheads excluding any fixed labour costs are expected to be $55,000 for the next year.

The following multi-product breakeven chart for Cardio Co has correctly been drawn:

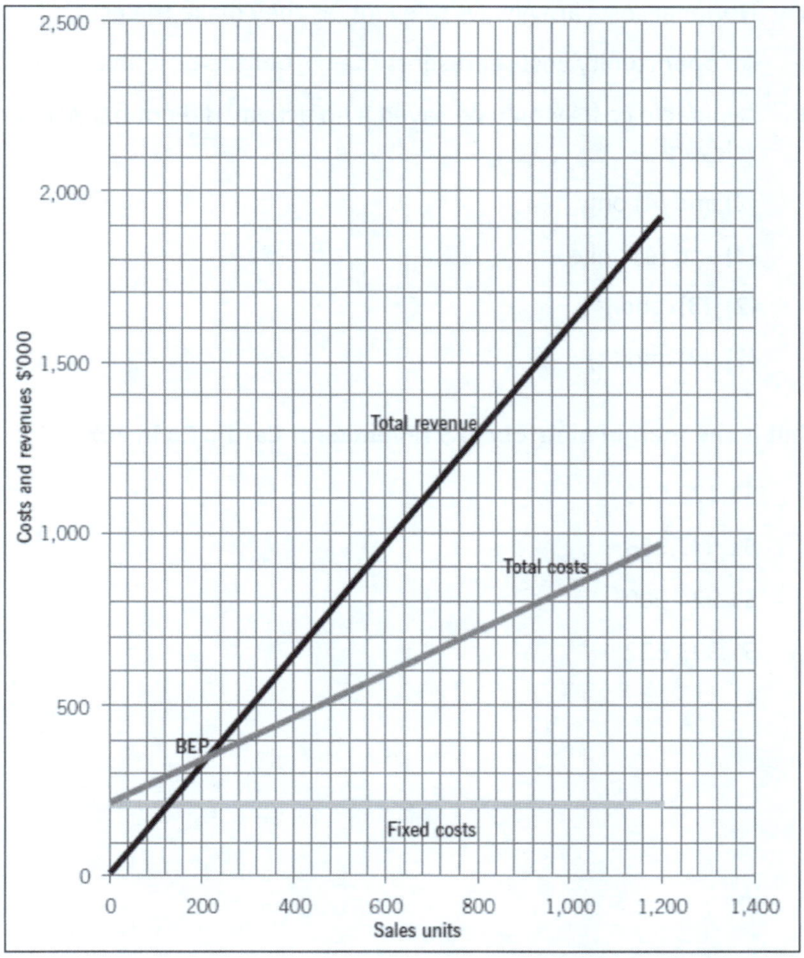

Cardio Co has recently received a request from a customer, Heart Co, to provide a one-off order of fitness machines (T, C and R), in excess of normal budgeted production for 20X6. The order would need to be completed within two weeks.

1 **Which of the following are valid factors to consider in the decision to cease the production of elliptical trainers at the end of 20X5?**

(1) The elliptical trainers made a loss in 20X5.

(2) The elliptical trainers made a positive contribution in the year just passed.

(3) The elliptical trainer market outlook in the long term looks very poor.

(4) Cardio Co also sells treadmills and many elliptical trainers buyers will also buy treadmills.

(5) The business was founded to produce and sell elliptical trainers.

A (3) and (4) only

B (1), (3), (4) and (5)

C (2), (3) and (4)

D None of the above

2 **Which of the following statements about relevant costing are true?**

(1) Fixed costs are always general in nature and therefore never relevant.

(2) Notional costs are always relevant, as they make the estimate more realistic.

(3) An opportunity cost represents the cost of the best alternative foregone.

(4) Avoidable costs would be saved if an activity did not happen, and therefore are relevant.

A (2) and (4) only

B (3) and (4) only

C (2), (3), and (4)

D (1), (2) and (4)

3 **What is the margin of safety in $ revenue for Cardio Co in 20X6?**

A $1,172,060

B $1,577,053

C $1,924,000

D $1,993,632

4 What would happen to the breakeven point if the products were sold in order of the most profitable products first?

A The breakeven point would be reached earlier.

B The breakeven point would be reached later.

C The breakeven point would be reached at the same time as in the graph above.

D The breakeven point would never be reached.

5 Which statement correctly describes the treatment of general fixed overheads when preparing the Heart Co quotation?

A The overheads should be excluded because they are a sunk cost.

B The overheads should be excluded because they are not incremental costs.

C The overheads should be included because they relate to production costs.

D The overheads should be included because all expenses should be recovered.

249 CARA CO (MARCH 2019)

Cara Co makes two products, the Seebach and the Herdorf.

To make a unit of each product the following resources are required:

	Seebach	**Herdorf**
Materials ($100 per kg)	5 kg	7 kg
Labour hours ($45 per hour)	2 hours	3 hours
Machine hours ($60 per hour)	3 hours	2 hours

Fixed overheads are $300,000 each month.

The contribution per unit made on each product is as follows:

	Seebach	**Herdorf**
Contribution ($ per unit)	250	315

The maximum demand each month is 4,000 units of Seebach and 3,000 units of Herdorf. The products and materials are perishable and inventories of raw materials or finished goods cannot be stored.

Cara Co has a legally binding obligation to produce a minimum of 2,000 units of Herdorf in each of months 1 and 2. There is no minimum production required in month 3.

The manufacturing manager is planning production volumes and the maximum availability of resources for months 1, 2 and 3 are as follows:

Month	**1**	**2**	**3**
Materials (kg)	34,000	42,000	35,000
Labour (hours)	18,000	12,000	24,000
Machine (hours)	18,000	19,000	12,000

For month 3 the following linear programming graph has been produced:

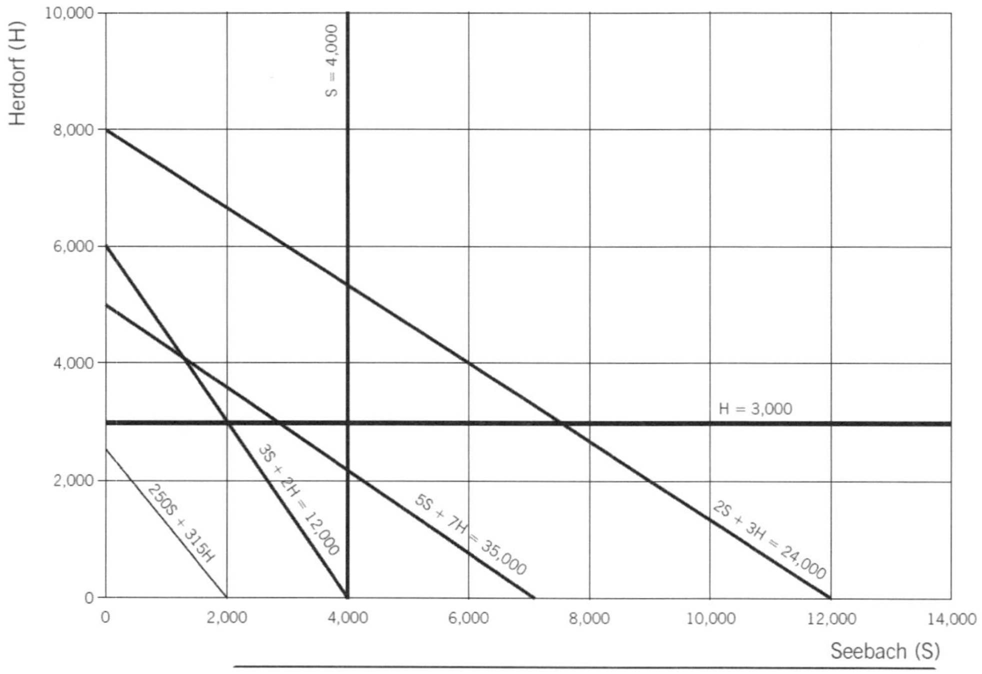

1 What is/are the limiting factor(s) in month 1?

A Materials, labour hours and machine hours

B Materials and machine hours only

C Materials only

D Labour hours only

2 The production manager has identified that the only limiting factor in month 2 is labour hours.

What is the production volume for Herdorf for month 2 (to the nearest whole unit)?

A 0

B 1,333

C 2,000

D 3,000

3 If the shadow price for month 2 is $125 per labour hour, which of the following statements is/are correct?

(1) The production manager would be willing to pay existing staff a maximum overtime premium of $125 per hour for the next 2,000 hours.

(2) The production manager would be willing to pay a maximum of $170 per hour for an additional 2,000 hours of temporary staff time.

A (1) only

B (2) only

C Both (1) and (2)

D Neither (1) nor (2)

4 What is the maximum profit which can be earned in month 3?

A $1,080,000

B $1,380,000

C $1,445,000

D $1,145,000

5 Which of the following interpretations of the linear programming graph produced for month 3 is/are correct?

(1) All other things being equal, unless demand increases for either product labour will be a slack variable.

(2) If more machine hours were made available in month 3 they would be used initially to make Herdorfs.

A (1) only

B (2) only

C Both (1) and (2)

D Neither (1) nor (2)

250 HOME ELECTRICS CO (MARCH/JUNE 2021)

Home Electrics Co manufactures electrical appliances for domestic use. It is made up of two divisions.

Small Appliances division

Two of the products manufactured by the Small Appliances division are the Blender (Product B) and the Toaster (Product T). The standard cost cards per unit for each of the products is as follows:

	B	**T**
	$	$
Selling Price	80	120
Direct Materials ($5 per kg)	10	15
Direct Labour ($7 per hour)	21	35
Variable Overheads	12	18
Fixed overheads	8	10
Profit	**29**	**42**

In the first quarter of the year the supply of materials was restricted to 2,000 kg per month. This was due to a global shortage.

It is now April and it has been identified that material will continue to be limited to 2,000 kg per month but also labour hours will be restricted to 3,200 hours per month. The management accountant has supplied formulas for the production constraints as follows:

Materials	2B + 3T = 2,000
Labour	3B + 5T = 3,200

Large Appliances division

This division also manufactures two products; a Freezer (Product F) which earns a contribution of $150 per unit and a Dishwasher (Product D) which earns a contribution of $200 per unit. Both products use the same resources, several of which are in short supply.

In April only 4,000 labour hours, 2,500 kg of material and 3,200 machine hours will be available. The management accountant has applied linear programming and defined the following constraints:

Materials	4F + 6D = 2,500
Labour	10F + 8D = 4,000
Machine time	5F + 10D = 3,200
Demand for D	250

Labour and machine time have been identified as the binding constraints and an optimum production plan of 240 units of F and 200 units of D has been calculated.

1 **What is the contribution per unit of limiting factor for Product T in the first quarter of the year (to the nearest whole $)?**

$_______

2 **Using simultaneous equations, what is the total contribution to be earned from Products B and T in April?**

A $28,400

B $35,600

C $62,000

D $77,200

3 **Which of the following statements about the use of linear programming to resolve limiting factor problems are true?**

(1) The linear programming method helps to identify the optimum selling price for a product.

(2) Slack occurs when more than the maximum available of the limited resource is required.

A (1) only

B (2) only

C Both (1) and (2)

D Neither (1) nor (2)

4 **What would be the shadow price of material in the Large Appliances division (to the nearest whole $)?**

$_______

5 **Which of the following statements about the linear programming method in the Large Appliances division are true?**

(1) Product D has a slack value.

(2) Contribution of $76,000 will be earned from the optimum production plan.

(3) Labour and machine time intersect at the optimum point if shown on a graph.

A (1), (2) and (3)

B (2) and (3) only

C (1) and (3) only

D (2) only

251 JEWEL CO (JUNE 2016, ADAPTED)

Jewel Co is setting up an online business importing and selling jewellery headphones. The cost of each set of headphones varies depending on the number purchased, although they can only be purchased in batches of 1,000 units. It also has to pay import taxes which vary according to the quantity purchased.

Jewel Co has already carried out some market research and identified that sales quantities are expected to vary depending on the price charged. Consequently, the following data has been established for the first month:

Number of batches imported and sold	Average cost per unit, including import taxes ($)	Total fixed costs per month ($)	Expected selling price per unit ($)
1	10.00	10,000	20
2	8.80	10,000	18
3	7.80	12,000	16
4	6.40	12,000	13
5	6.40	14,000	12

Most of Jewel Co's total fixed costs are set-up costs.

1 **How many batches should Jewel Co import and sell (to the nearest whole batch)?**
________ batches

2 **Which of the following statements(s) regarding Jewel Co's fixed costs is/are correct?**

(1) Jewel Co's fixed costs are stepped.

(2) Increasing batch sizes should reduce setup costs and therefore increase profits.

A (1) only

B (2) only

C Both (1) and (2)

D Neither (1) nor (2)

3 The following statements have been made about the tabular method used to establish an optimum price:

Which of the following statement(s) regarding Jewel Co's fixed costs is/are correct?

(1) With the tabular method, there must be a consistent relationship between price (P) and demand (Q), as well as a close relationship between demand (Q) and marginal costs (MC).

(2) The tabular method is only suitable for companies operating in a monopoly.

A (1) only

B (2) only

C Both (1) and (2)

D Neither (1) nor (2)

Earphones

Jewel Co is also producing luxury earphones and has entered two different new markets. In the USA, it is initially charging low prices so as to gain rapid market share while demand is relatively elastic. In Europe, it is initially charging high prices so as to earn maximum profits while demand is relatively inelastic.

Market research has revealed that the maximum demand for Jewel Co's earphones in the USA is 72,000 units per year, and that demand will reduce by 8,000 units for every $5 that the selling price is increased. Jewel Co has calculated that the profit-maximising level of sales for its earphones, for the coming year, is 32,000 units.

4 **Which price strategy is Jewel Co using in each market?**

A Penetration pricing in the USA and price skimming in Europe

B Price discrimination in the USA and penetration pricing in Europe

C Price skimming in the USA and penetration pricing in Europe

D Price skimming in the USA and price discrimination in Europe

5 **What is the optimum selling price at the profit-maximising level of sales (to the nearest $)? $__________**

252 SKULPT CO (SEPTEMBER/DECEMBER 2022)

Skulpt Co is a manufacturer of electronic goods. One electronic device it produces, and sells is the GSA. There are between 30 to 50 other suppliers of similar, but not identical, devices in Skulpt Co's markets. Each producer enjoys varying levels of customer and brand loyalty.

The current selling price for the GSA is $250 and Skulpt Co's directors are considering a reduction in price to $230. Market research commissioned by the company has suggested that the price elasticity of demand for the GSA is 1.25.

The same market research suggests that the price (P) schedule and marginal revenue (MR) schedule for the GSA in its current markets are as follows:

P = 450 – 0.2Q

MR = 450 – 0.4Q

Production and selling costs for one GSA are as follows:

	Cost per unit ($)
Variable production cost	30
Variable selling and distribution cost	24
Fixed production cost	40
Fixed selling and distribution cost	18
	112

New customer order

A new customer, LOK Co, has approached Skulpt Co with a bespoke, one-off order of 5,000 units of the GSA. The units will be produced in Skulpt Co's factory along with all of its usual production and delivered to LOK Co using Skulpt Co's usual distribution channels. The order is considered bespoke as LOK Co has requested some additional finishing in the production process, which will generate an extra production cost of $6 per unit. The units must also be delivered using a special packaging costing $2 per unit. The special packaging will be paid for and supplied by LOK Co.

The variable production cost of the GSA includes the current purchase price of $7 per unit for an electronic chip. As the GSA is a popular product the chips are in constant use and Skulpt Co has sufficient inventory of these chips to satisfy LOK Co's order. The chips in inventory were purchased several months ago at a discounted rate of $5 each.

A mark-up of 20% is usually added for all one-off orders.

New market

Skulpt Co wants to sell to the country of Harekish, which now allows the sale of the GSA following a change in its laws. Skulpt Co's objectives are to:

- Set a minimum acceptable price which is most likely to discourage new entrants; and
- Shorten the initial period of the product life cycle in Harekish to reach the growth and maturity stages quickly.

1 **Which of the following factors is LEAST likely to be considered by Skulpt Co when setting its prices in its home market?**

A Customer demand

B Manufacturing costs

C Competitors' prices

D Currency in its home market

2 **Which of the following statements about the price elasticity of demand for the GSA is true?**

A Its demand is price elastic and revenue will increase if the price is decreased to $230

B Its demand is price elastic and revenue will decrease if the price is decreased to $230

C Its demand is price inelastic and revenue will increase if the price is decreased to $230

D Its demand is price inelastic and revenue will decrease if the price is decreased to $230

3 **What is the profit-maximising price for the GSA (to the nearest whole $)?**

$ ________

4 **What is the minimum price per unit which could be set by Skulpt Co in respect of LOK Co's order of the GSA (to the nearest whole $)?**

$ ________

5 **Which TWO of the following pricing strategies are most appropriate for Skulpt Co in order to achieve its objectives in relation to selling the GSA in Harekish?**

A Transfer pricing

B Market skimming

C Market penetration

D Relevant cost pricing

E Price discrimination by product version

F Complementary product pricing

253 RUNF (MARCH/JUNE 2024)

Runf Co makes and sells a range of fitness equipment for use in gymnasiums and customers' homes. It currently produces a stationary fitness bicycle called the Quikcyc.

The Quikcyc has a demand function of P = 893 – 0.009Q and a variable cost per unit of $230.

The company has also been developing another type of stationary fitness bicycle called the Fitcyc, which it is about to launch. It has commissioned some research which has established that at a price of $500 the demand for the Fitcyc would be 20,000 units. The research also noted that for every $8 increase in price, demand for the Fitcyc would be expected to fall by 1,000 units.

It also sells 48,000 sets of hand weights per year. Based on this activity level, selling price and cost information for these weights is as follows:

	$ per set
Selling price	36
Variable cost	5
Fixed cost	2

The demand function for the hand weights is P = 84 – 0.001Q. Runf Co has 75,000 sets in inventory and wants to sell them all in the coming year.

1 **Using the optimal pricing approach, what should the selling price of the Quikcyc be in order to maximise profits?**

A $230

B $332

C $562

D $663

2 **Based on the research commissioned, at what selling price would demand for the Fitcyc be zero (to the nearest $)?**

$__________

3 **Runf Co sets a selling price in order to sell the 75,000 sets of hand weights in inventory, what would be the total profit earned?**

A $150,000

B $204,000

C $300,000

D $675,000

4 Runf Co has also recently developed a new electronic fitness device for tracking an individual's daily activity.

Which of the following facts about this new product would indicate that a market skimming pricing strategy would be suitable when it is launched?

(1) The fitness device has a three-year life-cycle.

(2) The company has incurred high development costs.

(3) The company wants to discourage new entrants into the market.

(4) The fitness device is currently the first of its kind.

A (1), (2), (3) and (4)

B (1) and (3) only

C (1), (2) and (4) only

D (2), (3) and (4) only

5 **Which of the following statements about price elasticity of demand (PED) is/are true?**

(1) PED is measured as 'the percentage change in price' divided by 'the percentage change in demand'.

(2) If the PED indicates that demand is elastic, prices should be increased in order to maximise profit.

A (1) only

B (2) only

C Neither (1) nor (2)

D Both (1) and (2)

254 GAM CO (JUNE 2014, ADAPTED)

Gam Co sells electronic equipment and is about to launch a new product onto the market. It needs to prepare its budget for the coming year and is trying to decide whether to launch the product at a price of $30, or $35 per unit. The following information has been obtained from market research:

Price per unit $30		**Price per unit $35**	
Probability	**Sales volume**	**Probability**	**Sales volume**
0.4	120,000	0.3	108,000
0.5	110,000	0.3	100,000
0.1	140,000	0.4	194,000

The six possible profit outcomes which could arise for Gam Co in the coming year have been correctly tabulated as follows:

Price per unit $30		**Price per unit $35**	
Sales volume	**Profit**	**Sales volume**	**Profit**
120,000	$930,000	108,000	$1,172,000
110,000	$740,000	100,000	$880,000
140,000	$1,310,000	194,000	$742,000

1 **What is the expected value of profit for the $30 price option?**

A $117,000

B $291,000

C $873,000

D $1,310,000

2 **What is the expected value of profit for the $35 price option?**

A $117,000

B $140,000

C $912,400

D $1,172,000

3 **Which is the correct definition of the maximin decision rule?**

A Under this rule, the decision-maker is an optimist who selects the alternative which maximises the maximum pay-off achievable.

B Under this rule, the decision-maker selects the alternative which maximises the minimum payoff achievable.

C Under this rule, the decision-maker selects the alternative which minimises the maximum regret.

D Under this rule, the decision-maker selects the alternative which minimises the minimum profit.

4 **Which price should be chosen by management if they use the maximin rule to decide which price should be charged?**

A $30

B $35

C Any price between $30 and $35

D Either $30 or $35, as it makes no difference to the profit

5 **Which price should be chosen by management if they use the maximax rule to decide which price should be charged?**

A $30

B $35

C Any price between $30 and $35

D Either $30 or $35, as it makes no difference to the profit

255 MYLO (SEPTEMBER 2016)

Mylo runs a cafeteria situated on the ground floor of a large corporate office block. Each of the five floors of the building are occupied and there are in total 1,240 employees.

Mylo sells lunches and snacks in the cafeteria. The lunch menu is freshly prepared each morning and Mylo has to decide how many meals to make each day. As the office block is located in the city centre, there are several other places situated around the building where staff can buy their lunch, so the level of demand for lunches in the cafeteria is uncertain.

Mylo has analysed daily sales over the previous six months and established four possible demand levels and their associated probabilities. He has produced the following payoff table to show the daily profits which could be earned from the lunch sales in the cafeteria:

Demand level	**Probability**		**Supply level**		
		450	620	775	960
		$	$	$	$
450	0.15	1,170	980	810	740
620	0.30	1,170	1,612	1,395	1,290
775	0.40	1,170	1,612	2,015	1,785
960	0.15	1,170	1,612	2,015	2,496

1 **If Mylo adopts a maximin approach to decision-making, which daily supply level will he choose?**

A 450 lunches

B 620 lunches

C 775 lunches

D 960 lunches

2 **If Mylo adopts a minimax regret approach to decision-making, which daily supply level will he choose?**

A 450 lunches

B 620 lunches

C 775 lunches

D 960 lunches

3 **Which of the following statements is/are true if Mylo chooses to use expected values to assist in his decision-making regarding the number of lunches to be provided?**

(1) Mylo would be considered to be taking a defensive and conservative approach to his decision.

(2) Expected values will ignore any variability which could occur across the range of possible outcomes.

(3) Expected values will not take into account the likelihood of the different outcomes occurring.

(4) Expected values can be applied by Mylo as he is evaluating a decision which occurs many times over.

A (1), (2) and (3)

B (2) and (4)

C (1) and (3) only

D (4) only

4 The human resources department has offered to undertake some research to help Mylo to predict the number of employees who will require lunch in the cafeteria each day. This information will allow Mylo to prepare an accurate number of lunches each day.

What is the maximum amount which Mylo would be willing to pay for this information (to the nearest whole $)?

A $191

B $359

C $478

D $175

5 Mylo is now considering investing in a speciality coffee machine. He has estimated the following daily results for the new machine:

	$
Sales (650 units)	1,300
Variable costs	(845)
Contribution	455
Incremental fixed costs	(70)
Profit	385

Which of the following statements are true regarding the sensitivity of this investment?

(1) The investment is more sensitive to a change in sales volume than sales price.

(2) If variable costs increase by 44% the investment will make a loss.

(3) The investment's sensitivity to incremental fixed costs is 550%.

(4) The margin of safety is 84.6%.

A (1), (2) and (3)

B (2) and (4)

C (1), (3) and (4)

D (3) and (4) only

256 HURSTMID CO (MARCH/JUNE 2025)

Hurstmid Co manufactures a range of domestic furniture. Its finance director is currently reviewing the financial performance of three types of chair which the company sells: the Comforo, the Leisuro and the Serenito.

Recent results

Results for the last trading period are as follows:

	Comforo	**Leisuro**	**Serenito**
	$'000	**$'000**	**$'000**
Revenue	4,500	1,700	1,200
Variable costs	(1,800)	(900)	(700)
Contribution	**2,700**	**800**	**500**
Attributable fixed costs	(1,000)	(900)	(400)
General fixed costs	(1,200)	(700)	(600)
Profit/(loss)	**500**	**(800)**	**(500)**

Hurstmid Co's finance director believes that it is clear from these recent results that the company should continue to sell the Comforo, but is unsure whether it should continue to produce the other two chairs.

Quotation from Hampar Co

Hurstmid Co's finance director is considering outsourcing the manufacture of some or all of the chairs and has received the following quotation from Hampar Co:

	$'000
Comforo	2,100
Leisuro	700
Serenito	1,200

Residential home order

Hurstmid Co has received a bulk order for the Comforo from a large group of residential homes. To be able to meet the order, the company will require additional machine capacity. It could use a machine which it purchased for $80,000 two years ago which now has a resale value of $90,000 and has a current replacement cost of $120,000. If this machine were used for the manufacture of other products, it could generate net income of $110,000.

Belgraff Co order

Belgraff Co wishes to place a special order for the Serenito chairs which it plans to use as part of its refurbishment of one of its largest offices. Hurstmid Co's finance director is considering charging a minimum price for this order in order to gain business from Belgraff Co. He believes that satisfactorily fulfilling the order will result in further, more profitable, orders in the future.

1 **Based only on the recent results provided, which, if any, of the chairs should Hurstmid Co cease to produce?**

A The Leisuro only

B The Serenito only

C Both the Leisuro and the Serenito

D Neither the Leisuro not the Serenito

2 **Which of the following, if any, would be valid reasons for Hurstmid Co to continue to manufacture a chair which was budgeted to make a loss?**

(1) The chair is a complementary product to other products.

(2) Selling the chair at a loss can be a way to gain market share.

A (1) only

B (2) only

C Both (1) and (2)

D Neither (1) nor (2)

3 **Based on the quotation from Hampar Co, which of the chairs should continue to be manufactured internally?**

A Serenito only.

B Comforo and Serenito.

C Comforo only.

D Comforo and Leisuro.

4 **What is the relevant cost of the machine required for the order for the residential homes?**

$ ___________

5 **Identify whether each statement about the minimum pricing approach suggested by the finance director for the order from Belgraff Co is true or false.**

	True	False
The costs which the minimum price should cover are incremental costs and opportunity costs only		
It can lead to the product's perceived value in the market being eroded		
The price can be easily raised on subsequent orders without affecting customer retention		

257 HORNGREN CO (MARCH/JUNE 2022)

Horngren Co manufactures a range of dairy products. It produces three types of yoghurt which it sells in 2 kg tubs to hotels and holiday resorts.

Details of demand, costs and selling prices for the three types of yoghurt are as follows:

Product	**Natural**	**Fruity**	**Luxury**
Maximum demand per month (units)	5,000	10,000	15,000
	$ per unit	**$ per unit**	**$ per unit**
Selling price	15	22	30
Direct Labour	4	8	12
Direct material	3	3.75	4.50
Fixed production overhead	1	4	6

Notes:

(1) Direct labour is paid at a rate of $8.00 per hour.

(2) Direct material costs are $1.50 per kg.

(3) The fixed production overhead is absorbed using a machine hours basis at a rate of $1 per hour. Fixed production overheads are a joint cost of the three products.

An external supplier has offered to supply units of Natural, Fruity and Luxury for $11, $17 and $25 per unit respectively.

Horngren Co predicts the following availability of resources over the next three months:

	Direct labour	**Direct material**	**Machine capacity**
Month 1	36,000 hours	75,000 kg	140,000 hours
Month 2	unlimited	unlimited	120,000 hours
Month 3	27,000 hours	unlimited	unlimited

Direct material and the products made are perishable and thus no inventory is held.

1 **For Month 1 rank the products in the order of preference for making internally.**

Product	Ranking
Natural	
Fruity	
Luxury	

2 **In Month 2 how many units of Fruity should Horngren Co buy from the external supplier assuming the company wants to maximise profit?**

____________ units

3 In Month 3 Horngren Co correctly calculates that it should be able to make 5,000 units of Natural, 15,000 units of Luxury and 2,000 units of Fruity internally. The balance of Fruity required should be bought from the external supplier.

How would this plan change if making Fruity internally incurred an incremental fixed cost of $8,000?

A The plan would not change

B All units of fruity would be bought externally

C All units of Fruity would be made internally

D 4,500 units of Fruity would be made internally

4 Horngren Co is considering outsourcing the management of its site, including security, cleaning and general maintenance work to a well-established facilities management company.

Which TWO of the following statements about this plan are correct?

A Economies of specialisation should mean that Horngren Co will make some cost savings

B Horngren Co will no longer need to monitor these areas of its organisation

C There will be an increase in Horngren Co management's control over these areas

D Management will be able to concentrate more on Horngren Co's core activities

5 **Which of the following statements about joint products is/are true?**

(1) Joint products are accounted for in the same way as by-products from a process.

(2) Joint products are indistinguishable from each other until the separation point.

A (1) only

B (2) only

C Both (1) and (2)

D Neither (1) nor (2)

BUDGETING AND CONTROL

258 LRA (JUNE 2015, ADAPTED)

Lesting Regional Authority (LRA) is responsible for the provision of a wide range of services in the Lesting region, which is based in the south of the country 'Alaia'. These services include, amongst other things, responsibility for residents' welfare, schools, housing, hospitals, roads and waste management. Over recent months the Lesting region experienced the hottest temperatures on record, resulting in several forest fires, which caused damage to several schools and some local roads. Unfortunately, these hot temperatures were then followed by flooding, which left a number of residents without homes and saw higher than usual numbers of admissions to hospitals due to the outbreak of disease. These hospitals were full and some patients were treated in tents. Residents have been complaining for some years that a new hospital is needed in the area.

Prior to these events, the LRA was proudly leading the way in a new approach to waste management, with the introduction of its new 'Waste Recycling Scheme.' Two years ago, it began phase 1 of the scheme and half of its residents were issued with different coloured waste bins for different types of waste. The final phase was due to begin in one month's time. The cost of providing the new waste bins is significant but LRA's focus has always been on the long-term savings both to the environment and in terms of reduced waste disposal costs.

The LRA is about to begin preparing its budget for the coming financial year, which starts in one month's time. Over recent years, zero-based budgeting (ZBB) has been introduced at a number of regional authorities in Alaia and, given the demand on resources which LRA faces this year, it is considering whether now would be a good time to introduce it.

1 What are the main steps involved in preparing a zero-based budget?

A Identifying previous inefficiencies, using adaptive management processes and avoiding wasteful expenditure in planning.

B Recognising different cost behaviour patterns, planning on a rolling basis and ignoring wasteful expenditure.

C Analysing the cost of each activity, identifying alternative methods and assessing the consequences of performing the activity at different levels.

D Updating the budget continually, setting performance standards and controlling performance monthly with the use of variance analysis.

2 Which TWO of the following statements are true?

(1) Now is a good time to introduce ZBB in LRA.

(2) The introduction of ZBB in any organisation is relatively straightforward.

(3) The introduction of ZBB in LRA would be lengthy and costly.

(4) A conflict situation may arise if ZBB is introduced in LRA.

A (1) and (2)

B (1) and (3)

C (3) and (4)

D (2) and (4)

3 Which of the following correctly describes a 'decision package' within the context of zero-based budgeting?

A A method of budgeting that requires each cost element to be specifically justified, as though the activities to which the budget relates were being undertaken for the first time.

B The decision or choice between making a product in-house or outsourcing and buying in.

C A method of budgeting based on an activity framework and utilising cost driver data in the budget-setting and variance feedback processes.

D A list of costs that will not result in an outflow of cash either now or in the future or result in a 'real' cash expenditure.

4 Which ONE of the following statements is true?

A If any of the activities or operations at LRA are wasteful, ZBB will not be able to identify these and remove them.

B With the implementation of ZBB, managers may become less motivated as they have had a key role in putting the budget together.

C ZBB would discourage a more questioning attitude and lead managers to just the status quo.

D Overall, ZBB at LRA will lead to a more efficient allocation of resources.

5 Which of the following describe difficulties in assessing performance in not-for-profit organisations?

(i) Benefits and costs are not always easy to quantify.

(ii) These organisations often have multiple stakeholders and therefore multiple objectives.

(iii) These organisations often have unlimited funds and are therefore not motivated to measure performance.

A (i) only

B (i) and (ii)

C (ii) only

D (ii) and (iii)

259 BOKCO (JUNE 2015, ADAPTED)

Bokco is a manufacturing company. It has a small permanent workforce, but it is also reliant on temporary workers, whom it hires on three-month contracts whenever production requirements increase. All buying of materials is the responsibility of the company's purchasing department. and the company's policy is to hold low levels of raw materials in order to minimise inventory holding costs.

Budgeting is done on spreadsheets and detailed variance reports are produced each month for sales, material costs and labour costs. Departmental managers are then paid a monthly bonus depending on the performance of their department.

Bokco is operating in a fast changing environment and its finance manager thinks the original standard costs are unrealistic. They are considering revising the budget by analysing existing variances into a planning and operational element would help to improve performance.

One month ago, Bokco began production of a new product. The standard cost card for one unit was drawn up to include a cost of $84 for labour, based on seven hours of labour at $12 per hour.

Actual output of the product during the first month of production was 460 units and the actual time taken to manufacture the product totalled 1,860 hours at a total cost of $26,040.

After being presented with some initial variance calculations, the production manager has realised that the standard time per unit of seven hours was the time taken to produce the first unit and that a learning rate of 90% should have been anticipated for the first 1,000 units of production.

The production manager has consequently been criticised by other departmental managers who have said that, 'He has no idea of all the problems this (i.e. the failure to anticipate the learning effect) has caused.'

Bokco uses cost plus pricing to set the selling prices for its products once an initial cost card has been drawn up. Prices are then reviewed on a quarterly basis.

1 Which TWO of the following statements about using spreadsheets in budgeting are true?

(1) Spreadsheets enable managers to consider many different budget options and also carry out sensitivity analysis on the budget figures.

(2) Minor errors in the spreadsheet cannot affect the validity of the data.

(3) Spreadsheets are able to take qualitative factors into account.

(4) The possibility of experimentation with data is so great that it is possible to lose sight of the original intention of the spreadsheet.

A (1) and (2)

B (1) and (4)

C (2) and (3)

D (3) and (4)

2 Which TWO of the following sentences about the manipulation issues involved in revising budgets are true?

(1) The establishment of ex-post budgets is very difficult. Managers whose performance is reported to be poor using such a budget are unlikely to accept them as performance measures because of the subjectivity in setting such budgets.

(2) Frequent demands for budget revisions may result in bias.

(3) The operational variances do not give a fair reflection of the actual results achieved in the actual conditions that existed.

(4) The analysis does not help in the standard-setting learning process.

A (1) and (2)

B (1) and (3)

C (2) and (3)

D (3) and (4)

3 **What is the labour efficiency planning variance AFTER taking account of the learning effect?**

Note: The learning index for a 90% learning curve is –0.1520.

A $1,360 F

B $1, 360 A

C $7,104 A

D $23,424 F

4 **What is the labour efficiency operational variance AFTER taking account of the learning effect?**

Note: The learning index for a 90% learning curve is –0.1520.

A $1,360 F

B $1, 360 A

C $7,104 A

D $23,424 F

5 **Which ONE of the following statements about the production manager's failure to anticipate the learning effect is true?**

A There will be no unnecessary extra labour costs.

B The selling price of the company's products would have been set too low.

C An adverse material price variance would have arisen.

D The sales manager's bonus would have still be guaranteed, in spite of the production manager's failure to anticipate the learning effect.

260 CORFE CO (SEPTEMBER 2016)

Corfe Co is a business which manufactures computer laptop batteries and it has developed a new battery which has a longer usage time than batteries currently available in laptops. The selling price of the battery is forecast to be $45.

The maximum production capacity of Corfe Co is 262,500 units. The company's management accountant is currently preparing an annual flexible budget and has collected the following information so far:

Production (units)	185,000	200,000	225,000
	$	$	$
Material costs	740,000	800,000	900,000
Labour costs	1,017,500	1,100,000	1,237,500
Fixed costs	750,000	750,000	750,000

In addition to the above costs, the management accountant estimates that for each increment of 50,000 units produced, one supervisor will need to be employed. A supervisor's annual salary is $35,000.

The production manager does not understand why the flexible budgets have been produced as they have always used a fixed budget previously.

1 **Assuming the budgeted figures are correct, what would the flexed total production cost be if production is 80% of maximum capacity?**

A $2,735,000

B $2,770,000

C $2,885,000

D $2,920,000

2 The management accountant has said that a machine maintenance cost was not included in the flexible budget but needs to be taken into account.

The new battery will be manufactured on a machine currently owned by Corfe Co which was previously used for a product which has now been discontinued. The management accountant estimates that every 1,000 units will take 14 hours to produce. The annual machine hours and maintenance costs for the machine for the last four years have been as follows:

	Machine time	**Maintenance costs**
	(hours)	($000)
Year 1	5,000	850
Year 2	4,400	735
Year 3	4,850	815
Year 4	1,800	450

What is the estimated maintenance cost if production of the battery is 80% of maximum capacity (to the nearest $000)?

A $575,000

B $593,000

C $500,000

D $735,000

3 In the first month of production of the new battery, actual sales were 18,000 units and the sales revenue achieved was $702,000. The budgeted sales units were 17,300.

Based on this information, which of the following statements is true?

A When the budget is flexed, the sales variance will include both the sales volume and sales price variances.

B When the budget is flexed, the sales variance will only include the sales volume variance.

C When the budget is flexed, the sales variance will only include the sales price variance.

D When the budget is flexed, the sales variance will include the sales mix and quantity variances and the sales price variance.

4 **Which of the following statements relating to the preparation of a flexible budget for the new battery are true?**

(1) The budget could be time-consuming to produce as splitting out semi-variable costs may not be straightforward.

(2) The range of output over which assumptions about how costs will behave could be difficult to determine.

(3) The flexible budget will give managers more opportunity to include budgetary slack than a fixed budget.

(4) The budget will encourage all activities and their value to the organisation to be reviewed and assessed.

A (1) and (2) only

B (1), (2) and (3)

C (1) and (4)

D (2), (3) and (4)

5 The management accountant intends to use a spreadsheet for the flexible budget in order to analyse performance of the new battery.

Which of the following statements are benefits regarding the use of spreadsheets for budgeting?

(1) The user can change input variables and a new version of the budget can be quickly produced.

(2) Errors in a formula can be easily traced and data can be difficult to corrupt in a spreadsheet.

(3) A spreadsheet can take account of qualitative factors to allow decisions to be fully evaluated.

(4) Managers can carry out sensitivity analysis more easily on a budget model which is held in a spreadsheet.

A (1), (3) and (4)

B (1), (2) and (4)

C (1) and (4) only

D (2) and (3)

261 BELLAMY CO

Bellamy Co is negotiating with marketing companies with regard to its marketing campaign on its 'Muse' product. Bellamy Co is uncertain as to what the total marketing costs will be each year. However, the following information is available, as the sales manager has provided the data for past marketing expenditure and sales on the 'Muse' product.

The sales manager has plotted both of these variables on a scatter plot with the marketing expenditure from the last 12 quarters on the x-axis, and the associated sales (in $000) on the y-axis:

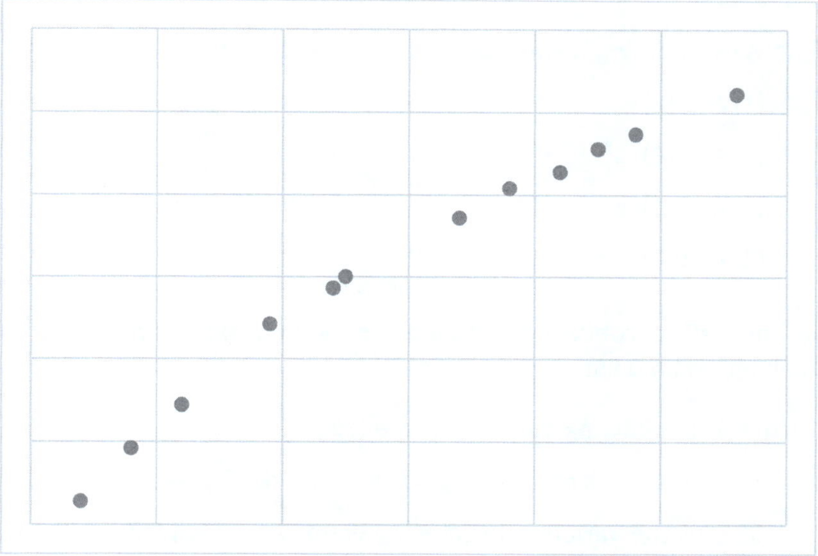

1 Which ONE of the following statements about the above graph is true?

A The graph shows a positive correlation, which means that low values of sales are associated with low values of marketing expenditure, and high values of sales are associated with high values of marketing expenditure.

B The graph shows a positive correlation, which means that low values of sales are associated with the high values of marketing expenditure, and high values of sales are associated with low values of marketing expenditure.

C The graph shows a negative correlation, which means that low values of sales are associated with the low values of marketing expenditure, and high values of sales are associated with high values of marketing expenditure.

D The graph shows a negative correlation, which means that low values of sales are associated with the high values of marketing expenditure, and high values of sales are associated with low values of marketing expenditure.

2 The linear relationship between marketing spend (X) and sales (Y) was correctly established by the sales manager as Y = 50,000 + 20X.

Which TWO of the following statements are true?

(1) For every $1,000 spent on marketing, sales revenue increases by $50,000 on average.

(2) When nothing is spent on marketing, the average sales level is $50,000.

(3) For every $1,000 spent on marketing, sales revenue increases by $20,000 on average.

(4) When nothing is spent on marketing, the average sales level is $20,000.

A (1) and (2)

B (1) and (4)

C (2) and (3)

D (3) and (4)

3 The correlation coefficient between marketing expenditure and sales revenue is calculated to be 0.85.

Which of the following statements are true?

A There is a weak relationship between marketing expenditure and sales revenue.

B 85% of the variation in sales revenue can be explained by the corresponding variation in marketing expenditure.

C 72% of the variation in sales revenue can be explained by the corresponding variation in marketing expenditure.

D Sales revenue will increase by 85% more than marketing expenditure will increase.

You have been asked to use regression analysis to forecast the impact of future marketing expenditure on sales.

4 **Which TWO of the following are underlying assumptions of forecasts made using regression analysis?**

(1) A curvilinear relationship exists between the two variables.

(2) The value of one variable can be predicted or estimated from the value of one other variable.

(3) A perfect linear relationship between the two variables.

(4) What has happened in the past will provide a reliable guide to the future.

A (1) and (2)

B (1) and (4)

C (2) and (4)

D (3) and (4)

5 **Which of the following would affect the reliability of a forecast using linear regression?**

(1) The amount of data on which the regression line is based.

(2) The assumption that the trend line applies outside the range of X values used to establish the line in the first place.

(3) The assumption that there is a linear relationship between the two variables.

(4) The coefficient of correlation.

A (1) and (2) only

B (3) and (4) only

C (1), (2), (3) only

D (1), (2), (3) and (4)

262 OBC (DECEMBER 2015, ADAPTED)

The Organic Bread Company (OBC) makes a range of breads for sale direct to the public. The production process begins with workers weighing out ingredients on electronic scales and then placing them in a machine for mixing. A worker then manually removes the dough from the machine and shapes it into loaves by hand, after which the bread is then placed into the oven for baking. All baked loaves are then inspected by OBC's quality inspector before they are packaged up and made ready for sale. Any loaves which fail the inspection are donated to a local food bank. The standard cost card for OBC's 'Mixed Bloomer', one of its most popular loaves, is as follows:

White flour	450 grams at $1.80 per kg	$0.81
Wholegrain flour	150 grams at $2.20 per kg	$0.33
Yeast	10 grams at $20 per kg	$0.20
Total	610 grams	$1.34

Budgeted production of Mixed Bloomers was 1,000 units for the quarter, although actual production was only 950 units. The total actual quantities used and their actual costs were:

	kgs	**$ per kg**
White flour	408.5	1.90
Wholegrain flour	152.0	2.10
Yeast	10.0	20.00
Total	570.5	

1 **What is the total material usage variance for OBC for the last quarter?**

A $3.30 favourable

B $20.90 favourable

C $20.90 adverse

D $34.20 favourable

2 **What is the total material mix variance for OBC for the last quarter?**

A $3.30 favourable

B $16.51 favourable

C $16.51 adverse

D $19.77 favourable

3 **What is the total material yield variance for OBC for the last quarter?**

A $3.30 favourable

B $16.51 favourable

C $16.51 adverse

D $19.77 favourable

4 **Which of the following statements below is/are true?**

(1) An adverse material mix variance may arise because the dough may not be removed completely out of the machine, leaving some dough behind.

(2) An adverse material yield variance may arise because handmade loaves may be slightly too large, meaning that fewer loaves can be baked.

A (1) only

B (2) only

C Both (1) and (2)

D Neither (1) nor (2)

5 **Which of the following statement(s) below is/are true?**

(1) Errors or changes in the mix may cause some loaves to be sub-standard and therefore rejected by the quality inspector.

(2) The loaves might be baked at the wrong temperature and therefore be rejected by the quality inspector.

A (1) only

B (2) only

C Both (1) and (2)

D Neither (1) nor (2)

263 VARIANCES – SALES

Fort Co produces and sells three models of family car: a basic model (the Drastic), an upgraded model (the Bomber) and a deluxe model (the Cracker). All of the cars are priced to achieve a 6% mark up on standard cost. For the month of June, Fort Co budgeted to sell 30,000 units of the Drastic and so have 10% market share of the budgeted sales at a price of $10,600 each. Fort Co actually achieved a 15% share of the market, though the market had actually contracted by 5%.

The following information is available for July.

	Drastic	**Bomber**	**Cracker**
Sales units:			
– Budgeted	27,000	15,000	18,000
– Actual	26,000	16,000	14,000
Budgeted sales price	**$10,600**	**$13,250**	**$16,960**

1 Which option correctly fills the gaps in the paragraph?

"The difference between the sales quantity and _____________ variances is that the standard _______________is considered in the former. The difference between standard and actual is _______________."

A volume, mix, ignored

B price, mix, calculated

C volume, quantity, ignored

D price, quantity, calculated

2 What is the favourable market share and adverse market size variance for the 'Drastic' (to the nearest $)?

Share $________ Favourable **Size $________ Adverse**

3 What is the total adverse sales mix variance for Fort Co (to the nearest $)? $________ Adverse

4 What is the total adverse sales quantity variance for Fort Co (to the nearest $)? $________ Adverse

5 Which TWO of the following statements are true?

(1) The sales mix variance would not give useful information to the management of Fort Co if the Cracker was a van.

(2) The sales mix variance will not be affected if the labour efficiency on the Drastic production line increases, all other factors remaining the same.

(3) The market share variance is a planning variance, not an operational variance.

(4) If the mix variance was calculated as a physical quantity, the answer would always be zero.

A (1) and (2)

B (2) and (3)

C (3) and (4)

D (1) and (4)

264 GRAYSHOTT CO (MARCH 2019)

Marcus manages production and sales of product MN at Grayshott Co. Marcus has been asked to attend a meeting with Grayshott Co's finance director to explain the results for product MN in the last quarter.

Budgeted and actual results for product MN were as follows:

	Budget	**Actual**
Sales volume (units)	40,000	38,000
	$000	$000
Revenue ($65 per unit)	2,600	2,394
Material (5.2 kg at $4 per kg)	(832)	(836)
Labour (2 hours at $8 per hour)	(640)	(798)
Variable overheads (2 hours at $4 per hour)	(320)	(399)
Fixed overheads	(220)	(220)
Profit	588	141

There was no opening and closing inventory in the last quarter. Grayshott Co operates a marginal costing system.

Marcus is angry about having to attend the meeting as he has no involvement in setting the original budget and he believes that the adverse results are due to the following circumstances which were beyond his control:

(1) A decision by Grayshott Co's board to increase wages meant that the actual labour rate per hour was 25% higher than budgeted. This decision was made in response to a request by the production department to enable it to meet a large, one-off customer order in the last quarter.

(2) Due to the closure of a key supplier, Grayshott Co agreed to a contract with an alternative supplier to pay 6% more per kg than the budgeted price for material. The actual cost per kg of material was $4.40.

(3) Difficult economic conditions meant that market demand for the MN was lower by 10%.

At present Grayshott Co does not operate a system of planning and operational variances and Marcus believes it should do so.

1 What was the market share variance for product MN for the last quarter?

A $40,400 Favourable

B $80,800 Adverse

C $29,400 Favourable

D $38,000 Adverse

2 What was the adverse materials price planning variance for product MN for the last quarter?

A $30,400

B $76,000

C $45,600

D $49,920

3 What was the labour rate operational variance for product MN for the last quarter?

A $159,600 Favourable

B $159,600 Adverse

C $160,000 Favourable

D $160,000 Adverse

4 Which of the following would explain a labour efficiency planning variance?

(1) A change in employment legislation requiring staff to take longer rest periods.

(2) Customers demanding higher quality products leading to a change in product design.

(3) The learning effect for labour being estimated incorrectly in the production budget.

A (1) and (2) only

B (2) and (3) only

C (3) only

D (1), (2) and (3)

5 Which of the following statements regarding the problems of introducing a system of planning and operational variances is/are true?

(1) Operational managers may argue that variances are due to the original budget being unrealistic.

(2) Operational managers may seek to blame uncontrollable external factors for the variances.

A (1) only

B (2) only

C Both (1) and (2)

D Neither (1) nor (2)

265 ROMEO CO (DECEMBER 2016)

Romeo Co is a business which makes and sells fresh pizza from a number of mobile food vans based at several key locations in the city centre. It offers a variety of toppings and dough bases for the pizzas and has a good reputation for providing a speedy service combined with hot, fresh and tasty food to customers.

Each van employs a chef who is responsible for making the pizzas to Romeo Co's recipes and two sales staff who serve the customers. All purchasing is done centrally to enable Romeo Co to negotiate bulk discounts and build relationships with suppliers.

Romeo Co operates a standard costing and variances system and the standard cost card for Romeo Co's basic tomato pizza is as follows:

Ingredient	**Weight** (kg)	**Price** ($ per kg)
Dough	0.20	7.60
Tomato sauce	0.08	2.50
Cheese	0.12	20.00
Herbs	0.02	8.40
	0.42	

In Month 3, Romeo Co produced and sold 90 basic tomato pizzas and actual results were as follows:

Ingredient	**Kgs bought and used**	**Actual cost per kg**
Dough	18.9	6.50
Tomato sauce	6.6	2.45
Cheese	14.5	21.00
Herbs	2.0	8.10
	42	

In Month 4, Romeo Co produced and sold 110 basic tomato pizzas. Actual results were as follows:

Ingredient	**Kgs bought and used**	**Actual cost per kg**
Dough	21.3	6.60
Tomato sauce	7.5	2.45
Cheese	14.2	20.00
Herbs	2.0	8.50
	45	

In Month 6, 100 basic tomato pizzas were made using a total of 42 kg of ingredients. A new chef at Romeo Co used the expected amount of dough and herbs but used less cheese and more tomato sauce per pizza than the standard. It was noticed that the sales of the basic tomato pizza had declined in the second half of the month.

1 **What was the total material price variance for Month 3?**

A $7.22 adverse

B $7.22 favourable

C $40.50 favourable

D $40.50 adverse

2 **What was the total materials mix variance for Month 3?**

A $81.02 adverse

B $41.92 adverse

C $42.88 adverse

D $38.14 adverse

3 **What was the materials yield variance for Month 4?**

Note: Calculate all workings to 2 decimal places.

A $12.21 favourable

B $11.63 favourable

C $21.95 adverse

D $9.75 adverse

4 In Month 5, Romeo Co reported a favourable materials mix variance for the basic tomato pizza.

Which of the following statements would explain why this variance has occurred?

A The proportion of the relatively expensive ingredients used in production was less than the standard.

B The prices paid for the ingredients used in the mix were lower than the standard prices.

C Each pizza used less of all the ingredients in actual production than expected.

D More pizzas were produced than expected given the level of ingredients input.

5 **Based on the above information about Month 6, which of the following statements are correct?**

(1) The actual cost per pizza in Month 6 was lower than the standard cost per pizza.

(2) The sales staff should lose their Month 6 bonus because of the reduced sales.

(3) The value of the ingredients usage variance and the mix variance are the same.

(4) The new chef will be responsible for the material price, mix and yield variances.

A (3) and (4)

B (1) and (2)

C (1) and (3)

D (2) and (4)

Section 3

CONSTRUCTED RESPONSE QUESTIONS – SECTION C

DECISION MAKING TECHNIQUES

266 BELLAHOUSTON CO (DECEMBER 2021)

Bellahouston Co manufactures three types of running shoes which it sells to sports clothing retailers: Road which are for running on roads, Spikes which are used for racing on athletics tracks, and Trail which are used for running off-road in rural locations. Each of these products use differing amounts of the same resources. Financial information and the resource requirements related to these products are as follows:

	Road	**Spikes**	**Trail**
	$	$	$
Selling price per pair of shoes	62.00	45.00	52.00
Variable costs per pair of shoes:			
Direct material ($5 per metre)	7.50	3.00	6.00
Direct labour ($7 per hour)	7.00	10.50	7.00
Machine hours ($10 per hour)	4.00	2.00	3.00
Fixed overheads absorbed per pair of shoes	4.00	6.00	4.00
Profit per pair of shoes	**39.50**	**23.50**	**32.00**

Fixed overheads are absorbed at a rate of $4 per direct labour hour. Bellahouston Co uses a just-in-time production system.

Demand and resource availability for March

Demand for the three products for the month of March is expected to be:

Road	2,300 pairs
Spikes	1,400 pairs
Trail	1,650 pairs

Bellahouston Co has received a special order from RunWild, which is not included in the demand estimates above. RunWild are a major sports retailer who have an extensive customer base and are known for stocking the most popular brands of sportswear. The order is to supply a maximum of 200 pairs of each type of shoe at a discount of $8.00 on the standard selling price.

RunWild will charge a financial penalty if the order is not fully complete in March. If this first order is successful, RunWild would be keen to enter into a regular supply contract.

Usually Bellahouston Co has sufficient resources to meet production, however during March the maximum availability for the following resources has been identified:

Direct material	7,200 metres
Direct labour	6,900 hours
Machine time	1,815 hours

Demand and resource availability for April

Bellahouston Co predicted that the resource availability in March would continue into April; however, it has been discovered that the availability of direct material and direct labour will be 15% less than in March. The available machine time and demand estimates are unchanged. RunWild would not be placing an order in April.

Required:

(a) (i) **Calculate the optimum production plan and the resulting total contribution earned for March, assuming that the order with RunWild is supplied in full.** **(7 marks)**

(ii) **Calculate the maximum financial penalty Bellahouston Co would be prepared to accept from RunWild, if it does not complete RunWild's order in full.** **(4 marks)**

(b) **Discuss whether Bellahouston Co should fulfil RunWild's order in full in March.** **(4 marks)**

(c) **Define the variables and formulate the constraints and objective function to be used in a linear programming model to determine the optimum usage of resources in April.** **(5 marks)**

(Total: 20 marks)

267 HEALTH NUTS (SEPTEMBER/DECEMBER 2020)

Health Nuts is a fitness centre, offering 'pay as you go' gym facilities. It has a fully fitted gym with the capacity to accommodate 200 users at one time. It also has 100 car parking spaces and an onsite café, both of which are only for customers using the gym. The fitness centre has shower facilities for customers and Health Nuts provides all customers with a clean towel to use on entry. It is open 360 days a year, from 7:00am until 9:00pm.

Customers pay $8.40 for access to the gym for one hour plus unlimited time in the café. If customers want to use the car park, they have to pay an additional $1 per visit and 80% of visiting customers use the car park. Health Nuts has been monitoring the number of customers attending throughout each day for the month of June, which was considered to be an average month, and for which Health Nuts was open for 30 days. It has determined that the average number of customers per day is 330 with 40 of these customers attending during the time of 9:00am to 5:00pm.

The total costs of the fitness centre for June, **excluding the café**, have also been recorded and analysed as follows:

Fixed costs per month	$48,000
Variable cost per customer	$1.20

On average, half of the customers also used the café in June, with an average spend per customer of $2.20. Of this spend, 60% is related to drinks, which have a profit margin of 60%, and the remainder is related to food items, which have a profit margin of 40%. The specific fixed costs associated with running the café are $3,600 for the month.

Crèche proposal

After reviewing all of the above information, the manager of Health Nuts has put together a proposal to close the café at the fitness centre and convert it into a crèche for children. This would mean that parents could leave their children in the crèche whilst they use the fitness centre between the hours of 9:00am and 5:00pm **only**. The charge for the crèche would be $4 per child, per hour.

Initial research suggests that customers have an average of two children each. The crèche is expected to attract new customers and increase the average number of customers between 9:00am and 5:00pm by 300%. Only these new customers will use the crèche facilities. Car park usage is expected to continue to be 80%. The fixed costs associated with running the crèche are estimated to be $8,000 per month, with a variable cost of $0.50 per child, per hour.

Required:

(a) **Calculate both the number of customers Health Nuts needs to break even and the margin of safety as a percentage of the month of June for:**

   (i) **The gym, and** **(3 marks)**

   (ii) **The café.** **(2 marks)**

(b) **Explain what each of your calculations in part (a) tells Health Nuts about the performance of the gym and the café.** **(3 marks)**

(c) **Calculate the budgeted total weighted average contribution/sales (C/S) ratio and the budgeted profit per month for Health Nuts if it closes the café and opens a crèche instead.** **(6 marks)**

(d) **Advise Health Nuts, considering both financial and non-financial factors, whether it should replace the café with a crèche, and whether the calculations in part (c) provide enough information to make such a decision.** **(6 marks)**

(Total: 20 marks)

268 COSMETICS CO (DECEMBER 2010, ADAPTED)

The Cosmetic Co is a company producing a variety of cosmetic creams and lotions. The creams and lotions are sold to a variety of retailers at a price of $23.20 for each jar of face cream and $16.80 for each bottle of body lotion. Each of the products has a variety of ingredients, with the key ones being silk powder, silk amino acids and aloe vera. Six months ago, silk worms were attacked by disease causing a huge reduction in the availability of silk powder and silk amino acids. The Cosmetic Co had to dramatically reduce production and make part of its workforce, which it had trained over a number of years, redundant.

The company now wants to increase production again by ensuring that it uses the limited ingredients available to maximise profits by selling the optimum mix of creams and lotions. Due to the redundancies made earlier in the year, supply of skilled labour is now limited in the short-term to 160 hours (9,600 minutes) per week, although unskilled labour is unlimited. The purchasing manager is confident that they can obtain 5,000 grams of silk powder and 1,600 grams of silk amino acids per week. All other ingredients are unlimited.

The following information is available for the two products:

	Cream	Lotion
Materials required: silk powder (at $2.20 per gram)	3 grams	2 grams
– silk amino acids (at $0.80 per gram)	1 gram	0.5 grams
– aloe vera (at $1.40 per gram)	4 grams	2 grams
Labour required: skilled ($12 per hour)	4 minutes	5 minutes
– unskilled (at $8 per hour)	3 minutes	1.5 minutes

Each jar of cream sold generates a contribution of $9 per unit, whilst each bottle of lotion generates a contribution of $8 per unit. The maximum demand for lotions is 2,000 bottles per week, although demand for creams is unlimited. Fixed costs total $1,800 per week. The company does not keep inventory although if a product is partially complete at the end of one week, its production will be completed in the following week.

The following graph has been accurately drawn:

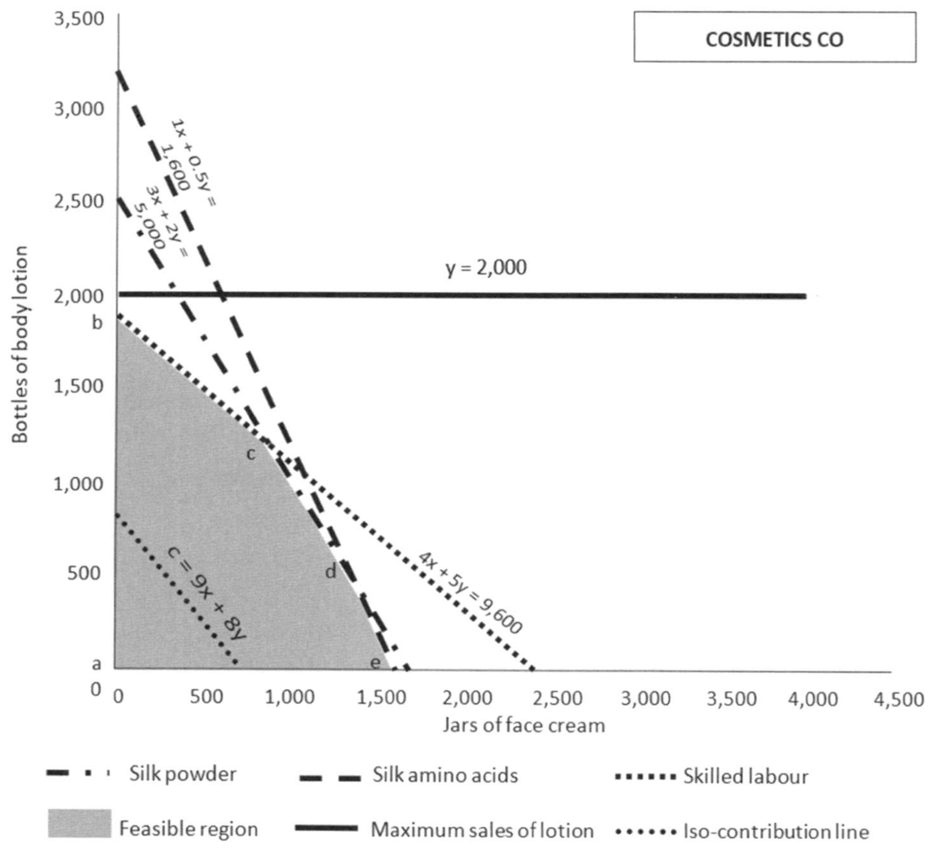

Required:

(a) **Calculate the optimum number of each product that the Cosmetics Co should make per week, assuming that it wishes to maximise contribution. Calculate the total contribution per week for the new production plan. All workings MUST be rounded to 2 decimal places.** **(14 marks)**

(b) **Calculate the shadow price for silk powder and the slack for silk amino acids. All workings MUST be rounded to 2 decimal places.** **(6 marks)**

(Total: 20 marks)

269 CUT AND STITCH (JUNE 2010)

Cut and Stitch (CS) make two types of suits using skilled tailors (labour) and a delicate and unique fabric (material). Both the tailors and the fabric are in short supply and so the accountant at CS has correctly produced a linear programming model to help decide the optimal production mix.

The model is as follows:

Variables:

Let W = the number of work suits produced

Let L = the number of lounge suits produced

Constraints

Tailors' time: $7W + 5L \leq 3{,}500$ (hours) – this is line T on the diagram

Fabric: $2W + 2L \leq 1{,}200$ (metres) – this is line F on the diagram

Production of work suits: $W \leq 400$ – this is line P on the diagram

Objective is to maximise contribution subject to:

$C = 48W + 40L$

On the diagram provided the accountant has correctly identified OABCD as the feasible region and point B as the optimal point.

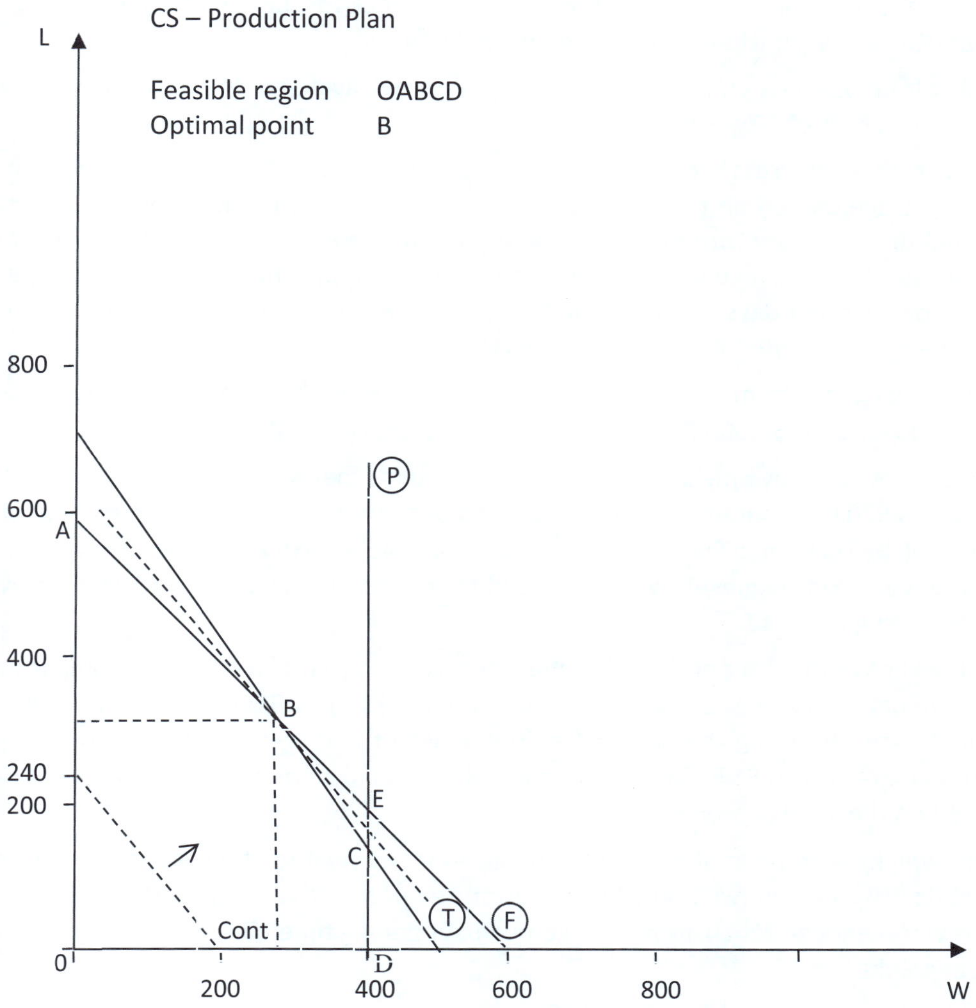

Required:

(a) Find by appropriate calculation the optimal production mix and related maximum contribution that could be earned by CS. **(4 marks)**

(b) Calculate the shadow prices of the fabric per metre and the tailor time per hour. **(6 marks)**

The tailors have offered to work an extra 500 hours provided that they are paid three times their normal rate of $1.50 per hour at $4.50 per hour.

Required:

(c) Briefly discuss whether CS should accept the offer of overtime at three times the normal rate. **(6 marks)**

(d) Calculate the new optimum production plan if maximum demand for W falls to 200 units. **(4 marks)**

(Total: 20 marks)

270 BITS AND PIECES (JUNE 2009)

Answer debrief

Bits and Pieces (B&P) operates a retail store selling spares and accessories for the car market. The store has previously only opened for six days per week for the 50 working weeks in the year, but B&P is now considering also opening on Sundays.

The sales of the business on Monday through to Saturday averages at $10,000 per day with average gross profit of 70% earned.

B&P expects that the gross profit % earned on a Sunday will be 20 percentage points lower than the average earned on the other days in the week. This is because they plan to offer substantial discounts and promotions on a Sunday to attract customers. Given the price reduction, Sunday sales revenues are expected to be 60% more than the average daily sales revenues for the other days. These Sunday sales estimates are for new customers only, with no allowance being made for those customers that may transfer from other days.

B&P buys all its goods from one supplier. This supplier gives a 5% discount on all purchases if annual spend exceeds $1,000,000.

It has been agreed to pay time and a half to sales assistants that work on Sundays. The normal hourly rate is $20 per hour. In total five sales assistants will be needed for the six hours that the store will be open on a Sunday. They will also be able to take a half-day off (four hours) during the week. Staffing levels will be allowed to reduce slightly during the week to avoid extra costs being incurred.

The staff will have to be supervised by a manager, currently employed by the company and paid an annual salary of $80,000. If the manager works on a Sunday, they will take the equivalent time off during the week when the assistant manager is available to cover for them at no extra cost to B&P. The manager will also be paid a bonus of 1% of the extra sales generated on the Sunday project.

The store will have to be lit at a cost of $30 per hour and heated at a cost of $45 per hour. The heating will come on two hours before the store opens in the 25 'winter' weeks to make sure it is warm enough for customers to come in at opening time. The store is not heated in the other weeks.

The rent of the store amounts to $420,000 annum.

Required:

(a) **Calculate whether the Sunday opening incremental revenue exceeds the incremental costs over a year (ignore inventory movements) and on this basis reach a conclusion as to whether Sunday opening is financially justifiable.** **(12 marks)**

(b) **Discuss whether the manager's pay deal (time off and bonus) is likely to motivate him.** **(4 marks)**

(c) **Briefly discuss whether offering substantial price discounts and promotions on Sunday is a good suggestion.** **(4 marks)**

(Total: 20 marks)

Calculate your allowed time, allocate the time to the separate parts..............

271 STAY CLEAN (DECEMBER 2009)

Stay Clean manufactures and sells a small range of kitchen equipment. Specifically the product range contains a dishwasher (DW), a washing machine (WM) and a tumble dryer (TD). The TD is of a rather old design and has for some time generated negative contribution. It is widely expected that in one year's time the market for this design of TD will cease, as people switch to a washing machine that can also dry clothes after the washing cycle has completed.

Stay Clean is trying to decide whether or not to cease the production of TD now **or** in 12 months' time when the new combined washing machine/drier will be ready. To help with this decision the following information has been provided:

1 The normal selling prices, annual sales volumes and total variable costs for the three products are as follows:

	DW	WM	TD
Selling price per unit	$200	$350	$80
Material cost per unit	$70	$100	$50
Labour cost per unit	$50	$80	$40
Contribution per unit	$80	$170	–$10
Annual sales	5,000 units	6,000 units	1,200 units

2 It is thought that some of the customers that buy a TD also buy a DW and a WM. It is estimated that 5% of the sales of WM and DW will be lost if the TD ceases to be produced.

3 All the direct labour force currently working on the TD will be made redundant immediately if TD is ceased now. This would cost $6,000 in redundancy payments. If Stay Clean waited for 12 months the existing labour force would be retained and retrained at a cost of $3,500 to enable them to produce the new washing/drying product. Recruitment and training costs of labour in 12 months' time would be $1,200 in the event that redundancy takes place now.

4 Stay Clean operates a just in time (JIT) policy and so all material cost would be saved on the TD for 12 months if TD production ceased now. Equally, the material costs relating to the lost sales on the WM and the DW would also be saved. However, the material supplier has a volume based discount scheme in place as follows:

Total annual expenditure ($)	Discount
0 – 600,000	0%
600,001 – 800,000	1%
800,001 – 9 00,000	2%
900,001 – 960,000	3%
960,001 and above	5%

Stay Clean uses this supplier for all its materials for all the products it manufactures. The figures given above in the cost per unit table for material cost per unit are net of any discount Stay Clean already qualifies for.

5 The space in the factory currently used for the TD will be sublet for 12 months on a short-term lease contract if production of TD stops now. The income from that contract will be $12,000.

6 The supervisor (currently classed as an overhead) supervises the production of all three products spending approximately 20% of their time on the TD production. They would continue to be fully employed if the TD ceases to be produced now.

Required:

(a) **Calculate whether or not it is worthwhile ceasing to produce the TD now rather than waiting 12 months (ignore any adjustment to allow for the time value of money).** **(13 marks)**

(b) **Explain two pricing strategies that could be used to improve the financial position of the business in the next 12 months assuming that the TD continues to be made in that period.** **(4 marks)**

(c) **Briefly describe three issues that Stay Clean should consider if it decides to outsource the manufacture of one of its future products.** **(3 marks)**

(Total: 20 marks)

272 MKL

Product 'M' is currently being tested by MKL and is to be launched in ten weeks' time. The 'M' is an innovative product which the company believes will change the entire market. The company has decided to use a market skimming approach to pricing this product during its introduction stage.

MKL continually reviews its product range and enhances its existing products by developing new models to satisfy the demands of its customers. The company intends to always have products at each stage of the product life cycle to ensure the company's continued presence in the market.

MKL is currently reviewing its two existing flagship products, Product K and Product L:

- Product K was introduced to the market some time ago and is now about to enter the maturity stage of its life cycle. The maturity stage is expected to last for ten weeks. Each unit has a variable cost of $38 and takes 1 standard hour to produce. The Managing Director is unsure which of four possible prices the company should charge during the next ten weeks. The following table shows the results of some market research into the level of weekly demand at alternative prices:

Selling price per unit	$100	$85	$80	$75
Weekly demand (units)	600	800	1,200	1,400

- Product L was introduced to the market two months ago using a penetration pricing policy and is now about to enter its growth stage. This stage is expected to last for 20 weeks. Each unit has a variable cost of $45 and takes 1.25 standard hours to produce. Market research has indicated that there is a linear relationship between its selling price and the number of units demanded, of the form P = a – bx. At a selling price of $100 per unit demand is expected to be 1,000 units per week. For every $10 increase in selling price the weekly demand will reduce by 200 units and for every $10 decrease in selling price the weekly demand will increase by 200 units.

The company currently has a production facility which has a capacity of 2,000 standard hours per week. This facility is being expanded but the extra capacity will not be available for ten weeks.

Required:

(a) Calculate which of the four selling prices should be charged for product K, in order to maximise its contribution during its maturity stage. (5 marks)

(b) Following on from your answer above in (a), calculate the selling price of product L during its growth stage. (8 marks)

(c) Compare and contrast penetration and skimming pricing strategies during the introduction stage, using product M to illustrate your answer. (7 marks)

(Total: 20 marks)

273 DAISY CO (SEPTEMBER/DECEMBER 2023)

Daisy Co is a large chemical company. One of its chemical processes produces two joint products: Nettle and Monkey. Each of these joint products can be sold at the end of the joint process (the separation point) or can be further processed into enhanced versions of the products, called Nettleplus and Monkeyplus.

The budget information relating to the joint process and further processing for period 3 is shown in the following table:

Budget information for period 3:

Total output of joint process (litres)	500,000	
Joint process costs:	$	
Direct material	6,310,000	
Variable overhead	2,000,000	
Total cost	8,310,000	
Joint products	**Nettle**	**Monkey**
Apportioned joint costs ($) (Note 1)	4,986,000	3,324,000
Output from joint process (litres)	300,000	200,000
Selling price at split off ($ per litre)	20.00	18.00
Selling price after further processing ($ per litre)	25.00	29.00
Further processing cost ($ per litre)	8.00	4.00
Normal loss in further processing (Note 2)	0	10%
Selling price of normal loss ($ per litre)	0	1.50

Note 1: Joint costs are apportioned on the basis of output.

Note 2: Normal losses occur at the end of further processing.

Daisy Co's production manager for this process needs to decide on the optimal production plan for period 3. She is unsure if either of the joint products should be further processed after the separation point and needs advice.

Period 4

In period 4, it has been decided that 280,000 litres of Nettle and 220,000 litres of Monkeyplus will be produced. The apportioned joint costs for period 4 are $4,500,000 for Nettle and $3,300,000 for Monkeyplus. The selling prices, further processing costs and normal loss details are the same as in period 3.

Information on costs and selling prices is collected by different departments within Daisy Co and is recorded on individual departmental spreadsheets and systems. This information is often not shared with other departments, so the production manager rarely has access to up-to-date information. She has heard of enterprise resource planning systems (ERPS) and wonders if one could be of use to Daisy Co.

Daisy Co carries no inventory.

Required:

(a) (i) Advise Daisy Co's production manager on whether either of the joint products should be further processed and calculate the optimal production plan for period 3. (7 marks)

(ii) Based on the optimal production plan given for period 4, prepare a profit statement showing each product's profit for period 4. (4 marks)

(b) Explain why joint processing costs are considered irrelevant when making the further processing decision but are considered relevant when assessing the profitability of the overall process. (3 marks)

(c) Discuss the benefits for Daisy Co of investing in an enterprise resource planning system. (6 marks)

(Total: 20 marks)

274 KEYTONE CO (SEPTEMBER/DECEMBER 2022)

Keytone Co is a recently established business specialising in the manufacture of a range of products for the fitness and health food market. It has recently developed a new product, 'Protein Power', which it is almost ready to launch. Keytone Co estimates that demand will be between 3,000 and 4,000 units per month, but Protein Power can only be manufactured in batches of 500 units. Therefore, Keytone Co must decide whether to manufacture 3,000, 3,500 or 4,000 units. Given the short shelf life of Protein Power, any units remaining unsold at the end of each month must be thrown away and have no scrap value.

The variable production cost of making one unit of Protein Power is as follows:

	$
Direct materials	6.20
Labour	2.70
Variable overhead	1.35

Protein Power will be processed on Machine X. Every time the machine is set up for a new batch of 500 units, it must be cleaned and inspected at a total cost of $240.

In addition to the above production costs, Keytone Co incurs selling and distribution costs of $0.90 for every unit sold.

Keytone Co has launched only one other similar product and, based on the information from that launch, has estimated that the probabilities associated with each demand level for Protein Power are as follows:

Probability	**Demand level (units)**
0.2	3,000
0.3	3,500
0.5	4,000

However, whilst Keytone Co believes that it could achieve a selling price of $35 per unit of Protein Power to sell up to 3,500 units, it would need to charge a lower selling price of $33 per unit, for ALL units sold, to achieve a sales volume above this.

The managing director is very risk averse and is concerned that the probabilities noted above may not be accurate. She has been in discussions with a local market research company who has offered to provide, for a fee, 100% accurate information about the actual demand level for Protein Power.

Required:

(a) **Construct a payoff table to show all the possible profit outcomes and recommend the level of production Keytone Co should choose based on expected values.** **(13 marks)**

(b) **Calculate the maximum fee which Keytone Co would be prepared to pay the market research company for the information about actual demand levels.** **(3 marks)**

(c) **Briefly discuss whether it is appropriate for the managing director to use expected values as a basis for making the decision about the production level of Protein Power and explain ONE alternative decision criterion which might be more useful.** **(4 marks)**

(Total: 20 marks)

275 TR CO (SEPTEMBER/DECEMBER 2017)

TR Co is a pharmaceutical company which researches, develops and manufactures a wide range of drugs. One of these drugs, 'Parapain', is a pain relief drug used for the treatment of headaches and until last month TR Co had a patent on Parapain which prevented other companies from manufacturing it. The patent has now expired and several competitors have already entered the market with similar versions of Parapain, which are made using the same active ingredients.

TR Co is reviewing its pricing policy in light of the changing market. It has carried out some market research in an attempt to establish an optimum price for Parapain. The research has established that for every $2 decrease in price, demand would be expected to increase by 5,000 batches, with maximum demand for Parapain being one million batches.

Each batch of Parapain is currently made using the following materials:

Material Z:	500 grams at $0.10 per gram
Material Y:	300 grams at $0.50 per gram

Each batch of Parapain requires 20 minutes of machine time to make and the variable running costs for machine time are $6 per hour. The fixed production overhead cost is expected to be $2 per batch for the period, based on a budgeted production level of 250,000 batches.

The skilled workers who have been working on Parapain until now are being moved onto the production of TR Co's new and unique anti-malaria drug which cost millions of dollars to develop. TR Co has obtained a patent for this revolutionary drug and it is expected to save millions of lives. No other similar drug exists and, whilst demand levels are unknown, the launch of the drug is eagerly anticipated all over the world.

Agency staff, who are completely new to the production of Parapain and cost $18 per hour, will be brought in to produce Parapain for the foreseeable future. Experience has shown there will be a significant learning curve involved in making Parapain as it is extremely difficult to handle. The first batch of Parapain made using one of the agency workers took 5 hours to make. However, it is believed that an 80% learning curve exists, in relation to production of the drug, and this will continue until the first 1,000 batches have been completed.

TR Co's management has said that any pricing decisions about Parapain should be based on the time it takes to make the 1,000th batch of the drug.

Note: The learning co-efficient, b = –0.321928

Required:

(a) **Calculate the optimum (profit-maximising) selling price for Parapain and the resulting annual profit which TR Co will make from charging this price.**

Note: if P = a – bQ, then MR = a – 2bQ **(12 marks)**

(b) **Discuss and recommend whether market penetration or market skimming would be the most suitable pricing strategy for TR Co when launching the new anti-malaria drug.** **(8 marks)**

(Total: 20 marks)

276 KAYLENE CO (SEPTEMBER/DECEMBER 2025)

Kaylene Co manufactures and sells washing machines. The company makes three different models of washing machine; two for household use (the 'Workhorse' and the 'Pristine') and one for industrial use (the 'Jumbo').

Selling price and cost information per unit for the three models is as follows:

	Workhorse ($)	Pristine ($)	Jumbo ($)
Selling price	400	600	1,250
Variable costs	170	230	580
Overhead allocation	200	250	500

The overhead allocation is an allocation of fixed costs, based on the expected amount of direct labour hours required to make each machine. Annual fixed costs for the current year, 20X9, are expected to be $1,375,000.

The number of washing machines expected to be manufactured, and sold, in 20X9 are:

Workhorse: 2,000

Pristine: 1,200

Jumbo: 800

This expected mix of sales is based on the mix of actual sales from 20X8, which has been maintained into the early part of 20X9.

A new chief executive officer (CEO) has recently joined Kaylene Co. He has been discussing possible opportunities for growth, and has set an annual profit target of $200,000 for next year.

The CEO has been discussing his plans with the other directors, and the following are extracts from a recent meeting:

Operations director: 'The production line is currently operating at around 80% of capacity, but I see little point making more machines if we cannot sell them.'

Marketing director: 'The market for washing machines is fairly mature now, and there is little opportunity for growth in the market as a whole. Competition in the household segment is particularly tough, but the hospitality industry is showing some growth, so there is potentially scope to increase the sales volume of the 'Jumbo' by selling to restaurants and hotels. However, we may need to lower the price to see any significant increase in sales volume.'

Required:

(a) **Calculate the contribution to sales ratio for each of the three models of washing machine and the overall weighted average contribution to sales ratio for Kaylene Co.**

Note: Show the contribution to sales ratios as decimal figures to three decimal places. **(3 marks)**

(b) **Calculate the margin of safety as a percentage for Kaylene Co AND explain the implications of the margin of safety (MOS) percentage for Kaylene Co.**

Note: Show the margin of safety (MOS) percentage to one decimal place. **(5 marks)**

(c) (i) **Based on the current selling prices, calculate the sales revenue required for Kaylene Co to achieve the CEO's target profit and discuss the feasibility of this profit target.** **(4 marks)**

(ii) **Explain the implications of increasing the sales volume of the Jumbo on the overall weighted average contribution to sales (C/S) ratio and the cost-volume-profit (CVP) analysis you have already performed for Kaylene Co.** **(4 marks)**

(b) **Discuss TWO limitations of cost-volume-profit (CVP) analysis for planning and decision-making.** **(4 marks)**

(Total: 20 marks)

277 THE ALKA HOTEL (JUNE 2018)

The Alka Hotel is situated in a major city close to many theatres and restaurants.

The Alka Hotel has 25 double bedrooms and it charges guests $180 per room per night, regardless of single or double occupancy. The hotel's variable cost is $60 per occupied room per night.

The Alka Hotel is open for 365 days a year and has a 70% budgeted occupancy rate. Fixed costs are budgeted at $600,000 a year and accrue evenly throughout the year.

During the first quarter (Q1) of the year the room occupancy rates are significantly below the levels expected at other times of the year with the Alka Hotel expecting to sell 900 occupied room nights during Q1. Options to improve profitability are being considered, including closing the hotel for the duration of Q1 or adopting one of two possible projects as follows:

Project 1 – Theatre package

For Q1 only the Alka Hotel management would offer guests a 'theatre package'. Couples who pay for two consecutive nights at a special rate of $67.50 per room night will also receive a pair of theatre tickets for a payment of $100. The theatre tickets are very good value and are the result of long negotiation between the Alka Hotel management and the local theatre.

The theatre tickets cost the Alka Hotel $95 a pair. The Alka Hotel's fixed costs specific to this project (marketing and administration) are budgeted at $20,000.

The hotel's management believes that the 'theatre package' will have no effect on their usual Q1 customers, who are all business travellers and who have no interest in theatre tickets, but will still require their usual rooms.

Project 2 – Restaurant

There is scope to extend the Alka Hotel and create enough space to operate a restaurant for the benefit of its guests. The annual costs, revenues and volumes for the combined restaurant and hotel are illustrated in the following graph.

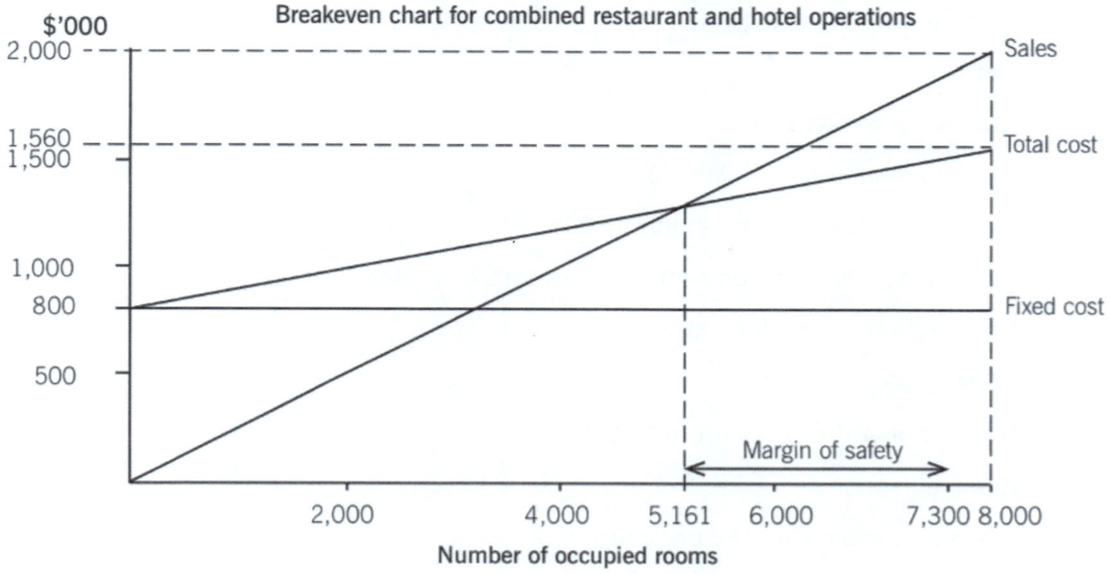

Note: The graph does not include the effect of the 'theatre package' offer.

Required:

(a) **Using the current annual budgeted figures, and ignoring the two proposed projects, calculate the breakeven number of occupied room nights and the margin of safety as a percentage.** **(4 marks)**

(b) **Ignoring the two proposed projects, calculate the budgeted profit or loss for Q1 and explain whether the hotel should close for the duration of Q1.** **(4 marks)**

(c) **Calculate the breakeven point in sales value of Project 1 and explain whether the hotel should adopt the project.** **(4 marks)**

(d) **Using the graph, quantify and comment upon the financial effect of Project 2 on the Alka Hotel.**

Note: There are up to four marks available for calculations. **(8 marks)**

(Total: 20 marks)

278 BELTON PARK RESORT (MARCH 2019)

Belton Park Resort is a new theme park resort located in the country of Beeland. The resort is made up of a theme park, a hotel and an indoor water park. The resort opened two months ago and is already very popular.

As all theme parks in Beeland are required, by law, to shut down in the colder month of January because of the risk of accidents, Belton Park Resort must decide whether to shut down the whole resort or just the theme park. It could choose to keep open the hotel and/or the water park.

Since Belton Park Resort has not been open for long, there is limited historical data available about costs and revenues. However, based on the last two months, the following average monthly data is available:

Hotel

Number of rooms 120

Average room rate per night $100

Average occupancy rate per month 90%

Average nightly spend on 'extras' per room $20

Contribution margin for 'extras'* 60%

Water park

Number of visitors per month 12,000

Admission price per visitor $21

Average spend on 'extras' per visitor $12

Contribution margin for 'extras'* 60%

*'Extras' includes anything purchased by the customer not included in the room rate or admission price.

Management estimates that, for January, the average room rate per night would need to decrease by 30% and the admission price for the water park by 20%. With such reductions, it is estimated that an occupancy rate of 50% would be achieved for the hotel and that the number of visitors to the water park would be 52% lower than current levels. The average nightly spend on 'extras' per room of $20 at the hotel and $12 per customer at the water park is expected to remain unchanged.

The running costs for the hotel and water park for each of the last two months are as follows:

	Notes	Hotel	Water park
		$	$
Staff costs	1	120,000	75,600
Maintenance costs	2	14,600	6,000
Power costs	3	20,000	18,000
Security costs	4	13,600	8,000
Water costs	5	12,900	12,100

Notes:

(1) Staff costs

Permanent staff

Included in the staff costs for the hotel is the salary of $30,000 per annum for the hotel manager and $24,000 per annum for the head chef. These are both permanent members of staff who are paid for the full year regardless of their working hours. The water park employs one permanent member of staff, the manager, on a salary of $24,000 who is also paid for the full year regardless of their working hours.

Temporary staff

The remaining staff costs relate to temporary staff who are only paid for the hours they work. If the hotel stays open in January, half of these staff members will continue to work their current hours because their jobs are largely unaffected by guest occupancy rates. However, the other half of the staff will work proportionately less hours to reflect the 50% occupancy rate in January as opposed to the 90% occupancy rate of the last two months. At the water park, the temporary staff's working hours will fall according to the number of visitors, hence a fall of 52% would be expected for January.

(2) Maintenance costs

Maintenance is undertaken by a local company, 'Techworks', which bills Belton Park Resort for all work carried out each month. If the hotel and water park are closed, Techworks will instead be paid a flat fee for the month of $4,000 for the hotel and $2,000 for the water park.

(3) Power costs

Electricity

Belton Park Resort pays a fixed monthly charge for electricity of $8,000 for the hotel and $7,000 for the water park, all year round.

Gas

The gas charges relate to heating and include a fixed charge of $2,200 per month for the hotel and $1,500 per month for the water park. The remainder of the gas charges is based solely on usage and would be expected to increase by 50% in January because of the colder weather.

(4) Security costs

If the hotel and water park close, no changes will be made to the current arrangements for security whilst the premises are empty.

(5) Water costs

It is estimated that water costs for the hotel would fall to $6,450 for the month if it remains open in January. However, the water costs for the water park would be expected to remain at their current level. If the hotel and water park were closed, all water would be turned off and no charges would arise.

Required:

(a) Calculate the incremental cash flows, for the month of January (31 days), if Belton Park Resort decides to keep open:

(i) the hotel

(ii) the water park.

In each case, state whether it should remain open or should close.

(15 marks)

(b) Discuss any other factors which Belton Park Resort should consider when making the decision in part (a). **(5 marks)**

(Total: 20 marks)

279 GLOBAL SCAN CO (SEPTEMBER/DECEMBER 2024)

Global Scan Co (GSC) is a company providing a wide range of private ultrasound scans for pregnancy, men's health, and women's health across Deeland. Each scan is carried out by someone called a 'sonographer', who is specially trained to carry out the scan and interpret the results.

GSC has 20 clinics in total, three of which (Darby, Leek and Nott) are based in the central region of Deeland within a 30-mile radius of each other. Recently, a new chief executive officer (CEO) has been appointed at GSC and he has asked for a review of the three clinics. He believes that it is unnecessary to have three clinics so close together and that at least one of them should be shut down at the end of the current financial year, 20X2. This is the earliest date that any of them could close due to the clinics' existing contractual obligations.

The following information for the financial year which has just ended, 20X1, has been provided for each of the three clinics concerned:

	Darby	**Leek**	**Nott**
Number of scans each year (Note 1)			
Pregnancy	2,200	2,650	3,820
Men's Health	640	865	980
Women's Health	1,765	1,130	1,990
Number of staff (Note 2)			
Junior sonographers	2	1	2
Senior sonographers	2	2	3
Other staff	8	6	10
Number of ultrasound machines (Note 3)	4	3	5
Other costs per month (Note 4)	56,000	45,000	62,000

Notes:

(1) The Darby and Leek clinics charge the same price per scan: $160 for a pregnancy scan, $200 for a men's health scan and $280 for a women's health scan. The Nott clinic charges 10% more. The number of scans performed is expected to fall by 20% in Darby and Leek in 20X2 but increase by 30% in Nott, which has more advanced scanning equipment.

(2) At the end of 20X1, junior sonographers earned a salary of $32,000 per annum each and senior sonographers earned $44,000 each. The average salary of 'other staff' at GSC was $18,000 per annum each. In addition to the salary cost, GSC has to pay a further amount of 13% of each employee's salary to the government as a contribution to the Deeland welfare system. All employees in Deeland are taxed at a flat rate of 30% on all of their salary before receiving it. The number of staff employed will remain the same in 20X2.

All employees at GSC receive a 5% pay rise at the beginning of the new financial year.

(3) All ultrasound machines, used to perform the scans, are hired out on five-year leases from a supplier. The lease payments for the Darby and Leek machines are $1,000 per month and those for the more advanced machines at Nott are $1,500 per month. If GSC wants to exit a lease agreement before the end of its term, it has to pay a substantial penalty.

(4) These costs include each clinic's specifically attributable overhead costs and a reapportionment of central head office (HO) costs for the support services it provides. The HO costs are reapportioned to each clinic on the basis of the total number of employees at the clinics. GSC as a whole has 150 employees. The total HO costs were $3m for 20X1 and are expected to remain unchanged in the next few years, even if one of the clinics is shut down. The clinic-specific overhead costs are also expected to remain the same in 20X2.

Required:

(a) Complete the statement provided for GSC for the year ending 31 December 20X2, showing the revenue and costs for each clinic in as much detail as possible. Recommend which clinic(s), if any, should be shut down at the end of 20X2.

(14 marks)

	Darby	Leek	Nott
	$	$	$
Sales revenue:			
Less expenses:			
Contribution			
Profit/(loss)			

(b) Discuss any other additional factors which GSC should consider before deciding to shut down any of the three clinics at the end of 20X2. **(6 marks)**

(Total: 20 marks)

BUDGETING AND CONTROL

280 STATIC CO (DECEMBER 2016)

Static Co is a multinational consumer goods company. Traditionally, the company has used a fixed annual budgeting process in which it sets quarterly sales revenue targets for each of its product lines. Historically, however, if a product line fails to reach its sales revenue target in any of the first three quarters, the company's sales director (SD) and finance director (FD) simply go back and reduce the sales revenue targets for the quarter just ended, to make it look like the target was reached. They then increase the target for the final quarter to include any shortfall in sales from earlier quarters.

During the last financial year ended 31 August 20X6, this practice meant that managers had to heavily discount many of their product lines in the final quarter in order to boost sales volumes and meet the increased targets. Even with the discounts, however, they still did not quite reach the targets. On the basis of the sales targets set at the beginning of that year, the company had also invested $6m in a new production line in January 20X6. However, to date, this new production line still has not been used. As a result of both these factors, Static Co saw a dramatic fall in return on investment from 16% to 8% in the year.

Consequently, the managing director (MD), the FD and the SD have all been dismissed. Two key members of the accounts department are also on sick leave due to stress and are not expected to return for some weeks. A new MD, who is inexperienced in this industry, has been appointed and is in the process of recruiting a new SD and a new FD. The MD has said:

'These mistakes could have been largely avoided if the company had been using rolling budgets, instead of manipulating fixed budgets. From now on, we will be using rolling budgets, updating our budgets on a quarterly basis, with immediate effect.'

The original fixed budget for the year ended 31 August 20X7, for which the first quarter (Q1) has just ended, is shown below:

Budget Y/E 31 August 20X7	**Q1**	**Q2**	**Q3**	**Q4**	**Total**
	$000	$000	$000	$000	$000
Revenue	13,425	13,694	13,967	14,247	55,333
Cost of sales	(8,055)	(8,216)	(8,380)	(8,548)	(33,199)
Gross profit	5,370	5,478	5,587	5,699	22,134
Distribution costs	(671)	(685)	(698)	(712)	(2,766)
Administration costs	(2,000)	(2,000)	(2,000)	(2,000)	(8,000)
Operating profit	2,699	2,793	2,889	2,987	11,368

The budget was based on the following assumptions:

(1) Sales volumes would grow by a fixed compound percentage each quarter.

(2) Gross profit margin would remain stable each quarter.

(3) Distribution costs would remain a fixed percentage of revenue each quarter.

(4) Administration costs would be fixed each quarter.

The actual results for the first quarter (Q1) have just been produced and are as follows:

Actual results	**Q1**
	$000
Revenue	14,096
Cost of sales	(8,740)
Gross profit	5,356
Distribution costs	(705)
Administration costs	(2,020)
Operating profit	2,631

The new MD believes that the difference between the actual and the budgeted sales figures for Q1 is a result of incorrect forecasting of prices, however, they are confident that the four assumptions the fixed budget was based on were correct and that the rolling budget should still be prepared using these assumptions.

Required:

(a) **Prepare Static Co's rolling budget for the next four quarters.** **(8 marks)**

(b) **Discuss the problems which have occurred at Static Co due to the previous budgeting process and the improvements which might now be seen through the use of realistic rolling budgets.** **(6 marks)**

(c) **Discuss the problems which may be encountered when Static Co tries to implement the new budgeting system.** **(6 marks)**

(Total: 20 marks)

281 YUMI CO (SEPTEMBER 2019)

Yumi Co owns a number of restaurants. It is a well-established company, and its restaurants have gained a favourable reputation for the quality of their meals.

Yumi Co's restaurants are all set in rural locations, where there is limited competition and this enabled them to develop a loyal customer base. Restaurants design their own menus and décor to fit with the requirements of their local market.

Yumi Co has been consistently profitable, however as is the case across the restaurant industry, profit margins are quite low and there is still a constant need for Yumi Co to monitor costs.

One of Yumi Co's restaurants is located in the small town of Cowly. Cowly has recently been the location for the filming of a popular television series and visitor numbers to the town have increased significantly as a result. Yumi Co's restaurant in Cowly has noticed a similar increase in customer numbers.

At the start of the current month a new restaurant opened in Cowly. The manager of Yumi Co's restaurant in Cowly has expressed concerns about the impact this new competitor will have on their ability to achieve profit targets for the rest of the year.

Budgets for all of Yumi Co's restaurants are prepared by the head office. At the start of each year, restaurant managers are given an annual budget, which is split into months. At the end of each month, the manager receives a statement comparing actual monthly performance against budget.

The statement for the Cowly restaurant for the most recent completed month is as follows:

	Actual	Budget	Variance
Number of customers	1,800	1,500	
	$	$	$
Revenue	87,300	75,000	12,300 F
Costs:			
Food and drink	26,100	22,500	3,600 A
Staff wages	38,250	31,500	6,750 A
Heat, light and power	8,100	7,500	600 A
Rent, rates and other overheads	12,600	12,000	600 A
Profit	**2,250**	**1,500**	**750 F**

Notes:

(1) Rent, rates and other overheads are apportioned to its restaurants by Yumi Co's head office, based on a fixed annual charge.

(2) All other budgeted costs are treated as variable costs, based on the expected number of customers.

Yumi Co currently adopts an incremental approach to budgeting, with the annual budget figures for each year being based on the previous year's figures. However, a new finance director has recently joined the company, and they have questioned whether this is suitable for all Yumi Co's restaurants.

The new finance director has also suggested that the company should adopt a more participative approach to budgeting.

Required:

(a) (i) Prepare a flexed budget for the Cowly restaurant. **(3 marks)**

(ii) With reference to your answer from part (i), explain the main weaknesses in the current monthly budget statements issued to the restaurants as a basis for managing performance. **(4 marks)**

(b) Discuss whether an incremental approach to budgeting is appropriate for Yumi Co. **(6 marks)**

(c) Define a participative approach to budgeting and explain the potential advantages and disadvantages of introducing this approach at Yumi Co. **(7 marks)**

(Total: 20 marks)

282 TREAD CO (MARCH/JUNE 2022)

Tread Co manufactures sports shoes and clothing. It is a relatively small company and has a good reputation for producing high quality products. In recent months, however, there have been an increasing number of customer complaints about quality problems with Tread Co's sports shoes.

Tread Co is profitable, but its finance director, who joined the company last year, believes there are inefficiencies in its operations and consequently it isn't as profitable as it could be.

The finance director believes that Tread Co's budgeting system is partly to blame for this. The company currently uses an incremental approach to budgeting, but the finance director believes activity-based budgeting would be more appropriate. He is analysing the production process for sports shoes to support his suggestion, and has asked for your help in connection with this.

Tread Co produces two different styles of sports shoe, the Deluxe and the Standard, and it has contracts to supply these to several large retail chains. Much of the production process is automated, and production occurs in batches. Similarly, goods are shipped to customers in batches. Demand is relatively constant throughout the year.

Operational data for each product is as follows:

	Deluxe	**Standard**
Monthly demand (pairs of shoes)	22,500	24,000
Pairs of shoes produced per production machine hour	250	300
Production batch size (pairs of shoes)	300	400
Shipment batch size (pairs of shoes)	125	150

The production line for sports shoes has a capacity of 175 production machine hours per month after allowing for set-up time.

In addition to the staff who work on the production line, Tread Co also employs two quality control inspectors and two shipping administrators. Each of these employees is contracted to work 150 hours per month, and their salaries are treated as overheads.

The quality control staff inspect a sample of sports shoes from each batch produced and the standard inspection time is 2.5 hours per batch produced.

The shipping administrators prepare the batches to be despatched to customers, and arrange the paperwork for the shipments. In total, this takes 0.75 hours per batch shipped.

Required:

(a) **Explain the main principles of activity-based budgeting.** **(5 marks)**

(b) **Calculate any spare capacity or shortage in the hours required to meet the expected monthly output for:**

- **Production machine time**
- **Quality control inspectors; and**
- **Shipping administrators.** **(8 marks)**

(c) **Discuss the implications of your findings in (b) for Tread Co's sports shoes production process.** **(7 marks)**

(Total: 20 marks)

283 QUALITY TYRE CO (MARCH/JUNE 2025)

Quality Tyre Co is based in Cassland and manufactures and sells two types of tyre for motor vehicles: the Basic and the Sport. It sells these tyres to commercial customers such as garages and car repair shops. The company has been using activity-based costing throughout 20X0 and is keen to take this one step further and begin using activity-based budgeting as well.

Details of some of last year's cost driver rates for overheads were as follows:

	$
Cost per material order	80
Cost per store requisition	14
Cost per machine set-up	120
Cost per quality control inspection	260
Cost per sales order	46
Cost per customer delivery	210

With the exception of customer delivery costs, all of these costs are expected to increase by inflation of 5% in the year ending 31 December 20X1. Customer delivery costs, however, are a semi-variable cost and the variable element relates to fuel, which is expected to increase by 10%, whilst the fixed cost element is expected to increase by 5%. Information for two different levels of activity for the total number of tyres is shown below:

Number of customer deliveries	1,300	800
Total delivery costs	$301,000	$266,000

The average order size for customers is 40 tyres and Quality Tyre Co arranges a specific delivery for each customer order.

Annual sales forecasts for the year ending 31 December 20X1 are as follows:

	Basic	**Sport**
Sales (tyres)	60,000	45,000

Opening inventory levels of tyres (finished goods) on 1 January 20X1 are as follows:

	Basic	**Sport**
Opening inventory	3,600	2,400

Quality Tyre Co's inventory policy for 20X2 is to hold enough inventory of tyres to meet the next month's sales demand. The forecast annual sales for 20X1 are expected to be the same in 20X2 and will occur evenly over the year.

Batch sizes are 200 for Basic and 450 for Sport and quality control checks take place on every 50th tyre. Every time a batch is complete, the machine used for manufacturing them needs to be set up again for the next batch.

In 20X0 the number of material orders and store requisitions was as follows:

	Basic	**Sport**
Number of material orders	1,800	1,460
Number of store requisitions	6,400	4,240

Quality Tyre Co introduced a new material ordering system several weeks ago, and whilst the exact effect of this is not known yet, the company estimates that there is a 50% probability that it will reduce the number of orders by 30% and a 50% probability that it will reduce them by 20%. Store requisition numbers are not expected to change.

Required:

(a) Using the template provided, complete the activity-based budget for overheads for Quality Tyre Co for the year ended 31 December 20X1. **(14 marks)**

	A	B	C	D
1	**Overheads budget**	**Basic**	**Sport**	**Total**
2		$	$	$
3	Material ordering costs			
4	Store requisition costs			
5	Machine set up costs			
6	Quality inspection costs			
7	Sales order costs			
8	Delivery costs			
9	**Total budgeted overheads**			

(b) Explain THREE difficulties which could be faced by an organisation when implementing an activity-based budgeting system. **(6 marks)**

(Total: 20 marks)

284 VENHOSP (MARCH/JUNE 2024)

Venhosp is an agency which supplies temporary staff providing catering and hospitality services for events at stadium venues in Deeland.

Demand for Venhosp's staff depends on the number of events taking place, and whether a venue selects Venhosp to supply staff for its events. As such, there is a strong correlation between the total number of events taking place in a period and the number of staff supplied by Venhosp.

There is intense competition between temporary staffing agencies in Deeland. All the agencies charge similar rates for the staff they provide, and there is little scope for any agency to increase the price it charges a stadium for staff. Venhosp's average charge-out rate for its staff was $16 per hour in 20X5, and that rate is expected to remain unchanged in 20X6.

Venhosp pays its staff $11.25 per hour, and on average they work eight hours per event day. They are only paid for the hours they work. By law, staffing agencies in Deeland also have to make additional contributions, directly to the government, at a rate of 10% on the amounts they pay to their staff.

The legal minimum wage in Deeland was $10.50 per hour in 20X5, but increased to $11 per hour from the start of 20X6. In recent years, there has been a shortage of workers prepared to work as temporary staff in catering and hospitality services in Deeland, because the work is seen as physically demanding and relatively poorly paid.

Venhosp's human resources (HR) director has suggested that the amount Venhosp pays its staff should be increased to $11.75. The chief executive officer (CEO) opposes the increase, saying it will reduce profits, but the HR director has argued that any decisions about pay rates need to take account of ethical issues, not just short-term financial ones.

Venhosp produces quarterly forecasts for its expected revenues and staff costs. These have already been produced for Quarters 1 to 3 for 20X6, but not yet for Quarter 4. The total number of stadium events scheduled for Quarter 4 20X6 is 114.

The CEO has asked you to prepare the forecast for Quarter 4 20X6, using least squares regression to forecast the demand for staff days expected in the quarter, and based on the current rates of pay.

Note: A 'staff day' constitutes one member of temporary staff being provided to a client for one day.

Summary of quarterly data for 20X2–20X5

Total number of events (Σx)	Total number of staff days (Σy)	Σx^2	Σy^2	Σxy
1,757	404,410	196,615	10,724,385,113	45,496,648

This is based on a sample size (n) of 16.

This is the data which the CEO wants you to use for the least squares regression calculation in **requirement (a) (i)**.

Required:

(a) (i) Use least squares regression, based on the quarterly data for 20X2-20X5, to calculate Venhosp's expected staff days in Quarter 4 20X6.

Note: Round your answer to the nearest full day. (5 marks)

(ii) Assume that your answer to (a)(i) gave you a figure of 30,000 expected staff days. Based on this figure, calculate Venhosp's forecast revenue, staff costs and gross profit (revenue less staff costs) for Quarter 4 20X6. (4 marks)

(iii) Calculate the correlation coefficient ('r') between the total number of events in Deeland, and Venhosp's staff days, based on the quarterly data for 20X2–20X5. (2 marks)

(b) Briefly discuss the limitations of regression analysis. (3 marks)

(c) Discuss THREE factors the board should consider when deciding whether to increase the hourly wage rate from $11.25 to $11.75, as the HR director has suggested. (6 marks)

(Total: 20 marks)

285 HENRY COMPANY (DECEMBER 2008)

Answer debrief

Henry Company (HC) provides skilled labour to the building trade. They have recently been asked by a builder to bid for a kitchen fitting contract for a new development of 600 identical apartments. HC has not worked for this builder before. Cost information for the new contract is as follows:

Labour for the contract is available. HC expects that the first kitchen will take 24 man-hours to fit but thereafter the time taken will be subject to a 95% learning rate. After 200 kitchens are fitted the learning rate will stop and the time taken for the 200th kitchen will be the time taken for all the remaining kitchens. Labour costs $15 per hour.

Overheads are absorbed on a labour hour basis. HC has collected overhead information for the last four months and this is shown below:

	Hours worked	**Overhead cost $**
Month 1	9,300	115,000
Month 2	9,200	113,600
Month 3	9,400	116,000
Month 4	9,600	116,800

HC normally works around 120,000 labour hours in a year.

HC uses the high low method to analyse overheads.

The learning curve equation is $y = ax^b$, where b = log r/log 2 = –0.074

Required:

(a) **Describe FIVE factors, other than the cost of labour and overheads mentioned above, that HC should take into consideration in calculating its bid.** **(5 marks)**

(b) **Calculate the total cost including all overheads for HC that it can use as a basis of the bid for the new apartment contract.** **(13 marks)**

(c) **If the second kitchen alone is expected to take 21.6 man-hours to fit demonstrate how the learning rate of 95% has been calculated.** **(2 marks)**

(Total: 20 marks)

286 MEDICAL TEMP CO (MARCH/JUNE 2021)

This part of the scenario relates to requirements (a) and (b).

Medical Temp Co (MTC) is one of several agencies in Sictopia supplying medical staff, both nurses and doctors, under temporary weekly contracts to local hospitals.

Information regarding the size of the market in Sictopia is as follows:

	Quarter 1	**Quarter 2**
	$m	$m
Size of national market for supply of temporary nurses	14	18.9
Size of national market for supply of temporary doctors	8	8.2

The increase in the national market for the supply of temporary nurses is due to a shortage of full-time nurses in Sictopia.

All agencies in Sictopia, including MTC, charge a single market rate for the supply of each type of staff $1,000 per week for supplying a nurse and $2,000 per week for supplying a doctor. In quarter 1, MTC held 30% of the market for the supply of temporary nurses, and 40% for the supply of temporary doctors.

MTC uses quarterly rolling budgets. At the end of quarter 1, it prepared its budgeted revenue figures for quarter 2. It based these budgeted figures on the assumption that the company would continue to maintain the market share it had in quarter 1. It also assumed that it would maintain its standard contribution margin of 80% for both nurses and doctors.

MTC's actual figures for quarter 2 are as follows:

	Actual
Total revenue from supply of nurses	\$5.3m
Total revenue from supply of doctors	\$3.6m
Actual contribution margin for both nurses and doctors	75%

This part of the scenario relates to requirement (c).

Cheat Co

The market size and market share variances have also been calculated for quarter 2 of one of MTC's competitors, Cheat Co. These variances are as follows:

	Nurses	**Doctors**	**Total**
	\$000	\$000	\$000
Market Size	185 A	724 A	909 A
Market Share	1,065 F	1,043 F	2,108 F

Cheat Co holds the same percentage of each market as MTC. It also uses rolling budgets and prepares its budgeted revenue figures using exactly the same assumptions as MTC. However, when Cheat Co's sales director had to provide the market size figures for quarter 2 to the accounts department, she deliberately reported these figures 30% lower by excluding the market segment relating to maternity units. The accounts department were unaware of this.

Required:

(a) **Explain why businesses calculate market size and market share variances.** **(4 marks)**

(b) **Calculate the total market size (planning) variance and the total market share (operational) variance for MTC for quarter 2.** **(10 marks)**

(c) **Discuss the actions of the sales director at Cheat Co and how this may have impacted on the variances which have been calculated.** **(6 marks)**

(Total: 20 marks)

287 CLEAR CO (MARCH/JULY 2020 SAMPLE EXAM)

Clear Co is an eye treatment specialist, founded in 20X4, which runs five clinics nationwide. It is based in Zeeland, a country in which 20% of the population is over 65 years old, compared to 15% ten years ago.

Clear Co offers two eye treatment procedures: laser treatment and lens treatment. Laser treatment is the less complex of the two procedures. Technology changes rapidly in this industry and as a result 90% of patients now qualify for laser treatment, compared to only 80% five years ago.

The remaining 10% of patients are only able to have lens treatment, of which there are two types: 'refractive lens exchange' (RLE) and 'implantable contact lenses' (ICL). Clear Co started providing RLE, a treatment most effective for patients aged 40 or older, in 20X4 when it was founded. Two years ago, it also began providing ICL, a treatment recommended for patients under the age of 40.

The market for eye treatment procedures in Zeeland is dominated by a few main suppliers, of which Clear Co is one. Until two years ago, Clear Co was the largest supplier but, following the merger of two other companies, it is now the second largest. The merged company, Eos Co, has recently released its financial statements for the year, showing profits which were 10% higher than forecast. Eos Co's press release stated that it has achieved this despite offering reduced prices for the ICL treatment. It has been able to offer reduced prices because of the economies of scale achieved by the merger.

The following information relates to the two types of lens treatments offered by Clear Co for the year just ended:

Lens treatment	**RLE**		**ICL**	
	Budget	**Actual**	**Budget**	**Actual**
Number of treatments	3,750	4,130	1,320	960
Selling price per treatment ($)	3,000	2,900	3,650	3,400
Variable cost treatment ($)	600	590	1,150	1,200

Required:

(a) **Calculate the following TOTAL variances for Clear Co's lens treatments:**

(i) **the sales mix contribution variance** **(4 marks)**

(ii) **the sales quantity contribution variance.** **(4 marks)**

(b) **Explain what each of the sales mix contribution variance and sales quantity contribution variance measures.** **(2 marks)**

(c) **Using your answer from part (a) and any other relevant calculations, discuss Clear Co's SALES performance for the year just ended.**

Note: There are up to four marks available for additional calculations relevant to SALES performance and six marks available for discussion. **(10 marks)**

(Total: 20 marks)

288 THE SCHOOL UNIFORM COMPANY (MARCH/JUNE 2017)

The School Uniform Company (SU Co) manufactures school uniforms. One of its largest contracts is with the Girls' Private School Trust (GPST), which has 35 schools across the country, all with the same school uniform.

After a recent review of the uniform at the GPST schools, the school's spring/summer dress has been re-designed to incorporate a dropped waistband. Each new dress now requires 2.2 metres of material, which is 10% more material than the previous style of dress required. However, a new material has also been chosen by the GPST which costs only $2.85 per metre which is 5% cheaper than the material used on the previous dresses. In February, the total amount of material used and purchased at this price was 54,560 metres.

The design of the new dresses has meant that a complicated new sewing technique needed to be used. Consequently, all staff required training before they could begin production. The manager of the sewing department expected each of the new dresses to take 10 minutes to make as compared to 8 minutes per dress for the old style. SU Co has 24 staff, each of whom works 160 hours per month and is paid a wage of $12 per hour. All staff worked all of their contracted hours in February on production of the GPST dresses and there was no idle time. No labour rate variance arose in February.

Activity levels for February were as follows:

Budgeted production and sales (units): 30,000

Actual production and sales (units): 24,000

The production manager at SU Co is responsible for all purchasing and production issues which occur.

SU Co uses standard costing and usually, every time a design change takes place, the standard cost card is updated prior to production commencing.

However, the company accountant responsible for updating the standards has been off sick for the last two months. Consequently, the standard cost card for the new dress has not yet been updated.

Required:

(a) Calculate the material variances in as much detail as the information allows for the month of February. **(7 marks)**

(b) Calculate the labour efficiency variances in as much detail as the information allows for the month of February. **(5 marks)**

(c) Assess the performance of the production manager for the month of February. **(8 marks)**

(Total: 20 marks)

289 KAPPA CO (SEPTEMBER 2018)

Kappa Co produces Omega, an animal feed made by mixing and heating three ingredients: Alpha, Beta and Gamma. The company uses a standard costing system to monitor its costs.

The standard material cost for 100 kg of Omega is as follows:

Input	**Kg**	**Cost per kg**	**Cost per 100 kg of Omega**
		($)	($)
Alpha	40	2.00	80.00
Beta	60	5.00	300.00
Gamma	20	1.00	20.00
Total	120		400.00

Notes:

(1) The mixing and heating process is subject to a standard evaporation loss.

(2) Alpha, Beta and Gamma are agricultural products and their quality and price varies significantly from year to year. Standard prices are set at the average market price over the last five years. Kappa Co has a purchasing manager who is responsible for pricing and supplier contracts.

(3) The standard mix is set by the finance department. The last time this was done was at the product launch which was five years ago. It has not changed since.

Last month 4,600 kg of Omega was produced, using the following inputs:

Input	Kg	Cost per kg	Total cost
		$	$
Alpha	2,200	1.80	3,960
Beta	2,500	6.00	15,000
Gamma	920	1.00	920
Total	5,620		19,880

At the end of each month, the production manager receives a standard cost operating statement from Kappa Co's performance manager. The statement contains material price and usage variances, labour rate and efficiency variances, and overhead expenditure and efficiency variances for the previous month. No commentary on the variances is given and the production manager receives no other feedback on the efficiency of the Omega process.

Required:

(a) Calculate the following variances for the last month:

(i) the material usage variance for each ingredient and in total **(4 marks)**

(ii) the total material mix variance **(4 marks)**

(iii) the total material yield variance. **(3 marks)**

(b) Discuss the problems with the current system of calculating and reporting variances for assessing the performance of the production manager. **(9 marks)**

(Total: 20 marks)

290 VEGAN CO (MARCH/JUNE 2023)

Vegan Co is based in Zeeland and manufactures a wide range of non-meat and non-dairy products, which it supplies to retailers. Its mission is:

'To produce high quality, cruelty-free products sourced from local ingredients.'

Vegan Co uses a just-in-time system and holds no inventories. Its best-selling product is soya milk and for the month of November, production levels were as follows:

	Budgeted production level (units)	Actual production level (units)
Soya Milk	440,000	480,000

The main ingredients used in soya milk are soybeans and sugar, both of which are grown within 50 km of Vegan Co's premises. Vegan Co markets its soya milk on this basis, making it appeal to customers committed to caring for the environment.

Extracts from the standard cost card per unit of soya milk for November are shown below:

	Quantity	**Cost per kg**
Soybeans	0.200 kg (200 grams)	$5.90
Sugar	0.012 kg (12 grams)	$1.80

Vegan Co used 94,000 kg of soybeans and 5,280 kg of sugar in its actual production of soya milk in November. The actual cost to Vegan Co of soybeans in November was $5.70 per kg and the actual cost of sugar was $1.90 per kg. The market price in Zeeland for soybeans decreased by 10% in November, but for sugar it increased by 20%. This was due to an unusually cooler winter, which had a positive effect on soybean crops but a negative one on sugar crops. The purchasing manager is responsible for negotiating prices with suppliers.

Vegan Co made a change to the standard mix at the beginning of November, reducing sugar to 10 grams per unit in order to comply with new government legislation. To try to maintain the consistency of the milk, Vegan Co also decreased the soybeans content from 200 grams per unit to 190 grams per unit at the same time. The production manager is responsible for the product mix at Vegan Co.

None of the above changes to prices and quantities were reflected in the standard cost card for November, which is prepared by the accounts department and updated twice a year, despite both the purchasing and production managers stating that this is not frequent enough.

Required:

(a) For EACH ingredient (soybeans and sugar), calculate the following variances for the month of November:

(i) Material price planning variance. (3 marks)

(ii) Material price operational variance. (3 marks)

(iii) Material usage planning variance. (3 marks)

(iv) Material usage operational variance. (3 marks)

(b) Assess the performance of both the production manager and the purchasing manager for the month of November.

Note: There are up to two marks available for additional calculations. (8 marks)

(Total: 20 marks)

PERFORMANCE MEASUREMENT AND CONTROL

291 MAN CO (JUNE 2016)

A manufacturing company, Man Co, has two divisions: Division L and Division M. Both divisions make a single standardised product. Division L makes component L, which is supplied to both Division M and external customers. Division M makes product M using one unit of component L and other materials. It then sells the completed product M to external customers. To date, Division M has always bought component L from Division L.

The following information is available:

	Component L	Product M
	$	$
Selling price	40	96
Direct materials:		
Component L		(40)
Other	(12)	(17)
Direct labour	(6)	(9)
Variable overheads	(2)	(3)
Selling and distribution costs	(4)	(1)
Contribution per unit before fixed costs	16	26
Annual fixed costs	$500,000	$200,000
Annual external demand (units)	160,000	120,000
Capacity of plant	300,000	130,000

Division L charges the same price for component L to both Division M and external customers. However, it does not incur the selling and distribution costs when transferring internally.

Division M has just been approached by a new supplier who has offered to supply it with component L for $37 per unit. Prior to this offer, the cheapest price which Division M could have bought component L for from outside the group was $42 per unit.

It is head office policy to let the divisions operate autonomously without interference at all.

Required:

(a) **Calculate the incremental profit/(loss) per component for the group if Division M accepts the new supplier's offer and recommend how many components Division L should sell to Division M if group profits are to be maximised.** **(3 marks)**

(b) **Using the quantities calculated in (a) and the current transfer price, calculate the total annual profits of each division and the group as a whole.** **(6 marks)**

(c) **Discuss the problems which will arise if the transfer price remains unchanged and advise the divisions on a suitable alternative transfer price for component L.** **(6 marks)**

(Total: 15 marks)

292 BEST NIGHT CO (MARCH 2019)

Best Night Co operates a chain of 30 hotels across the country of Essland. It prides itself on the comfort of the rooms in its hotels and the quality of service it offers to guests.

The majority of Best Night Co's hotels are located in major cities and have previously been successful in attracting business customers. In recent years, however, the number of business customers has started to decline as a result of tough economic conditions in Essland.

Best Night Co's policy is to set standard prices for the rooms in each of its hotels, with that price reflecting the hotel's location and taking account of competitors' prices. However, hotel managers have the authority to offer discounts to regular customers, and to reduce prices when occupancy rates in their hotel are expected to be low. The average standard price per night, across all the hotels, was $140 in 20X7, compared to $135 in 20X6. In addition to room bookings, the hotels also generate revenue from the additional services available to customers, such as restaurants and bars.

Summary from Best Night Co's management accounts:

	Year ended 30 June 20X7	**Year ended 30 June 20X6**
	$000	$000
Revenue – Rooms at standard price per night	111,890	104,976
Room discounts or rate reductions given	(16,783)	(11,540)
Other revenue: food, drink	24,270	23,185
	———	———
Total revenue	119,377	116,621
Operating costs	(95,462)	(92,379)
	———	———
Operating profit	23,915	24,242
	———	———

Oher performance information:

	Year ended 30 June 20X7	**Year ended 30 June 20X6**
	$000	$000
Capital employed (Note 1)	$39.5m	$39.1m
Average occupancy rates (Note 2)	74%	72%
Average customer satisfaction score (Note 3)	4.2	4.5

Note 1: Capital employed is calculated using the depreciated cost of non-current assets at all Best Night Co's hotels.

Note 2: Occupancy rates for the year ended 30 June 20X7 were budgeted to be 72%.

Note 3: Customer satisfaction scores are graded on a scale of 1–5 where '5' represents 'Excellent'. On average, in any given town in Essland, the top 10% of hotels earn a score of 4.5 or above and the top 25% of hotels earn a score of 4.2 or above.

Two themes are becoming increasingly frequent in the comments Best Night Co's customers make alongside the scores:

1 Repeat customers have said that the standard of service in recent visits has not been as good as in previous visits.

2 The rooms need redecorating, and the fixtures and fittings need replacing. For example, the beds need new mattresses to improve the level of comfort they provide. Best Night Co had planned a two-year refurbishment programme beginning in 20X7 of all the rooms in each hotel. However, this programme has been put on hold, due to the current economic conditions, and in order to reduce expenditure.

Required:

Using the information provided, discuss Best Night Co's financial and non-financial performance for the year ended 30 June 20X7. Note: There are 5 marks available for calculations and 15 marks available for discussion.

(Total: 20 marks)

293 YETGO CO (SEPTEMBER/DECEMBER 2024)

Yetgo Co operates a chain of 23 vacation resorts each of which contains bedrooms, restaurants and leisure facilities, and has been trading for ten years. All of Yetgo Co's resorts are run as investment centres and the managers receive bonuses based on the return on investment (ROI) that their resort achieves.

The first two resorts in the chain were built in the same year by Yetgo Co. They are identical in terms of the design, construction and number of buildings. They were built in different locations in the same country and named after these locations, Yuri and Lux.

In recent years the area surrounding the Yuri resort has become highly fashionable and a much sought after destination for holidaymakers. The manager has made no significant capital investment in the resort for over two years. The area in which the Lux resort is based in is in decline and is a much less popular destination for holidaymakers. In an attempt to maintain custom the manager at Lux has invested in high quality spa and gym equipment, as well as ensuring that all operations are run as efficiently as possible.

An extract of the current year's budget for the Yuri and Lux resorts is as follows:

	Yuri	**Lux**
	$	$
Turnover	350,000	420,000
Operating costs (excluding depreciation)	200,000	200,000
Depreciation (controllable non-current assets)	26,000	60,000
Tax	51,000	66,000
Profit after tax	**73,000**	**94,000**
Controllable non-current assets	350,000	700,000
Inventory	90,000	40,000
Receivables	90,000	70,000
Payables	40,000	40,000
Net controllable assets	**490,000**	**770,000**

For each whole percentage point achieved above a 22% ROI managers are paid a bonus of $5,000. The resort ROI is calculated on controllable assets only, which therefore exclude the largest proportion of the resorts' assets, namely the land and buildings. In the past five years the manager at Yuri has been awarded large bonuses, whereas the manager at Lux has received no bonus.

Yetgo Co's average financial ratios are as follows:

Inventory holding period	80 days
Receivables collection period	60 days
Operating profit margin	36%
Current ratio	3:1

Yuri resort investment opportunity

The manager at Yuri has an opportunity to invest in state of the art solarium equipment at a cost of $20,000. The equipment will be used for three years before being sold for $5,000. The solarium will generate $8,000 net cash inflow each year.

Yetgo Co has a 10% cost of capital.

Required:

(a) Calculate the receivables collection period, operating profit margin and current ratio for both the Yuri and Lux resorts and comment on their relative performance. **(7 marks)**

(b) (i) Calculate the return on investment (ROI) of both the Yuri and Lux resorts and state which manager, if any, will receive a bonus this year. **(3 marks)**

(ii) Explain the problems with the current bonus system at Yetgo Co. **(6 marks)**

(c) Calculate the Yuri resort's divisional ROI if the new investment opportunity goes ahead and explain whether Yuri's manager will make a decision on the investment opportunity which is in the best interest of Yetgo Co. **(4 marks)**

(Total: 20 marks)

294 SPORTS CO (SEPTEMBER/DECEMBER 2017)

Sports Co is a large manufacturing company specialising in the manufacture of a wide range of sports clothing and equipment. The company has two divisions: Clothing (division C) and Equipment (division E). Each division operates with little intervention from Head Office and divisional managers have autonomy to make decisions about long-term investments.

Sports Co measures the performance of its divisions using return on investment (ROI), calculated using controllable profit and average divisional net assets. The target ROI for each of the divisions is 18%. If the divisions meet or exceed this target the divisional managers receive a bonus.

Last year, an investment which was expected to meet the target ROI was rejected by one of the divisional managers because it would have reduced the division's overall ROI. Consequently, Sports Co is considering the introduction of a new performance measure, residual income (RI), in order to discourage this dysfunctional behaviour in the future. Like ROI, this would be calculated using controllable profit and average divisional net assets.

The draft operating statement for the year, prepared by the company's trainee accountant, is shown below:

	Division C	**Division E**
	$000	$000
Sales revenue	3,800	8,400
Less variable costs	(1,400)	(3,030)
Contribution	**2,400**	**5,370**
Less fixed costs	(945)	(1,420)
Net profit	**1,455**	**3,950**
Opening divisional controllable net assets	13,000	24,000
Closing divisional controllable net assets	9,000	30,000

Notes:

(1) Included in the fixed costs are depreciation costs of $165,000 and $460,000 for divisions C and E respectively. 30% of the depreciation costs in each division relates to assets controlled but not owned by Head Office. Division E invested $2m in plant and machinery at the beginning of the year, which is included in the net assets figures above, and uses the reducing balance method to depreciate assets. Division C, which uses the straight-line method, made no significant additions to non-current assets. It is the policy of both divisions to charge a full year's depreciation in the year of acquisition.

(2) Head Office recharges all of its costs to the two divisions. These have been included in the fixed costs and amount to $620,000 for division C and $700,000 for division E.

(3) Sports Co has a cost of capital of 12%.

Required:

(a) (i) Calculate the return on investment (ROI) for each of the two divisions of Sports Co. **(6 marks)**

(ii) Discuss the performance of the two divisions for the year, including the main reasons why their ROI results differ from each other. Explain the impact the difference in ROI could have on the behaviour of the manager of the worst performing division. **(6 marks)**

(b) (i) Calculate the residual income (RI) for each of the two divisions of Sports Co and briefly comment on the results of this performance measure. **(4 marks)**

(ii) Explain the advantages and disadvantages of using residual income (RI) to measure divisional performance. **(4 marks)**

(Total: 20 marks)

295 THE PORTABLE GARAGE COMPANY (JUNE 2018)

The Portable Garage Co (PGC) is a company specialising in the manufacture and sale of a range of products for motorists. It is split into two divisions: the battery division (Division B) and the adaptor division (Division A). Division B sells one product – portable battery chargers for motorists which can be attached to a car's own battery and used to start up the engine when the car's own battery fails. Division A sells adaptors which are used by customers to charge mobile devices and laptops by attaching them to the car's internal power source.

Recently, Division B has upgraded its portable battery so it can also be used to rapidly charge mobile devices and laptops. The mobile device or laptop must be attached to the battery using a special adaptor which is supplied to the customer with the battery. Division B currently buys the adaptors from Division A, which also sells them externally to other companies.

The following data is available for both divisions:

Division B

Selling price for each portable battery, including adaptor	$180
Costs per battery:	
Adaptor from Division A	$13
Other materials from external suppliers	$45
Labour costs	$35
Annual fixed overheads	$5,460,000
Annual production and sales of portable batteries (units)	150,000
Maximum annual market demand for portable batteries (units)	180,000

Division A

Selling price per adaptor to Division B	$13
Selling price per adaptor to external customers	$15
Costs per adaptor:	
Materials	$3
Labour costs	$4
Annual fixed overheads	$2,200,000
Current annual production capacity and sales of adaptors – both internal and external sales (units)	350,000
Maximum annual external demand for adaptors (units)	200,000

In addition to the materials and labour costs above, Division A incurs a variable cost of $1 per adaptor for all adaptors it sells externally.

Currently, Head Office's purchasing policy only allows Division B to purchase the adaptors from Division A but Division A has refused to sell Division B any more than the current level of adaptors it supplies to it.

The manager of Division B is unhappy. They have a special industry contact who they could buy the adaptors from at exactly the same price charged by Division A if they were given the autonomy to purchase from outside the group.

After discussions with both of the divisional managers and to ensure that the managers are not demotivated, Head Office has now agreed to change the purchasing policy to allow Division B to buy externally, provided that it optimises the profits of the group as a whole.

Required:

(a) Under the current transfer pricing system, prepare a profit statement showing the profit for each of the divisions and for The Portable Garage Co (PGC) as a whole. Your sales and costs figures should be split into external sales and inter-divisional transfers, where appropriate. ⊞ **(9 marks)**

(b) Assuming that the new group purchasing policy will ensure the optimisation of group profits, calculate and discuss the number of adaptors which Division B should buy from Division A and the number of adaptors which Division A should sell to external customers.

Note: There are 3 marks available for calculations and 3 marks for discussion.

(6 marks)

Assume now that no external supplier exists for the adaptors which Division B uses.

(c) Calculate and discuss what the minimum transfer price per unit would be for any additional adaptors supplied above the current level by Division A to Division B so that Division B can meet its maximum annual demand for the new portable batteries.

Note: There are 2 marks available for calculations and 3 marks available for discussion.

(5 marks)

(Total: 20 marks)

296 CTD

CTD has two divisions – FD and TM. FD is an iron foundry division which produces mouldings that have a limited external market and are also transferred to TM division. TM division uses the mouldings to produce a piece of agricultural equipment called the 'TX' which is sold externally. Each TX requires one moulding. Both divisions produce only one type of product.

The performance of each Divisional Manager is evaluated individually on the basis of the residual income (RI) of his or her division. The company's average annual 12% cost of capital is used to calculate the finance charges. If their own target residual income is achieved, each Divisional Manager is awarded a bonus equal to 5% of his or her residual income. All bonuses are paid out of Head Office profits.

The following budgeted information is available for the forthcoming year:

	TM division **TX per unit**	**FD division** **Moulding per unit**
External selling price ($)	500	80
Variable production cost ($)	*366	40
Fixed production overheads ($)	60	20
Gross profit ($)	74	20
Variable selling and distribution cost ($)	25	**4
Fixed administration overhead ($)	25	4
Net profit ($)	24	12
Normal capacity (units)	15,000	20,000
Maximum production capacity (units)	15,000	25,000
Sales to external customers (units)	15,000	5,000
Capital employed	$1,500,000	$750,000
Target RI	$105,000	$85,000

* The variable production cost of TX includes the cost of an FD moulding.

** External sales only of the mouldings incur a variable selling and distribution cost of $4 per unit.

FD division currently transfers 15,000 mouldings to TM division at a transfer price equal to the total production cost plus 10%. Fixed costs are absorbed on the basis of normal capacity.

Required:

(a) Calculate the bonus each Divisional Manager would receive under the current transfer pricing policy and discuss any implications that the current performance evaluation system may have for each division and for the company as a whole.

(14 marks)

(b) Both Divisional Managers want to achieve their respective residual income targets. Based on the budgeted figures, calculate:

(i) the maximum transfer price per unit that the Divisional Manager of TM division would pay

(ii) the minimum transfer price per unit that the Divisional Manager of FD division would accept.

(6 marks)

(Total: 20 marks)

297 ROTECH (JUNE 2014)

Answer debrief

The Rotech group comprises two companies, W Co and C Co.

W Co is a trading company with two divisions: The Design division, which designs wind turbines and supplies the designs to customers under licences and the Gearbox division, which manufactures gearboxes for the car industry.

C Co manufactures components for gearboxes. It sells the components globally and also supplies W Co with components for its Gearbox manufacturing division. The financial results for the two companies for the year ended 31 May 2014 are as follows:

	W Co		**C Co**
	Design Division	**Gearbox Division**	
	$000	$000	$000
External sales	14,300	25,535	8,010
Sales to Gearbox division			7,550
			15,560
Cost of sales	(4,900)	(16,200)*	(5,280)
Administration costs	(3,400)	(4,200)	(2,600)
Distribution costs	–	(1,260)	(670)
Operating profit	6,000	3,875	7,010
Capital employed	23,540	32,320	82,975

* Includes cost of components purchased from C Co.

Required:

(a) **Discuss the performance of C Co and each division of W Co, calculating and using the following three performance measures:**

(i) **Return on capital employed (ROCE)**

(ii) **Asset turnover**

(iii) **Operating profit margin.**

Note: There are 4.5 marks available for calculations and 5.5 marks available for discussion. **(10 marks)**

(b) C Co is currently working to full capacity. The Rotech group's policy is that group companies and divisions must always make internal sales first before selling outside the group. Similarly, purchases must be made from within the group wherever possible. However, the group divisions and companies are allowed to negotiate their own transfer prices without interference from Head Office.

C Co has always charged the same price to the Gearbox division as it does to its external customers. However, after being offered a 5% lower price for similar components from an external supplier, the manager of the Gearbox division feels strongly that the transfer price is too high and should be reduced. C Co currently satisfies 60% of the external demand for its components. Its variable costs represent 40% of revenue.

Required:

Advise, using suitable calculations, the total transfer price or prices at which the components should be supplied to the Gearbox division from C Co.

(10 marks)

(Total: 20 marks)

Calculate your allowed time, allocate the time to the separate parts..............

298 KLEN CO (SEPTEMBER/DECEMBER 2025)

Klen Co, manufactures industrial washing machines used by hotels across the world. It is based in the country of Deeland, but has manufacturing plants in a number of countries.

Klen Co's goal is to be the leading global industrial washing machine manufacturer, generating value for customers and shareholders through a commitment to quality, innovation and respect for the planet.

In 20X5, the global economy suffered a severe downturn, and sales of new machines fell significantly. However, Klen Co's chief executive officer (CEO) is confident that the company's reputation for quality, and its commitment to embracing new technologies, will help it strengthen its competitiveness and market position as the global economy recovers from the downturn.

Klen Co's commitment to technology is evident both in its manufacturing process, which is highly automated, and also in the design of its machines. It has been a market leader in the development of the most energy efficient machines with its ECO10 range of machines being the most energy efficient machine available in the market.

Klen Co's board uses a balanced scorecard to measure the company's performance, with the following objectives and measures for each of the perspectives:

Perspective	Objectives	Measures
Financial	Sustain growth	Revenue growth (%)
	Maintain profitability	Operating profit ($m)
Customer	Strengthen market position	Market share (%)
	Delight customers	% of customers who recommend Klen Co
Internal business process	Reduce machine downtime	Machine downtime (hours)
	Reduce defect rates	% of manufactured machines with defects
Innovation and learning	Increase productivity	Average output (machines) per employee
	Promote innovation	ECO10 machines as a % of machines produced

Performance Information

Summary performance information for Klen Co for the years to 30 June 20X5 and 30 June 20X4 is shown below:

Financial information	**Note**	**20X5 ($m)**	**20X4 ($m)**	**Change**
Revenue	1	107,209	117,995	-9.1%
Operating costs (excluding depreciation)		88,669	99,528	-10.9%
Depreciation		10,390	9,785	6.2%

Non-financial information	**Note**	**20X5**	**20X4**	**Change**
Average number of employees		61,860	71,200	-13.10%
Machines manufactured by Klen Co		3,763,400	4,249,600	-11.40%
of which:				
Traditional machines		2,012,236	2,517,264	-20.10%
ECO10 machines		1,751,164	1,732,336	1.10%
Downtime (hours)	2	5,956	6,354	-6.30%
Machines with defects	3	24,086	29,322	-17.90%
% of customers who recommend Klen Co		59%	56%	5.40%

Notes:

(1) Total global revenue from new machine sales in the year to 30 June 20X5 was $1,600,134m. The corresponding figure for the year to 30 June 20X4 was $1,815,308m.

(2) 'Downtime' measures any time when production is stopped, either due to technical failure, maintenance or unavailability of inputs (materials, labour).

(3) 'Machines with defects' means the number of machines manufactured in the year which have had defects reported by a customer within 12 months of buying them. Industry figures for both 20X5 and 20X4 show that, on average, customers reported a defect in 1.33% of new machines within 12 months of buying them. This figure has remained largely unchanged for a number of years.

Klen Co's assistant management accountant has started preparing the results for the year to 30 June 20X5, but has not yet calculated all of the figures required for the balanced scorecard.

Required:

(a) Using the template provided, calculate the performance measures for the year to 30 June 20X5, and the prior year figures for the year to 30 June 20X4. **(5 marks)**

	A	B	C
1	**Klen Co - Balanced Scorecard**		
2			
3	**Measures**	**20X5**	**20X4**
4	**Financial**		
5	Revenue growth (%)	-9.10%	n/a
6	Operating profit ($m)		
7	**Customer**		
8	Market share (%)		
9	% of customers who recommend Klen	59.0%	56.0%
10	**Internal business process**		
11	Downtime (hours)	5,956	6,354
12	% of manufactured machines with defects		
13	**Innovation and learning**		
14	Average output (machines per employee)		
15	ECO10 machines as % of machines produced		

(b) Using the performance measures given in Klen Co's balanced scorecard, and your calculations from part (a), analyse Klen Co's performance for the year to 30 June 20X5.

Note: A maximum of 3 marks will be given for additional calculations performed (1 mark per calculation). **(15 marks)**

(Total: 20 marks)

299 MEDCOMP (MARCH/JUNE 2021)

Medcomp is a charity based in Ceeland. It provides medical treatment to prevent and cure blindness caused by cataracts, to thousands of people in less developed countries. This disease is relatively easy to cure when treatment is available; but the majority of people who need treatment cannot afford to pay for it. For over 10 years Medcomp has provided free treatment from 12 treatment centres based in fixed locations worldwide.

Medcomp employs a small number of paid permanent staff who consist of medical practitioners, medical administrators and fundraisers; but the majority of its workforce is voluntary The charity has built relationships with several teaching hospitals in Ceeland, from where it recruits newly qualified doctors and nurses. These doctors and nurses volunteer to work unpaid for a year in Medcomp's treatment centres before returning home to work in one of Ceeland's many hospitals. Medcomp believes that using newly qualified medical staff will promote the use of the most effective and up-to-date techniques and procedures.

Financial donations are sourced from large businesses in Ceeland and most of the equipment and other medical supplies needed are donated by hospitals and manufacturers. Thus, it is rare for the treatment centres to run short of supplies.

Medcomp keeps accounts with a year end of 31 August as well as detailed operating data. Data extracts from its management accounts for the current year (20X8) and from 20X7 and 20X6 are as follows:

	20X8	**20X7**	**20X6**
Average Size of Donation ($)	600	535	500
Number of Donations	2,850	3,000	2,950
Total Operating Costs ($000s)	1,730	1,550	1,430
New procedures as a percentage of total procedures **(Note)**	20%	5%	5%
Number of treatments performed	5,600	5,000	4,600
Number of successful treatments	4,312	4,300	4,002
Average number of days taken to deliver drugs and equipment to treatment centres	7	7	7

Note: New procedures are procedures which are introduced within the year.

Medcomp is about to introduce a balanced scorecard to help implement its strategy and measure performance. The critical success factors (CSFs), which relate to the four perspectives of the balanced scorecard have been identified as: positive cash flow, innovation, medical effectiveness and functional efficiency.

Required:

(a) **For each perspective of the balanced scorecard, select the appropriate critical success factor (CSF) which relates to the perspective, suggest ONE key performance indicator (KPI) which will help to measure the CSF and use the KPI to analyse Medcomp's performance from 20X6 to 20X8.** **(16 marks)**

Note: Use the balanced scorecard template provided below to structure your answer.

FINANCIAL	**CSF:**
	KPI:
	Performance Analysis:

CUSTOMER	**CSF:**
	KPI:
	Performance Analysis:
INTERNAL BUSINESS PROCESS	**CSF:**
	KPI:
	Performance Analysis:
LEARNING AND GROWTH	**CSF:**
	KPI:
	Performance Analysis:

(b) **Explain the benefits of an organisation using the balanced scorecard to measure performance instead of using solely financial measures.** **(4 marks)**

(Total: 20 marks)

300 HAMMOCK CO (MARCH/JULY 2020 SAMPLE EXAM)

Hammock Co own and operate a small chain of four luxury vacation resorts. All four resorts are located on islands that enjoy a hot, sunny climate for nine months of the year. Each resort has gourmet restaurants, water sports and spa facilities, as well as sun terraces and pools.

Hammock Co's management currently focus on two distinct stakeholder groups: shareholders and customers, and has two objectives:

1 to make a profit long term and

2 to create customer loyalty

All operational (non-management) staff at the resorts receive comprehensive training and are employed in secure, long-term contracts, which is unusual in this industry.

Guests who visit the resorts pay one upfront fee and then enjoy unlimited food, drink and use of the resort facilities. When a guest arrives at a resort they are personally greeted by a concierge, offered a drink and cold towel while their luggage is transferred to their luxury room. All rooms are scrupulously clean and contain complimentary drinks, snacks, toiletries, bathrobes and slippers. The rooms are all equipped with appliances, which Hammocks Co's management believe that guests need during their stay, including satellite television, coffee-maker, refrigerator and hairdryer. If a guest requests something that is not available in the room, a call to the reception ensures that it arrives within ten minutes.

An extract from Hammock Co's management accounting data is as follows:

	Budget 20X7	Actual 20X7 (*)	Actual 20X6	Actual 20X6 Competitor 'Loungers'
Average number of guests per week	2,000	1,960	1,940	1,700
Average revenue per week ($)	4,000,000	3,920,000	3,880,000	3,060,000
Average staff costs per week				
– Maintenance ($)	480,000	480,000	470,588	455,000
– Service ($)	960,000	960,000	941,176	800,000
Average weekly spend on repairs ($)	200,000	160,000	196,078	180,000
Ratio of operational staff to guests	1.50	1.53	1.50	1.30
Average rooms available per week **	1,200	1,200	1,200	1,100
Market share %	29	28	29	23

* The actual 20X7 figures are based on the year to date figures (ten weeks)

** Rooms are designed for double occupancy

Note: general inflation is 2% higher in 20X7

Extracts from TripEvent, an influential online customer forum:

'I love Hammock Co; the service and attention to detail is exemplary and the resorts are always pristine. However, their competitor 'Loungers' has full body dryers, ionised water taps and a range of professional haircare equipment in all their rooms.'

'Our third time back to Hammocks Co this year and we continue to be amazed by the wonderful level of service. One thing though is the menus don't seem to have changed from one visit to the next.'

'We booked Hammocks Co on the spur of the moment but then found that we couldn't get a flight. We called Hammocks Co's administrative centre to change our booking to another resort where we could get a flight to and were told that it would not be a problem. However, it took two more calls and three emails to get confirmation and then our credit card was charged twice in error. Of course it was eventually all resolved, the incorrect charge refunded, a complimentary limousine provided to and from the airport and we received the most amazing customer service at the resort, but it was frustrating at the time.'

'When I made my booking I was assured that my bed would be made with the special anti-allergenic bedding which I need for a good night's sleep and that my favourite blend of tea would be available. When I arrived, neither of these requirements were met. To be fair to Hammocks Co though, everything was in order two hours later when I went to bed.'

Required:

(a) Based on the limited information available, discuss the performance of Hammocks Co in light of its two existing objectives. **(8 marks)**

(b) (i) Explain TWO advantages of Hammocks Co using the balanced scorecard approach to performance management. **(3 marks)**

(ii) Suggest and justify ONE goal and TWO performance measures for each of the TWO perspectives of the balanced scorecard which are not currently addressed by Hammock Co's objectives. **(9 marks)**

(Total: 20 marks)

301 LEMIC AIR CO (SEPTEMBER/DECEMBER 2023)

Lemic Air was established 50 years ago in the country of Surland as a 'premium' airline. Following a global recession, it relaunched itself as a 'low cost' airline two years ago, focussing on providing seats on flights at the lowest possible price. It currently has a 35% share of the 'low cost' airline market in Surland; its largest competitor has a 40% market share.

Lemic Air's 'low cost' approach includes:

(1)	Leasing planes with seats placed close together in order to fit more seats in. The engine in these planes uses a cheaper grade of fuel which is more polluting to the environment.
(2)	Permitting only one piece of 'hand luggage' per customer (that is, luggage that can be carried on board the plane). Any additional bags have to be placed in the plane's luggage hold area, which is never full, at a cost of $50 per item. On average, customers pay for 0.7 luggage 'hold bags' per person compared to an industry average on 'low cost' airlines of 0.92.
(3)	Using 'ground boarding', which uses buses, often left with their engines running for some time, to transport passengers between the airport terminal building and the plane. This is cheaper than using 'passenger loading bridges', which are far more environmentally-friendly.
(4)	Requiring customers to pay a fee of $30 each if they want to choose a pre-allocated seat. 25% of customers choose this option (industry average is 32%).

(5)	Offering only online check-in for flights to passengers free of charge. In person check-in incurs a fee for the passenger but the fee only partially covers the cost of check-in for Lemic Air. It also leads to longer queues for those customers who just need to drop their bags off at the same customer service desk. This has led to complaints by customers who prefer the automated machines offered by competitors for both check-in and bag drop offs.
(6)	Improving cleanliness of planes, a reason for past customer complaints, whilst also attempting to reduce the minimum 'ground turnaround time' (time on the tarmac between flights) by using cabin crew to clean planes. Average turnaround time in the industry is 50 minutes per flight.
(7)	Making sure that prices are equal to or less than those of competitors so that flight occupancy rate is high (88% at Lemic Air in the last year).

Staffing issues have led to 220 flight cancellations in the last year, which has led to huge volumes of complaints and Lemic Air having to pay compensation to customers totalling $1.2 million in the last year. Lemic Air's CEO is hoping to start cross-training staff so that they can work both on the planes and in the airport.

All customers who have travelled on a Lemic Air flight are asked to complete a questionnaire asking key questions about comfort, cleanliness, delays etc.

Required:

(a) **For each of the SIX dimensions of Fitzgerald & Moon's Building Block model, identify one objective together with one corresponding performance indicator which could be used by Lemic Air to measure its performance. The objectives and measures should be specifically relevant to Lemic Air. Justify your choice of objective and measure for each dimension.**

Note: Use the template provided. **(15 marks)**

(b) **Discuss the issues that Lemic Air faces with regard to the management of its environmental costs.** **(5 marks)**

(Total: 20 marks)

Dimension: Financial Performance
Objective:
Performance indicator:
Justification:

Dimension: Competition
Objective:
Performance indicator:
Justification:

Dimension: Quality
Objective: Performance indicator: Justification:
Dimension: Innovation
Objective: Performance indicator: Justification:
Dimension: Flexibility
Objective: Performance indicator: Justification:
Dimension: Resource Utilisation
Objective: Performance indicator: Justification:

302 CAROLINE CO (MARCH/JUNE 2024)

Caroline Co is a decentralised company which manufactures and sells radios. It has two divisions: the Radio Division, which manufactures the radios, and the Packaging Division, which produces the boxes in which the radios are packaged. The Packaging Division has no external market for its boxes.

The expected costs and volume of sales of the two divisions are as follows:

	Packaging Division	Radio Division
Market price ($/unit)		220
Variable cost ($/unit)	1	120
Annual fixed costs ($)	80,000	500,000
Annual sales (units)	20,000	20,000

The current transfer price for the boxes is based on the **full cost** of a box plus a mark-up of 20%.

Recently, an external packaging company has offered to supply the Radio Division with boxes of the same specification as those produced by the Packaging Division at a cost of $4 per box. The manager of the Radio Division has proposed two alternative responses to this offer:

1 The Packaging Division should be asked to reduce the transfer price on the boxes to $4 per box, in which case the Radio Division would continue to buy from the Packaging Division.

2 If the Packaging Division is not prepared to match the external supplier's price, then it should be closed, and all boxes required should be purchased externally.

The Packaging Division's fixed costs relate mainly to long-term lease payments and only $20,000 per year of its fixed costs could be avoided if it were closed.

Required:

(a) Prepare a profit statement for each of the two divisions and for Caroline Co as a whole, under the current transfer pricing arrangements.

Note: Your sales and costs figures should be split into external sales and inter-divisional transfers where appropriate. (6 marks)

(b) (i) Calculate the effect on the profits of each division and Caroline Co as a whole if a transfer price of $4 per box is used. (4 marks)

(ii) Calculate the effect on the profits of Caroline Co as a whole if the Packaging Division is closed and all boxes are purchased externally. (4 marks)

(c) Discuss the advantages and disadvantages to Caroline Co of using a transfer price of $4 per box. (6 marks)

(Total: 20 marks)

303 ROBINHOLT UNIVERSITY (SEPTEMBER 2019)

Robinholt University is one of the largest and most popular universities in the country of Richpori. It had 27,000 registered students in 20X6, whereas in 20X5, the number of registered students was only 24,000. Robinholt University managed to increase its student numbers in 20X6 by making the entry requirements for students slightly lower than in previous years. All courses at the university last for three years.

Robinholt University has five strategic aims:

1. To provide education which promotes intellectual initiative and produces confident and ambitious graduates who have reached the highest academic standards to prepare them for success in life and the workplace.
2. To provide an organised, efficient learning environment with access to cutting edge technology and facilities.
3. To be a leader in sustainable business practices which protect the environment and support local people.
4. To provide attractive, innovative conference and event facilities, attracting clients both nationally and internationally.
5. To be recognised both nationally and internationally for the scope and relevance of their research.

Extracts from the university's statement of profit or loss for the last two years are as follows:

	20X6 $ million	**20X5** $ million
Income		
Tuition fees	148.0	135.6
Research grants	3.5	4.5
Conferences and other events	18.0	16.0
Total income	**169.5**	**156.1**
Expenditure		
Academic staff costs	80.8	76.2
Administration staff costs	50.4	48
Premises, facilities and technology costs	7.6	8.4
Event and conference costs	8.3	8.0
Research grants	3.1	4.0
Sustainability and community assistance	1.2	2.4
Total expenditure	**151.4**	**147.0**
Surplus	**18.1**	**9.1**

Every year, final year students complete an external survey run by the National Organisation for Students. In this, they have to agree or disagree with statements made. Extracts from this for the last two years are shown below (the percentage rates show the number of students who agreed with the statements made):

	20X6	20X5
Teaching		
(1) The course is intellectually stimulating and quality of teaching high	83%	86%
Academic support		
(2) I have received good advice and support with my studies from academic staff	82%	86%
Organisation and management		
(3) The course is well organised and its administration is good	81%	90%
Learning resources		
(4) The standard of rooms, facilities and equipment is good	83%	92%
Personal development		
(5) The course has helped me develop as a person	82%	80%
Overall satisfaction		
(6) Overall, I am satisfied with the quality of the course	81%	83%

The 'overall satisfaction' percentage is used by the Education Authority to set the maximum level of tuition fees that a university can charge each year and is seen as the main measure of success both internally and externally.

Other key information

	20X6	20X5
Students graduating with a First Class Honours degree (highest class attainable)	20%	28%
Employers happy with the graduates from Robinholt University	72%	75%
Ratio of students to staff members	40:1	35:1
Staff retention rate	75%	90%

The staff retention rate in 20X5 was consistent with previous years. Data gathered from students who graduated in 20X5 showed that 65% of students found a graduate job within one year of leaving compared to 68% of 20X4's graduates.

In 20X5, Robinholt University won the 'Green Environmental' award for their campuses, which all have extensive recycling facilities. Students were also involved in a local 'Grow to Give' food sharing project that year, which provided thousands of pounds worth of fresh produce to food banks offering food to poorer residents. Due to staff shortages, the university was not involved in this project in 20X6. The recycling bins have also been abandoned because of the cost of using them.

Every year, the University Research Council issues a range of prestigious awards for contributions to research. One of Robinholt University's main competitors in the area won an award in 20X5 for their contribution to some pioneering research on genetics. Robinholt University has yet to win an award for research. However, in 20X5 it did win an 'Innovation' award for its new, innovative conference facilities which have attracted a number of new clients in the last year.

Required:

Using Robinholt University's five strategic aims, assess its performance for 20X6.

Note: There are 4 marks available for calculations and 16 marks for discussion. Use the headings in the template provided below to structure your answer.

(1) To provide education which promotes intellectual initiative and produces confident and ambitious graduates who have reached the highest academic standards to prepare them for success in life and the workplace
(2) To provide an organised, efficient learning environment with access to cutting edge technology and facilities
(3) To be a leader in sustainable business practices which protect the environment and support local people
(4) To provide attractive, innovative conference and event facilities, attracting clients both nationally and internationally
(5) To be recognised both nationally and internationally for the scope and relevance of their research
Overall satisfaction

(Total: 20 marks)

304 TONFORD SCHOOL (SEPTEMBER/DECEMBER 2020)

All schools in the country of Ducland are funded by the state and are accountable to the Department of Education (DoE) which oversees educational standards and monitors performance of the schools.

The DoE's objectives, which are also the objectives for all the schools in Ducland, are to:

1. Strive for continuous improvement in performance standards
2. Provide a supportive learning environment, which encourages a high standard of pupil achievement
3. Ensure pupils are prepared for adult life and have the skills and character necessary to contribute to society and the economy
4. Provide all children with access to high quality education, regardless of their location or background.

Summary performance data for each school is accessible via the DoE's website. Parents in Ducland have the right to choose which school their child should attend and many parents use the performance data to help with their selection.

Inspectors from the DoE visit each school in Ducland at the end of every five years. The DoE believes that to gain a better insight into the quality of the teaching and learning environment, inspectors should attend a selection of lessons and speak to some of the pupils.

Tonford School has recently had its inspection visit, and the school's data entry on the DoE's website has been updated following that visit. The revised entry is shown below:

Performance factor	**Notes**	**Tonford School actual (20X7)**	**National target (20X7)**	**Tonford School actual (20X2)**
Exam results	1	62%	65%	64%
Pupil progress	2	0.4	0.25	0.3
Inspection grade	3, 4	Very Good	Good	Good
Pupil numbers	–	662	n/a	627
Number of teaching staff	5	35	n/a	33

Notes:

(1) The 'exam results' indicator shows the percentage of pupils leaving school with at least five final exams including compulsory subjects of mathematics, science and languages at Grade A-C (the top three grades).

(2) 'Pupil progress' is an indicator of how well pupils have performed in compulsory subjects in their final exams at age 16 compared to their performance in intermediate exams at age 11.

Academic grades are given numerical values, and the 'pupil progress' score is the movement in the average of pupils' grades. Scores typically range between –0.5 and +0.5.

(3) There are six inspection grades: excellent; very good; good; average; poor and very poor.

(4) The inspector's summary report for Tonford School concluded: "There is a very strong sense of community values and citizenship. Pupils appear to have a genuine respect for their teachers, and for one another, despite their diverse backgrounds."

(5) The DoE recommends that the pupil/teacher ratio should be less than 22:1.

Required:

(a) Explain the problems which not-for-profit organisations face as a result of having multiple objectives. **(4 marks)**

(b) Assess Tonford School's performance against the objectives set by the DoE, using the performance data published on the DoE's website. **(12 marks)**

Note: Use the four objectives in the template provided below to structure your answer.

Objective 1 – Strive for continuous improvement in performance standards.
Objective 2 – Provide a supportive learning environment, which encourages a high standard of pupil achievement.
Objective 3 – Ensure pupils are prepared for adult life and have the skills and character necessary to contribute to society and the economy.
Objective 4 – Provide all children with access to high quality education, regardless of their location or background.

(c) Explain the difficulties in assessing performance of schools in Ducland due to the qualitative nature of their objectives. **(4 marks)**

(Total: 20 marks)

305 MOBE (JUNE 2015 ADAPTED)

Mobe Co manufactures electronic mobility scooters. The company is split into two divisions: the scooter division (Division S) and the motor division (Division M). Division M supplies electronic motors to both Division S and to external customers. The two divisions run as autonomously as possible, subject to the group's current policy that Division M must make internal sales first before selling outside the group; and that Division S must always buy its motors from Division M. However, this company policy, together with the transfer price which Division M charges Division S, is currently under review.

Details of the two divisions are given below.

Division S

Division S's budget for the coming year shows that 35,000 electronic motors will be needed. An external supplier could supply these to Division S for $800 each.

Division M

Division M has the capacity to produce a total of 60,000 electronic motors per year. Details of Division M's budget which has just been prepared for the forthcoming year, are as follows:

Budgeted sales volumes (units)	60,000
Selling price per unit for external sales of motors	$850
Variable cost per unit for external sales of motors	$770

The variable cost per unit for motors sold to Division S is $30 per unit lower due to cost savings on distribution and packaging.

Maximum external demand for the motors is 30,000 units per year.

Required:

(a) Assuming that the group's current policy could be changed, advise, using suitable calculations, the number of motors which Division M should supply to Division S in order to maximise group profits. Recommend the transfer price or prices at which these internal sales should take place. (10 marks)

Note: All relevant workings must be shown

(b) Each of Mobe's divisions is managed by a divisional manager who has the power to make all investment decisions within the division. The cost of capital for both divisions is 12%. Historically, investment decisions have been made by calculating the return on investment (ROI) of any opportunities and at present, the return on investment of each division is 16%.

A new manager who has recently been appointed in division S has argued that using residual income to make investment decisions would result in 'better goal congruence' throughout the company.

Each division is currently considering the following separate investments:

	Division S	Division M
Capital required for investment	$82,800	$40,600
Sales generated by investment	$44,600	$21,800
Net profit margin	28%	33%

Required:

(i) Calculate the return on investment for each of the two divisions. (2 marks)

(ii) Calculate the residual income for each of the two divisions. (4 marks)

(iii) Comment on the results, taking into consideration the managers views about residual income. (4 marks)

(Total: 20 marks)

306 FLAG CO (SEPTEMBER/DECEMBER 2021)

The country of Jayland has two airlines, Flag Co, its national airline, and Budget Co, a recent entrant into the market.

Flag Co

Flag Co was government owned until ten years ago but is now operated as a private company. Its mission is 'to be the airline of choice for long distance travellers'. It charges premium fares and operates routes from Jayland's capital city to the major airports serving the largest cities around the world. Many of its flights have durations greater than 12 hours The majority of its passengers are travelling on business and are prepared to pay high prices, however the demand for business travel is very sensitive to economic conditions. Its fleet of aircraft is regarded as 'ageing' by industry analysts.

Budget Co

Budget Co was founded by a wealthy entrepreneur who invested their personal fortune in the company's equity. Its mission is 'to be the lowest fare airline on any route we serve'. It offers flights to destinations up to three hours travel from Jayland. Its fleet of aircraft are generally less than two years old. Most of its passengers are holiday-makers and the demand for its flights appears to be relatively insensitive to economic conditions.

The following information is available for both companies:

Statement of profit or loss extract for the year end 31 December 20X6	**Flag Co**	**Budget Co**
	$m	$m
Total revenue	11,333	6,654
Operating profit	1,239	404
Finance costs	250	50
Other non-operating costs	130	76
Profit before tax	**859**	**278**

Statement of financial position (summarised) for the year end 31 December 20X6	**Flag Co**	**Budget Co**
	$m	$m
Non-current assets	11,972	3,177
Current assets **(Note 1)**	3,404	885
Total assets	**15,376**	**4,062**
Total equity	4,598	1,945
Non-current liabilities	5,078	1,001
Current liabilities	5,700	1,116
Total liabilities and shareholders' equity	**15,376**	**4,062**

Note 1: Current assets include inventory of $2.1m and $1.1m respectively.

Other information for year end 31 December 20X6	Flag Co	Budget Co
Aviation fuel litres consumed (millions)	2,434	1,246
Available seat kilometres (millions)	21,423	14,953
Passenger seat kilometres (millions)	14,201	14,206
Operating gearing (contribution/profit before interest and tax)	950%	820%

Required:

(a) Analyse the financial performance of the two airlines, including reasons for the differences in the two businesses' performance. (14 marks)

Note: Use the headings profitability, liquidity and risk to structure your answer. There are up to six marks available for calculations.

(b) Briefly explain how Fitzgerald and Moon's building block model could be used to manage the performance of a service business. (6 marks)

(Total: 20 marks)

307 CLEAN FEET CO (MARCH/JUNE 2022)

Clean Feet Co is a large supplier of environmentally-friendly products. The company is split into two divisions: the Household Goods division (Division HG) and the Personal Care division (Division PC). The two divisional managers are responsible for generating revenues and controlling costs. Both of them make all of their sales and purchases on credit, having negotiated 30-day credit terms with both customers and suppliers. Whilst the divisional managers can authorise capital expenditure up to $50,000, any expenditure over this amount is controlled by Head Office. All of the Head Office running costs are shared equally between the two divisions and are included in their 'indirect costs' below.

The performance of each division is assessed by Head Office using return on investment (ROI) based on net assets. Each of the divisional managers is paid an annual salary of $180,000 plus an annual bonus based on the ROI achieved by their division. Each division is expected to achieve a minimum ROI of 15% for which no bonus is payable, however, for every whole percentage point above this that the divisions achieve, the managers accrue a bonus of 3% of the annual salary. The maximum bonus which can be earned is 10% of the annual salary.

During the year ending 31 August 20X9, Head Office decided to invest $2m in a new computer system in Division HG. This was against the advice of the divisional manager and caused a lot of disruption to customer orders. Due to these issues, Head Office decided that a similar planned installation would not take place at Division PC.

The following data relates to the year ending 31 August 20X9:

	Division HG	**Division PC**
Sales	12,655	22,834
Direct costs	5,796	11,134
Indirect costs	4,023	6,078
Non-current Assets	14,570	20,698
Inventory	1,286	1,984
Cash	650	–
Trade receivables	1,040	3,753
Trade Payables	800	2,230
Overdraft	–	1,650
Number of orders completed within 7 days of the order being placed		
y/e 31 August 20X9	80%	95%
y/e 31 August 20X8	99%	97%
Customer complaints as percentage of total sales volume		
y/e 31 August 20X9	2%	1%
y/e 31 August 20X8	0.2%	0.5%
Staff turnover rate		
y/e 31 August 20X9	2%	18%
y/e 31 August 20X8	2%	8%

Required:

(a) For each of the divisions, calculate:

(i) the return on investment (ROI) for the year ending 31 August 20X9

(ii) the amount of bonus which each of the managers will receive for the year ending 31 August 20X9. **(4 marks)**

(b) Using your answer to part (a) and the data provided, assess the performance of each of the divisions, including the management of working capital. **(12 marks)**

Note: There are four marks available for calculations and eight marks for discussion.

(c) Discuss whether using return on investment (ROI) as a basis for assessing divisional performance and calculating bonuses at Clean Feet Co is appropriate, taking into consideration any issues which it may cause. **(4 marks)**

(Total: 20 marks)

308 WYELAND (SEPTEMBER/DECEMBER 2022)

The government of Wyeland is trying to reduce spending on public services as part of its effort to reduce the country's overall budget deficit. As a result, the government has announced plans to reduce the total budget for Wyeland's police forces by 3% for the year ended 30 June 20X8.

The Chief Police Officer, the most senior police officer in Wyeland, has reacted angrily to this announcement. They have stated that funding cuts like this will inevitably lead to a reduction in the number of police officers and a reduction in the level of service that the police forces across the country can provide.

Police forces in Wyeland are organised on a regional basis, but the overall aim of all the police forces in the country is 'to provide a value for money service to ensure the safety and security of communities across the country.'

In support of this overall aim, all of the police forces also have the following three objectives:

1 To reduce rates of crime

2 To identify offenders (those who carry out crimes) and bring them to justice

3 To provide the best possible protection and support for individuals and communities

There is a national target that 50% of crimes should be solved within one year of being reported.

At the end of the year, the performance of all the police forces is reviewed, and this review process is currently underway. Selected performance data for three of the regions for the year ended 30 June 20X8 is as follows:

	Northern	Central	Southern
Number of crimes reported in year	112,380	84,300	88,620
Number of crimes solved within 12 months of report	56,980	48,560	46,735
Number of police force employees	11,025	10,300	11,060
Annual cost of police force ($m)	735	685	715
Total population of the region	2,250,000	1,900,000	2,080,000

Required:

(a) Explain the terms economy, efficiency and effectiveness (3Es) in a value for money context. **(3 marks)**

(b) Using the 3Es headings in the template provided, assess the performance of each of the Northern, Central and Southern police forces in Wyeland for the year ended 30 June 20X8. **(17 marks)**

Note: There are 5 marks available for calculations and 12 marks available for discussion.

Northern region	
Economy	
Efficiency	
Effectiveness	

Central region	
Economy	

Efficiency	
Effectiveness	

Southern region	
Economy	
Efficiency	

Effectiveness	

(Total: 20 marks)

309 TROT CO (MARCH/JUNE 2023)

Trot Co is an owner-managed travel company operating in the country of Veeland where the domestic currency is Veeland $ (V$). It offers a range of package holidays to customers and the holiday price it charges to customers includes flights, transfers to and from resorts and accommodation costs.

The market is extremely competitive. Until recently, the company only offered holidays to Europe. However, following a consistent 5% annual decline in the European holiday market over the last two years, Trot Co decided to extend its coverage to North America from the beginning of 20X7. Flights to North America from Veeland are longer than flights to Europe from Veeland.

It is now the end of 20X7 and the following information is available.

At the beginning of 20X7, following the company's expansion into North America, Trot Co made an arrangement with a North American television station to place an advert every month. Each advert costs V$600. At the same time, Trot Co reduced its level of advertising in Veeland.

Six months ago, political unrest in Veeland caused the V$ to fall in value by an average of 25% against all other currencies. Trot Co pays for all flights, immediately when the customer makes a booking, in V$.

During the year, it also began using a new booking agent for flights who promised more competitive prices. Customers usually book their holidays at least six months in advance of their departure and are required to pay for their holidays in full at the time of booking in V$. The costs of accommodation and transfers are always paid by Trot Co in the currency of the country being visited and these costs are paid once the customer's holiday is complete.

Midway through 20X7, one of Trot Co's employees was awarded a V$22,000 compensation payment after a court decided that she was unfairly dismissed. All remaining staff were given a 10% pay rise with immediate effect in an attempt to reassure them.

Trot Co is financed partly by medium-term loans. One of the loans came to an end three months ago and the company therefore had to renegotiate a new loan. The new loan incurred a V$3,000 finance fee and a higher interest rate than the old loan. The new loan also covered the purchase of a new V$2,000 computerised billing system which was expected to reduce administration costs by 50%.

The results of Trot Co for the last two years are as follows:

	20X7		20X6	
	V$	V$	V$	V$
Revenue:				
Europe	512,000		640,000	
North America	256,000		0	
		768,000		640,000
Less: Cost of sales				
Flights	138,240		128,000	
Accommodation	384,000		256,000	
Transfers	96,000		64,000	
		(618,240)		(448,000)
Gross Profit		**149,760**		**192,000**
Less: Expenses				
Office rent	20,400		20,000	
Salaries	52,500		50,000	
Advertising	15,300		10,200	
Administration	12,600		14,000	
Finance costs	12,960		8,100	
Miscellaneous	48,000		12,000	
		(161,760)		(114,300)
Net Profit/(loss)		**(12,000)**		**77,700**

The owner of Trot Co has looked at 20X7's results and is extremely disappointed. Having seen that the business has made a loss, he feels like the whole expansion into North America was a bad idea.

Required:

Discuss the performance of Trot Co for 20X7.

Note: There are 6 marks for calculations and 14 marks for discussion.

(Total: 20 marks)

310 EASTERN HOSPITALS TRUST (MARCH/JUNE 2025)

The Eastern Hospitals Trust (EHT) is responsible for running three hospitals in the east of the country of Azuland. These hospitals are called the Mid-East, the North-East and the South-East.

EHT's overall objective is that its hospitals should '**provide top-quality medical services which are quick to access and supported by excellent patient care.**'

EHT is funded by the government of Azuland and does not charge patients for the services its hospitals offer, which include patient referral by a doctor and emergency treatment.

In recent years, government expenditure in Azuland has been significantly higher than tax revenues, and the government is trying to reduce public spending. As a result, EHT's funding has been reduced.

EHT's chief executive has raised concerns that these funding cuts could lead to a reduction in the number of staff employed at the hospitals which may affect the quality of care they provide to their patients.

The following table shows the actual results for the last financial year for the three hospitals compared against the key performance indicators EHT uses to assess hospital performance. The results have been verified by EHT's auditors.

	Note	Mid-East	North-East	South-East
% of emergency patients treated within four hours	1	94.0	89.5	91.0
% of non-emergency patient appointments scheduled within 12 weeks	2	95.0	91.0	92.5
% of patients who describe services as 'Excellent'	3	46.0	56.5	55.4
Quality Rating score	4	4.5	5.0	4.9
Average cost per patient ($000)		16.8	21.3	18.1
Overspend compared to budget ($000)		143.0	156.0	531.0

Notes

(1) All hospitals in Azuland have a target of treating emergency patients within four hours of them arriving at the hospital.

(2) The target for non-emergency patients is that they should attend their first hospital appointment within 12 weeks of being referred by their doctor.

(3) At the end of their treatment, patients (or their relatives if a patient is unable to respond directly) are asked to assess whether their quality of care has been 'Excellent', 'Very good', 'Good', 'Average' or 'Poor'.

(4) The Quality Rating is an assessment made by independent, external medical professionals who observe the quality of a sample of the medical procedures being carried out in a hospital. A score of 5 denotes 'Excellent' while 1 denotes 'Poor'.

Required:

(a) (i) **Define economy, efficiency and effectiveness (3 E's) in a value for money context.** **(3 marks)**

(ii) **Explain why it is important that EHT uses a balanced mix of performance measures across the 3 E's.** **(4 marks)**

(b) **Discuss the performance of the three hospitals using the performance data provided.**

Note: Use the headings Economy, Efficiency and Effectiveness to structure your answer. **(9 marks)**

(c) **Discuss TWO challenges EHT might face when measuring the performance of its overall objective.** **(4 marks)**

(Total: 20 marks)

Section 4

ANSWERS TO OBJECTIVE TEST QUESTIONS – SECTION A

MANAGEMENT INFORMATION SYSTEMS AND DATA ANALYTICS

MANAGEMENT INFORMATION SYSTEMS

1 The second and third statements are correct.

A lack of compatibility with existing or other systems is a typical risk or disadvantage of new information system investments. Increased training for staff to become familiar with the system is also considered a disadvantage of a new information system.

2 **B**

An extranet can limit both the amount of information available and the users who have access to it. Giving access to an intranet would open access to more information than the airline would desire to give access to. The internet is more commonly used to give public information to everyone. Emails are unlikely to provide real time information.

3 **A**

A memory stick is much more likely to get mislaid and compromise security than a password protected laptop. It is likely that memory sticks could get lost or that information is left on home computers.

In the context of the scenario all the other options are good practice.

4 **C**

The other statements are not true. Robust security procedures (such as strong passwords) can limit access to a wireless network. Wireless networks can often cover larger distances than wired networks (for example, nurses are likely to be able to access data in rooms where there are no wired access points). There will be no requirement to buy new user devices (although many businesses who switch to wireless technology choose to do so); existing user devices should work with both wired and wireless technology.

But wireless networks can be prone to interference from other devices and networks which can result in them being less stable than wired networks.

5 D

A universal password would apply to everyone and therefore there would be no way to trace the person responsible for printing/transferring or amending the information.

The other three options are common methods for securing the confidentiality of information.

6 C

Statement (1) is correct. Networked computers can share hardware, such as printers and software, such as accountancy packages. Networks can also share data.

Statement (2) is incorrect. An intranet is an internal network that can be used to share information and communication within the organisation. An extranet would be used to communicate with suppliers.

Statement (3) is correct. Adding additional cabling to a wired network can be disruptive and costly. Wireless networks do not need additional cabling and new users can be added relatively easily.

Statement (4) is correct. Organisations can use the internet to, for example, monitor social media which is a useful way to measure customer interest.

7 B

Data visualisation is based on the data available so it can only be as accurate as the original data. Visualisation does not improve this accuracy.

8 B, E

9 A

10 A

Monitoring the usage and access logs on a regular basis would have revealed that the human resource director's account was being accessed whilst they were on vacation and that confidential information was being looked at and copied. This would have enabled the company to investigate immediately and the individual could have been identified sooner, which could have prevented the sensitive information from being divulged to everyone in the company.

Selecting options B, C and D would have been ineffective in this instance. Even if certain information was restricted to only director level, or that the information the director had access to, was on a separate server, or that the director was prompted regularly to change passwords; none of these controls would have helped as the director had shared his confidential account details with the junior employee.

11 B, D

This is an unusual scenario for information security, and one that is not often encountered in the workplace, as there is no use of networked technology. Hence, the common controls of firewalls and anti-spyware may not be suitable.

It is essential that the information provided in a scenario is carefully read and interpreted, and that assumptions are not made as to the suitability of generic approaches. The ability to apply generic concepts to a specified scenario is a key one in the Performance Management exam.

In this situation as the computers used by the consultant are non-networked a firewall and anti-spyware are not needed to preserve security at the consultant end.

The consultants will need lockable cabinets/safes for the hard copy design documents to be kept secure, along with any hard drives awaiting dispatch back to Bazile Co. Bazile Co will need similar secure storage for the receipt of items from the consultants.

A confidentiality contract will serve as a legal support to protect the commercially sensitive information.

12 B

Many cloud services are provided by external third parties, and therefore reliance on these suppliers will be increased.

13 B

'Acceptable' is not part of the ACCURATE mnemonic.

14 C

The increase in costs is less than $3,700. It is unlikely that cost of preparing the report would be beneficial even if all of the increase was due to increased printing of emails.

15 C

Summarised information is characteristic of strategic reports, as is external information on local competition. Operational reports are likely to be produced frequently (sometimes daily) and contain accurate information on a business' current position.

USES AND CONTROL OF INFORMATION

16 C

Strategic reports typically display highly summarised showing overall trends, with options to 'drill down' to obtain detail.

17 A

Long-term forecasts are usually associated with strategic planning.

18

	Suited to all levels of management	Not suited to all levels of management
A Management Information System producing management accounts showing margins for individual customers	✓	
A Customer Relationship Management system tracking the acquisition, retention and extension of all customers	✓	
An Executive Information System giving access to internal and external information in summarised form, with the option to drill down to a greater level of activity		✓

EIS systems are usually suited to Senior Executives and strategic planning.

19 D

The tracking and summarising of critical strategic information is done by an Executive Information System (EIS).

The other three options are all likely to be potential benefits which would result from the introduction of an ERPS.

20 D

Option A is a Customer Relationship Management system. Option B is an Enterprise Resource Management system, and option C is an example of a Management Information System.

21 B

The report is a typical example of an output from a Management Information System.

22 B

Option A is Data mining. Option C is a Customer Relationship Management system. Option D is a Transaction Processing System.

BIG DATA AND DATA ANALYTICS

23 D

The first three options are typical characteristics of big data. Vicinity is not normally a word that would be associated with big data.

24 The second and third statements are correct

One of the 'V's' of big data is its velocity – it is created and can change very quickly. Another 'V' is its variety which suggests that it can take multiple forms.

Statement 1 is not correct. Another 'V' that is associated with big data is its veracity – it is often difficult to assess its reliability and accuracy and there is no reason why it should be considered more reliable than other sources of data.

Statement 4 is not correct. Big data does not simply refer to financial numbers nor do the numbers themselves have to be big.

25 D

If organisations analyse big data they can often better understand areas such as customer tastes, potential changes in the market or potential problems in supply chains. If this data is used accurately it can allow the organisation to react in quicker and better ways than rivals and to achieve a competitive advantage.

Option A is not correct. Big data can be useful for any size of organisations. Even the smallest of organisations, can analyse, say, the data contained on their social media feeds.

Options B and C are not correct. Big data refers to any unstructured data, not just data stored or contained on the internet. Many organisations find that they already hold lots of data on customers but it just hasn't been structured yet. This also explains why the data may have been generated internally.

26 A

Using big data allow organisations to react more quickly than rivals in the marketplace giving them a competitive edge. This can be achieved by better tracking of consumer trends as well as the actions of competitors themselves. The actions and changes of competitors can be accounted for by examining data on rivals such as their public announcements and market expectations.

27 The second and third statements are correct

Statement 1 is not correct. One of the criticisms in analysing big data is that it still requires interpretation. This is only of value to the organisation if the analyst also has a deep understanding of the industry.

Statement 4 is not correct. Firstly, analysing all available big data would be almost impossible and certainly very expensive. But it is not all likely to be of use to an organisation. For example, a small accountancy practice would gain little benefit in analysing big data on the potential benefits of future space travel.

28 B

Big data should be used alongside traditional sources of data to make business decisions. There is no reason for traditional sources of data such as economic data, sales trends etc. to be ignored.

The other statements are risks of using big data analytics in making business decisions.

SPECIALIST COST AND MANAGEMENT ACCOUNTING TECHNIQUES

ACTIVITY-BASED COSTING

29 The third and fourth statements are correct.

ABC does not affect the prime cost of products. It will however give better details on indirect costs which will be shared between products on a fairer basis (thus impacting on the total production cost of each product and potentially the selling price of each product). This is also likely to make cost control of indirect overheads easier.

30 **$71.43**

Alpha batches (2,500/500) = 5; therefore inspections required for Alpha (5 × 4) = 20

Zeta batches (8,000/1,000) = 8; therefore inspections required for Zeta (8 × 1) = 8

OAR = $250,000/28 = $8,928.57

Alpha cost/unit = (20 × $8,928.57)/2,500 units = $71.43

31 **D**

Statement (1) provides a definition of a cost driver. Cost drivers for long-term variable overhead costs will be the volume of a particular activity to which the cost driver relates, so Statement (2) is correct.

Statement (3) is also correct. In traditional absorption costing, standard high-volume products receive a higher amount of overhead costs than with ABC. ABC allows for the unusually high costs of support activities for low-volume products (such as relatively higher set-up costs, order processing costs and so on).

32 **$0.50**

Cost driver = number of set-ups	Cost pool = $12,000
Total set-ups = 20 (for A) + 4 (for B) = 24	Rate = $12,000/24 = $500 per set-up
Cost for A = $500 × 20 set-ups = $10,000	Per unit=$10,000/20,000 = $0.50

33 **A**

Statement (2) is not correct. Although the OAR is calculated in the same way as the absorption costing OAR, a separate OAR will be calculated for each cost pool.

34 **$0.60**

Cost driver = number of set-ups

Cost pool = $84,000

Total set-ups= 20 (for A) + 8 (for B) = 28

Rate =$84,000/28 = $3,000 per set-up

Cost for B = $3,000 × 8 set-ups = $24,000

Per unit = $24,000/40,000 = $0.60.

35 $31.82

$$\text{Overhead absorption rate} = \frac{\text{Total overhead cost}}{\text{Total number of direct labour hours}}$$

$$\text{Overhead absorption rate} = \frac{\$420{,}000}{66{,}000\ \text{Direct labour hours}}$$

Overhead absorption rate = $6.36 per labour hour. Alpha uses 5 direct labour hours per unit so will have an overhead cost per unit of 5 hours × $6.36 per hour = $31.82.

36 C

The overhead cost per unit for each unit of product Beta will be the same as product Alpha (see calculations in Q above), as both products use the same number of labour hours (5 hours).

37 C

	Volume related	**Purchasing related**	**Set-up related**
Costs	$100,000	$145,000	$175,000
Consumption of activities (cost drivers)	66,000 labour hours	160 purchase orders	100 set-ups
Cost per unit of cost driver	$1.5151 per labour hour	$906.25 per purchase order	$1,750 per set-up
Costs per product			
Product Alpha:	6,000 labour hours cost: $9,090.91	75 purchase orders cost: $67,968.75	40 set-ups cost: $70,000
Product Beta:	60,000 labour hours cost: $90,909.09	85 purchase orders cost: $77,031.25	60 set-up cost: $105,000

Total overhead cost for Alpha = $9,090.91 + $67,968.75 + $70,000 = $147,060. Spread over 1,200 units, this represents a cost per unit of $122.55 approx.

38 B

Total material budget ((1,000 units × $10) + (2,000 units × $20)) = $50,000 Fixed costs related to material handling = $100,000

OAR = $2/$ of material

Product B = $2 × $20 = $40

Total labour budget ((1,000 units × $5) + (2,000 units × $20) = $45,000 General fixed costs = $180,000

OAR = $4/$ of labour

Product B = $4 × $20 = $80

Total fixed overhead cost per unit of Product B ($40 + $80) = $120.

39 Increase, Increase, Decrease

	Increase	Decrease
Product X	✓	
Product Y	✓	
Product Z		✓

Absorption costing

Since the time per unit is the same for each product, the overheads per unit will also be the same.

$156,000 ÷ 6,000 units = $26

Activity based costing

Number of deliveries for X (1,000/200)	5
Number of deliveries for Y (2,000/400)	5
Number of deliveries for Z (3,000/1,000)	3
Total	**13**

Cost per delivery = $156,000/13 = $12,000

Cost per unit of X = ($12,000/1,000 units) × 5 deliveries = $60

Increase = $60 – $26 = $34.

Cost per unit of Y = ($12,000/2,000 units) × 5 deliveries = $30

Increase = $30 – $26 = $4.

Cost per unit of Z = ($12,000/3,000 units) × 3 deliveries = $12

Decrease = $26 – $12 = $14.

40 **B**

Total set-ups = Budget production/batch size × set-ups per batch

D (100,000/100 × 3)	3,000
R (100,000/50 × 4)	8,000
P (50,000/25 × 6)	12,000
	23,000

Cost per set-up = $150,000/23,000 = $6.52

Therefore cost per unit of R = $6.52 × 8,000 set-ups/100,000 units = $0.52.

TARGET COSTING

41 D

Answer A is not correct: increasing the selling price is not possible, the industry is competitive so product will not sell effectively at higher prices.

Answer B ('Reduce the expectation gap by reducing the selling price') is not target costing.

Answer C ('Reducing the desired margin on the product') is not possible either: shareholders are demanding and would expect a good return.

42 The maximum rate per hour is **$12.40**

	$
Selling price	56.00
Profit (56 × 25/125)	11.20
Target cost	**44.80**
Material cost (16 × 10/8)	20.00
Labour – 2 hours	24.80
Labour rate per hour = 24.80/2	$12.40

43 B

Variance analysis is not relevant to target costing as it is a technique used for cost control at the production phase of the product life cycle. It is a feedback control tool by nature and target costing is feedforward.

Value analysis can be used to identify where small cost reductions can be applied to close a cost gap once production commences.

Functional analysis can be used at the product design stage. It ensures that a cost gap is reached or to ensure that the product design is one which includes only features which customers want.

Activity analysis identifies and describes activities in an organisation and evaluates their impact on operations to assess where improvements can be made.

44 D

Sales revenue 500 units @ $250	$125,000
Return on investment required 15% × $250,000	$37,500
Total cost allowed	$87.500
Target cost per unit	$175

45 D

It is simultaneous as there is no delay between the service being provided by the optician and consumed by the patient.

46 The correct answer is

Step 1 Develop the product concept

Step 2 Set the selling price

Step 3 Determine the profit margin

Step 4 Cost the product

Step 5 Identify the cost gap

Step 6 Use functional and value analysis

Traditional pricing techniques such as cost-plus take the production costs of a product and add on a required mark-up or margin to arrive at the selling price. Target costing works in a different way in that it consults the external market to ascertain the selling price that the market would accept.

Once a product concept has been developed, the company will take this to the market and use the feedback gathered to set the selling price. The company will then apply its required profit margin to this selling price and calculate the target production cost. This is the maximum cost that the company can incur in the production of the product and still earn the required margin. This target cost is then compared to the calculated cost of production and any cost gap is identified. The company must then use techniques such as functional and value analysis in order to close the cost gap.

LIFE-CYCLE COSTING

47 C

Variable production costs ($2.30 × 2,000) + ($1.80 × 5,000) + ($1.20 × 7,000) = $22,000

Variable selling costs ($0.50 × 2,000) + ($0.40 × 5,000) + ($0.40 × 7,000) = $5,800

Fixed production costs = $10,500; Fixed selling costs = $4,700

Administrative costs = $2,100

Total costs = $45,100

Cost per unit = $45,100/14,000 units = $3.22

48 C

OAR for fixed production overheads ($72 million/96 million hours) = $0.75 per hour

Total manufacturing costs (300,000 units × $20) = $6,000,000

Total design, depreciation and decommissioning costs = $1,320,000

Total fixed production overheads (300,000 units × 4 hours × $0.75) = $900,000

Total life-cycle costs = $8,220,000 and life-cycle cost per unit ($8,220,000/300,000 units) = $27.40

49 D

Life-cycle costs calculated as follows:

	Calculation	Total cost ($000)
R&D		950
Marketing	$230k + $120k + $20k + $5k	375
Production cost	$450 × 10k + $430 × 12k + $290 × 11.1k + $290 × 3k	13,749
Warranty costs	$30 × 10k + $30 × 12k + $40 × 11.1k + $45 × 3k	1,239
End of life		125
Total life-cycle costs		**16,438**

Total units = 10k +12k + 11.1k + 3k = 36.1k

Life-cycle cost per unit = $16,438k ÷ 36.1k = $455.35

This is more than the average price of $420 that consumers are willing to pay. So statement (1) is true.

More R&D would reduce defects in future years and therefore reduce warranty costs, so Statement (2) is also true.

50 Benefits are:

- It provides a true financial cost of a product
- Expensive errors can be avoided in that potentially failing products can be avoided
- Lower costs can be achieved earlier by designing out costs
- Better selling prices can be set.

Note: Shortening the length of a lifecycle is not desirable and decline (for most products) inevitable.

51 A

1 This is true, justifying the time and effort of life cycle costing.

2 As above.

3 This is not true: life cycle costing is not about setting selling prices, it is about linking total revenues to total costs. Even if it were about setting a selling price, the early sales may well be at a loss since it is TOTAL revenues and costs that are considered. Furthermore, the pre-launch costs are sunk at launch and are therefore irrelevant when setting a selling price.

4 This is true. The deliberate attempt to maximise profitability is the key to life cycle costing.

52 B

53 A

The original life cycle cost per unit = ($43,000 + (20,000 × $15) + $30,000)/20,000 = $18.65

THROUGHPUT ACCOUNTING

54 C

Overall the cost per unit should reduce, and so the measure for throughput should improve.

A is wrong as the TPAR measures return based on the slowest machine not the fastest. B is wrong since rent has increased so the TPAR will worsen from its current level. D is wrong since we cannot meet demand even at the moment so reducing prices will reduce throughput per unit without any extra sales level benefit.

55

	Product X	Product Y	Product Z
Throughput per unit (selling price – direct material cost)	$20	$30	$4
Machine hours per unit	10	20	2.5
Return per hour (throughput per unit ÷ machine hours per unit)	**$2**	**$1.5**	**$1.6**

As all three products are mutually exclusive, the company would choose to make X as it has the highest throughput return per hour of $2.

Changes to the selling price and material cost of Product X and Product Z will only change the TPAR if the values change enough to mean that the company would prefer to make that product instead of product X. This means the products' return per hour after the changes would need to be more than $2 per hour.

Option 1: return per hour = ($22–$16)/2.5 = $2.4. This would improve the company's TA ratio as now Z would be made instead of X and the TPAR would be higher.

Option 2: return per hour = ($44–$10)/20 = $1.7. This would not improve the company's TA ratio.

Option 3: return per hour = ($20–$15.2)/2.5 = $1.92. This would not improve the company's TA ratio.

Option 4: return per hour = (40–9.5)/20 = $1.525. This would not improve the company's TA ratio.

Of the four possible options, only increasing the selling price of product Z by 10% would give a higher throughput return per hour of $2.40.

	Would improve the company's existing TA ratio?	**Would NOT improve the company's existing TA ratio?**
Increase the selling price of product Z by 10%	✓	
Increase the selling price of product Y by 10%		✓
Reduce the material cost of product Z by 5%		✓
Reduce the material cost of product Y by 5%		✓

56 $60.00

The first step is to identify the bottleneck.

Process P output is 6 × 8 × 0.9 = 43.2 per hour. Process Q output is 9 × 6 × 0.85 = 45.9 per hour. In the absence of other information, then process P is slower, and so is the bottleneck.

Cloud:

Throughput:	$
Selling price ($20 × 0.85)	17.00
Material cost	5.00
Throughput per unit	12.00
Time in process P (hrs)	0.2
TP per hour	60.00

57 D

As the products are all produced in the same factory the cost per machine hour will be the same across all the products so they can be ranked on their throughput return per machine hour (otherwise they should be ranked on their throughput accounting ratio).

Product	**Production rate per machine hour (units)**	**Throughput per unit (selling price – material cost) ($)**	**Throughput per machine hour ($)**	**Ranking of products**
W	200	230	(200 × $230) = 46,000	3rd
X	500	95	(500 × $95) = 47,500	2nd
Y	400	110	(400 × $110) = 44,000	4th
Z	350	140	(350 × $140) = 49,000	1st

The products would be ranked in order: Z, X, W and Y. Product Y would be ranked forth (last).

58 A

Tutorial note

This question tested candidates' knowledge of throughput accounting, and specifically how throughput can be improved. It is also a good example of a question where it's important not to rush – all of the possible answers could improve throughput, depending on what our bottleneck (limiting factor) is – Process 1, 2 or 3. If none of the processes are limited, then increasing demand would improve throughput.

Throughput is determined by the bottleneck resource. Process 2 is the bottleneck as it has insufficient time to meet demand.

The only option to improve Process 2 is to improve the efficiency of the maintenance routine. All the other three options either increase the time available on non-bottleneck resources or increase demand for an increase in supply which cannot be achieved.

59 D

All of these points are true, except D.

Throughput accounting was designed as a performance measurement tool, not a decision-making tool.

One of its advantages is that it will be used by managers to make decisions that have outcomes that are goal congruent with corporate aims. However, it was designed as a performance measurement tool.

ENVIRONMENTAL ACCOUNTING

Tutorial note

A technical article 'Environmental Management Accounting' has been published on the ACCA website – make sure you read it as part of your revision.

60 B, H

Waste water has been produced which is a failure cost, but it has been cleaned **before** leaving the factory, making it an internal failure cost.

Likewise, waste exhaust gases have been produced, but these have been captured and recycled within the factory.

Environmental prevention costs relate to activities or measure which aim to avoid the pollution or wastage occurring. Insulation of heating pipes in the factory to reduce heat loss and fitting of carbon filters to machine processes to reduce carbon emissions would come under this heading.

Environmental detection costs relate to the costs incurred to test the levels of emissions and wastage to ensure that the organisation is being compliant with internal standards and external regulations. Quality control inspections to monitor pollution levels in water leaving a production process and power usage measuring system to monitor energy consumption within the factory would come under this heading.

External failure costs relate to pollution which has affected the outside environment. Payment of fines for breaching environmental regulations in the industry and public relations costs to remedy reputational damage caused by accidental river pollution would be examples of environmental external failure costs.

61 D

Revised tables:

INPUTS

Description	**Comment**	**Weight (kg)**	**USD value**
Materials		1,000	(50,000)
System costs	Labour, utilities, etc.	–	(35,000)
Total			(85,000)

OUTPUTS

Description	**Comment**	**Weight (kg)**	**USD value**
Good output	Expected good output is 76% of input and can be sold for $120 per kg	760	91,200
Waste	Expected waste is 4% of input and must be scrapped at a cost of $10 per kg	40	(400)
Scrap	Expected scrap is 20% of input and can be sold for $15 per kg	200	3,000
Total		1,000	93,800

Revised profit = 93,800 – 85,000 = $8,800

This gives an increase of $2,800

Alternative answer

Impact on profit = extra revenue + cost savings + extra costs

= (60 × 120) + (60 × 10) – 5,000

= $2,800

62 D

Under a system of flow cost accounting material flows are divided into three categories – material, system, and delivery and disposal.

63 Only the first two statements are true.

64 $22,000

Input materials and system costs work out as $80 per kg.

This means that the total input costs to be allocated to waste and scrap = 300 × 80 = (24,000)

Overall net cost of waste and scrap = 3,000 – 1,000 – 24,000 = (22,000)

65 The first and third statements are true.

Manufacturing costs are categorised into material costs, system costs and delivery and disposal costs. After dividing material flows into three categories (material, system and delivery and disposal costs), flow cost accounting calculates the values and costs of each of these three flows. Output costs are allocated between positive products (good finished output) and negative product costs (costs of waste and emissions).

The second statement is not correct: this is a definition of the input/output analysis method of accounting for environmental costs.

The fourth statement is not correct: The aim of flow cost accounting is to reduce the quantity of materials which, as well as having a positive effect on the environment, should have a positive effect on a business' total costs in the long run.

66 D

67 D

Waste flows are not a category used within flow cost accounting, however, the other three categories are.

68 B

Environmental costs can be very long-term, are often not split out in accounting systems and may be hidden. All of this makes accounting for environmental costs difficult. The size of the costs should have no impact on the accountants ability to deal with the costs and is not a valid reason for the difficulties in dealing with environmental costs.

69 C

Measuring the various aspects of TBL (such as the organisation's impact on the planet and people) can be very subjective. Often the measures are difficult and time-consuming to monitor and report on.

DECISION-MAKING TECHNIQUES

RELEVANT COST ANALYSIS

70 B

The original cost is an historic cost and therefore not relevant. There is no intention to replace material X. There are two options for material X, scrap at a value of 50p per kg or use as a replacement for material Y, which would save $4 per kg ($6 – $2). The latter is the preferable option so the relevant cost is $4 per kg for 10 kgs = $40.

71 C

Labour is in short supply so there is an opportunity cost. The contribution from Contract Z will still be earned but will be delayed. The relevant cost is therefore the wages earned plus the penalty fee.

($15 × 100) + ($1,000) = $2,500

72 C

Since material J is in regular use and is readily available in the market, its relevant cost is the replacement price of $8/kg.

So 2,000 kgs × $8/kg = $16,000

73 A

3,700 kg × $3.80 + 500 kg × $6.30 = $17,210

Tutorial note

The company needs 4,200 kg. It has 3,700 kg in inventory. It will therefore need to buy 500 kg and these can be bought for $6.30 per kg. The tricky bit is the value to the company of the 3,700 kg in inventory. The $4.50 original price is of course a sunk cost and cannot be relevant. The inventory can be sold for $3.20 per kg, so this is its very minimum value.

The inventory is worth $3.20 per kg unless the company has an even better alternative – and there is a better alternative. The company can take the inventory and, by spending $3.70 per kg on it, can turn it into something worth $7.50 per kg. If something will be worth $7.50 if we spend $3.70 on it, then it is at present worth $3.80. This then is the value of the inventory to the company and to fulfil the contract the company will use 3,700 kg of inventory with a value of $3.80 per kg.

74 C

The relevant cash flow is:

Lost disposal proceeds (net)	$10,300
Additional costs of set up	$1,300
Total	$11,600

75 A

The relevant cash flow is:

Extra variable overheads: 450 hours × $4/hr	$1,800
Rent	$1,200
Total	$3,000

Fixed costs are not incremental and idle time would normally mean that the machines are not in use are so are not an incurred cost.

76 D

The options are:

Agency 600 × $9/hr =	$5,400
Internal transfer 600 × (7 + 3) =	$6,000
Hire new $1,200 + (600 × $6/hr)	$4,800

Cleverclogs would select the lower of the costs and so this is the relevant cash flow.

77 B

The book value is not relevant as it is a sunk cost. The relevant cost of the paper in inventory is the resale value as that is its next best use. The remaining material required must be bought at the replacement cost of $26.

100 reams @ $10	$1,000
150 reams @ $26	$3,900
	$4,900

COST VOLUME PROFIT ANALYSIS

78 B

Two units of Y and one unit of X would give total contribution of $18. Weighted average contribution per unit = $18/3 units = $6

Sales units to achieve target profit = ($90,000 + $45,000)/$6 = 22,500

79 B

Current breakeven point is: $640,000/40 =	16,000 units
New breakeven point is: $400,000/35 =	11,429 units
Change in level of breakeven is 16,000 – 11,429 =	4,571 units
Current contribution is: $60 – $20 =	$40
New contribution is $60 – $20 – $5 =	$35

Operating gearing reduces with less fixed costs in a business.

80 18,637 units

Number of units required to make target profit = fixed costs + target profit/contribution per unit of P1.

Fixed costs = ($1.2 × 10,000) + ($1 × 12,500) – $2,500 = $22,000.

Contribution per unit of P = $3.20 + $1.20 = $4.40.

($22,000 + $60,000)/$4.40 = 18,637 units rounded up.

81 C

Contribution: $5,000,000 – ($1,400,000 + $400,000) =	$3,200,000
For 20,000 units, that is a contribution of	$160 per unit
Fixed costs amount to $1,600,000 + $1,200,000 =	$2,800,000
BEP units = FC/Unit contribution i.e. $2,800,000/$160 =	17,500

82

Selling price per unit ($36/0.75) =	$48
Contribution per unit $48 – $36 =	$12
Fixed costs	$18,000
Therefore, breakeven point (units) is $18,000/$12 =	1,500

83 D

If budgeted sales increase to 40,000 units, then budgeted profit will increase by $100,000. This is because 10,000 more units will be sold at a contribution per unit of $10. The fixed costs would not be expected to change.

84 D

	Now	**Revised**
	$	$
Selling price	20	21.60
Variable cost	8	8.416
	12	13.184

Breakeven volume now: $79,104/$12 = 6,592

Breakeven volume revised: $79,104/$13.184 = 6,000

Decrease in breakeven volume = 592/6,592 × 100% = 9%

85 D

The breakeven revenue (BER) = Fixed costs/average CS ratio

BER = $1,400,000/0.2375 (W1) = $5,894,737

(W1)

	Product F $	**Product G** $	**Total** $
Budget revenue	6,000,000	2,000,000	8,000,000
Contribution	1,500,000	400,000	1,900,000
C/S	0.25	0.2	
Average C/S			0.2375

86 C

Because the C/S ratio of product G is lower than F the change in mix would reduce the average C/S ratio. As a consequence, the breakeven revenue would increase by an amount but not by the amount of extra sales of product G. This is not relevant.

87 A

The shaded area on the breakeven chart represents loss.

88 B

The fixed costs are at the point where the profit line meets the vertical axis.

89 B

Statement (1) is correct. The line which passes through the origin indicates the sales revenue at various levels of activity. At an activity level of 10,000 units, the sales revenue is $100,000, therefore the selling price is $10 per unit.

Statement (2) is incorrect. The sloping line which intercepts the vertical axis at $30,000 shows the total cost at various levels of activity. The total cost for 10,000 units is $80,000, from which we subtract the $30,000 fixed costs.

Statement (3) is correct. The fixed cost is the cost incurred at zero activity, and is shown as a horizontal line at $30,000.

Statement (4) is incorrect. The profit for 10,000 units is the difference between the sales value $100,000 and the total cost of $80,000, which amounts to $20,000.

90 The second and third statements '3,152 units of sales are required to achieve a profit of $100,000 next month' and 'Monthly fixed costs amount to $136,400' are correct.

Fixed overheads every month amount to $22 fixed overhead per unit × 6,200 units = $136,400

The key to calculating the breakeven point is to determine the contribution per unit.

Contribution per unit = sales price – variable costs

Contribution per unit = $199 – $54 – $50 – $20

Contribution per unit = $75

Breakeven point in units = (Fixed costs/contribution per unit)

Breakeven point in units = $136,400/$75

Breakeven point in units = 1,819 units (and so the first statement is not correct.)

To achieve a profit of $100,000 next month:

Units of sales required = (Fixed costs + target profit)/unit contribution

Units of sales required = ($136,400 + $100,000)/$75

Units of sales required = 3,152

$$\text{Margin of safety expressed as a \%} = \frac{\text{Budgeted sales} - \text{breakeven sales}}{\text{Budgeted sales}} \times 100$$

Margin of safety = (6,200 units – 1,819 units)/6,200 units = 71% (and so the fourth statement is not correct.)

91 The first two statements are correct: point A is the breakeven point if the company's products are sold in order of their C/S ratio, and point B is the breakeven point if the company's products are sold in the budgeted sales mix.

Statement 3 is not correct. Changing the product mix in favour of Product 3, that has a negative contribution and reduces the cumulative profit, would impact negatively on the overall c/s ratio.

Statement 4 is not correct: if all three products are produced, then the company can expect a profit (not revenue) of $350,000.

92 **58.3%**

The breakeven revenue is FC/CS = $1,600,000/0.4 =	$4,000,000
Budget revenue is FC × 6 = $1,600,000 × 6 =	$9,600,000
Margin of safety is = (9,600,000 – 4,000,000)/9,600,000 =	58.3%

LIMITING FACTORS

93 Should be produced, Should not be produced, Should not be produced, Should be produced

	Should be produced	Should not be produced
Product A	✓	
Product B		✓
Product C		✓
Product D	✓	

Product	A	B	C	D
Selling price per unit	$160	$214	$100	$140
Raw material costs	$24	$56	$22	$40
Direct labour cost at $11 per hour	$66	$88	$33	$22
Variable overhead cost	$24	$18	$24	$18
Contribution per unit	$46	$52	$21	$60
	———	———	———	———
Direct labour hours per unit	6	8	3	2
Contribution per labour hour	$7.67	$6.50	$7	$30
	———	———	———	———
Rank	2	4	3	1
Normal monthly hours (total units × hours per unit)	1,800	1,000	720	800

If the strike goes ahead, only 2,160 labour hours will be available. Therefore make all of Product D, then 1,360 hours' worth of Product A (2,160 – 800 hrs).

94 8,000

The optimal production plan will have to be determined by using a simultaneous equations technique.

If the unskilled labour function is multiplied by 3:

Skilled labour: $6X + 4Y \leq 62,000$

Unskilled labour: $6X + 15Y \leq 150,000$

Deducting one from the other, leaves:

$11Y = 88,000$

$Y = 8,000$

95 A

If the values for R and N are substituted into the constraints:

Labour required = (3 × 500) + (2 × 400) = 2,300 hours which is less than what is available so there is slack.

Machine time required = (0.5 × 500) + (0.4 × 400) = 410 hours which is exactly what is available and so there is no slack.

96 D

The company maximises contribution by producing Qutwo. Contribution per unit of material is:

$\frac{\$8.50}{2.5 \text{ kg}}$ = \$3.40 and this is the shadow price.

97 C

A shadow price for a scarce resource is its opportunity cost. It is the amount of contribution that would be lost if one unit less of that resource were available. It is similarly the amount of additional contribution that would be earned if one unit more of that resource were available. (This is on the assumption that the scarce resource is available at its normal variable cost.)

98 D

	R	S	T
	$	$	$
Contribution per unit			
$(100 – 15 – 20 – 15)	50		
$(150 – 30 – 35 – 20)		65	
$(160 – 25 – 30 – 22)			83
Direct labour cost per unit	20	35	30
Contribution per $1 of direct labour	2.50	1.85	2.77
Profitability ranking	2nd	3rd	1st

99 B

By definition, a shadow price is the amount by which contribution will increase if an extra kg of material becomes available. 20 × $2.80 = $56.

Tutorial note

In this question, the shadow price is $2.80 per unit, and therefore if 20 kgs of additional material Z becomes available, the increase in contribution would be $56 (20 × $2.80). The answer is therefore B. In the first distractor A, the cost of the material (20 kg × $2) has also been added to the $56. This is because a common mistake made is to add the cost of the material in too.

Similarly, in distractor C, the $40 has been deducted from the $56 leaving a figure of $16. This is because candidates often fail to realise that the shadow price is the amount over and above the normal cost that one would be prepared to pay for an extra unit of scarce material if it becomes available. Therefore, this would lead candidates to think that contribution would only increase by $0.80 ($2.80 – $2) for each extra kg of material Z that becomes available resulting in a total increase in contribution of only $16.

100 A

The slope of the iso-contribution line will be determined by the relative contribution per unit of each product. If it is very flat, the product on the vertical axis must have a higher contribution than the product on the horizontal axis.

101 The first statement is not true: linear programming is only suitable when there are two products.

The second statement is not true: : there needs to be more than one limiting factor, but it is not essential for one of these two to be the level of demand.

The third statement is correct: fixed costs do not change and do not need to be considered.

The fourth statement is correct: a steady state being reached means that variable costs are constant.

102 C

The optimal production plan will have to be determined by using a simultaneous equations technique.

If the Material X function is multiplied by 2:

Material X: 2A + 4B = 16,000

Material Y: 2A + B = 13,000

Deducting one from the other, leaves:

3B = 3,000

B = 1,000

Substituting this into one of the equations:

2A + (4 × 1,000) = 16,000

2A = 12,000

A = 6,000

103 Only direct labour hours will have a shadow price.

Only resources that meet at the optimal point will have a shadow price. This is at point B, where the direct labour line meets line R. The other constraints lines are above this point and there therefore must be surplus of these resources available. Resources that have a surplus do not have a shadow price.

PRICING DECISIONS

104 D

Penetration pricing involves setting a low price when a product is first launched in order to obtain strong demand.

It is particularly useful if significant economies of scale can be achieved from a high volume of output and if demand is highly elastic and so would respond well to low prices.

105 C

106 The second and third options are valid. If demand is inelastic or the product life cycle is short, a price skimming approach would be more appropriate.

107 B

108 B

From the formula provided, we can see a = 1,500 and b = –0.01

At the profit maximising point, MR = MC, where MR = a + 2bQ

MR = $1,500 – 0.02Q

MC = $200

Set MR = MC in order to maximise profit, and find profit maximising quantity:

1,500 – 0.02Q = 200

0.02Q = 1,300

Q = 65,000 units

Substitute Q = 65,000 in to the demand equation to find profit maximising price:

P = $1,500 – (0.01 × 65,000)

P = $850

Finally work out the maximum profit:

	$
Revenue ($850 × 65,000)	55,250,000
Variable costs ($200 × 65,000)	(13,000,000)
Fixed costs	(20,000,000)
Maximum total profit	**22,250,000**

109 C

Prime cost + 80% = 12 × (1.8) = $21.6

MC + 60% = 15 × (1.6) = $24.00

TAC + 20% = 21 × (1.2) = $25.20

Net margin would mean 21 × 100/86 = $24.40

110 C

b = –20/1,000 or –0.02

By substitution:

400 = a – 0.02 (5,000)

a = $500

MR = $500 – 0.04Q

MC = $200

Set MR = MC in order to profit maximise thus:

500 – 0.04Q = 200

–0.04 Q = – 300

Q = 7,500

Substitute Q = 7,500 in to the demand equation thus:

P = $500 – 0.02 (7,500)

P = $350

111 The correct options are price skimming, complimentary product pricing and price discrimination. Without brand loyalty or a long shelf life then a strategy of penetration is unlikely to work. Additionally the uniqueness of the product prevents low prices.

112 B

The demand formula is P = a + bQ, with b = change of price/change of demand quantity

b = –20/500 = –0.04

By substitution:

400 = a –0.04 (5,000)

400 = a – 200

a = 600

Hence: P = 600 – 0.04Q

113 $340

The demand formula is P = a + bQ, with b = change of price/change of demand quantity

b = –20/500 = –0.04

By substitution:

400 = a –0.04 (5,000)

400 = a – 200

a = 600

Hence: P = 600 – 0.04Q

MR = 600 – 0.08Q

MC = 80

For profit maximisation MR = MC

600 – 0.08Q = 80

Q = –520/–0.08 = 6,500

Again by substitution:

P = 600 – 0.04 (6,500) so P = $340

MAKE-OR-BUY AND OTHER SHORT TERM DECISIONS

114 The correct items are:

- The variable costs of purchase from the new supplier
- The level of discount available from the new supplier
- The redundancy payments to the supervisor of the product in question
- The materials no longer bought to manufacture the product

115 The correct factors to include are:

- The market outlook in the long term looks very poor
- The business also sells pens and many diary buyers will often also buy a pen

The following were NOT to be included:

- The diaries made a loss in the year just passed is a sunk event
- The diaries made a positive contribution in the year just passed is a sunk event
- The budget for next year shows a loss includes fixed costs and these are not relevant
- The business was founded to produce and sell diaries – things change!

116 Before further processing, the sales value of X (10,000 units × $1.20) = $12,000

After further processing:

Sales value of Z (8,000 units × $2.25) = $18,000

Further processing costs ((10,000 units of X × $0.50) + $1,600) = $6,600

This gives a net return of $11,400 which is **$600 less** than the sales value of X.

117 D

Tutorial note

If we manufacture internally, we will incur labour costs of $4.00. Internal manufacture means we couldn't use our labour hours to make 'another item' that would bring us $10 contribution, but that takes twice as long to make as it incurs labour costs of $8.00.

So, this $10 per unit is the 'contribution foregone' but the contribution foregone per labour hour is $10/2 = $5.00. This is part of the relevant cost of manufacturing internally, to which we must add the cost of labour of $4 in our calculations.

	$
Direct material	3.00
Direct labour (W1)	9.00
Variable overhead	1.00
Specific fixed cost	2.50
	15.50

(W1) Relevant cost = Contribution Forgone + Direct labour = $10/2 + $4 = $9

DEALING WITH RISK AND UNCERTAINTY IN DECISION-MAKING

118 A pessimistic buyer would seek to achieve the best results if the worst happens. They would adopt the maximin approach, which involves selecting the alternative that maximises the minimum payoff achievable. The minimum payoffs for each truck are as follows:

Truck A – Minimum $1,400

Truck B – Minimum $1,800

Truck C – Minimum $3,600

Therefore, the 'C' series truck would be chosen.

119 'A' series

This maximises the average daily contribution if the growth rate is forty per cent.

120 'C'

Regret table		**Type of truck**		
		A Series	**B Series**	**C Series**
		$	$	$
Growth rate	15%	1,200	1,800	0
	30%	3,100	2,600	0
	40%	0	2,100	1,000
Max Regret		3,100	2,600	1,000

121 'C'

Expected value calculations:

A Series: ($2,400 × 0.4) + ($1,400 × 0.25) + ($4,900 × 0.35) = $3,025

B Series: ($1,800 × 0.4) + ($1,900 × 0.25) + ($2,800 × 0.35) = $2,175

C Series: ($3,600 × 0.4) + ($4,500 × 0.25) + ($3,900 × 0.35) = $3,930

122 A

The first two statements are correct. Statement 3 is not correct. Sensitivity analysis only identifies how far a variable needs to change, it does not look at the probability of such a change. Statement 4 is not correct. Sensitivity analysis assumes that changes to variables can be made independently: for example, material prices will change independently of other variables; but it is simulation that allows more than one variable to be changed at a time.

123 True, True, Not True, True

	True	Not true
Simulation models the behaviour of a system.	✓	
Simulation models can be used to study alternative solutions to a problem.	✓	
The equations describing the operating characteristics of the system are known.		✓
A simulation model cannot prescribe what should be done about a problem.	✓	

124 The second and fourth options are correct.

The expected value does not give an indication of the dispersion of the possible outcomes; a standard deviation would need to be calculated, so option 2 is correct.

The expected value is an amalgamation of several possible outcomes and their associated probabilities so it may not correspond to any of the actual possible outcomes, so option 4 is correct.

125 A

New profit figures before salary paid:

Good manager: $180,000 × 1.3 = $234,000 Average manager: $180,000 × 1.2 = $216,000 Poor: $180,000 × 1.1 = $198,000

EV of profits = (0.35 × $234,000) + (0.45 × $216,000) + (0.2 × $198,000) = $81,900 + $97,200 + $39,600 = $218,700

Deduct salary cost and EV with manager = $178,700

Therefore do not employ manager as profits will fall by $1,300.

126 D

Perfect information is certain to be right about the future. Imperfect information may predict wrongly.

127 A

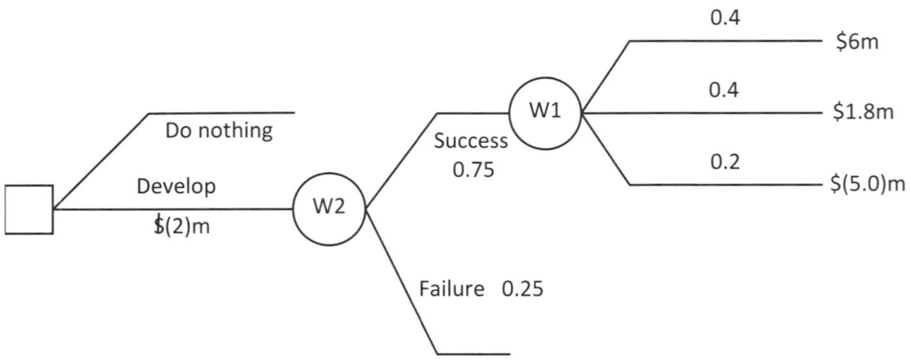

(W1) EV	=	($6m × 0.4) + ($1.8m × 0.4) – ($5m × 0.2)
	=	$2.12m
(W2) EV	=	($2.12m × 0.75) + ($Nil × 0.25)
	=	$1.59m
Net benefit:		$1.59m – $2m = ($0.41m)

128 $600

Without information, the expected profits are:

Product X: $20,000 × 0.2 + $15,000 × 0.5 + $6,000 × 0.3 = $13,300

Product Y: $17,000 × 0.2 + $16,000 × 0.5 + $7,000 × 0.3 = $13,500

So without information, product Y would be selected.

With perfect information, product X would be selected if the market was good, and product Y in the other two cases. The expected value would then be:

$20,000 × 0.2 + $16,000 × 0.5 + $7,000 × 0.3 = $14,100

The expected value of perfect information is therefore $14,100 – $13,500

= $600

129 B

This is an example of sensitivity analysis.

For the project to no longer be worthwhile the expected value would have to fall to $0.

If we make L = the loss made when interest rates fall and restate the expected value calculation we get the following:

EV = (0.3 × 200,000) – (0.7 × L)

If EV falls to zero, (0.3 × 200,000) – 0.7L = 0

Multiplying this out we get:

60,000 – 0.7L = 0

0.7L = 60,000

L = 60,000/0.7

L = 85,714

130 B

Expected value at point A = [(0.60 × 42) – (0.4 × 20)] = $17.2m

Expected value at point B = the higher of (17.2m – 9m) and 15m = 15m

Expected value at point C = [(0.7 × 15m) – (0.3 × 4m)] = $9.3m

The expected value at point D = 9.3m – 5m = $4.3m

131 A

Motivational and measurement research are forms of field research which is considered to be a form of primary research.

BUDGETING AND CONTROL

BUDGETARY SYSTEMS AND TYPES OF BUDGET

132 A

(2) is wrong – activities drive costs and the aim is to control the causes (drivers) of costs, rather than the costs themselves. This, in turn, will ensure that the costs are better managed, and better understood.

133 B

(1) is wrong – it would fall under strategic planning.

134 A

135 C

(1) is wrong, it that would be feedback control. (2) is also wrong, feed-forward control occurs before actual results come through as it is based on forecast results.

136 Incremental budgets are appropriate when applied to stationary costs, the business is stable and for administration costs when the experience of managers is limited.

137 D

An incremental budget starts with the current period's budget and 'builds' on this to produce the budget for the next period.

138 B

139 A

Beyond budgeting makes greater use of rolling budgets to create an environment of continuous planning. It also has more local budget setting (rather than a top-down approach), uses a greater number of targets (rather than simply focusing on financial targets) and seeks continuous improvements (rather than standardisation).

140

	E	F	G	
Budgeted number of batches to be produced:	75,000/200	120,000/60	60,000/30	
	= 375	= 2,000	= 2,000	
Machine set-ups per batch:	5	3	9	
Total machine set-ups	1,875	6,000	18,000	**25,875**

Budgeted cost per set-up: $180,000/25,875 = $6.96 per set-up

Therefore the budgeted machine set-up cost per unit of F produced is:

($6.96 × 3)/60 = $0.35 per unit or $6.96 × 6,000/120,000 = **$0.35 per unit**

141 D

142 The third and fourth statements are correct. In beyond budgeting, planning is performed more regularly. Also, as targets become more challenging and more market focused they stretch staff and encourage staff to find better ways to do things, to innovate and improve. They also make the organisation more customer focused by focusing on areas that concern customers such as quality.

Statement 1 is not correct. Because there is less centralised (top-down) budgeting it is much harder to coordinate activities.

Statement 2 is not correct. Beyond budgeting will require the creation and implementation of more performance measures and will require more up-to-date information and more regularly planning. All of this will be difficult and expensive to introduce.

143 A

This is an example of feed-forward control, as the manager is using a forecast to assist in making a future decision.

144 D

A flexible budget controls operational efficiency by producing a realistic budget cost allowance for the actual level of activity achieved. This allows a more meaningful control comparison with the actual results. Statement (i) is therefore correct.

Incremental budgeting uses the current period's results as a base and adjusts this to allow for any known changes, including the cost increases caused by extra planned units of activity. Statement (ii) is therefore incorrect.

In a rolling budget system an extra quarter is added to the end of the budget when the most recent quarter has expired. The remaining budget might be updated at this point. Statement (iii) is therefore incorrect.

145 C

146 ZBB is useful for support expenses as they are discretionary and it can be used to link strategic goals to specific functional areas, so statements 1 and 2 are correct.

147 A

(2) is not correct. ABB can provide useful information for a total quality management programme (TQM) by relating the cost of an activity to the level of service provided and asking the user departments if they feel they are getting a cost-effective service.

QUANTITATIVE TECHNIQUES

148 B

460 – 400 = 60 clients

\$40,000 – \$36,880 = \$3,120

VC per unit = \$3,120/60 = \$52

Therefore FC = \$40,000 – (460 × \$52) = \$16,080

149 B

	Cumulative average time per unit	No of units	Total time
For first 7 units: $y = 6 \times 7^{-0.415}$	2.676	× 7 =	18.72982
For first 6 units: $y = 6 \times 6^{-0.415}$	2.8525	× 6 =	17.11472
Time for 7th Assignment			1.6151

Answer 1.62 hours to nearest 0.01 hours

150 D

Using the learning curve model $Y = ax^b$

Cumulative average time per unit, $Y = 50 \times 17^{-0.234}$ = 25.7659 hours per unit

Total time = 25.7659 × 17 units = **438.02 to the nearest 0.01 hours**

151 92%

Batches	Total time	Average time/unit
1	500	500
2		$500 \times r$
4		$500 \times r^2$
8		$500 \times r^3$
16	5,731	$500 \times r^4$

For 16 units, total time is 5,371. Average time = 5,731/16 = 358.1875

$Y = ar^n$

1 to 16 is 4 doublings so 358.1875 = $500 \times r^4$

r^4 = 358.1875/500 = 0.716375

$r = \sqrt[4]{0.716375}$ = 0.92 = 92%.

152 $34,400

A high low method analysis will first of all split out the budgeted VC and FC:

	Units	$ Cost
High	1,400	31,600
Low	1,000	30,000
Increment	400	1,600

VC per unit is $1,600/400 = $4/u

Substitution in high:

TC = FC + VC

TC = FC + (1,400 × 4)

31,600 = FC + 5,600

FC = $26,000

For 2,100 units, Fixed costs	= $26,000
VC (2,100 × 4)	= $8,400
Total	= $34,400

153 95%

Units	Total time	Average time/unit
1	100	100
2	190	95

Learning rate is based on the improvement in the average 95/100 = 95%

154 $41,509

Key answer tips

We must work in batches here, where 1 batch = 50 units

Time for the first order:

$Y = ax^b$

$Y = 400 \times 12^{-0.152}$

Y = 274.17285 hours

Total time = 3,290.07 hours

Time for first 1,400 units (28 batches)

$Y = ax^b$

$Y = 400 \times 28^{-0.152}$

Y = 241.04158 hours

Total time = 6,749.16 hours

Time for second order = 6,749.16 – 3,290.07 = 3,459.09 hours

Cost of second order = 3,459.09 × $12/hr = $41,509.08

155 84.3%

$100r^2 = (100 + 70 + 59 + 55)/4$, giving r = 84.3%

Tutorial note

We could also explain this answer as follows: by the time we have produced two units, we have an average per unit of (100 minutes + 70 minutes)/2 units = 85%. If we were to stop there, the rate of learning would be 85%.

By the time we have got to 4 units, we have an average of (100 minutes + 70 minutes + 59 minutes + 55 minutes)/4 units = 71 minutes. These 71 minutes represent (71/85) = 83.53% of the previous average of 85 minutes.

The overall rate of learning is an average of these two rates of learning, so we have (85% + 83.53%)/2 = 84.265, say 84.3%.

156 9.98 minutes

Using the learning curve model $Y = ax^b$

	Cumulative average minutes	Total minutes
For the 3rd unit	$Y = 22 \times 3^{-0.3219} = 15.45$	$\times 3 = 46.34$
For the 4th unit	$Y = 22 \times 4^{-0.3219} = 14.08$	$\times 4 = 56.32$

Therefore the time for the 4th unit is 56.32 – 46.34 = 9.98 minutes.

157 D

Year 7, quarter 3 is period 27

Trend sales = 25,000 + 6,500 (27)

= 200,500 units

Adjusted for seasonal variations = 200,500 units × 150% = 300,750 units

158 D

The sales revenue 'y' is dependent on the money spent on advertising. The more advertising money is spent, the higher the sales revenue should be. If there is no advertising spend at all, sales revenue can still be forecast at a 'constant' of $150,000.

159 C

'y' total expected overhead costs = $127,000 +18.6 × 4,600 labour hours = $212,560

This is calculated using a line of best fit based on 20X5 prices; we need to use an index of 225 for 20X6 when the expected cost index is 225

'y' total expected overhead costs 20X6 = $212,560 × (225/205) = $233,298

160 $39,000

Orders = [100,000 + (30 × 240)] × 1.08 = 115,776

Overhead cost = $10,000 + ($0.25 × 115,776) = $38,944

161

Quarter 2 average seasonal variation	**-1,250**
Quarter 2 20X2 seasonally adjusted forecast sales units	**574**

Firstly, we can identify the missing average seasonal variation for quarter 2 by ensuring that the average seasonal variations in the additive model sum to zero. The total of the provided average seasonal variations = 1,450 – 1,000 + 800 = +1,250. Therefore, the quarter 2 seasonal variation must be -1,250.

The sales volume forecast = trend + seasonal variation under the additive model. Quarter 2 20X2 is where x = 6 in the trend expression. Therefore, the trend = 1,800 + (4 x 6) = 1,824.

Applying the quarter 2 seasonal variation will give the required sales forecast to be 1,824 – 1,250 = 574 units.

162

	Correct?
89% of the variation in production costs from one month to the next can be explained by corresponding variation in output.	✓
Costs increase as output increases.	
The linear relationship between output and costs is very strong.	✓
An increase of 100% in output is associated with an increase of 89% in costs.	
An increase of 89% in output is associated with an increase of 100% in costs.	

A coefficient of determination between output and production costs, tells us that 89% of the variation in production costs from one month to the next can be explained by corresponding variation in output. It also tells us that the linear relationship between output and costs is very strong. Only a positive correlation can tell us that costs increase as output increases and we cannot assume this from the coefficient of determination.

163 B, D

One assumption of simple linear regression is that the dependent variable is only affected by one independent variable. Therefore 'It can account for the effect of multiple independent variables' is incorrect.

Another assumption is that what happened in the past will continue into the future. Therefore 'It assumes that historical data is a reliable guide to the future' is correct.

Simple linear regression is suitable when there is correlation between two variables. It can be positive or negative correlation. Therefore 'It is not suitable when the variables show strong negative correlation' is incorrect.

Interpolation means forecasting within the range of the original data whereas extrapolation means forecasting outside the range of the original data. Forecasting within the range is more reliable because there is data to back up the forecast. It is more difficult to be sure what the results will be if they are outside the range recorded in the past. 'Cost forecasts using extrapolation are less accurate than those using interpolation' is therefore correct.

STANDARD COSTING

164 A

Option B is a current standard, option C is an ideal standard and option D is an attainable standard.

165 The first and fourth statements are true.

The second statement is not correct. Standards can include allowances for inefficiencies in operations, through the use of attainable standards.

The third statement is not correct either, standards and budgets are both used for planning and control purposes.

166 C

167 C

The standard labour rate should be the expected rate/hour, but allowing for standard levels of idle time. For example, if the work force is paid $9 per hour but idle time of 10% is expected, the standard labour rate will be $10 per hour, not $9.

168 C

169 The correct items are: exchange rate movements, increased demand for the material, world oil price rises.

Extra discounts would reduce prices and give a favourable variance. Dividends do not normally count as a cost to a business, and extra supply would normally reduce prices not increase them.

MIX AND YIELD VARIANCES

170 The correct answers are 'Inadequate training of newly recruited staff in the production department', and 'Change in the production process causing extra losses of materials'.

'Selection of a new supplier offering similar quality for lower prices' would lead to a favourable variance for the materials purchasing manager. No impact on usage or production performance as the quality is similar.

'Movements in the exchange rates causing more expensive materials' would lead to an adverse variance for the materials purchasing manager. No impact on usage or production.

'Machine breakdown due to delays in the annual maintenance schedule' would not lead to an adverse usage variance as no materials would be used during the delays.

'Reduced quality materials bought' this would impact the materials usage variance, but would be indicative of the poor performance of the materials purchasing manager, as it is out of the production manager's control.

171 A

A favourable material mix variance is more likely to lead to an adverse material yield variance.

172 C

A planning variance must be caused by an unexpected/unplanned change. If the government unexpectedly increases labour rates then the plan will become outdated and a planning variance will arise.

A planning variance will not always be adverse just because labour rates have increased; there may be no planning variance at all or the planning variance may be favourable if the increase is less than was expected.

A change in production policy by a labour manager is not a planning decision but an operational one.

Whilst the relationship with the variable overhead planning variance may be true, it would not hold for a labour rate planning variance.

173 B

174 $18,000

Original standard hours for actual output = 3 hours × 900 services = 2,700 hours

Revised standard hours for actual output = 3.5 hours × 900 services = 3,150 hours

Variance in hours = 2,700 – 3,150 = 450 adverse

Value of the variance = 450 × $40 = $18,000 adverse

175 A

3,000 units should use 10 kg each (3,000 × 10) = 30,000 kg 3,000 units did use = 29,000 kg

Difference = 1,000 kg favourable

Valued at $6.80 per kg ($68/10 kg)

Variance = $6,800 favourable

176 $72

The planning variance was $40,000 Favourable. This amounts to $2 per hour.

If the revised standard rate per hour was $70 then, for a favourable variance, the original planned rate must have been $2 higher than this.

The original standard rate per hour must have been $72.

177 C

	Material A	**Material B**	**Material C**	**Total**
	kg	kg	kg	kg
Actual input	13,200	7,600	5,600	26,400
Actual input in std proportions				⇓
50:40:20	12,000	9,600	4,800	⇐ 26,400
Difference in quantity	1,200 A	2,000 F	800 A	
× Standard price	× 10	× 5	× 9	
Mix variance	$12,000 A	$10,000 F	$7,200 A	$9,200 A

Key answer tips

An alternative calculation of the mix variance above can be done, using the standard average price per kilogram, as presented below.

$$\text{Std weighted average price per kg} = \frac{(50 \times 10) + (40 \times 5) + (20 \times 9)}{50 + 40 + 20 \text{ kg}} = \$8/\text{kg}$$

	Material A	Material B	Material C	Total
	kg	kg	kg	kg
Actual input	13,200	7,600	5,600	26,400
Actual input in std proportions				⇓
50:40:20	12,000	9,600	4,800	⇐ 26,400
	———	———	———	———
Difference in quantity	1,200	(2,000)	800	
× Difference in price				
(weighted average std price – Ind. material std price)				
× (8 – 10)	x – 2			
× (8 – 5) × 3		x–3		
× (8 – 9)			x – 1	
	———	———	———	
Mix variance	$2,400 A	$6,000 A	$800 A	$9,200 A
	———	———	———	———

178 $11.41

	AQAM	AQSM	Difference	Standard	Variance	
	Kgs	Kgs	Kgs	$/kg	$	
Lettuce	62	45.94	–16.06	0.20	–3.21	A
Peppers	81	76.56	–4.44	0.40	–1.78	A
Beetroot	102	122.50	20.50	0.80	16.40	F
	245	**245**	**Material Mix variance**		**11.41**	**F**

Standard mix:

Lettuce	$\frac{30}{160}$	18.75%
Peppers	$\frac{50}{160}$	31.25%
Beetroot	$\frac{80}{160}$	50%

179 B

Actual yield	1,500.00
Standard yield	1,531.25
Difference	31.25
Standard cost of a plate	0.09
Yield variance = 31.25 × 0.09 =	2.8125 A
Standard yield is 245,000 × 1/160 =	1,531.25

Standard cost of a plate is:

	Quantity (g)	Price ($)	Cost ($)
Lettuce	30	0.0002	0.006
Peppers	50	0.0004	0.020
Beetroot	80	0.0008	0.064
Standard cost:			0.09

180 A

	$
Actual usage in standard proportions	
D = 4,000 litres at $9 per litre	= 36,000
E = 3,500 litres at $5 per litre	= 17,500
F = 2,500 litres at $2 per litre	= 5,000
10,000 litres	58,500
Actual usage in actual proportions	
D = 4,300 litres at $9 per litre	38,700
E = 3,600 litres at $5 per litre	18,000
F = 2,100 litres at $2 per litre	4,200
	60,900

Mix variance is 58,500 – 60,900 = $2,400 Adverse

181 A

The operational labour efficiency variance uses the revised standard time of 12 minutes.

	$	
SHSR		
$\frac{12}{60}$ × 370 × $10/hr =	740	Efficiency $60 A
AHSR		
80 hrs × $10/hr =	800	

SALES MIX AND QUANTITY VARIANCES

182 The sales price variance is $19,800 Adv

AQ × AP = 13,200 × 23.50 =	310,200
AQ × SP = 13,200 × 25.00 =	330,000
Price variance =	19,800 Adv

183 The sales volume variance is $6,000 Fav

AQ × SC = 13,200 × 5 =	66,000
BQ × SC = 12,000 × 5 =	60,000
Volume variance =	6,000 Fav

184 $50,000

	Actual mix	Standard mix	Standard contribution from actual mix $	Standard contribution from standard mix $
Type A	200,000	150,000	800,000	600,000
Type B	40,000	90,000	200,000	450,000
	240,000	240,000	1,000,000	1,050,000
Difference in contribution			50,000 Adv	

Since Yellow uses MC then the variance should be calculated at standard contribution.

185 $87,500

Total actual sales	240,000
Total budget sales	220,000
Difference	20,000
Average standard contribution	
((5 × 4) + (3 × 5))/8 = 4.375	$4.375
Favourable variance is	$87,500

186

Tutorial note

A sales mix variance indicates the effect on profit of changing the mix of actual sales from the standard mix. Looking a July's budgeted sales levels, we can see that the standard mix of sales is one 'X' for two 'Y's, It means that we expect that every time an 'X' is sold, two units of 'Y' will be sold at the same time. The least profitable unit, 'X', represents a third of the budgeted sales volume.

The actual sales mix is 1'X' for four 'Y's, and is different from the budgeted sales mix. The least profitable unit, 'X', represents a fifth of sales volume. To calculate Jones' sales mix variance, we can use the 'Toolbox' method detailed in your ACCA Performance Management Study Text.

	Actual Quantities, Actual Mix	Actual Quantities, Standard Mix	Difference	At standard profit	Variance
	AQAM	AQSM			
Product X	2,000 units	3,333 units	–1,333	$4	($5,332) A
Product Y	8,000 units	6,667 units	1,333	$6	$7,998 F
	10,000 units	**10,000 units**	**0**		**$2,667 F**

187 A

The sales quantity variance is the difference between the actual sales volume in the standard mix and budgeted sales, valued at the standard profit per unit:

	X	Y	Z	Total
Budgeted sales units, in standard mix	1,000 units (1/6 of total)	2,000 units (1/3 of total)	3,000 units (1/2 of total)	6,000 units
Actual sales volume, in standard mix 1/6; 1/3;1/2	991.67	1,983.33	2,975	5,950
Difference in units	8.33 ADV	16.67 ADV	25 ADV	
Standard profit per unit, as per question	$2	$5	$2	
Variance	$16.67 ADV	$83.34 ADV	$50 ADV	**$150 ADV**

PLANNING AND OPERATIONAL VARIANCES

188 C

Statement 1 is not true: the publication of material price planning variances should not always lead to automatic updates of standard costs. There must be a good reason for deciding that the original standard cost is unrealistic.

Statement 2 is not true either. Although planning variances are not usually the responsibility of operational managers, these variances do need to be investigated by senior management when they are substantial, so that lessons may be learned for the future.

189 D

	Budget units	**Actual units**	**Change**
Sales	504,000	532,000	Up 5.55%
Market share	18%	20%	Up 2%
Market size	2,800,000	2,660,000	Down 5%

190 C

	Budget units	**Revised units**	**Actual units**	**Change**
Sales	504,000	478,800	532,000	Up 5.55%
Market share	18%	18%	20%	Up 2%
Market size	2,800,000		2,660,000	Down 5%

Market size variance is (478,800 – 504,000) × $12 = $302,400 Adv

191 B

Market share variance compares revised sales volume to actual sales volume.

Revised sales volume (300,000 units × 2%) = 6,000 units Actual sales volume = 5,600 units

Difference = 400 units adverse

Valued at standard contribution of $1,000

Variance = $400,000 adverse

192 C

An operational variance compares revised price to actual price.

20,000 kg should cost $0.40 per kg at the revised price (20,000 kg × $0.40) = $8,000 20,000 kg did cost $0.42 per kg (20,000 kg × $0.42) = $8,400

Variance = $400 adverse

193 A

The material price when flexed is higher than budget whilst the external environment shows that prices are reducing. This indicates that although suppliers lowered their prices, the manager has still overspent which indicates poor performance.

When sales volumes and prices are flexed, it can be seen that the manager has performed better.

194 D

PERFORMANCE ANALYSIS

195 B

The materials mix variance could be affected or influenced by decisions outside the production manager's control, for example the quality of the materials purchased may change the mix.

196 C

PERFORMANCE MEASUREMENT AND CONTROL

PERFORMANCE ANALYSIS IN PRIVATE SECTOR, PUBLIC SECTOR AND NOT-FOR-PROFIT ORGANISATIONS

197 B

198 D

Measuring the budgeted number of quotations actually issued would be monitoring the output and activity of the department but it would not be helpful in improving the department's performance in terms of the accuracy or speed of quotations in the scenario described.

199 'Customer satisfaction ratings' and 'customer retention rates'

'Customer profitability analysis' results belong to the financial quadrant. 'Customer ordering processing times' belongs to the 'Internal business process' quadrant.

200 Innovation and learning perspective

201 D

'Number of returns in the month' is an absolute measure and not appropriate to measure 'quality'. 'Number of faulty goods returned as a percentage of number of orders received in the month' is not a bad measure, but orders may not have been delivered; 'Average customer satisfaction rating where customers were asked a range of questions including quality, delivery and customer service' seems to lack focus as a measure.

202 The correct items are Competitive Performance, Innovation, Financial Performance, Resource utilisation, Flexibility and Quality of Service.

203 A

Co X (2,140/20,000) × 100 = 10.7%

Co Y (2,180/26,000) × 100 = 8.38%

204 C

Company B has a higher asset turnover and is therefore using its assets more efficiently than A. The two companies have the same ROCE and are therefore generating the same profit from every $1 of asset employed. The profit of the two companies is the same but company A has a higher profit margin and is therefore controlling its costs better than company B. The calculations are:

	Co A	**Co B**
ROCE	20% (10,000/50,000 × 100)	20% (10,000/50,000 × 100)
Profit margin	20% (10,000/50,000 × 100)	5% (10,000/200,000 × 100)
Asset turnover	1 (50,000/50,000)	4 (200,000/50,000)

205 C

Inventory holding period = 44,000/324,500 × 365 days = 49 days

Average inventories/COS × 365

Average inventories = (50,000 + 38,000)/2 = 44,000

Current ratio = 108,000/56,000 = 1.93:1

Current assets: Current liabilities

Current assets = Trade receivables 60,000 + Prepayments 4,000 + Cash in hand 6,000 + Closing inventories 38,000 = 108,000

Current liabilities = Bank overdraft 8,000 + Trade payables 40,000 + Accruals 3,000 + Declared dividends 5,000 = 56,000

206 Accountable, Accountable, Accountable, Not accountable

	Accountable	**Not accountable**
The generation of revenues	✓	
Transfer prices	✓	
Management of working capital	✓	
Apportioned head office costs		✓

The manager will be accountable for the generation of revenues, transfer prices and management of working capital as they have control over these areas. The manager will not be accountable for the apportioned head office costs as they have no control over those.

207 A

The quick ratio (acid test) is similar to the current ratio, but inventory is removed from the current assets due to its poor liquidity in the short term.

$$\textit{Acid test (or 'quick') ratio} = \frac{\textit{Current assets} - \textit{Inventory}}{\textit{Current liabilities}}$$

Binny's Co sales are all for cash, and therefore its 'Current Assets' figures will not include any receivables.

$$\text{Current ratio 3.2} = \frac{\text{Cash + Inventory}}{\text{Current liabilities}}$$

$$\text{Current ratio 3.2} = \frac{\text{Cash \$40,000 + Inventory \$160,000 (W1)}}{\text{Current liabilities 62,500 (W2)}}$$

$$\text{Therefore, acid test (or 'quick' ratio)} = \frac{\text{Cash \$40,000}}{\text{Current liabilities \$62,500}} = 0.64$$

Working 1 – Inventory

$$\text{Cost of sales} = \frac{\text{\$960,000 annual sales} \times 100}{150} = \$640,000$$

$$\text{Inventory holding period 90 days} = \frac{\text{Inventory}}{\text{Cost of sales}} \times 360$$

$$\text{Inventory} = \frac{\text{90 days} \times \$640,000}{360} = \$160,000$$

Working 2 – Current liabilities

$$\textbf{Current ratio 3.2} = \frac{\text{\$40,000 cash + \$160,000 inventory}}{\text{Current liabilities}}$$

$$\text{So current liabilities} = \frac{\$200,000}{3.2} = \$62,500$$

DIVISIONAL PERFORMANCE AND TRANSFER PRICING

208 B

Increase in variable costs from buying in (2,200 units × $40 ($140 – $100)) = $88,000

Less the specific fixed costs saved if A is shut down = ($10,000)

Decrease in profit = $78,000

209 Would choose to invest, would not choose to invest

	Would choose to invest in the project	**Would choose not to invest in the project**
Division A	✓	
Division B		✓

Division A: Profit = $14.4 m × 30% = $4.32 m

Imputed interest charge = $32.6 m × 10% = $3.26 m

Residual income = $1.06 m

Division B: Profit = $8.8 m × 24% = $2.112 m

Imputed interest charge = $22.2 m × 10% = $2.22 m

Residual income = $(0.108) m

210 $10.50

Tutorial note

Division A can sell all of its output on the outside market at $12 per unit. Any internal transfer will be at the expense of external sales. However, the external sales also include a packaging cost of $1.50 per unit which is not incurred on an internal transfer and this saving can be passed on to the buying division. Therefore, the correct transfer price from a decision-making point of view is $12 (the market price) – $1.50 (the saving in packaging cost) = $10.50.

211 $830 m

Controllable profit is 1,200 + 90 + 30 + 50 =	$1,370m
Assets at start of year are	$4,500m
Notional interest charges at 12% (4,500 × 0.12)	$540m
Residual Income	$830m

212

$$\text{ROCE} = \frac{\text{Profit before interest and tax}}{\text{Capital employed}} = \frac{500}{2{,}400} = 20.8\%$$

Capital employed is equity + long-term debt = 1,500 + 900 = 2,400

or

Total assets less current liabilities = 3,400 – 1,000 = 2,400

213 C

$236,000

	$000
Profit	500
Imputed interest 11% × 2,400	(264)
Residual income	236

214 28.0%

ROI = 1,370/4,890 = 28.0%

215 19.8%

Tutorial note

Firstly, a machine with carrying value of $40k was sold for $50k. This will reduce non-current assets by $40k and, as we are told this was a cash transaction, increase cash by $50k – increasing net assets by $10k. As a profit has been made on disposal, it will also increase profits by $10k. Secondly, another machine was purchased for $250k. This will increase non-current assets by $250k, but as this was also a cash transaction, decrease cash by $250k, so no net effect. As no depreciation is charged on either machine there is no further effect. The net effect is therefore +10k to both profit and net assets, so the ROI is ($200k/$1,010k) × 100% = 19.8%.

Revised annual profit = $190,000 + $10,000 profit on the sale of the asset = $200,000

Revised net assets = $1,000,000 – $40,000 carrying value + $50,000 cash – $250,000 cash + $250,000 asset = $1,010,000 ROI = ($200,000/$1,010,000) × 100 = 19.8%

Tutorial note

Do not make the mistake of omitting the profit on disposal from profits and increasing net assets by the $250k machine purchase, but not subtracting the cash.

216 B

Statement (1) is not true: a price above variable costs will generate a positive contribution but will not necessarily cover fixed costs and make a profit, so will not always be accepted.

217 B

Using the opportunity cost approach to transfer pricing, the minimum price charged by the transferring division must be the marginal (variable) cost of producing X + the contribution that is lost from selling however many units of Y could have been made for each X.

'Division A has limited skilled labour' means that skilled labour is a scarce resource. If Division A now has to make X instead of Y, it will lose the contribution it currently makes on Product Y. This contribution is equal to $600 selling price – $200 Material costs – $80 labour costs = $320.

It takes 4 hours to make a Y and 6 hours to make an X. So, every time we (in Division A) make an X, we will not make 1.5Ys because of the shortage of skilled labour. So we lose 1.5 Y × Contribution per unit $320 = $480.

We add to this lost contribution a marginal cost of making an X of $150 (material) + $120 (labour).

Total transfer price = $480 + $150 + $120 = $750

Tutorial note

There is an alternative to approaching this question. You could calculate the contribution per labour hour for Y and then multiplying this by the number of hours X uses. It is the contribution per labour hour that is relevant, because of the fact that it is labour that is in short supply.

Product	**Y in $**
Selling Price per unit	600
Less Direct Materials (4 kgs)	200
Less Direct Labour (4 hours)	80
Contribution per unit	320
Contribution per labour hour for Y	80

Therefore, if Division A is to be no worse off by selling Product X to Division B instead of Product Y externally, the contribution per labour hour from selling X must also be $80. The opportunity cost is therefore $80 per labour hour.

Since it uses 6 labour hours to make one unit, one unit must generate a contribution (i.e. opportunity cost in this context) of 6 × $80 i.e. $480. To arrive at a minimum transfer price, the marginal cost of producing X must be added. Total variable cost per unit of X = $150 + $120. Therefore, the minimum transfer price is $750.

218 $12.90

We must set a price high enough for TM to cover its costs, but not so high that RM cannot make a profit.

For TM, an item sold externally has VC of 60% × $24.00 = $14.40. Of this, $1.50 will not be incurred on an internal transfer so it is not relevant here, VC on internal transfer = $14.40 – $1.50= $12.90. We do not know RM's cost structure, so we leave the price at $12.90; this will ensure that RM is not discouraged from taking an internal transfer when it is profitable to do so.

PERFORMANCE ANALYSIS ISSUES IN NON-FOR-PROFIT ORGANISATIONS AND THE PUBLIC SECTOR

219 B

(1) is not correct: Output does not usually have a market value, and it is therefore more difficult to measure efficiency.

220 Economy, Efficiency, Effectiveness

	Economy	Efficiency	Effectiveness
Target (1)	✓		
Target (2)		✓	
Target (3)			✓

221 A

Reducing mortality rates is likely to be a stated objective of the hospital and as such is a measure of output, or effectiveness. Cost per patient is a measure of output related to input i.e. efficiency.

222 B

Multiple objectives often conflict and therefore do not ensure goal congruence between stakeholders, therefore Statement 1 is incorrect. This then can lead to the need for compromise between objectives which can be problematic, therefore Statement 2 is correct.

223 C

Exam success will be a given objective of a school, so it is a measure of effectiveness.

224 D

225 The correct answers are:

Economy
Direct staff cost as a percentage of contract income
Food cost per meal served to residents
Efficiency
Temporary staff usage (hours) as a percentage of total staff hours
Number of voids (the number of empty beds as a percentage of total
Effectiveness
Achieving the CHQC's designated standard of care for the elderly
Staff turnover

Economy is an input measure and considers whether the resources used are being acquired at the required quality for the cheapest price. Efficiency links inputs and outputs and considers whether the maximum outputs are being achieved given the level of inputs. Effectiveness measures outputs and considers if the overall objectives are being met.

So, staff costs and food costs should be measured against the budgets set and are economy measures. The use of temporary staff and having empty beds are efficiency measures as they measure how well resources are being used. Finally, providing good quality care to meet the regulator's requirements is a measure of effectiveness. As relationships are key to providing good care then low staff turnover will facilitate that.

EXTERNAL CONSIDERATIONS AND THE IMPACT ON PERFORMANCE

226 D

There is nothing to suggest that imposed standards are more likely to be achieved. Where managers are allowed to participate in the setting of standards, they are usually more motivated and this can lead to more acceptance of these standards.

Managers should be targeted on factors which they can control, and be set targets which are specific to their business area.

It is recognised that ideal standard do not generally motivate, therefore standards are generally set at an achievable level with some stretch built in.

227 A, B and D

It is important to take account of all stakeholders when setting performance targets.

Government policy can have an impact on the internal performance of a business.

228 A

Managers should also have targets which are based on the overall performance of the company and not solely based on their own responsibility centre to aid goal congruence.

Capital investment decisions may be reviewed centrally and judged on the basis of net present value (NPV).

Setting targets involving the overall performance of the company may not be motivating if poorly performing managers are rewarded in the same way as managers who are performing well.

229 C

It is important that performance measures are set to encourage the long term growth of the company. A focus on short term profit could result in risky and dysfunctional behaviour.

The government is also interested in many other aspects including price stability, economic growth and compliance with laws.

Companies have a range of stakeholders, all of which can affect the company and should be considered. Some of these stakeholders are external such as the government, the general public and pressure groups.

Section 5

ANSWERS TO OBJECTIVE TEST CASE STUDY QUESTIONS – SECTION B

SPECIALIST COST AND MANAGEMENT ACCOUNTING TECHNIQUES

230 MIDHURST CO (SEPTEMBER/DECEMBER 2020)

1 A, C

Statements A and C are correct as capital expenditure is likely to increase at the introduction stage and the majority of a product's costs are determined at the outset.

Statement B defines the decline stage of the product lifecycle and Statement D defines the maturity stage.

2 D

To calculate a cost per unit using life-cycle costing, the first step is to calculate the total cost over the full life-cycle of the product.

The total cost of the new product (in $000s) is:

$6,200 + $33,450 + $177,685 + ($42 × 10,000) + $98,470 +($9 × 10,000) + $10,300 + ($4 × 10,000) + $7,790 + $23,450 = **$907,345**

To calculate the cost per unit, divide the total cost by the number of units to be produced over the life-cycle of the product:

$907,345,000/10,000 = **$90,735**.

If A was selected, the variable costs per unit were omitted from the total cost.

If B was selected, the total production cost was used, and all non-production costs were excluded.

If C was selected, the administration costs were excluded.

3 $6,940

Current variable material cost per unit = 20% × $42,000 = $8,400

Revised variable material cost per unit = (85% × ($8,400 – $2,000)) + (75% × $2,000) = **$6,940**

4 C

Normally product development occurs at the maturity phase in order to extend the profitable stage of the life-cycle. This is usually done by adding enhancements or new features.

5 B

Statement 3 is an advantage of target costing and not life-cycle costing.

231 DUFF CO (JUNE 2014, ADAPTED)

1 A

Product	**Z**
Direct materials	\$28.00
Direct labour	\$24.00
Overhead (\$9.70 × 2 DL hours)	\$19.40
Full cost per unit	\$71.40

2 B

Full budgeted production cost per unit using activity based costing

Product	**X**	**Y**	**Z**	**Total**
Number of batches (i.e. set ups)	**40**	**20**	**55**	**115**
Number of purchase orders per batch	4	5	4	
Total number of orders	**160**	**100**	**220**	**480**
Total machine hours	**30,000**	**20,000**	**30,800**	**80,800**

Cost driver rates:

Cost per machine set up	\$280,000/115 = \$2,434.78
Cost per order	\$316,000/480 = \$658.33
Cost per machine hour	(\$420,000 + \$361,400)/80,800 = \$9.67

Allocation of overheads to product X:

Product	**X**
	\$
Machine set up costs (\$2,434.78 × 40)	**97,391**
Material ordering costs (\$658.33 × 160)	**105,333**
Machine running and facility costs (\$9.67 × 30,000)	**290,100**
Total	**492,824**
Number of units produced	**20,000**
Overhead cost per unit	**\$24.64**

3 **B**

Total cost per unit:	$ per unit
Direct materials	28
Direct labour	24
Overhead	26.21
ABC cost per unit	78.21

4 **D**

All statements are correct.

5 **B**

Statement (1) is not true. When activity based costing is used, the cost for product X is very similar to that cost calculated using full absorption costing. This means that the price for product X is likely to remain unchanged, because cost plus pricing is being used.

Statement (2) is correct. Demand for product X is relatively elastic but since no change in price is expected, sales volumes are likely to remain the same if ABC is introduced.

Statement (3) is correct. The cost for product Y is almost $10 per unit less using ABC. This means that the price of product Y will go down if cost plus pricing is used.

Statement (4) is incorrect. Given that demand for product Y is also elastic, like demand for product X, a reduced selling price is likely to give rise to increased sales volumes.

232 BECKLEY HILL (JUNE 2015, ADAPTED)

1 **C**

	Procedure A	**Procedure B**
Total cost per procedure, as per question	$2,475.85	$4,735.85
Less: Surgical time and materials (direct cost)	($1,200)	($2,640)
Less: Anaesthesia time and materials (direct cost)	($800)	($1,620)
Overhead cost per procedure	$475.85	$475.85

2 **A**

$$\text{Administration cost per hour} = \frac{\text{Total admin cost}}{\text{Total number of admin hours}}$$

Administration cost per hour =

$$\frac{\$1,870,160}{(1 \text{ hour} \times 14,600 \text{ procedures 'A'}) + (1.5 \text{ hours} \times 22,400 \text{ procedures 'B'})}$$

Administration cost per hour = $38.80

3 D

> ***Tutorial note***
>
> *Make sure you use the number of patient hours, not admin hours, to answer this question.*

$$\text{Nursing cost per hour} = \frac{\text{Total nursing cost}}{\text{Total number of patient hours}}$$

$$\text{Nursing cost per hour} = \frac{\$6{,}215{,}616}{(24 \text{ hours} \times 14{,}600) + (48 \text{ hours} \times 22{,}400)}$$

Nursing cost per hour = $4.36 per patient hour

4 A

Only statement (1) is correct. When activity-based costing (ABC) is used, the cost for Procedure A is approximately $2,297 as compared to the approximate $2,476 currently calculated by BH. For Procedure B, the cost using ABC is approximately $4,853 as compared to the approximate current cost of $4,736. Hence, the cost of Procedure A goes down using ABC and the cost of Procedure B goes up. This reflects the fact that the largest proportion of the overhead costs is the nursing and general facility costs. Both of these are driven by the number of patient hours for each procedure. Procedure B has twice as many patient hours as Procedure A.

5 C

Both statements are correct. ABC can be a lot of work to implement, and whilst the comparative costs are different, they are not significantly different. Given that ABC is costly to implement, it may be that a similar allocation in overheads can be achieved simply by using a fairer basis to absorb the costs. If patient hours are used as the basis of absorption instead of simply dividing the overheads by the number of procedures, the costs for Procedures A and B would be $2,296 and $4,853:

$17,606,352/1,425,600 hours = $12.35 per hour.

Therefore absorption cost for A = $1,200 + $800 + (24 × $12.35) = $2,296.

Same calculation for B but with 48 hours instead.

Hence, the same result can be achieved without going to all of the time and expense of using ABC. Therefore BH should not adopt ABC but use this more accurate basis of absorbing overheads instead.

233 ABKABER PLC

1 B

Total overhead cost	=	\$2,400,000 + \$6,000,000 + \$3,600,000
	=	\$12,000,000
Total labour hours	=	200,000 + 220,000 + 80,000
	=	500,000
Overhead absorption rate/labour hour	=	\$12,000,000/500,000 = \$24

	Sunshine	**Roadster**	**Fireball**
Direct labour hours	200,000	220,000	80,000
	\$	\$	\$
Overheads (\$24/direct labour hour)	**4,800,000**	**5,280,000**	**1,920,000**

2 C

Number of deliveries to retailers	100 + 80 + 70	=	250
Cost driver rate for deliveries	\$2,400,000/250	=	\$9,600
Number of set-ups	35 + 40 + 25	=	100
Cost driver rate for set-ups	\$6,000,000/100	=	\$60,000
Number of purchase orders	400 + 300 + 100	=	800
Cost driver rate for purchase orders	\$3,600,000/800	=	\$4,500

Overheads	**Fireball**
	\$
Deliveries (\$9,600 × 70)	672,000
Set-ups at (\$60,000 × 25)	1,500,000
Purchase orders (\$4,500 × 100)	450,000
Total overheads attributed	**2,622,000**

3 B

Both methods are acceptable, but ABC can give more detailed information about the overhead costs per products, so it would be unwise for management to ignore the useful additional information that ABC can provide.

Using ABC will give a lower profit to the Fireball as more overheads are attributed to it.

Reducing labour hours would reduce the overheads attributed to the product under the existing method, but is not focussing on what is driving the overheads which is deliveries, set-ups, and purchases processes.

4 D

(1) is false – ABC can provide management with more accurate information as it gives a more accurate cost per unit. This can improve management decisions such as whether the Fireball product is viable.

(2) is false – ABC can help with determining a more accurate incremental cost, however it's accuracy depends on identifying appropriate cost drivers.

(3) is true.

5 D

It is difficult to achieve complete accuracy with ABC as it depends on the accuracy of the cost drivers identified.

ABC is more accurate, but is more expensive and time consuming than traditional methods.

ABC is more useful when overheads are a large proportion of the costs, as accurate attribution of those overheads will have a more significant impact on the cost per product in this instance.

234 RAASAY (SEPTEMBER/DECEMBER 2023)

1 A

The profit per unit of a Jazz guitar = selling price – prime cost – overheads. The selling price and prime cost per unit are given, but the overhead cost per unit needs to be calculated. Overheads are absorbed on a revenue basis.

The overhead absorption rate (OAR) = total overheads/total revenue:

Total overheads = ($40,810 + $120,540 + $643,100) = $804,450

Total revenue = ($620 × 5,000) + ($700 × 6,000) + ($450 × 3,000) = $8,650,000

OAR = $804,450/$8,650,000 = $0.093 per $ revenue

The profit per unit of a Jazz guitar = $620 – $370 – ($620 × 0.093) = $192.34

If you answered:

Option B, this is the selling price less prime costs.

Option C, this is the prime costs less overheads.

Option D, this is just the overhead figure.

2 **$9.80**

The machine set-up for a Rock guitar

= (cost per machine set-up × number of set-ups for all Rock guitars)/total number of Rock guitars produced

The cost per machine set-up = total machine set-up costs/total number of set-ups

The total number of set-ups:

Product	**Jazz**	**Rock**	**Classic**	**Total**
Batches	(5,000/100) = 50	(6,000/150) = 40	(3,000/200) = 15	
Set-ups per batch	3	5	4	
Total machine set-ups	150	200	60	**410**

The cost per machine set-up = $120,540/410 = $294 per set-up

The total machine cost for a Rock guitar = ($294 × 200)/6,000 = **$9.80**

3 **A**

The component processing cost for a Classic guitar

= (cost per component processing hour × processing time per Classic guitar)

The cost per processing hour

= total component processing costs/total processing time (hours)

The total processing time (hours):

Product	**Jazz**	**Rock**	**Classic**	**Total**
Number of units	5,000	6,000	3,000	
Processing time per unit (hours)	4	5	3	
Total processing time (hours)	20,000	30,000	9,000	**59,000**

The cost per processing hour = $643,100/59,000 = $10.90 per hour.

The total component processing cost for a Classic guitar = $10.90 × 3 = **$32.70**

If you answered:

Option B is the processing time per unit for the Classic guitar.

Option C is the total processing cost for Classic guitars ($10.90/hour × 9,000 hours = $98,100) divided by the total production units for all three guitars (5,000 + 6,000 + 3,000 = 14,000).

Option D arises where batch size is incorrectly used as driver.

4 **D**

ABC is limited in as much as it will still have an element of arbitrary allocation – not all costs can be definitively linked to a cost driver, therefore statement A is incorrect.

ABC gives more accurate costing when overheads are a large proportion of total costs therefore statement B is incorrect.

Absorption costing also includes fixed overheads so there can be no advantage to using ABC and short-term decision-making often assesses fixed cost as irrelevant, therefore statement C is incorrect.

5 **The correct matching is:**

Cost Driver	Activity
Number of material movements	Material Handling
Number of warranties handled	Customer Service
Number of service requests	IT support
Number of purchase orders	Procurement
Number of machine hours	Maintenance

In each case the cost driver has been selected as one that reflects the nature of the activity, and one that if increased would lead to additional activity costs to be incurred.

It is necessary to use business organisational knowledge to accurately identify activities with the cost drivers; such as procurement involves raising purchase orders for goods or services and customer service is likely to be dealing with warranty claims for faulty products.

235 GADGET CO (DECEMBER 2010 ADAPTED)

1 B

Cost per unit under full absorption costing

Total annual overhead costs:	$
Machine set up costs	26,550
Machine running costs	66,400
Procurement costs	48,000
Delivery costs	54,320
	195,270

Overhead absorption rate:

	A	B	C	Total
Production volumes	15,000	12,000	18,000	45,000

Therefore, overhead absorption rate = $195,270/45,000 = $4.34 per unit

So statement (i) is **true.**

Machine running costs:

	A	B	C	Total
Machine hours per unit	0.5	0.7	0.9	
Production and sales volumes (units)	15,000	12,000	18,000	
Total machine hours	7,500	8,400	16,200	32,100

Therefore, cost driver rate for machine running costs = $66,400/32,100 = $2.07 per hour

Therefore each unit would absorb $2.07/hour × 0.9 hours per unit = $1.86 per unit.

So statement (ii) is **false**.

2 B

Overhead absorption rate:

	A	**B**	**C**	**Total**
Production volumes	15,000	12,000	18,000	
Labour hours per unit	0.1	0.15	0.2	
Total labour hours	1,500	1,800	3,600	6,900

Therefore, overhead absorption rate = $195,270/6,900 = $28.30 per hour.

Cost per unit for product A

	A
	$
Raw materials	2.4
Direct labour ($14.80 × 0.1hrs)	1.48
Overhead ($28.30 × 0.1hrs)	2.83
Full cost per unit	**6.71**

3 C

Cost per unit using full absorption costing

Cost drivers:

Cost pools	**$**	**Cost driver**
Machine set up costs	26,550	36 production runs (16 + 12 + 8)
Machine running costs	66,400	32,100 machine hours (7,500 + 8,400 + 16,200)
Procurement costs	48,000	94 purchase orders (24 + 28 + 42)
Delivery costs	54,320	140 deliveries (48 + 30 + 62)
	195,270	

Cost per machine set up	$26,550/36 = $737.50
Cost per machine hour	$66,400/32,100 = $2.0685
Cost per order	$48,000/94 = $510.6383
Cost per delivery	$54,320/140 = $388

Allocation of overheads to each product:

	B
	$
Machine set up costs ($737.50 × 12)	8,850
Machine running costs ($2.0685 × 8,400)	17,375
Procurement costs ($510.6383 × 28)	14,298
Delivery costs ($388 × 30)	11,640
Total overhead cost for Product B	52,163
Number of units produced	12,000

Overhead cost per unit (52,163/12,000) = $4.35

4 D

Statement (i) is false – whilst product C makes a loss under traditional absorption costing ($13 – $13.42 = –$0.42), with the more accurate overhead apportionment under ABC it makes a profit ($13 – $12.48 = $0.52). So shifting to ABC would help Gadget to see that product C is financially viable.

Statement (ii) is true – the lower number of productions runs has reduced the machine set up cost overhead allocation to product C under ABC, compared with traditional absorption costing. This is reflected in the full unit cost being lower under ABC.

Statement (iii) is false – switching to ABC costing means product C goes from making a loss, to making a profit, so this would change management's decision about whether to continue producing product C, and how much to produce.

5 B

Both statements are false. ABC often makes a difference, but not always. ABM, which uses ABC, suggests that by reducing or changing activity levels, then cost reduction of fixed costs is possible.

236 DARASK CO (SEPTEMBER/DECEMBER 2021)

1 B

Statement 1 is incorrect as, although just-in-time (JIT) is often associated with cost reduction and performance improvement, there is no prerequisite that JIT must be in operation for target costing to be useful, as long as there is scope to reduce costs sustainably in other ways.

Statement 2 is correct, but some candidates will believe that target costing, life cycle costing and planning are alternatives to each other.

2 $264

	$m
Variable cost ($123 × 80m)	9,840
Fixed cost (given)	3,360
	13,200
Mark-up	× 1.6
	21,120

$21,120m ÷ 80m units = **$264**

3 B

	Sales units (millions)	Sales Price ($)	Revenue ($m)
Introduction	8	425	3,400
Growth	14	300	4,200
Maturity	56	220	12,320
Decline	2	120	240
Target revenue			20,160
Target cost (Balance)			**(11,088)**
Target profit (45% × $20,160m)			9,072

Cost gap = $13,000m – $11,088m = **$1,912m**

4 C

Increasing capacity and building inventory are non-value adding activities unless the additional production can be sold.

Boosting marketing spend to sell more units may be tempting but it does not address the cost gap.

Quality assurance inspections eliminate waste and reduces cost so is the only potential option to reduce the cost gap.

5 D

Director X is wrong as it is possible to estimate target selling prices for services (many organisations do) even if target costs may be more difficult to establish.

Director Y is wrong because a high degree of variability makes it difficult to determine a target that can be achieved through cost reduction. Designing costs out of a new mobile phone can be done because it is a standardised product so once it is designed the cost reduction can be realised. If a service is so variable then it is less obvious as to what is required to fulfil each customer's needs so a target cost can be difficult to meet.

Director Z is correct as services are intangible and determining a service unit is not always possible.

237 HELOT CO (SEPTEMBER 2016)

1 D

Target costing does encourage looking at customer requirements early on so that features valued by customers are included, so Statement 2 is correct. It will also force the company to closely assess the design and is likely to be successful if costs are designed out at this stage rather than later once production has started, so Statement 4 is correct.

Statement 1 explains a benefit of flow cost accounting. Statement 3 explains the concept of throughput accounting.

2 A

Target price is $45 and the profit margin is 35% which results in a target cost of $29.25. The current estimated cost can be calculated as:

Production costs per unit	$
Direct material	3.00
Direct labour	2.50
Direct machining	5.05
Set-up	0.45
Inspection and testing	4.30
Total non-production costs per unit	
Design (salaries and technology) (2,500K ÷ 350K)	7.14
Marketing consultants (1,700K ÷ 350K)	4.86
Distribution (1,400K ÷ 350K)	4.00
Current total cost per unit	**31.30**

$31.30 – $29.25 results in a cost gap of $2.05.

3 Not appropriate, Appropriate, Not appropriate, Appropriate.

	An appropriate way to close a cost gap	**Not an appropriate way to close a cost gap**
Buy cheaper, lower grade plastic for the game discs and cases.		✓
Using standard components wherever possible in production.	✓	
Employ more trainee game designers on lower salaries.		✓
Use the company's own online gaming websites for marketing.	✓	

Using more standardised components and using its own websites for marketing will reduce processing and marketing costs.

Using cheaper materials and trainee designers will reduce costs but could impact the quality and customer perception of the product which would impact the target price.

4 C

The change in the learning rate will increase the current estimated cost which will increase the cost gap.

The target cost will be unaffected as this is based on the target selling price and profit margin; neither of which are changing.

5 B

Services do use more labour relative to materials.

The other three statements are incorrect as uniformity is not a characteristic of services, there is no transfer of ownership and although it is difficult to standardise a service due to the human influence, target costing can still be used.

Tutorial note

The characteristics of target costing in service industries are frequently highlighted by the examining team as an absolute must-know. Make sure you learn them before attempting the exam.

238 CHEMICAL FREE CLEAN CO (DECEMBER 2015, ADAPTED)

1 A

A product or service is developed which is perceived to be needed by customers and therefore will attract adequate sales volumes. A target price is then set based on the customers' perceived value of the product. This will therefore be a market based price. The required target operating profit per unit is then calculated. This may be based on either return on sales or return on investment. The target cost is derived by subtracting the target profit from the target price. If there is a cost gap, attempts will be made to close the gap.

2 The second and fourth statements are correct.

The five characteristics of services that make target costing more difficult in service industries include: intangibility, simultaneity (in Statement 2), heterogeneity, perishability (in Statement 4) and no transfer of ownership.

3 C $3.37

We start with the market price of $20 per hour as this is the same as our competitors. $23 is too high and led to C Co losing customers.

We than deduct the required profit to get the target cost:

	$
Sales price	20.00
Required profit ($2.5m ÷ 462,000)	(5.41)
Target cost	14.59

To work out the cost gap, we need to compare this target cost to the estimated cost of one hour of cleaning:

Estimated cost

	$
Labour cost	10.00
Average cleaning product cost per labour hour	4.42
Fixed operating costs per unit ($1,635,480 ÷ 462,000)	3.54
Total operating cost per hour	17.96

Therefore the cost gap can be calculated as:

Cost gap = Estimated cost – target cost

= $17.96 – $14.59

= **$3.37**

4 B and D

A is not correct: a dominant company will find target costing less useful than a business faced with competitive pressures.

C is not correct either: ignoring the market price in such a competitive market will only lead to C Co's erosion of market share.

5 C

Both statements are correct.

239 PRINTER UNIVERSE CO (SEPTEMBER/DECEMBER 2025)

1 D

Feed-forward control is the correct answer as target costing helps take corrective action before production starts to ensure a cost gap can be closed.

2 $380

Selling Price = $500

Target profit is the higher of the higher of 25% profit mark-up and 20% of investment per unit.

25% mark-up = $500 × 25/125 = $100 per unit

Return on investment = ($300,000 × 20%)/500 = $120 per unit

Hence, target profit is $120 per unit.

Therefore, target cost = selling price – target profit = $500 - $120 = $380 per unit of Zone.

3 A

Firstly, calculate the target cost = $110 × 0.75 = $82.50

The current cost is $10 + $16 + ($64 × 0.5) + ($20 × 1.5) = $88

So the cost gap is $88 – $82.50 = $5.50

If we look at the total actual cost without the ink which is $56, the difference to target cost is $82.50 – $56 = $26.50 which is how much the ink required for the cartridge can cost.

The ink required per cartridge is 0.5 gram so the cost per gram is $53.

4 C, D

Accepting a lower profit margin and negotiating a bulk discount are two ways to close the cost gap.

Increasing the selling price isn't viable as it is set in reference to the market, and reducing the amount of ink would mean the cartridge wouldn't last so long and so would impact the perceived quality of the product.

5 **C**

Services are heterogenous, not homogenous. This means that the service may differ depending on the situation. This variability makes predictability impossible, which is what makes it difficult to apply target costing.

As services provided by the after-sales service department are intangible experiences rather than physical outputs, it is difficult to specify all the components that make up the service, and so it is difficult to define the costs.

As services are produced and consumed at the same time, during the customer interaction, it becomes difficult to apply target costing as there is little (if any) chance to pre-design the service in the way you would with a physical product. Target costing requires a stable, predictable output so costs can be set and managed in advance.

As unused service capacity cannot be stored and used at a later date (i.e. services are perishable), target costing becomes difficult as it assumes stable, predictable output levels do that costs can be planned and controlled, but perishability makes demand and costs far less predictable.

240 VOLT CO (MARCH 2019)

Tutorial note

Make sure you read through the technical article on lifecycle costing published on the ACCA website in the Performance Management (PM) section.

1 **C**

Nuclear station	$
Operating costs, net of depreciation: ($486 m –$175 m) × 40 years	12,440 m
Building costs	7,000 m
Decommissioning costs	12,000 m
Total costs	$31,440 m
9,000 gigawatts per year × 40 years	360,000 gigawatts
Cost per Gigawatt $31,440m/360,000 gigawatt	$87,333

2 **B**

Statement (1) is not correct: increasing the useful life of the station will decrease the average annual cost. The operating cost will be incurred every year, thus increasing the total life-cycle costs.

Statement (2) is correct. If the decommissioning cost is reduced, this will reduce the total life-cycle costs.

3 C

Environmental internal failure costs are those costs incurred from performing activities that have produced contaminants and waste that have not been discharged into the environment.

We are told that 'the decommissioning cost' is incurred by Volt Co as a result of its activities; It relates to the cost of safely disposing of spent nuclear fuel', and by 'safely' we may deduct that the fuel has not been discharged into the environment, it is being disposed of in a safe manner to ensure that it does not become a cost borne by society as a whole.

4 B

Tutorial note

The total lifecycle cost of $55,000 per gigawatt is split into operating costs ($40,000 per gigawatt) and non-operating costs ($15,000 per gigawatt). An operating margin is calculated after deducting operating costs only.

1,750 Gigawatts per year × 20 years = 35,000 gigawatts in total over the life of the wind station.

		$
Total operating costs over the life of the wind station	35,000 gigawatts × $40,000	(1,400 m)
Operating profit (operating margin)	1,400 × (40/60)	$933.33 m
Less:		
Non-operating costs	35,000 gigawatts × $15,000	($525m)
Lifetime profit		$408.33 m

An alternative debrief, starting from the selling price based on an operating margin of 40%, reads as follows:

		$
Selling price per gigawatt	$40,000/0.60	$66,667 m
Lifetime profit per gigawatt	($66,667 – $55,000)	$11,667 m
Total Lifetime profit	1,750 Gigawatts × $11,667 × 20 years	$408.33 m

5 B

Statements (1) and (2) are benefits of life-cycle costing for Volt Co.

Statement (3) describes a benefit of activity-based costing (ABC), and is not correct: although life-cycle costing tracks the actual costs and revenues attributable to each product from 'cradle to grave' (thereby enabling a product's true profitability to be determined at the end of its economic life), it does not give a better understanding of the actual causes of overhead costs.

Statement 4 describes a benefit of relevant costing, and is not correct either: The objective of LCC is to select the most cost-effective approach, so that the lowest long-term cost of ownership is achieved; but short-term decision making, that focuses on cost control, is not served by the adoption of lifecycle costing.

241 SHOE CO (JUNE 2016, ADAPTED)

1 **The third and fourth statements are correct.**

2 **$6,960,000**

Total sales revenue		$34,300,000
Less costs:		
Development and design costs		($5,600,000)
Patent application costs (including $20K)		($500,000)
Patent renewal costs – 2 years		($400,000)
Total material costs	[(280,000 × $16) + (420,000 × $14)]	($10,360,000)
Total labour costs	[(280,000 × $8) + (420,000 × $7)]	($5,180,000)
Fixed production overheads		($3,800,000)
Selling and distribution costs		($1,500,000)
Profit		$6,960,000

3 **The third and fourth statements are correct.**

Statement (1) is not correct: identifying the costs of environment-related activities is difficult. Statement (2) is not correct either: EMA generates and analyses both financial and non-financial information in order to support internal environmental management processes.

4 **C**

Expected marketing cost in year 1: (0.2 × $2.2m) + (0.5 × $2.6m) + (0.3 × $2.9m) = $2.61m

Expected marketing cost year 2: (0.3 × $1.8m) + (0.4 × $2.1m) + (0.3 × $2.3m) = $2.07m

Total expected marketing cost = $4.68m

5 **D**

242 SWEET TREATS BAKERY (DECEMBER 2016)

Tutorial note

The Examiner has reported that performance was weaker in December 2016 on this scenario question, which tested throughput accounting in a situation where resources were scarce. It was interesting that this technique involved an understanding of limiting factor analysis. Understanding is particularly lacking in this area, so make sure you give it the time it deserves in your revision plan.

1 **B**

Process	**Available minutes**	**Brownies**	**Muffins**	**Cupcakes**	**Total minutes required**
Weighing	240	60	45	100	205
Mixing	180	80	48	60	188
Baking	1,440	480	330	600	1,410

The bottleneck is the mixing process as 188 minutes are required to meet maximum demand but there are only 180 minutes available.

Note: Four batches of brownies need to be made in order to have sufficient cakes to meet maximum demand as the cakes must be made in their batch sizes.

2 **A**

	Brownies	**Muffins**	**Cupcakes**
Throughput contribution ($)	50	37.5	35
Mixing minutes	20	16	12
Throughput per mixing minute ($)	2.50	2.34	2.91
Ranking	2	3	1

Optimal production plan:

Fulfil customer order	**Number of cakes**	**Mixing minutes**
1 batch of cupcakes	20	12
1 batch of brownies	40	20
1 batch of muffins	30	16
General production (based on ranking)		
4 batches of cupcakes	80	48
1 batch of brownies	40	20

Therefore the bakery should produce 80 brownies, 30 muffins and 100 cupcakes.

3 **Will not improve, Will improve, Will not improve, Will improve.**

	Will improve the TPAR	**Will not improve the TPAR**
The café customer will be given a loyalty discount.		✓
A bulk discount on flour and sugar is available from suppliers.	✓	
There is additional demand for the cupcakes in the market.		✓
The rent of the premises has been reduced for the next year.	✓	

Reduction in rent and discounts on materials will reduce costs and will improve the TPAR.

Giving a customer a loyalty discount will reduce sales revenue and as a result the TPAR. Demand for cupcakes can increase but it will not impact the TPAR as demand is not the restriction.

4 **C**

Each oven has a capacity of eight hours and each cupcake batch takes two hours, so four extra batches can be made. Extra throughput = four batches × $35 = $140.

Less the hire costs will result in an additional profit of $95

5 **A**

As the TPAR exceeds 1, then the throughout contribution exceeds operating costs, so Statement 1 is false. Less idle time on a non-bottleneck process would not improve the TPAR, so Statement 2 is false.

Improving efficiency during the weighing process would improve the TPAR as any actions to improve throughput on a bottleneck will improve the TPAR, so Statement 3 is true.

243 BRICK BY BRICK (JUNE 2010 ADAPTED)

1 **D**

Costs and quoted prices for the GC using labour hours to absorb overheads:

		GC
		$
Materials		3,500
Labour	300 hrs × $15/hr	4,500
Overheads	300 hrs × $10/hr (W1)	3,000
Total cost		11,000
Quoted price		16,500

Workings:

(W1) Overhead absorption rate is calculated as $400,000/40,000 hrs = $10/hr

2 B

Costs for the EX using ABC to absorb overheads:

			EX
			$
Materials			8,000
Labour		500 hrs × $15/hr	7,500
Overheads			
– Supervisor	(W2) and (W3)		1,080
– Planers	(W2) and (W3)		1,400
– Property	(W2) and (W3)		3,000
Total cost			20,980

(W2)

	Costs	**Number of drivers**	**Cost per driver**
Supervisor	90,000	500	180
Planners	70,000	250	280
Property	240,000	40,000	6

(W3)

	Supervisor	**Planner**	**Property**
Cost per driver (W2)	$180	$280	$6
EX overhead using ABC	180 × 6 = 1,080	280 × 5 = 1,400	6 × 500 = 3,000

3 C

Statement A is incorrect. Whilst increasing the quoted price of the EX by 2% will retain the mark up percentage, the total profits from EX may not be maintained as the increase in price may make the product less appealing to customers, or they may switch to competitor products, reducing sales volumes. So overall total profits may not be maintained, despite the profit per unit being the same.

This also explains why statement D is incorrect. Keeping the existing mark ups will make the GC more competitive as the quoted price will reduce, but the EX becomes less competitive.

Statement B is incorrect. Reducing labour hours would reduce the overheads attributed to EX under the existing method, but is not focussing on what is driving the overheads which is site visits, and planning documents.

4 C

Both statements are true.

As marginal costing does not incorporate fixed costs into the unit cost, budget volume is not necessary to calculate a unit cost.

By focussing only on marginal costs, there is a risk the service is priced at a price that covers marginal costs, and is low enough to be more competitive. The total contribution may not necessarily cover fixed costs and therefore, there is a risk that management's pricing decisions will not lead to an overall profit, especially when overheads are large.

5 B, D and E are correct.

If budgeted level of activity differs from actual level of activity, over-absorption or under-absorption of overheads may occur under ABC just as under absorption costing. This will have to be accounted for when reconciling the budgeted and actual profit under ABC. Hence, this answer option is incorrect.

ABC leads to a rational absorption of overheads and therefore it is particularly useful when overheads are high in the overall cost structure of a business. Hence, this answer option is correct.

ABC can be applied to both manufacturing and service industry. In fact, ABC is relevant in service industries where overheads account for a significant share of the total cost. Hence, this answer option is incorrect.

Marginal costing takes into account only variable costs whereas ABC accounts for all costs when computing the cost of a product. This means that ABC gives a better reflection of the true cost of a product unlike marginal costing which computes a lower cost. Hence, this answer option is correct.

ABC absorbs costs on the basis of cost driver units consumed in the making of a product or provision of a service. Cost drivers are specific actions that cause the costs to be incurred. As a result, ABC helps to understand what really drives costs. In contrast, absorption costing absorbs costs using rather generic or blanket factors for absorbing overheads. This does not help to ascertain what is driving costs. Hence, this answer option is correct.

ABC considers all costs, including fixed costs, when computing the cost of a product or service. This means ABC treats fixed costs as product costs. On the other hand, marginal costing does not absorb any fixed costs when computing the cost of a product; in fact, it treats all fixed costs as period costs i.e. relating to a specific time period. Hence, this answer option is incorrect.

244 GOODTYME CO (SEPTEMBER/DECEMBER 2024)

1 C

Under the theory of constraints, a business should attempt to elevate a bottleneck resource to a level where it ceases to be a bottleneck. At that point, there will be a new bottleneck from another resource, hence statement 1 is correct.

Throughput accounting aims to make optimal use of the bottleneck resource, but limit the usage of non-bottleneck resources to the level required to maximise throughput. This avoids waste such as the creation of work in progress. Statement 2 is therefore incorrect.

In throughput accounting, work in progress is valued at the cost of materials only, as no value is considered to be added to it until it is completed and sold, so statement 3 is correct.

2 **B**

Throughput accounting ratio (TPAR) is calculated by dividing the throughput per assembly machine hour by the factory cost per assembly machine hour.

Throughput per clock is equal to sales price less materials = $40.00 – $15.50 = $24.50.

It takes 20 minutes of assembly machine time, the bottleneck resource, to make each clock. So, throughput per assembly machine hour = $24.50 / (20/60) = $73.50 per hour.

Total factory cost per clock is equal to the total of all factory costs apart from materials = $6.60 + $3.00 + $2.40 = $12.00.

Factory cost per assembly machine hour = $12.00 / (20/60) = $36.00.

So, TPAR = $73.50 / $36.00 = 2.04 to two decimal places.

3

	Increase	**Decrease**
Improving the effectiveness and efficiency of the maintenance process to increase available machine hours	✓	
Payment of overtime at time and a third to increase the number of labour hours available		✓
Negotiating a contract to buy materials at a lower price from a new supplier	✓	
Changing electricity suppliers to one charging a lower standing charge per day for factory power	✓	

To approach this question it is necessary to refer to the calculation of the TPAR = throughput per assembly machine hour / factory cost per assembly machine hour. Any action that increases the throughput per assembly machine hour or decreases the factory cost per assembly machine hour will lead to an increase in the TPAR and vice versa.

Making more machine hours available means the total factory operating costs, which are treated as fixed under throughput accounting, would be spread over an increased number of hours. This would lead to a reduction in the factory cost per assembly machine hour and hence an increase in the throughput accounting ratio.

Paying labour at a higher rate per hour would increase the factory cost and hence cause the throughput accounting ratio to fall.

Buying materials from a cheaper supplier would increase throughput and hence increase the throughput accounting ratio.

Changing electricity suppliers would reduce the factory costs, therefore improving the throughput accounting ratio.

4 **D**

Production would be ranked based upon throughput per assembly machine hour, so it is necessary to calculate this for all three watches.

	GL	RT	SM
Sales price per unit	$36.00	$26.00	$22.00
Materials per unit	$14.70	$10.30	$8.80
Throughput per unit	**$21.30**	**$15.70**	**$13.20**
Assembly machine time (minutes)	24	18	15
Assembly machine time (hours)	0.4	0.3	0.25
Throughput per assembly machine hour	**$53.25**	**$52.33**	**$52.80**
Ranking for production	**1st**	**3rd**	**2nd**

5 **D**

The new stopwatch has a TPAR of 1.75. This indicates that the throughput per hour (throughput contribution) is greater than the factory cost per hour (operating costs) so statement 1 is incorrect.

The TPAR calculation uses total factory cost per hour, and so would exclude any non-production costs such as advertising costs. Statement 2 is therefore incorrect.

DECISION-MAKING TECHNIQUES

245 SIP CO

Tutorial note

There is a lot of information in this question and a lot to do for the marks available. Questions in the exam are unlikely to have this level of detail but the question should still allow you to practice applying your knowledge in these areas.

1 **Upholstery fabric** = \$85 × 20 + \$7.50 × 20 = **\$1,850**

Do not include the retainer as this is paid whether or not the refurbishment goes ahead.

Galley = \$4,000 + 40 × \$15 + 0.9 × 2,000 = **\$6,400**

This is cheaper than the new galley of \$6,500

2 **A**

If the teak in inventory is used, the relevant cost is sale proceeds lost plus the cost of sanding – \$95 + \$14 = \$109. This is cheaper than buying new teak. The remaining 5m will need to be bought. All the teak needs staining and the machine resetting.

Relevant cost = 5 × \$109 + 5 × \$110 + \$4.50 × 10 + \$80 = \$1,220

3 **Skilled labour \$2,640 Unskilled labour \$648**

The existing skilled labour can be used costing (\$25 + \$6) × 100 = \$3,100

OR new labour can be hired and trained costing \$25 × 100 + \$14 ×10 = \$2,640

Take the cheaper cost.

The unskilled workers are guaranteed work for \$420/\$12 = 35 hours.

They are currently working \$372/\$12 = 31 hours. Therefore there are 4 hours per week per worker spare capacity. There are 5 workers therefore 20 hours a week will have no cost, leaving 36 hours to be paid for at time and a half.

36 × \$12 × 1.5 = \$648

4 **Committed, Notional, Committed**

	Committed	**Notional**
Factory rates	✓	
Depreciation		✓
Interest	✓	

5 **The second and third statements are correct.**

246 HARE EVENTS (DECEMBER 2016)

1 B

Total fixed costs = $385,000

Contribution per marathon entry [$55 – ($15.8+$2.4)] = $36.80

BEP = $385,000/$36.80 = 10,462 entries

Margin of safety (20,000 – 10,462)/20,000 = 47.7%

2 C

Revenue	**Full marathon**	**Half marathon**	**Total**
Price	55	30	
Sales volume	20,000	14,000	
Total Revenue	1,100,000	420,000	1,520,000
Sales mix	72.4%	27.6%	

Variable costs	**Full marathon**	**Half marathon**	**Total**
Race packs	15.8	10.8	
Water stations	2.4	1.2	
Variable cost per entry	18.2	12	
Sales volume	20,000	14,000	
Total variable costs	364,000	168,000	532,000

Weighted average C/S ratio = (1,520,000 – 532,000)/(1,520,000) = 65%

Break Even Revenue = $385,000/65% = $592,308

3 A

Revenue to achieve target profit = ($500,000 + $385,000)/65% = $1,361,538

Sales needed of each event based on original sales mix:

Full Marathon 72.4% × $1,361,538 = $985,324

In units: $985,324/$55 = 17,915 entries

Half marathon 27.6% × $1,361,538 = $376,214

In units: $376,214/$30 = 12,540 entries

4 Will not change, Will change.

	Will change	Will not change
Breakeven volume		✓
Breakeven revenue	✓	

Current contribution = $12

Current BEP = $48,000/$12 = 4,000 units

Current BER = $48,000/($12/$20) = $80,000

Revised contribution (($20 × 1.1) – ($8 × 1.1) = $13.20

Revised fixed costs = $48,000 × 1.1 = $52,800

Revised BEP = $52,800/$13.20 = 4,000 units

Revised BER = $52,800/($13.20/$22) = $88,000

The BEP has not changed but the BER has increased by 10%.

5 C

CVP analysis assumes no movement in inventory and the C/S ratio can be used to indicate the relative profitability of different products, so Statements 1 and 2 are correct.

247 RACQUETZ CO (MARCH/JUNE 2023)

1 D

To calculate the weighted average contribution to sales ratio, divide the total contribution for all products with the total sales revenue for all products. The sales volume ratio of 4:2:1 should be used for the quantities of each product. It is easier to do this calculation using a table.

	Badminton racquets	Tennis racquets	Squash racquets	Total
Sales mix	4	2	1	
Contribution per unit	10	15	8	
Total contribution	**40**	**30**	**8**	**78**
Sales revenue per unit	21	30	24	
Total sales revenue	**84**	**60**	**24**	**168**

C/S ratio = 78/168 = **46.4%**

Option A used the weighted average variable cost over the weighted average sales revenue.

Option B did not weight the contribution or the sales revenue.

Option C used variable costs over sales revenue and did not weight the variable costs or the sales revenue.

2 **A**

Firstly, calculate the total sales revenue required to break even. This can be calculated as: fixed costs/C/S ratio. Use the weighted average C/S ratio, which is given in the question, of 52.21%.

Total sales revenue required to break even = $604,750/0.5221 = $1,158,303

The next step is to calculate the split of this total for each product. This is based on the proportion of total sales revenue for each product. As in question 1, the sales volume ratio should be used as the quantity for each product.

	Badminton racquets	**Tennis racquets**	**Total**
Sales mix	3	5	
Selling price per unit	22	32	
Total Revenue	**66**	**160**	**226**

Sales revenue from badminton racquets: $1,158,303 × 66/226 = **$338,265**

Sales revenue from tennis racquets: $1,158,303 × 160/226 = **$820,038**

Option B calculated the correct breakeven sales revenue, but used revenue per unit to proportion this to each product.

Option C calculated the correct breakeven sales revenue, but used the sales volume ratio to proportion this to each product.

Option D incorrectly calculated the breakeven sales revenue by multiplying the fixed costs by the C/S.

3 **D**

This question requires the calculation of the total sales revenue required to make a profit of $450,800. This can be calculated as: (fixed costs + required profit)/C/S ratio. The weighted average C/S ratio of 52.21% given in the question should be used.

Total sales revenue required to make a profit of $450,800 = $(604,750 + 450,800)/ 0.5221 = $2,021,739. The answer should be rounded to the nearest $000, so $2,022,000.

Option A deducted the target profit from fixed costs instead of adding it.

Option B multiplied by the C/S ratio rather than dividing.

Option C omitted the fixed costs.

4 **B**

The best way to tackle this type of question is to consider each statement while examining the graph.

Statement 1: The shape of the graph shows that this is false. The graph is bow-shaped which assumes that the company sells its most profitable product first and then its next most profitable product, and so on. The higher the C/S ratio, the steeper the gradient of the line and the higher the profit of a product, therefore the chart shows that tennis racquets are more profitable than badminton racquets as they have a higher C/S ratio.

Statement 2: The straight line on the graph assumes a constant sales mix and the line crosses the x-axis at the breakeven point. The line crosses the x-axis at approximately $1,300,000 therefore statement 2 is true.

Statement 3: The top of the line can be read on the y-axis as $740,000, but this is the approximate profit for 20X3, not the contribution, therefore statement 3 is false.

Statement 4: Both the bow shaped line and the straight line cross the y-axis at $600,000 which is the fixed cost amount therefore statement 4 is true.

5 C

It is important to read the requirement carefully here as the question is looking for facts which means that the use of CVP will be limited.

Statement 1: CVP analysis assumes that racquet sales prices will be the same at all levels of activity. This is not the case for badminton racquets if discounts are being given at the World Championship event, therefore statement 1 is true.

Statement 2: CVP analysis assumes that variable costs per racquet are the same at all levels of output. As the racquets are improved, the variable costs per racquet are likely to change and economies of scale may also be achieved. Therefore statement 2 is true.

Statement 3: CVP analysis assumes that costs can be divided into a component that is fixed and a component that is variable. This assumption is true for Racquetz Co therefore statement 3 is false as this is not a limitation.

248 CARDIO CO (DECEMBER 2015, ADAPTED)

1 A

Statements (1) and (2) are not valid: 'the elliptical trainers made a loss in 2015' and 'the elliptical trainers made a positive contribution in the year just passed' are sunk events.

Statement (5) is not valid either: businesses evolve and the fact that the business was founded to produce and sell elliptical trainers is irrelevant in this decision.

2 B

Statement (1) is not correct: fixed costs can be incremental to a decision, and in those circumstances would be relevant. Statement (2) is not correct either: notional costs are used to make cost estimates more realistic; however, they are not real cash flows and are not considered to be relevant.

3 B

	T	C	R
	$	$	$
Selling price	1,600	1,800	1,400
Material	(430)	(500)	(360)
Labour 40%	(88)	(96)	(76)
Variable overheads	(110)	($120)	(95)
Contribution	972	1,084	869
Sales units	420	400	380
Total contribution	$408,240	$433,600	$330,220

Total contribution achieved by all three products = \$408,240 + \$433,600 + \$330,220 = \$1,172,060

Margin of safety = budgeted sales – breakeven sales

Budgeted sales revenue = \$1,924,000

Fixed labour costs = {(420 × \$220) + (400 × \$240) + (380 × \$190)} × 0.6 = \$156,360.

Therefore total fixed costs = \$156,360 + \$55,000 = \$211,360.

$$\text{Breakeven sales revenue} = \frac{\text{Fixed costs}}{\text{Weighted average C/S ratio}}$$

$$\text{Breakeven sales revenue} = \frac{\$211{,}360}{60.92\%}$$

Breakeven sales revenue = \$346,947.

Therefore margin of safety = \$1,924,000 – \$346,947 = \$1,577,053.

4 A

If the more profitable products are sold first, this means that the company will cover its fixed costs more quickly. Consequently, the breakeven point will be reached earlier, i.e. fewer sales will need to be made in order to break even. So, the breakeven point will be lower.

5 B

The general fixed overheads should be excluded as they are not incremental, i.e. they are not arising specifically as a result of this order. They are not sunk as they are not past costs.

249 CARA CO (MARCH 2019)

1 C

'Materials' is the only limiting factor in Month 1, as more is needed than is available. To satisfy the maximum demand in Month 1 would require:

	4,000 units of 'Seebach'	**3,000 units of 'Herdorf'**	**Total resource needed**	**Total maximum resource available**
Materials	5 kgs per unit × 4,000 units = 20,000 kgs	7 kgs per unit × 3,000 units = 21,000 kgs	41,000 kgs	34,000 kgs
Labour hours	2 hours per unit × 4,000 units = 8,000 hours	3 hours per unit × 3,000 units = 9,000 hours	17,000 hours	18,000 hours
Machine hours	3 hours per unit × 4,000 units = 12,000 hours	2 hours per unit × 3,000 units = 6,000 hours	18,000 hours	18,000 hours

2 C

	Seebach	Herdorf
	$	$
Contribution per unit	250	315
Number of labour hours per unit	2	3
Contribution per labour hour:	**125**	**105**
Ranking	1st	2nd

Only the legally binding production of 2,000 units of 'Herdorf' should be honoured in Month 2. It would use up 2,000 × 3 hours = 6,000 hours. The remaining 6,000 hours should be used to produce the top ranking product, the Seebach.

3 C

Both statements are correct.

The shadow price is the contribution earned from having one extra unit of limited resource available and is also the extra, on top of the existing cost for that limited resource, which a company would be willing to pay to acquire that extra resource. If the shadow price is $125 per labour hour, it would mean that Cara Co would be willing to pay $125 of overtime premium per hour for the next 2,000 hours. The maximum hourly rate Cara Co would be willing to pay would be ($45 + $125) $170 for an additional 2,000 hours of temporary staff.

4 D

Tutorial note

Although you will not be asked to produce a linear programming graph in the exam, you must be able to read a lot of information from one.

The iso-contribution line can be dragged towards the optimum production point within the feasible region. The optimum point is found at the intersection of the lines 'H=3,000' and '3S + 2H = 12,000'.

This corresponds to a production of 2,000 units of 'Seebach' and 3,000 units of 'Herdorf'.

	Seebach	Herdorf	
	$	$	
Contribution per unit	250	315	
Total number of units as per graph	2,000	3,000	
Total contribution	500,000	945,000	$1,445,000
Fixed costs (monthly)			$300,000

Therefore profit = $1,445,000 – $300,000 = $1,145,000.

5 A

Statement (1) is correct: the line representing the labour constraint '2S + 3H = 24,000' does not delimit the feasible area, and therefore labour is not a scarce resource in Month 3. It can be therefore described as a slack variable.

Statement (2) is not correct: the current number of machine hours satisfies the maximum demand of Herdorfs (3,000 units) and if more machine hours were to become available in Month 3, they should be used to make more of the other product (the Seebach).

250 HOME ELECTRICS CO (MARCH/JUNE 2021)

1 $17

From the scenario, it is stated that the limiting factor for Product T in the first quarter was direct materials. The calculation is therefore the contribution per kg of direct materials.

Selling Price	$120
Variable Cost ($15 + $35 + $18)	$(68)
Contribution	$52
Kgs of material required per unit	3 kgs
Contribution per kg of material ($52/3 kgs)	**$17.33**

The answer is to be provided to the nearest whole $, therefore $17.

2 B

The constraint equations are given:

Materials 2B + 3T = 2,000 (1)

Labour 3B + 5T = 3,200 (2)

To solve the simultaneous equations, we must multiply the equations so that we end up with the value of Bs or the value of Ts the same. We could multiply equation (1) by 5 and (2) by 3 to give:

10B + 15T = 10,000 (3)

9B + 15T = 9,600 (4)

Now we can eliminate the Ts by deducting equation (4) from equation (3). This leaves us with

1B = 400.

We can calculate the value of T, by using B = 400 in any of the equations. Using equation (1):

(2 × 400) + 3T = 2,000

800 + 3T = 2,000

3T = 1,200

Therefore, T = 400

Now that we know the quantities of B and T, we can calculate the total contribution.

The contribution of B = ($80 – $10 – $21 – $12) = $37.

The contribution of T = ($120 – $15 – $35 – $18) = $52.

The total contribution is therefore (37 × 400) + (52 × 400) = $35,600.

3 **D**

The first statement is incorrect. Linear programming identifies the optimum number of units of each product to produce, not the optimum selling price.

The second statement is incorrect. Slack occurs when less of the limited resource is required than is available. When slack occurs, there will be some of the resource left over after production of the optimum production plan.

4 **$0**

There are three constraints for the Large Appliances division (labour hours, material and machine hours). It is stated in the scenario that labour and machine time have been identified as the binding constraints. This suggests that material is NOT a binding constraint, and therefore will have a shadow price of $0. Only binding constraints will have a shadow price.

5 **A**

1. Product D has a slack value. At the optimum solution, the demand for product D is 250, while the output is 200. Product D has unfulfilled demand at the optimum solution, so it has a slack value. This statement is true.
2. Contribution of $76,000 will be earned from the optimum production plan. The optimum production plan is to produce 240 units of product F and 200 units of product D. The total contribution will be (240 × $150) + (200 × $200) = $76,000. This statement is true.
3. Labour and machine time intersect at the optimum point if shown on a graph. As labour and machine time are the binding constraints, they will be the vertex where the optimum point occurs on a linear programming graph. This statement is true.

251 JEWEL CO (JUNE 2016, ADAPTED)

1 4 batches

Tutorial note

The tabular approach to finding the optimum price Jewel Co should charge is required here. In this exam, pricing questions tend to test the algebraic method (MR=MC), cost-plus and pricing strategies – the tabular method appears less frequently. However, it is impossible to answer this question using the algebraic method, because of the changing fixed costs.

The other trap to avoid here is to calculate the profit per unit for each demand level. This is meaningless for comparison, as it's better to sell 2,000 units for a profit of $1.50 per unit than 1,000 units for a profit of $2 per unit.

Total profit = Total sales revenue – total variable costs – total fixed costs

Batches sold	Total revenue	Total variable costs	Total fixed costs per month	Total profit
		$	$	$
1	1,000 units × $20 = $20,000	1,000 units × $10 = $10,000	10,000	0
2	2,000 units × $18 = $36,000	2,000 units × $8.80 = $17,600	10,000	8,400
3	3,000 units × $16 = $48,000	3,000 units × $7.80 = $23,400	12,000	12,600
4	4,000 units × $13 = $52,000	4,000 units × $6.40 = $25,600	12,000	14,400
5	5,000 units × $12 = $60,000	5,000 units × $6.40 = $32,000	14,000	14,000

The highest total profit is achieved when 4 batches (4,000 units) are sold.

2 C

Statement (1) is correct. Jewel Co's fixed costs fit the stepped costs definition – a type of fixed cost that is only fixed within certain levels of activity. Once the upper limit of an activity level is reached then anew higher level of fixed cost becomes relevant.

Statement (2) is also correct. Working on the principle that large cost savings are likely to be found in large cost elements, management's attention should start to focus on how these set-up costs could be reduced. Is there any reason why the headphones units have to be produced in batches of only 1,000? A larger batch size would reduce those set-up costs.

3 B

Statement (1) is not correct. It is the algebraic model that requires a consistent relationship between price (P) and demand (Q), so that a demand equation can be established, usually in the form P = a – bQ. Similarly, there must be a clear relationship between demand and marginal cost, usually satisfied by constant variable cost per unit and constant fixed costs.

Statement (2) is correct. The model is only suitable for companies operating in a monopoly, because any 'optimum' price might become irrelevant if competitors charge significantly lower prices and as Jewel Co is only setting up an online business, it is probably not a monopoly.

4 A

5 $25

When P= 0, demand (Q) = 72,000 units

P = a – bQ

Find b:

b = change in price/change in quantity = 5/8,000 = 0.000625

Find a:

P = a – 0.000625Q

Substitute in P = 0, Q = 72,000

0 = a – (0.000625 × 72,000)

a = 45

So demand function is:

P = 45 – 0.000625Q

If optimum profit maximising quantity is 32,000 then optimum price is:

P = 45 – (0.000625 × 32,000)

P = $25

252 SKULPT CO (SEPTEMBER/DECEMBER 2022)

1 D

The question asks about setting the price in the home market, and which of the factors would have the LEAST impact.

There are no currency issues to consider if we are only looking only at the home market. This is the least likely to concern the company when setting the price in the home country.

Customer demand – This is driven largely by price and so would be a key factor in setting the price.

Manufacturing Costs – Businesses must cover their costs in the long run so costs are also a key factor in setting prices.

Competitors' prices – In this market although the products are not identical, any large deviations in prices between competitors will see some customers move to the cheaper products when they are similar. This is therefore also a key factor.

2 A

If demand is price elastic the percentage of units demanded changes at a greater rate than the price per unit. If the price goes down the number of units sold (demanded) goes up by a greater amount, so the revenue will increase.

3 $252

Profit is maximised when marginal revenue (MR) = marginal cost (MC).

MR = 450 – 0.4Q

MC = variable costs = $30 + $24 = $54

So:

54 = 450 – 0.4Q

Q = (450 – 54)/0.4

Q = 990

Using price equation at profit maximising Q:

P = 450 – 0.2Q

P = 450 – (0.2 × 990)

P = $252

4 $60

A minimum price requirement relates to relevant cost. Relevant costs are future incremental costs, which will only be incurred if the contract for LOK Co is fulfilled.

In this question, the best approach is to go through each cost given and decide whether or not it is relevant to the one-off order for LOK Co.

In terms of the production and selling costs, the full cost per unit of one GSA is $112, but the only relevant costs are the variable production costs ($30) and the variable selling and distribution costs ($24). The total fixed production and fixed selling and distribution costs will not change as a result of the LOK Co order.

Considering the other costs, the LOK Co order requires extra finishing which will generate additional production costs of $6 per unit. This is a relevant cost as it would not be incurred if the LOK Co order is not fulfilled.

The $2 required for the additional packaging will be paid for and supplied by LOK Co so should not be included in the minimum price to be charged by Skulpt Co.

The electronic chip cost of $7 is included in the variable cost of $30 so should not be double counted.

The mark-up of 20% should not be included in the calculation of the minimum price.

The minimum price for the LOK Co order is therefore (30 + 24 + 6) = $60.

5 C and D

Skulpt Co's objectives are to discourage new entrants and shorten the initial period of the product life cycle.

Market penetration pricing involves setting an initially low price in order to grow the customer base quickly. This would allow Skulpt Co to shorten the initial period of the product life cycle and reach the growth and maturity stages quickly.

Using a relevant costing approach would result in arriving at the minimum price for the GSA, which would fit with objective of setting a minimum acceptable price to discourage new entrants.

Market skimming involves setting an initially high price which can be lowered at a later stage. This would not assist Skulpt Co in meeting its objectives.

Skulpt Co is following a price discrimination strategy but based on location rather than product version.

Transfer pricing and complementary product pricing are not suitable for Skulpt Co's objectives.

253 RUNF (MARCH/JUNE 2024)

1 C

Profit will be maximised when marginal revenue (MR) = marginal cost (MC).

In a question such as this we can substitute variable cost for marginal cost, which for the Quikcyc is given as $230.

The demand function (P = a – bQ) has been provided as P = 893 – 0.009Q. Marginal revenue is found as MR = a – 2bQ.

Marginal revenue (MR)

MR = 893 – 0.018Q

Marginal cost (MC) = $230

Equate MC and MR to find profit maximising quantity:

230 = 893 – 0.018Q

Rearrange and solve for Q:

0.018Q = 893 – 230

0.018Q = 663

Q = 36,833

Use Q = 36,833 in price equation to find optimum profit maximising price:

P = 893 – (0.009 × 36,833)

Solve for P:

P = $562

If you answered:

Option A – Correct calculation of Q, but incorrect equation used for price.

Option B – Arranged incorrectly hence wrong value of Q, and subsequent price.

Option D – Correct calculation of Q, but then used incorrectly to obtain price.

2 **$660**

P = a – bQ is the demand function, a straight line relationship. The value of 'a' reflects the price at which the quantity demanded is zero (it is the intercept on the y axis). So, we need to find 'a'.

Firstly the value of 'b' has to be calculated from the information provided relating to the impact of price changes on the demand for the Fitcyc.

b = change in price/change in quantity = 8/1,000 = 0.008.

So using the price/demand combination provided for the product ($500 price will lead to sales of 20,000 units) 'a' can be calculated through substitution.

P = a – bQ

500 = a – (0.008 × 20,000) = 660

The price at which demand will be zero is $660.

3 **B**

The demand function for hand weights is given as P = 84 – 0.001Q. The price at which 75,000 sets can be sold is calculated from this.

P = 84 – (0.001 × 75,000) = 9. Price of $9 is required to sell the 75,000 sets.

Total contribution = ($9 – $5) × 75,000 = $300,000.

Total fixed cost can be calculated at the activity level of 48,000 sets = $2 × 48,000 = $96,000.

Profit = $300,000 – $96,000 = **$204,000**.

If you answered:

Option A – incorrect fixed cost used to calculate profit

Option C – total sales value calculated as opposed to profit

Option D – total contribution calculated but fixed costs not deducted

4 **C**

Statement 1 means that the device has a short life-cycle. Price skimming is suitable as profits can be made relatively quickly.

Statement 2 means that Runf Co will want to recover costs quickly. Price skimming is therefore favourable.

Statement 4 means that the device is innovative. Customers are likely to pay a high price for something which is new and different and so price skimming is favourable.

Statement 3 does not favour a market skimming pricing policy. Potential competitors will be attracted to the idea of producing their own version of the device in order to obtain high profits. Discouraging new entrants is usually a reason to adopt a penetration strategy.

5 C

Statement 1 is false as PED is calculated by percentage change in demand/percentage change in price, the inverse of that which has been suggested.

Statement 2 is false because elastic demand means that customers are sensitive to price changes. Therefore, a price increase would lead to a proportionately larger fall in demand, and hence have a negative impact on total revenue.

254 GAM CO (JUNE 2014, ADAPTED)

1 C

Price per unit $30			
Sales volume	**Profit**	**Probability**	**EV of profit**
120,000	$930,000	0.4	$372,000
110,000	$740,000	0.5	$370,000
140,000	$1,310,000	0.1	$131,000
		EV of profit	$873,000

2 C

Price per unit $35			
Sales volume	**Profit**	**Probability**	**EV of profit**
120,000	$1,172,000	0.3	$351,600
110,000	$880,000	0.3	$264,000
140,000	$742,000	0.4	$296,800
		EV of profit	$912,400

3 B

Under the maximin rule, the decision-maker selects the alternative which maximises the minimum payoff achievable.

4 B

Under this rule, the decision-maker selects the alternative which offers the most attractive worst outcome, i.e. the alternative which maximises the minimum profit. In the case of Gam Co, this would be the price of $35 as the lowest profit here is $742,000, as compared to a lowest profit of $740,000 at a price of $30.

5 A

The maximax rule involves selecting the alternative ($30 or $35 selling price) that maximises the maximum payoff available, which in this case is $1,310,000. Therefore, a price per unit of $30 should be selected.

255 MYLO (SEPTEMBER 2016)

1 A

The maximin rule selects the maximum of the minimum outcomes for each supply level. For Mylo the minimum outcomes are:

450 lunches – $1,170

620 lunches – $980

775 lunches – $810

960 lunches – $740

The maximum of these is at a supply level of 450 lunches.

2 D

The minimax regret rule selects the minimum of the maximum regrets.

Demand level	**Supply level**			
	450	620	775	960
	$	$	$	$
450		190	360	430
620	442	–	217	322
775	845	403	–	230
960	1,326	884	481	–
Max regret	1,326	884	481	430

The minimum of the maximum regrets is $430, so suggests a supply level of 960 lunches.

3 B

Expected values do not take into account the variability which could occur across a range of outcomes; a standard deviation would need to be calculated to assess that, so Statement 2 is correct.

Expected values are particularly useful for repeated decisions where the expected value will be the long-run average, so Statement 4 is correct.

Expected values are associated with risk-neutral decision-makers. A defensive or conservative decision-maker is risk averse, so Statement 1 is incorrect.

Expected values will take into account the likelihood of different outcomes occurring as this is part of the calculation, so Statement 3 is incorrect.

4 A

This requires the calculation of the value of perfect information (VOPI).

Expected value with perfect information = (0.15 × $1,170) + (0.30 × $1,612) + (0.40 × $2,015) + (0.15 × $2,496) = $1,839.50

Expected value without perfect information would be the highest of the expected values for the supply levels = $1,648.25 (at a supply level of 775 lunches).

The value of perfect information is the difference between the expected value with perfect information and the expected value without perfect information = $1,839.50 – $1,648.25 = $191.25, therefore $191 to nearest whole $.

5 D

The investment's sensitivity to fixed costs is 550% ((385/70) × 100), so Statement 3 is correct.

The margin of safety is 84.6%. Budgeted sales are 650 units and BEP sales are 100 units (70/0.7), therefore the margin of safety is 550 units which equates to 84.6% of the budgeted sales, so Statement 4 is therefore correct.

The investment is more sensitive to a change in sales price of 29.6%, so Statement 1 is incorrect.

If variable costs increased by 44%, it would still make a very small profit, so Statement 2 is incorrect.

256 HURSTMID CO (MARCH/JUNE 2025)

1 A

This decision relies on identification of the relevant costs and revenues were a product range to be discontinued. Revenue and variable costs will be considered relevant to this decision, as would attributable fixed costs since if the product is no longer made these cash flows would cease.

Therefore, on this basis it is necessary to calculate the relevant profit or loss for each product as revenue, less variable costs, less attributable fixed costs. Any product that generates a relevant loss should be discontinued as if its production were to cease Hurstmid would be better off.

For the Leisuro the figure is a loss of $100 ($800 – $900), for the Serenito the figure is a profit of $100 ($500 – $400), hence the correct answers is to cease production of the Leisuro only.

2 C

If the chair is complementary to other (profitable) products, ceasing to sell the chair could affect the profitability of the other products so this is correct.

Selling at a loss can be a deliberate strategy to increase market share so this is correct.

3 A

A make-or-buy decision can be made by either comparing the relevant costs of each option, or by calculating the net cost from one option.

If a chair type is purchased from Hampar the relevant cost would be the purchase price quoted. If a chair type is to be manufactured internally the relevant costs would be the variable cost incurred plus the attributable fixed cost.

Net cost of internal manufacture is calculated as follows:

	Comforo	**Leisuro**	**Serenito**
	$'000	**$'000**	**$'000**
Variable costs	1,800	900	700
Attributable fixed costs	1,000	900	400
Less saved purchase cost (from Hampar)	(2,100)	(700)	(1,200)
Net cost of internal manufacture	**700**	**1,100**	**(100)**

Serenito is the only product where there is a benefit to be found from continuing to manufacture internally. For the other two products there would be a net saving if they were to be purchased from Hampar.

4 **$110,000**

The original purchase price of $80,000 is not relevant to the decision as this cost is historic and therefore sunk.

The machine is in use by the company at present generating a net income of $110,000, higher than its value if sold of $90,000. To utilise this machine for the residential home order Hurstmid would have to either cease production of other products, thereby losing the $110,000 net income, or purchase a new machine at a cost of $120,000. The lower of these options is the $110,000 which is therefore the relevant cost of this asset.

5

	True	**False**
The costs which the minimum price should cover are incremental costs and opportunity costs only	✓	
It can lead to the product's perceived value in the market being eroded	✓	
The price can be easily raised on subsequent orders without affecting customer retention		✓

A minimum price is based on relevant costs, which would be the total of incremental and opportunity costs only.

Setting a minimum price to gain business can lead to the perceived value of a product being eroded as customers can view cheap as being consistent with low quality.

It can actually be difficult to increase the price of subsequent orders if the minimum price sets the expectation of the customers, hence this last statement is false.

257 HORNGREN CO (MARCH/JUNE 2022)

1 1st: Luxury, 2nd: Fruity, 3rd: Natural

First, establish which of direct labour, direct material or machine capacity is the limiting factor.

	Required	**Available**
Direct labour	(5,000 × 4/8) + (10,000 × 8/8) + (15,000 × 12/8) = 35,000 hours	36,000 hours
Direct material	(5,000 × 3/1.50) + (10,000 × 3.75/1.50) + (15,000 × 4.5/1.50) = 80,000 kg	75,000 kg
Machine capacity	(5,000 × 1/1) + (10,000 × 4/1) + (15,000 × 6/1) = 135,000 hours	140,000 hours

Therefore, direct material is the limiting factor. Now rank the products based on their contribution per unit of limiting factor.

Product	**Natural**	**Fruity**	**Luxury**
Contribution ($)	8.00	10.25	13.50
Material kg per unit	2 kg	2.5 kg	3 kg
Contribution per kg of material ($)	4.00	4.10	4.50
Ranking	**3**	**2**	**1**

2 3,750 units

In month 2 the limiting factor is machine capacity. Calculate the ranking of the products based on the cost saved by making per unit of limiting factor.

Product	**Natural**	**Fruity**	**Luxury**
Buy in cost ($)	11.00	17.00	25.00
Variable cost of making ($)	7.00	11.75	16.50
Cost saved by making ($)	4.00	5.25	8.50
Machine hours per unit	1 hour	4 hours	6.00
Cost saved per machine hour ($)	4.00	1.31	1.42
Ranking	**1**	**3**	**2**

This shows that the products should be made in the order of Natural, Luxury then Fruity.

Machine hours available	120,000
Make 5,000 units of Natural (use 5,000 × 1 hour)	5,000
Make 15,000 units of Luxury (use 15,000 × 6 hours)	90,000
Remaining hours available for Fruity	25,000

The remaining hours are enough to make (25,000/4) = 6,250 units. Therefore, buy in (10,000 – 6,250) **= 3,750 units**.

3 A

Making Fruity internally gives a saving on variable cost of $5.25 per unit ($17 – $11.75). As 2,000 units are being made internally, this saves ($5.25 × 2,000) = $10,500 which is more than the incremental fixed cost. The plan would therefore be unchanged.

4 A and D

Because of its specialisation the facilities management company might be able to do the job cheaper than Horngren Co, allowing Horngren Co to make some cost savings.

By outsourcing these functions, Horngren Co's management will have more time to focus on its core business activities.

B is incorrect as services provided by outside suppliers will still need to be monitored by Horngren Co to ensure they are being done to the standards required.

C is incorrect as much of the control over these activities will be passed to the external party, and Horngren Co's management's control is likely to decrease.

5 B

Statement (1) is not true. Joint products are accounted for separately in the accounts and are not treated in the same way as by-product.

Statement (2) is true. Joint products are normally only identifiable at their split-off/separation point.

BUDGETING AND CONTROL

258 LRA (JUNE 2015, ADAPTED)

1 C

2 C

Statement (1) is not correct: At present, the LRA finds itself facing particularly difficult circumstances. The fires and the floods have meant that urgent expenditure is now needed on schools, roads and hospitals which would not have been required if these environmental problems had not occurred. Lesting is facing a crisis situation and the main question is therefore whether this is a good time to introduce anything new at the LRA when it already faces so many challenges.

Statement (2) is not correct: the introduction of ZBB in any organisation is difficult at any time because of the fact that the process requires far more skills than, for example, incremental budgeting. Managers would definitely need some specialist training as they simply will not have the skills which they would need in order to construct decision packages. This then would have further implications in terms of time and cost, and, at the moment, both of these are more limited than ever for the LRA.

Statement (3) is correct: with ZBB, the whole budgeting process becomes a lot more cumbersome as it has to be started from scratch. There is a lot of paperwork involved and the whole process of identifying decision packages and determining their costs and benefits is extremely time-consuming. There are often too many decision packages to evaluate and there is frequently insufficient information for them to be ranked. The LRA provides a wide range of services and it is therefore obvious that this would be a really lengthy and costly process to introduce. At the moment, some residents are homeless and several schools have been damaged by fire. How can one rank one as more important than the other when both are equally important for the community?

Statement (4) is correct: ZBB can cause conflict to arise as departments compete for the resources available. Since expenditure is urgently required for schools, roads and hospitals, it is likely that these would be ranked above expenditure on the recycling scheme. In fact, the final phase of the scheme may well be postponed. This is likely to cause conflict between departments as those staff and managers involved in the recycling scheme will be disappointed if the final phase has to be postponed.

3 A

4 D

ZBB will respond to changes in the economic environment since the budget starts from scratch each year and takes into account the environment at that time. This is particularly relevant this year after the fires and the floods. Without ZBB, adequate consideration may not be given to whether the waste management scheme should continue but, if ZBB is used, the scheme will probably be postponed as it is unlikely to rank as high as expenditure needed for schools, housing and hospitals. – If any of the activities or operations at LRA are wasteful, ZBB should be able to identify these and remove them. This is particularly important now when the LRA faces so many demands on its resources. – Managers may become more motivated as they have had a key role in putting the budget together. – It encourages a more questioning attitude rather than just accepting the status quo. – Overall, it leads to a more efficient allocation of resources. – All of the organisations activities and operations are reviewed in depth.

5 B

259 BOKCO (JUNE 2015, ADAPTED)

1 B

Statement (2) is not true: a minor error in the design of the model at any point can affect the validity of data throughout the spreadsheet. Even if the spreadsheet is properly designed in the first place, it is very easy to corrupt a model by accidentally inputting data in the wrong place.

Statement (3) is not correct either: spreadsheets cannot take account of qualitative factors that are always, by definition, difficult to quantify.

2 A

Statement (3) is not correct: the operational variances do give a fair reflection of the actual results achieved in the actual conditions that existed. Statement (4) is not correct either: the analysis helps in the standard-setting learning process , which will hopefully result in more useful standards in the future.

3 D

Revised hours for actual production: Cumulative time per hour for 460 units is calculated by using the learning curve formula: $Y = ax^b$

a = 7

x = 460

b = –0.1520 Therefore $y = 7 \times 460^{-0.1520} = 2.7565054$

Therefore revised time for 460 units = 1,268 hours.

Labour efficiency planning variance (Standard hours for actual production – revised hours for actual production) × std rate = ([460 × 7] – 1,268) × $12 = $23,424F

4 C

Labour efficiency operational variance (Revised hours for actual production – actual hours for actual production) × std rate (1,268 – 1,860) × $12 = $7,104A

5 C

Option A is not correct: there **will** be unnecessary extra labour costs. Bokco will have hired too many temporary staff because of the fact that the new product can actually be produced more quickly than originally thought. Given that these staff are hired on three-month contracts, Bokco will presumably have to pay the staff for the full three months even if all of them are not needed.

Option B is therefore not correct either: since Bokco uses cost plus pricing for its products, the price for the product will have been set too high. This means that sales volumes may well have been lower than they otherwise might have been, leading to lost revenue for the company and maybe even failure of the new product launch altogether. This will continue to be the case for the next two months unless the price review is moved forward.

Option C is correct: since production is actually happening more quickly than anticipated, the company may well have run out of raw materials, leading to a stop in production. Idle time is a waste of resources and costs money. If there have been stockouts, the buying department may have incurred additional costs for expedited deliveries or may have been forced to use more expensive suppliers. This would have made the material price variance adverse and negatively affected the buying department's manager bonus.

Option D is not correct: the sales manager will be held responsible for the poorer sales of the product, which will probably be reflected in an adverse sales volume variance. This means that they may lose their bonus through no fault of their own.

260 CORFE CO (SEPTEMBER 2016)

1 D

An 80% activity level is 210,000 units.

Material and labour costs are both variable. Material is $4 per unit and labour is $5.50 per unit. Total variable costs = $9.50 × 210,000 units = $1,995,000

Fixed costs = $750,000

Supervision = $175,000 as five supervisors will be required for a production level of 210,000 units.

Total annual budgeted cost allowance = $1,995,000 + $750,000 + $175,000 = $2,920,000

2 B

Variable cost per hour ($850,000 – $450,000)/(5,000 hours – 1,800 hours) = $125 per hour Fixed cost ($850,000 – (5,000 hours × $125)) = $225,000.

Number of machine hours required for production = 210 batches × 14 hours = 2,940 hours.

Total cost ($225,000 + (2,940 hours × $125)) = $592,500, therefore $593,000 to the nearest $000

3 C

If the budget is flexed, then the effect on sales revenue of the difference between budgeted and actual sales volumes is removed and the variance which is left is the sales price variance.

4 A

Flexible budgeting can be time-consuming to produce as splitting out semi-variable costs could be problematic, so Statement 1 is correct.

Estimating how costs behave over different levels of activity can be difficult to predict, so Statement 2 is correct. A flexible budget will not encourage slack compared to a fixed budget, so Statement 3 is incorrect.

It is a zero-based budget, not a flexible budget, which assesses all activities for their value to the organisation, so Statement 4 is incorrect.

5 C

Spreadsheets can be used to change input variables and new versions of the budgets can be more quickly produced, so Statement 1 is correct.

Sensitivity analysis is also easier to do as variables are more easily changed and manipulated to assess their impact, so Statement 4 is correct.

A common problem of spreadsheets is that it is difficult to trace errors in a spreadsheet and data can be easily corrupted if a cell is changed or data is input in the wrong place, so Statement 2 is incorrect.

Spreadsheets do not show qualitative factors; they show predominantly quantitative data, so Statement 3 is incorrect.

261 BELLAMY CO

1 A

The graph shows a positive correlation, which means that low values of sales are associated with low values of marketing expenditure, and high values of sales are associated with high values of marketing expenditure.

2 C

When there is no marketing expenditure, X = 0, and Y = \$50,000 + (20 × 0) = \$50,000.

If \$1,000 extra is spent on marketing, sales will increase by 20 × \$1,000 = \$20,000.

3 C

Coefficient of determination $r^2 = 0.85^2 = 0.72$

4 C

5 D

All of the stated factors can affect the accuracy of the forecast.

262 OBC (DECEMBER 2015, ADAPTED)

1 A

	Actual quantity used	Standard price	Total
White flour	408.50 Kgs	\$1.80	\$735.30
Wholegrain flour	152 kgs	\$2.20	\$334.40
Yeast	10 kgs	\$20.00	\$200.00
Actual quantity at standard price (AQ SP)			**\$1,269.70**
Standard quantity at standard price (SQ SP)	950 loaves	\$1.34	**\$1,273**
Variance			**\$3.3 F**

2 C

Ingredient	**AQAM** (kgs)	**AQSM** (kgs)	**Difference** (kgs)	**Standard cost** (\$/kgs)	**Variance** (\$)
White flour	408.50	420.86	12.36 F	1.80	22.25 F
Wholemeal flour	152	140.29	11.71 A	2.20	25.76 A
Yeast	10	9.35	0.65 A	20	13 A
	570.5	570.5			**16.51 A**

Tutorial note

These numbers in the 'Actual Quantity – Standard Mix (AQSM)' column are calculated by taking the actual input in total (that is, 570.5 kgs) from the previous column AQAM, and copying it across to the second column AQSM. Then, work it back in the standard proportions. For example, the standard proportion for 'white flour' is 450 grams out of 610; We take that (450/610) as a proportion and multiply it by the actual total of 570.5 kgs, giving us a standard proportion for white flour, on the actual weight, of (450/610) × 570.5 = 420.89 kgs.

3 D

Method 1: the 'Total' method

Actual output (given)	950 loaves
Expected output from actual input	570,500 g/610 g per loaf = 935.25 loaves
Difference	14.75 loaves F
Standard cost per loaf	$1.34
Variance	**$19.77 F**

Method 2: the 'Individual' method:

Ingredient	**SQSM** (kgs)	**AQSM** (kgs)	**Difference** (kgs)	**Standard cost** ($/kg)	**Variance** ($)
White flour	427.50	420.861	6.639 F	1.80	11.95 F
Wholemeal flour	142.50	140.287	2.213 F	2.20	4.87 F
Yeast	9.50	9.352	0.148 F	20	2.96 F
	579.5 kgs (*)	570.5 kgs			**19.78 F**

(*) 610 g standard weight per loaf × 950 loaves = 579,500 g or 579.5 kgs

4 B

Statement (1) is not correct: if some mix was left behind, it is the efficiency of turning the inputs into outputs that would be diminished. Therefore, it would be the yield variance that is affected, not the mix variance.

5 C

Both statements are correct: Errors in the quality or proportions of ingredients will make the items sub-standard and therefore rejected by the quality inspector.

When baked at the wrong temperature and therefore be rejected by the quality inspector if they are burnt, or undercooked.

263 VARIANCES – SALES

1 **A**

"The difference between the sales quantity and **volume** variances is that the standard **mix** is considered in the former. The difference between standard and actual is **ignored**."

2

Profit per unit =	10,600 – (10,600/1.06) = $600
Actual market size =	(30,000/0.1) × 0.95 = 285,000
Sales expected	0.1 × 285,000 = 28,500 units
Actual sales	285,000 × 0.15 = 42,750
So:	
Market size variance	(30,000 – 28,500) × $600 = **$900,000** Adverse
Market share variance	(28,500 – 42,750) × $600 = **$8,550,000** Favourable

3 **$708,000 Adverse**

4 **$2,982,000 Adverse**

Tutorial note

The standard margins (SM) per unit can be calculated as follows:

$10,600 – (10,600/1.06) = $600 (Drastic)

$13,250 – (13,250/1.06) = $750 (Bomber)

$16,960 – (16,960/1.06) = $960 (Cracker)

	AQ and AM	Standard Margin		
Drastic	26,000	600	**$41,040,000**	
Bomber	16,000	750		
Cracker	14,000	960		
	56,000			**$708,000 Adv**

	AQ and SM	Standard Margin		
Drastic	25,200	600	**$41,748,000**	
Bomber	14,000	750		
Cracker	16,800	960		
	56,000			**$2,982,000 Adv**

	SQ and SM	Standard Margin	
Drastic	27,000	600	**$44,730,000**
Bomber	15,000	750	
Cracker	18,000	960	
	60,000		

5 **D**

264 GRAYSHOTT CO (MARCH 2019)

1 A

Tutorial note

Grayshott operates a marginal costing system and therefore we understand 'standard contribution'(and not standard profit) to be the 'standard margin' here.

In view of the 'difficult economic conditions', we must revise the market demand with a decrease of 10%; this means the revised market demand should be 40,000 units × (1 – 10%), so 36,000 units.

Standard margin (per unit):

	$
Selling price	65.00
Material cost (5.2 kgs × $4 per kg)	(20.80)
Labour (2 hours × $8 per hour)	(16.00)
Variable overheads (2 hours × $4 per hour)	(8.00)
Contribution	20.20

Market share variance: (38,000 units – 36,000 units) × $20.20 = $40,400 favourable

2 C

Tutorial note

We are told here that the actual cost of materials amounted to $4.40 per kilogram. As the total actual expenditure was $836,000, we must have purchased $836,000/$4.40 = 190,000 kilograms of materials.

Original standard price $4 per kilogram of material

Revised standard price $4 × (1 + 6%) = $4.24 per kilogram of material

Based on actual purchases of materials:

190,000 kilograms should have cost 190,000 × $4.00 (old standard) = $760,000

190,000 kilograms should have cost 190,000 × $4.24 (revised standard) = $805,600
Variance = $760,000 – $805,600 = $45,600 Adverse

3 B

The budgeted labour rate per hour was, as per question, $8 per hour.

The actual labour rate per hour was 25% higher than the standard of $8 per hour; this means that the actual labour rate per hour was $8 × (1+25%) = $10. This is an adverse operational difference of $2 per hour.

Number of hours worked (based on actual performance) = ($798,000/$10) = 79,800 hours.

79,800 hours × $2.00 per hour adverse = $159,600 adverse.

4 D

All statements are correct. Labour efficiency planning variance will occur when the standard hours have to be revised due to factors which are beyond the control of the operational managers. All the factors would require the original standard hours to be revised and would therefore cause a labour efficiency planning variance.

5 C

Both statements are correct and are known issues with the introduction of a system of planning and operating variances.

265 ROMEO CO (DECEMBER 2016)

1 B

Dough 18.9 kg × ($7.60 – $6.50) = $20.79 favourable

Tomato sauce 6.6 kg × ($2.50 – $2.45) = $0.33 favourable

Cheese 14.5 kg × ($20.00 – $21.00) = $14.50 adverse

Herbs 2 kg × ($8.40 – $8.10) = $0.60 favourable

Total material price variance = $7.22 favourable

2 D

	AQSM	**AQAM**	**Diff**	**Std**	**Variance**
	kg	kg	kg	**cost**	$
Dough	20	18.9	1.1 F	7.60	8.36 F
Sauce	8	6.6	1.4 F	2.50	3.50 F
Cheese	12	14.5	2.5 A	20.00	50.00 A
Herbs	2	2		8.40	
	42	42			38.14 A

3 A

	SQSM	**AQSM**	**Diff**	**Std**	**Variance**
	kg	kg	kg	**cost**	$
Dough	22	21.43	0.57 F	7.60	4.33 F
Sauce	8.8	8.57	0.23 F	2.50	0.58 F
Cheese	13.2	12.86	0.34 F	20.00	6.80 F
Herbs	2.2	2.14	0.06 F	8.40	0.50 F
	46.2	45			12.21 F

4 A

A favourable mix variance indicates that a higher proportion of cheaper ingredients were used in production compared to the standard mix.

5 C

The actual cost per pizza will be lower than the standard cost per pizza because expensive cheese has been replaced with cheaper tomato sauce.

The usage variance equals the mix and yield variances. The yield variance will be zero as 100 pizzas used 42 kg, so the mix and usage variances will be the same.

Sales staff should not automatically lose their bonus as the reduced sales could be a result of the change in mix affecting the quality of the pizza and the new chef will only be responsible for the mix and yield variances as they have no control over the purchase costs of ingredients.

Section 6

ANSWERS TO CONSTRUCTED RESPONSE QUESTIONS – SECTION C

DECISION MAKING TECHNIQUES

266 BELLAHOUSTON CO (DECEMBER 2021)

(a) (i) **Identify the limiting factor**

	Road	**Spikes**	**Trail**	**Total**
Direct material/pair	1.5	0.6	1.2	6,930
Direct Labour/pair	1	1.5	1	6,750
Machine time/pair	0.4	0.2	0.3	1,875

Based on the above, machine time is the limiting factor.

Calculate the contribution per unit of limiting factor and rank the products:

	Road	**Spikes**	**Trail**
Contribution per pair of shoes ($)	43.50	29.50	36.00
Machine hours required	0.40	0.20	0.30
Contribution per machine hour ($)	108.75	147.50	120.00
Ranking	3	1	2

Prepare the optimum production plan and calculate resultant total contribution earned:

	Machine hours used (1,815 available)	**Contribution per pair of shoes ($)**	**Total contribution ($)**
Fulfil customer order:			
200 Road	80	35.50	7,100
200 Spikes	40	21.50	4,300
200 Trail	60	28.00	5,600
	1,635 hours remaining		
Apply ranking:			
1,400 Spikes – 1st	280	29.50	41,300
1,650 Trail – 2nd	495	36.00	59,400
2,150 Road – 3rd	860 (β)	43.50	93,525
			211,225

(ii) **Calculate the profit maximising mix:**

	Machine hours used (1,815 available)	Contribution per pair of shoes ($)	Total contribution ($)
Apply ranking for the general sales in March:			
1,400 Spikes	280	29.50	41,300
1,650 Trail	495	36.00	59,400
2,300 Road	920	43.50	100,050
Apply ranking for special order:			
200 Spikes	40	21.50	4,300
200 Trail	60	28.00	5,600
50 Road	20 (β)	35.50	1,775
			212,425

The loss of contribution from fulfilling RunWild's order is $1,200 ($212,425 – $211,225), therefore the maximum financial penalty acceptable would be $1,200.

Alternative approach:

If RunWild's order could only be partially completed, then Bellahouston Co would divert machine hours from making Road shoes for the specific order to making Road shoes for general sale to other retailers. The number of Road shoes for general sale in part (a)(i) fails to meet demand by 150 pairs of shoes and the difference in the contribution earned from making them available for general sale and not to RunWild is $8 per pair. Therefore, the difference in the contribution earned is $1,200 (150 pairs of Road shoes × $8), which would be the maximum financial penalty Bellahouston Co would be willing to accept.

(b) Although the contribution earned is higher if the order is only partially completed, if Bellahouston Co does not fully complete the order, then RunWild may not enter into a regular supply contract and future sales revenue would therefore be lost. In addition, the customer base and reputation of RunWild will help to market Bellahouston Co's products and increase awareness of their products. This benefit will also be lost if RunWild choose not to order from Bellahouston Co again.

It would also not be good for Bellahouston Co's existing reputation if it becomes known for not fulfilling its obligations. This could make other sports retailers reluctant to order from them. It might also impact the end-customer's perception of their product if they cannot buy Bellahouston Co's running shoes due to a lack of availability.

(c) **Define the variables:**

R = number of pairs of Road shoes

S = number of pairs of Spikes shoes

T = number of pairs of Trail shoes

Constraints:

Direct material	1.5R + 0.6S + 1.2T ≤ 6,120
Direct labour	1R + 1.5S + 1T ≤ 5,865
Machine time	0.4R + 0.2S + 0.3T ≤ 1,815
Demand	R ≤ 2,300
	S ≤ 1,400
	T ≤ 1,650
Non-negativity	R, S, T ≥ 0

Objective function:

C = 43.50R+ 29.50S + 36.00T

ACCA Marking scheme			
			Marks
(a)	(i)	Production plan	7
	(ii)	Financial penalty	4
(b)		Discussion	4
(c)		Linear programming	5
Total			**20**

267 HEALTH NUTS (SEPTEMBER/DECEMBER 2020)

(a) (i) The gym

Break-even Point

Average sales revenue per customer	$
Gym entry	8.40
Car park expected value (0.8 × $1)	0.80
	9.20
Variable cost	(1.20)
Contribution per customer	**8.00**
Total fixed costs	48,000
Break-even point ($48,000 ÷ $8)	**6,000 units**

Margin of Safety

Average number of customers per day	330
No of days in the month	30
Total customers in June (330 × 30)	**9,900**
Margin of Safety (customers) (9,900 – 6,000)	3,900
Margin of Safety (%) [(9,900 – 6,000) ÷ 9,900]	**39.39%**

(ii) The cafe

Break-even Point

Average contribution per customer	$
Drinks ($2.20 × 60% × 60%)	0.792
Food ($2.20 × 40% × 40%)	0.352
	1.144
Total fixed costs	3,600
Break-even point = ($3,600 ÷ $1.144)	**3,147 units**

Margin of Safety

Total customers in June (9,900 ÷ 2)	**4,950**
Margin of Safety (customers) = (4,950 – 3,147)	1,803
Margin of Safety (%) = [(4,950 – 3,147) ÷ 4,950	**36.43%**

(b) The gym needs 6,000 customers per month and the café needs 3,147 customers per month in order to cover its fixed costs.

Each $1 of contribution after this point generates profit.

Whether or not these figures are particularly high can be gauged by comparing them to the expected (or, in this case, actual) customers in one month and this is where the margin of safety is useful. Both the margin of safety for the gym and the café are quite similar, at approximately 39% and 36% respectively. This tells Health Nuts the extent to which it can feel confident about covering its fixed costs and making a profit. In this instance, its margin of safety is such that, even if its customer numbers went down by over one third it could still cover its fixed costs.

(c)

Total sales/contribution from gym

Original number of customers	330
New customers	120
Total customers per day	**450**
Number of days in the month	30
Total customers for the month (450 × 30)	**13,500**
Total sales from gym entry and car park (13,500 × $9.20)	**$124,200**
Total contribution (13,500 × $8)	**$108,000**

Total sales/contribution from crèche	
Total customers using the crèche per day	120
Number of days in the month	30
Total customers for the month (120 × 30)	3,600
Total number of children per month (3,600 × 2)	**7,200**
Total sales from crèche (7,200 × $4)	**$28,800**
Total contribution (7,200 × ($4 – $0.5))	**$25,200**
Total sales from gym and crèche	**$153,000**
Total contribution from gym and crèche	**$133,200**
Weighted average C/S ratio ($133,200 ÷ $153,000)	**87.06%**

Budgeted profit per month including crèche	$
Total contribution	133,200
Less: total fixed costs	(56,000)
Budgeted profit	**77,200**

(d)

	$
Total contribution from gym ($8 × 9,900)	79,200
Total contribution from cafe ($1.144 × 4,950)	5,663
Less: total fixed costs (48,000 + 3,600)	(51,600)
Budgeted profit	**33,263**

With the crèche, profit will increase from $33,263 to $77,200 per month, an increase of $43,937. Therefore, from a purely financial point of view, the crèche would seem like a good idea.

However, there are various other factors that need to be taken into account:

Details of how much the conversion from the café to the crèche will cost has not been provided. The investment would need to be appraised using a technique like NPV to assess its financial viability.

The research for the revised customer numbers is only initial. Is this data realistic and can it be relied on? There is no information about how Health Nuts got this research.

The opening of a crèche could put off other customers, who want to exercise in a child-free environment, from using the gym during the day. There is no indication that Health Nuts have taken this into account.

Similarly, closing the café could upset many other customers at all times of day and lead to the loss of their business.

The calculations so far performed are not therefore enough to make this decision.

268 COSMETICS CO (DECEMBER 2010, ADAPTED)

(a) Optimum production plan

Define the variables

Let x = no. of jars of face cream to be produced

Let y = no. of bottles of body lotion to be produced

Let C = contribution

State the objective function

The objective is to maximise contribution, C

C = 9x + 8y

State the constraints

Silk powder	$3x + 2y \leq 5{,}000$
Silk amino acids	$1x + 0.5y \leq 1{,}600$
Skilled labour	$4x + 5y \leq 9{,}600$

Non-negativity constraints:

$x, y \geq 0$

Sales constraint:

$y \leq 2{,}000$

On the graph

Silk powder	3x + 2y = 5,000
Silk amino acids	1x + 0.5y = 1,600
Skilled labour	4x + 5y = 9,600

Solve using iso-contribution line

Using the iso-contribution line, the furthest vertex from the origin is point 'c', the intersection of the constraints for skilled labour and silk powder.

Solving the simultaneous equations for these constraints:

4x + 5y = 9,600 × 3

3x + 2y = 5,000 × 4

12x + 15y = 28,800 12x + 8y = 20,000

Subtract the second one from the first one 7y = 8,800, therefore y = **1,257.14**.

If y = 1,257.14 and:

4x + 5y = 9,600

Then 5 × 1,257.14 + 4x = 9,600

Therefore x = 828.58

If C = 9x + 8y

C = $7,457.22 + $10,057.12 = $17,514.34

(b) Shadow prices and slack

The shadow price for silk powder can be found by solving the two simultaneous equations intersecting at point c, whilst adding one more hour to the equation for silk powder.

4x + 5y = 9,600 × 3

3x + 2y = 5,001 × 4

12x + 15y = 28,800

12x + 8y = 20,004

Subtract the second one from the first one

7y = 8,796, therefore y = 1,256.57

3x + (2 × 1,256.57) = 5,001.

Therefore x = 829.29

C = (9 × 829.29) + (8 × 1,256.57) = $17,516.17

Original contribution = $17,514.34

Therefore shadow price for silk powder is $1.83 per gram.

The slack for amino acids can be calculated as follows:

(828.58 × 1) + (0.5 × 1,257.14) = 1,457.15 grams used.

Available = 1,600 grams.

Therefore slack = 142.85 grams.

Marking scheme			
			Marks
(a)	Optimum production plan		
	Defining constraint for silk powder		1
	Defining constraint for amino acids		1
	Defining constraint for labour		1
	Non-negativity constraint		1
	Sales constraint: x		1
	Sales constraint: y		1
	Iso-contribution line worked out		1
	Optimum point identified		2
	Equations solved at optimum point		3
	Total contribution		2
		Maximum	**14**
(b)	Shadow prices and slack		
	Shadow price		4
	Slack		2
		Maximum	**6**
Total			**20**

269 CUT AND STITCH (JUNE 2010)

(a) The optimal production mix can be found by solving the two equations given for F and T.

7W + 5L = 3,500

2W + 2L = 1,200

Multiplying the second equation by 2.5 produces:

7W + 5L = 3,500

5W + 5L = 3,000

2W = 500

W = 250

Substituting W = 250 in the fabric equation produces:

2 × 250 + 2L = 1,200

2L = 700

L = 350

The optimal solution is when 250 work suits are produced and 350 lounge suits are produced. **The contribution gained is $26,000**:

C = 48W + 40L

C = (48 × 250) + (40 × 350)

C = 26,000

(b) The shadow prices can be found by adding one unit to each constraint in turn.

Shadow price of T

7W + 5L = 3,501

2W + 2L = 1,200

Again multiplying the second equation by 2.5 produces:

7W + 5L = 3,501

5W + 5L = 3,000

2W = 501

= 250.5

Substituting W = 250.5 in the fabric equation produces:

(2 × 250.5) + 2L = 1,200

2L = 1,200 – 501

L = 349.5

Contribution earned at this point would be = (48 × 250.5) + (40 × 349.5) = 26,004 which is an increase of $4.

Hence the shadow price of T is $4 per hour.

Shadow price of F

7W + 5L = 3,500

2W + 2L = 1,201

Again multiplying the second equation by 2.5 produces:

7W + 5L = 3,500.0

5W + 5L = 3,002.5

2W = 497.5

W = 248.75

Substituting W = 248.75 in the fabric equation produces:

(2 × 248.75) + 2L = 1,201

2L = 1,201 – 497.5

L = 351.75

Contribution earned at this point would be = (48 × 248.75) + (40 × 351.75) = 26,010, which is an increase of $10. Hence the shadow price of F is $10 per metre.

(c) The shadow price represents the maximum premium above the normal rate a business should be willing to pay for more of a scarce resource. It is equal to the increased contribution that can be gained from gaining that extra resource.

The shadow price of labour here is $4 per hour. The tailors have offered to work for $4.50 – a premium of $3.00 per hour. At first glance the offer seems to be acceptable.

However, many businesses pay overtime at the rate of time and a half and some negotiation should be possible to create a win/win situation. Equally some consideration should be given to the quality aspect here. If excessive extra hours are worked then tiredness can reduce the quality of the work produced.

(d) If maximum demand for W falls to 200 units, the constraint for W will move left to 200 on the × axis of the graph. The new optimum point will then be at the intersection of:

W = 200 and

2W + 2L = 1,200

Solving these equations simultaneously, if:

W = 200, then (2 × 200) + 2L = 1,200

Therefore L = 400.

So, the new production plan will be to make 400L and 200W

Marking scheme			
			Marks
(a)	Optimal point calculation		3
	Contribution		1
		Maximum	**4**
(b)	For each shadow price		3
		Maximum	**6**
(c)	Rate discussion		3
	Other factors e.g. tiredness, negotiation		3
		Maximum	**6**
(d)	Find optimum point		1
	Solve 2 equations		2
	Conclusion		1
		Maximum	**4**
Total			**20**

270 BITS AND PIECES (JUNE 2009)

(a) The decision to open on Sundays is to be based on incremental revenue and incremental costs:

	Ref	$	$
Incremental revenue	(W1)		800,000
Incremental costs			
Cost of sales	(W2)	335,000	
Staff	(W3)	45,000	
Lighting	(W4)	9,000	
Heating	(W5)	9,000	
Manager's bonus	(W6)	8,000	
Total costs			(406,000)
Net incremental revenue			394,000

Conclusion

On the basis of the above it is clear that the incremental revenue exceeds the incremental costs and therefore it is financially justifiable.

Workings

(W1) Incremental revenue

Day	**Sales**	**Gross profit**	**Gross profit**	**Cost of Sales**
	$	%	$	$
Average	10,000	70%		
Sunday (+60% of average)	16,000	50%	8,000	8,000
Annually (50 days)	800,000		400,000	400,000
Current results (300 days)	3,000,000	70.0%	2,100,000	
New results	3,800,000	65.8%	2,500,000	

(W2) Purchasing and discount on purchasing

Extra purchasing from Sunday trading is $800,000 – $400,000 = $400,000

Current annual purchasing is $18,000 × 50 = $900,000

New annual purchasing is ($900,000 + $400,000) × 0.95 = $1,235,000

Incremental cost is $1,235,000 – $900,000 = $335,000 (a $65,000 discount)

(W3) Staff costs

Staff costs on a Sunday are 5 staff × 6 hours × $20 per hour × 1.5 = $900 per day
Annual cost is $900 × 50 days = $45,000

(W4) Lighting costs

Lighting costs are 6 hours × $30 per hour × 50 days = $9,000

(W5) Heating costs

Heating cost in winter is 8 hours × $45 per hour × 25 days = $9,000

(W6) Manager's bonus

This is based on the incremental revenue $800,000 × 1% = $8,000 (or $160 per day)

Tutorial note

Only relevant cash flows should be taken into consideration when making this decision, i.e. the future incremental cash flows that occur as a result of Sunday opening. Prepare a summary of the relevant cash flows and reference in workings, where required.

(b) The manager's rewards can be summarised as follows:

Time off

This appears far from generous. The other staff are being paid time and a half and yet the manager does not appear to have this option and also is only being given time off in lieu (TOIL) at normal rates. Some managers may want their time back as TOIL so as to spend time with family or social friends; others may want the cash to spend. One would have thought some flexibility would have been sensible if the manager is to be motivated properly.

Bonus

The bonus can be calculated at $8,000 per annum (W6); on a day worked basis, this is $160 per day. This is less than that being paid to normal staff; at time and a half they earn 6 hours × $20 × 1.5 = $180 per day. It is very unlikely to be enough to keep the presumably better qualified manager happy. Indeed the bonus is dependent on the level of new sales and so there is an element of risk involved for the manager. Generally speaking higher risk for lower returns is far from motivating.

The level of sales could of course be much bigger than is currently predicted. However, given the uplift on normal average daily sales is already +60%, this is unlikely to be significant.

(c) Discounts and promotion

When new products or in this case opening times are launched then some form of market stimulant is often necessary. B&P has chosen to offer substantial discounts and promotions. There are various issues here:

Changing buying patterns: It is possible that customers might delay a purchase a day or two in order to buy on a Sunday. This would cost the business since the margin earned on Sunday is predicted to be 20% points lower than on other days.

Complaints: Customers that have already bought an item on another day might complain when they see the same product on sale for much less when they come back in for something else on a Sunday. Businesses need to be strong in this regard in that they have to retain control over their pricing policy. Studies have shown that only a small proportion of people will actually complain in this situation. More might not, though, be caught out twice and hence will change the timing of purchases (as above).

Quality: The price of an item can say something about its quality. Low prices tend to suggest poor quality and vice versa. B&P should be careful so as not to suggest that lower prices do not damage the reputation of the business as regards quality.

Marking scheme

		Marks
(a)	Existing total sales	1.0
	New sales	1.0
	Incremental sales	1.0
	Existing purchasing	2.0
	Discount allowed for	1.0
	Incremental Sunday purchasing costs	1.0
	Staff cost	2.0
	Lighting cost	1.0
	Heating cost	1.0
	Manager's bonus	1.0
(b)	Time off at normal rate not time and a half	1.0
	Lack of flexibility	1.0
	Bonus per day worked calculation and comment	1.0
	Risk	1.0
(c)	Changing customer buying pattern	2.0
	Complaints risk	2.0
	Quality link	2.0
	Maximum	**4**
Total		**20**

Examiner's comments (extract)

This question (in the second two parts) required some common business sense. This is sadly lacking in many. The manager's pay deal offered them less money per hour than the staff (on current prediction of incremental sales) and time off on a one to one basis when the staff got time and a half. Most managers would be savvy enough to recognise a poor deal when they saw it. Equally a weekend day is for many a family day and a day off in the week is a poor substitute for that.

The offering of substantial discounts may well encourage sales (a mark earning point). However, surely it is likely that customers could switch from weekday shopping to weekend shopping to save money. Surprisingly few realised this.

Marks gained for part (a) were reasonable with incremental sales, staff costs, and lighting being done correctly by most candidates. For some reason the incremental heating cost was incorrectly calculated by many, with candidates electing to heat the stores all year as opposed to just the winter months as stated in the question.

There were two sunk costs to be excluded (rent and supervisor salary). It is always advisable for a candidate to indicate that the cost is to be excluded rather than simply not mention it at all.

Very few realised that the manager's pay deal was not overly generous both in terms of time off and the amount of cash on offer. Many candidates seemed to think that the mere existence of time off and the offer of money was enough to motivate. The amount of time off and cash was ignored. This is again naive, demonstrating a lack of understanding or experience.

271 STAY CLEAN (DECEMBER 2009)

(a) The relevant costs of the decision to cease the manufacture of the TD are needed:

Cost or Revenue	**Working reference**	**Amount** ($)
Lost revenue	Note 1	(96,000)
Saved labour cost	Note 2	48,000
Lost contribution from other products	Note 3	(118,500)
Redundancy and recruitment costs	Note 4	(3,700)
Supplier payments saved	Note 5	88,500
Sublet income		12,000
Supervisor	Note 6	0
Net cash flow		(69,700)

Conclusion: It is not worthwhile ceasing to produce the TD now.

Note 1: All sales of the TD will be lost for the next 12 months, this will lose revenue of 1,200 units × $80 = $96,000.

Note 2: All normal labour costs will be saved at 1,200 units × $40 = $48,000.

Note 3: Related product sales will be lost. This will cost the business 5% × ((5,000u × $150) + (6,000u × $270)) = $118,500 in contribution (material costs are dealt with separately below).

Note 4: If TD is ceased now, then:

Redundancy cost	($6,000)
Retraining saved	$3,500
Recruitment cost	($1,200)
Total cost	($3,700)

Note 5: Supplier payments:

	DW ($)	WM ($)	TD ($)	Net cost ($)	Discount level	Gross cost ($)
Current buying cost	350,000	600,000	60,000	1,010,000	5%	1,063,158
Loss of TD			(60,000)	(60,000)	5%	(63,158)
Loss of related sales at cost	(17,500)	(30,000)		(47,500)	5%	(50,000)
New buying cost				921,500	3%	950,000
Difference in net cost				88,500		

Note 6: There will be no saving or cost here as the supervisor will continue to be fully employed.

An alternative approach is possible to the above problem:

Cash flow	**Ref**	**Amount** ($)
Lost contribution – TD	Note 7	12,000
Lost contribution – other products	Note 8	(71,000)
Redundancy and recruitment	Note 4 above	(3,700)
Lost discount	Note 9	(19,000)
Sublet income		12,000
Supervisor	Note 6 above	0
Net cash flow		(69,700)

Note 7: There will be a saving on the contribution lost on the TD of 1,200 units × $10 per unit = –$12,000

Note 8: The loss of sales of other products will cost a lost contribution of 5% ((5,000 × $80) + (6,000 × $170)) = $71,000

Note 9:

	DW	WM	TD	Total (net)	Discount	Total gross
Current buying cost	350,000	600,000	60,000	1,010,000	5%	1,063,158
Saved cost	(17,500)	(30,000)	(60,000)			
New buying cost	332,500	570,000	0	902,500	5%	950,000
				921,500	3%	950,000
Lost discount				(19,000)		

(b) Complementary pricing

Since the washing machine and the tumble dryer are products that tend to be used together, Stay Clean could link their sales with a complementary price. For example they could offer customers a discount on the second product bought, so if they buy (say) a TD for $80 then they can get a WM for (say) $320. Overall then Stay Clean make a positive contribution of $130 (320 + 80 – 180 – 90).

Product line pricing

All the products tend to be related to each other and used in the utility room or kitchen. Some sales will involve all three products if customers are upgrading their utility room or kitchen for example. A package price could be offered and as long as Stay Clean make a contribution on the overall deal then they will be better off.

(c) Outsourcing requires consideration of a number of issues (only 3 required):

- The cost of manufacture should be compared to cost of buying in from the outsourcer. If the outsourcer can provide the same products cheaper than it is perhaps preferable.
- The reliability of the outsourcer should be assessed. If products are delivered late then the ultimate customer could be disappointed. This could damage the goodwill or brand of the business.
- The quality of work that the outsourcer produces needs to be considered. Cheaper products can often be at the expense of poor quality of materials or assembly.
- The loss of control over the manufacturing process can reduce the flexibility that Stay Clean has over current production. If Stay Clean wanted, say, to change the colour of a product then at present it should be able to do that. Having contracted with an outsourcer this may be more difficult or involve penalties.

272 MKL

(a) The selling price that should be charged for Product K is the one that maximises total contribution, i.e. a price of $75 for a demand of 1,400 units:

Selling price per unit	**$100**	**$85**	**$80**	**$75**
Variable cost	$38	$38	$38	$38
Unit contribution	$62	$47	$42	$37
Demand units	600 units	800 units	1,200 units	1,400 units
Total Weekly contribution	**$37,200**	**$37,600**	**$50,400**	**$51,800**

(b) 1,400 units of Product K will use up 1,400 standard hours; in order to utilise all of the spare capacity, we now need to use 600 hours for Product L, for the first 10 weeks.

$\frac{600 \text{ hours}}{1.25 \text{ hours}}$ = 480 units will use all the spare capacity.

To maximise profits, the optimum price P will be expressed as P = a – bQ.

Here, a = $\$100 + (\frac{1,000}{200} \times \$10)$

So a = $150 and b = $\frac{\$10}{200}$ 0.05

P = $150 – 0.05Q

P = $150 – 0.05 × 480 units

P = $126 for the first 10 weeks.

For the following 10 weeks when the extra capacity becomes available, the optimum price P will be expressed as P = a – bQ and we need to equate MC = MR to maximise profits, with

MR = a – 2bQ.

Profit maximised when MC = MR, i.e. when $45 = a – 2bQ

When $45 = $150 – 0.10Q i.e. when Q =1,050 units and P = $150 – 0.05 × 1,050

P = $97.50

(c) **Skimming**

Given that the product is innovative and unlike any current products on the market, then a skimming strategy would seem a very good fit. As the product in new and exciting, charging a high early price would help target the early adopters in the introduction stage. This would also have the advantage of allowing product M to be produced in relatively low volumes, whilst still generating good cashflows to recoup the substantial R&D and launch costs traditionally linked to this kind of products.

Finally, as the market is untested for the product, it allows the firm to start with a high intro price and adjust downwards accordingly.

Penetration pricing

This tactic represents the alternative approach when launching a new product; it involves charging an initial low price to quickly gain market share. It offers the advantage of scaring off potential entrants to the market and may allow the firm to exploit economies of scale. However, given that our product M is differentiated and there will be little, if any, immediate competition, we think the company is right to adopt a skimming strategy for its pricing.

273 DAISY CO (SEPTEMBER/DECEMBER 2023)

(a) (i) **Optimal production plan**

Further processing decision

	Nettle	**Monkey**
	$	$
Revenue at separation point	6,000,000	3,600,000
Revenue after further processing	7,500,000	5,220,000
	1,500,000	1,620,000
Revenue from normal losses		30,000
Incremental revenue	1,500,000	1,650,000
Incremental costs	(2,400,000)	(800,000)
Incremental profit	(900,000)	850,000

Working

Revenue from normal losses = 200,000 × 10% × $1.50 = $30,000

Produce 300,000 litres of Nettle and sell it at the separation point because the incremental revenue earned from further processing Nettle is less than the incremental cost.

Produce 200,000 litres of Monkey which will be further processed into 180,000 (200,000 × 90%) litres of Monkeyplus because the incremental revenue earned from further processing Monkey exceeds the incremental cost.

The optimal production plan is 300,000 litres of Nettle and 180,000 litres of Monkeyplus.

(ii) Profit statement for optimal production plan

Production	280,000	220,000
Sales	280,000	198,000
	Nettle	**Monkeyplus**
	$	$
Sales revenue	5,600,000	5,742,000
Apportioned joint cost	(4,500,000)	(3,300,000)
Further processing cost		(880,000)
Revenue from sale of normal losses		33,000
Profit	**1,100,000**	**1,595,000**

Workings

Sales revenue Nettle: 280,000 litres × $20 = $5,600,000

Sales revenue Monkeyplus: 220,000 × 0.9 × $29 = $5,742,000

Revenue from normal losses = 220,000 × 10% × $1.5 = $33,000

(b) When making a decision on whether to further process two joint products, the costs incurred to bring those products to the separation point have already been incurred and so are sunk costs. In addition, as the products are not separately identifiable before the separation point, any apportionment of joint costs to joint products is necessarily arbitrary. The only relevant costs in a further processing decision are those which are incurred after the separation point.

Joint processing costs are, however, relevant to assessing whether the whole process is viable, as the total costs to ready the products for sale need to be compared to the revenues earned to determine if the overall process generates a profit. In addition, the joint costs are avoidable if the joint process is closed.

(c) Enterprise resource planning (ERP) systems are modular software packages which are designed to integrate the key functions of an organisation (sales, manufacturing, planning, human resources, finance, purchasing, etc.), so that a single software system can serve the needs of all functional areas. This integration is achieved by setting up a database which can be shared by all application programs.

The major benefit of ERP systems is that information is visible and can be shared between different departments across the organisation. This would give the production manager access to price and cost data which is currently held within separate departments. ERP systems work in real time, meaning that the exact status of all key variables will be available to users at all times. Both of these improvements will allow the production manager to make more timely and effective decisions in relation to when to further process joint products.

ERP systems allow reports to be run across departments which can allow Daisy Co to analyse and compare functions. This could give Daisy Co information about the efficiency of different processes and help to identify where improvements could be made, e.g. is there a way to reduce the loss when further processing Monkey?

It can also eliminate repetitive manual tasks which can free up managers to focus on value-adding activities, e.g. the sales team can focus on building customer relationships instead of maintaining spreadsheets.

Improved information comes at a cost. ERP systems can be very expensive to set up and Daisy Co should conduct a cost benefit analysis before investing in such a system. If Daisy Co spends more money managing all of the different departmental systems than it would on a centralised system, then it could find that it saves on IT costs overall.

Marking scheme				
				Marks
(a)	(i)	Optimal plan		4
	(ii)	Profit statement		7
			Maximum	11
(b)	Explanation			3
(c)	ERPS			6
Total				**20**

274 KEYTONE CO (SEPTEMBER/DECEMBER 2022)

(a)

Pay off table

	Demand	Probability	Supply 3,000	Supply 3,500	Supply 4,000
	3,000	0.2	70,110	64,745	59,380
	3,500	0.3	70,110	81,795	76,430
	4,000	0.5	70,110	81,795	85,480
Expected value (EV) of profit ($)			70,110	78,385	77,545

Keytone Co should choose to produce 3,500 units as this production level gives the highest expected value (EV) of profit.

Workings

(W1) Make and sell 3,000 units (maximum which can be sold)

	$
Net sales proceeds (W4)	102,300
Variable costs (W5)	(30,750)
Stepped fixed costs (W6)	(1,440)
	70,110

(W2) Make 3,500 units but sell 3,000 units

	$
Net sales proceeds (W4)	102,300
Variable costs (W5)	(35,875)
Stepped fixed costs (W6)	(1,680)
	64,745

Make and sell 3,500 units (maximum which can be sold)

	$
Net sales proceeds (W4)	119,350
Variable costs (W5)	(35,875)
Stepped fixed costs (W6)	(1,680)
	81,795

Making the same profit if demand is 4,000 units.

(W3) Make 4,000 units and sell 3,000 units

	$
Net sales proceeds (W4)	102,300
Variable costs (W5)	(41,000)
Stepped fixed costs (W6)	(1,920)
	59,380

Make 4,000 units and sell 4,000 units (maximum which can be sold)

	$
Net sales proceeds (W4)	128,400
Variable costs (W5)	(41,000)
Stepped fixed costs (W6)	(1,920)
	85,480

(W4) Net sale proceeds

Per unit up to 3,500 units

	$
Sales price	35.00
Less selling and distribution costs	(0.90)
	34.10

Per unit over 3,500 units

	$
Sales price	33.00
Less selling and distribution costs	(0.90)
	32.10

Total sales revenue

Units	$
3,000	102,300
3,500	119,350
4,000	128,400

(W5) Variable costs per unit (at all volumes)

	$
Direct materials	6.20
Labour	2.70
Variable overheads	1.35
Total variable cost per unit produced	10.25

Total variable costs

	$
3,000	30,750
3,500	35,875
4,000	41,000

(W6) Stepped fixed costs

Machine cleaning and inspection costs for 3,000 units

Set ups required: 3,000 units/500 units	6
× $240 for each set up	$1,440

Machine cleaning and inspection costs for 3,500 units

Set ups required: 3,500 units/500 units	7
× $240 for each	$1,680

Machine cleaning and inspection costs for 4,000 units

Set ups required: 4,000 units/500 units	7
× $240 for each set up	$1,920

(b) Fee for the market research

EV of profit before perfect information by choosing to supply 3,500 units

EV of profit after perfect information

	Probability (p)	**Outcome (x) $**	**Px $**
Demand 3,000 so choose to supply 3,000	0.2	70,110	14,022
Demand 3,500 so choose to supply 3,500	0.3	81,795	24,539
Demand 4,000 so choose to supply 4,000	0.5	85,480	42,740
EV of profit with perfect information			81,301
Difference between EVs of profit			2,916

Maximum fee would therefore be $2,916

(c) Expected value is a long-run weighted average of the outcomes of a decision that is repeated time and time again. Since it is just an average, the actual outcomes will vary and none of them may be the same as the average calculated. It is therefore useful for a risk neutral decision-maker who is neither seeking nor avoiding risk and will be happy with the average outcome. It is also dependent on the accuracy of the probabilities applied to the outcomes.

The decision about how much Protein Power to produce is a repeated decision, so in this regard the use of expected value would seem appropriate. The managing director is, however, already concerned about the accuracy of the probabilities and looking to buy additional research, so the method does not seem appropriate in light of those concerns. Also, the managing director of the company is risk averse, not risk neutral, so it may be better to use a criterion like maximin. Using maximin, the decision-maker looks at the lowest outcome at each supply level and picks the supply level with the highest of the lowest outcomes, thus minimising any losses.

Marking scheme		
		Marks
(a)	Payoff table	12.5
	Decision	0.5
		13
(b)	Maximum fee	**3**
(c)	EV discussion	3
	Alternative	1
		4
Total		**20**

275 TR CO (SEPTEMBER/DECEMBER 2017)

(a) Step 1: Establish the demand function

Tutorial note

The first skill tested here is the choice of the right pricing method. As students are given information about how changes in price will affect demand, it is the MR = MC method (as opposed to the tabular method) that must be picked.

Students are expected to recognise that information about the learning effect must be taken into account to calculate labour costs and, in turn, establish the 'Marginal Cost' component of their pricing calculations.

b = change in price/change in quantity

b = $2/5,000 units = 0.0004

The maximum demand for Parapain is 1,000,000 units, so where P = 0, Q = 1,000,000, so 'a' is established by substituting these values for P and Q into the demand function:

0 = a – (0.0004 × 1,000,000)

0 = a – 400

Therefore a = 400 and the demand function is therefore: P = 400 – 0. 0004Q

Step 2: Establish the marginal cost

		Total in $
Material Z	500 g × $0.10	50
Material Y	300 g × $0.50	150
Labour	Working 1	6.6039
Machine running cost	(20/60) × $6.00	2
Total marginal cost per batch		208.6039

Note: Fixed overheads have been ignored as they are not part of the marginal cost.

The marginal cost will now be rounded down to $208.60 per batch.

Working 1: Labour

The labour cost of the 1,000th unit needs to be calculated as follows as this is the basis TR Co will determine the price for Parapain:

Learning curve formula: $Y = aX^b$

'a' is the cost for the first batch: 5 hours × $18 = $90

If X = 1,000 batches and b = –0.321928, then $Y = 90 \times 1{,}000^{-0.321928} = 9.7377411$

Total cost for 1,000 batches = $9,737.7411

If X = 999 batches, then $Y = 90 \times 999^{-0.321928} = 9.7408781$

Total cost for 999 batches = $9,731.1372

Therefore the cost of the 1,000 batches ($9,737.7411 – $9,731.1372) = $6.6039

Step 3: Establish the marginal revenue function: MR = a – 2bQ

Equate MC and MR and insert the values for 'a' and 'b' from the demand function in step 1.

208.60 = 400 – (2 × 0.0004 × Q)

Step 4: Solve the MR function to determine optimum quantity, Q

208.60 = 400 – 0.0008Q

0.0008Q = 191.4

Q = 239,250 batches

Step 5: Insert the value of Q from step 4 into the demand function determined in step 1 and calculate the optimum price

P = 400 – (0.0004 × 239,250)

P = $304.30

Step 6: Calculate profit

	Total in $
Revenue (239,250 batches × $304.30)	72,803,775
Variable cost (239,250 batches × $208.60)	(49,907,550)
Fixed costs (250,000 batches × $2)	(500,000)
Profit	22,396,225

(b) Market penetration pricing

Tutorial note

Requirement (b) asked discussions and recommendations; for students wondering where to start, pros and cons of different strategies are a good point to make initially. It is interesting to notice that even if all information pointed towards skimming as the strategy of choice, students would have not maximised marks unless market penetration was mentioned, too.

With penetration pricing, a low price would initially be charged for the anti-malaria drug. The ideology behind this is that the price will make the product accessible to a larger number of buyers and therefore the high sales will compensate for the lower prices being charged. The anti-malaria drug would rapidly become accepted as the only drug worth buying, i.e. it would gain rapid acceptance in the marketplace.

The circumstances which would favour a penetration pricing policy are:

- Highly elastic demand for the anti-malaria drug, i.e. the lower the price, the higher the demand. There is no evidence that this is the case.
- If significant economies of scale could be achieved by TR Co so that higher sales volumes would result in sizeable reductions in costs. It cannot be determined if this is the case here.

- If TR Co was actively trying to discourage new entrants into the market, however in this case, new entrants cannot enter the market anyway due to the patent.
- If TR Co wished to shorten the initial period of the drug's life-cycle so as to enter the growth and maturity stages quickly but there is no evidence the company wish to do this.

Market skimming pricing

With market skimming, high charges would initially be charged for the anti-malaria drug rather than low prices. This would enable TR Co to take advantage of the unique nature of the product. The most suitable conditions for this strategy are:

- The product has a short life cycle and high development costs which need to be recovered. There is no information about the drug's life cycle but development costs have been high.
- Since high prices attract competitors, there needs to be barriers to entry if competitors are to be deterred. In TR Co's case it has a patent for the drug and also the high development costs could act as a barrier.
- Where high prices in the early stages of a product's life cycle are expected to generate high initial cash flows, this will help TR Co recover the high development costs it has incurred.

Recommendation

Given the unique nature of the drug and the barriers to entry, a market skimming pricing strategy would appear to be the far more suitable pricing strategy. Also, whilst there is demand curve data, it is unknown how reliable this data is, in which case a skimming strategy may be the safer option.

Marking scheme

			Marks
(a)	Demand function		1.5
	Marginal cost/batch		2.5
	Labour 1,000th batch		3.5
	Establishing MR function		0.5
	Solve MR to find Q		1.0
	Use demand function and Q to find P		1.0
	Contribution based on P and Q		1.0
	Deduction of fixed costs		0.5
	Profit		0.5
		Maximum	**12**
(b)	Penetration pricing		3
	Skimming pricing		3
	Other relevant comments/recommendation		2
		Maximum	**8**
Total			**20**

276 KAYLENE CO (SEPTEMBER/DECEMBER 2025)

(a)

	Workhorse	Pristine	Jumbo	Kaylene Co
Selling price ($)	400	600	1,250	
Variable cost ($)	(170)	(230)	(580)	
Contribution per unit ($)	230	370	670	
Expected sales	2,000	1,200	800	
Total contribution ($)	460,000	444,000	536,000	1,440,000
Total Revenue ($)	800,000	720,000	1,000,000	2,520,000
C/S ratio	**0.575**	**0.617**	**0.536**	**0.571**

(b) Breakeven Sales Revenue = Fixed Costs/CS ratio

= 1,375,000/0.571

= $2,408,056

Margin of safety = (Expected sales – breakeven sales)/expected sales

= ($2,520,000 – $2,408,056)/$2,520,000

= 4.4%

Implications of margin of safety

The margin of safety indicates that if actual revenues fall by 4.4% or more, Kaylene Co will become loss-making (assuming that annual fixed costs and the contribution to sales ratio both remain unchanged). 4.4% is a very low margin of safety.

The mature nature of the market, and the intense competition within it, increases the chances of sales falling. If this happens, the low margin of safety means there is a high risk that Kaylene Co will no longer break even. These concerns are likely to reinforce the CEO's desire to find opportunities for growth.

(c) **(i)** **Sales revenue required to achieve target profit:**

= (Fixed costs + required profit)/CS ratio

= ($1,375,000 + $200,000)/0.571

= $2,758,319

Feasibility of CEO's target

In order to achieve the target profit of $200,000, Kaylene Co's revenue will need to increase by about 9.5% (from $2,520,000 to $2,758,319).

Kaylene Co's production line is currently operating at 80% of capacity, so there is sufficient spare capacity to meet this increase in production.

However, the more challenging issue is whether Kaylene Co will be able to increase demand for its washing machines by 9.5% overall given the lack of growth, and intense levels of competition in the market. This would appear to be a very challenging target.

(ii) Implications of increasing the sales volumes of the 'Jumbo'

Kaylene Co achieves the lowest contribution to sales (C/S) ratio on the 'Jumbo'. Therefore, if the proportion of 'Jumbo' sold increases, Kaylene Co's overall weighted average C/S ratio will fall.

This fall will be even greater if the selling price has to be reduced in order to boost demand. Consequently, the increase in the number of machines sold will need to be more than 9.5% to achieve the target profit figure of $200,000.

If the C/S ratio falls, the total revenue Kaylene Co needs to earn in order to break even will increase. Given Kaylene Co's low margin of safety at present, initiatives which increase break-even sales could be seen as risky.

(d) Limitations of cost-volume profit (CVP) analysis

The limitations of CVP analysis arise from the assumptions which are made in it:

Mix remains constant – CVP assumes that where a company makes multiple products, the mix remains constant. The C/S ratio varies across different products, so as the mix changes the break-even point (or the level of sales required to achieve a target profit) will also change.

All variables apart from volume remain constant – CVP assumes that volume is the only factor which causes revenues and costs to change, but in practice this may not be the case. For example, a company may need to reduce the unit price of its products in order to increase sales. Alternatively, as production volumes increase, a company might benefit from economies of scale.

Fixed costs – CVP also assumes that fixed costs remain fixed. However, at a general level, some fixed costs (e.g. business rates) may increase over time, and would need to be accounted for when calculating figures such as break-even sales or C/S ratios.

Cost classification – CVP assumes that costs can be divided into costs which are either fixed or variable. In reality, however, some costs may be semi-variable, or some might be stepped. If a business grows significantly, this could lead to an increase in costs previously classified as 'fixed' but which should actually be classified as 'stepped' rather than wholly 'fixed'.

Production and sales – There is an assumption that production volumes are equal to sales volumes. However, this is not necessarily the case, and many businesses do not sell all the units they produce in a period, meaning that inventory levels will change.

Note: Only TWO limitations were required here.

Marking scheme

		Marks
(a)	Calculations	3
(b)	Margin of safety – calculations	3
	Implications	2
(c)	**(i)** Target sales revenue – calculations	2
	Discussion	2
	(ii) Implications	4
(d)	TWO Limitations (2 marks each)	4
	Other relevant comments/recommendation	2
Total		**20**

277 THE ALKA HOTEL (JUNE 2018)

(a) Breakeven point (in occupied room nights) = Fixed cost/contribution per room

$600,000/($180 – $60) = 5,000 occupied room nights

Margin of safety = (Budgeted room occupancy – breakeven room occupancy)/budgeted room occupancy

Total rooms available per annum: 365 days × 25 rooms = 9,125 rooms

Budgeted occupancy level: 9,125 × 70% = 6,387.5 rooms

Margin of safety: (6,387.5 – 5,000)/6,387.5 = 21.72%

(b) Profit or loss for Q1

	$
Contribution (900 rooms × $120)	108,000
Fixed costs (($600,000/12) × 3)	(150,000)
Loss	(42,000)

The Alka Hotel should not close in Q1. The fixed costs will still be incurred and closure would result in lost contribution of $108,000. This in turn would result in a decrease in annual profits of $108,000. In addition, the hotel could lose customers at other times of the year, particularly their regular business customers, who may perceive the hotel as being unreliable.

(c) Contribution/sales ratio of Project 1

	$
Sales value of two room nights (2 × $67.50)	135
Sales value of a pair of theatre tickets	100
	235
Variable cost of two room nights (2 × $60)	(120)
Variable cost of a pair of theatre tickets	(95)
Contribution	20

C/S ratio (20/235) = 8.51%

Breakeven point in revenue ($20,000/0.0851) = $235,000

Alternatively:

Contribution per theatre package sold = $20

Breakeven point in theatre packages ($20,000/$20) = 1,000

Breakeven point in revenue (1,000 × $235) = $235,000

The unit contribution per theatre package is low and it requires a large number of sales to break even. Each theatre package would require two room nights to be sold which would mean 2,000 room nights needed in Q1 to break even. The available rooms for Q1 are only 2,281.25 (9,125/4) and the Alka Hotel has already sold 900 rooms, so there is insufficient capacity. Based on this, Project 1 is not viable at the quoted prices.

(d) Project 2 will cause the fixed costs of the hotel to rise from $600,000 per annum to $800,000 per annum for the hotel and restaurant combined. This is an annual increase of $200,000.

Revenue per occupied room will rise from $180 to $250 ($2,000,000/8,000 rooms) which reflects the extra guest expenditure in the restaurant.

The total cost predicted at a level of 8,000 occupied rooms is $1,560,000 which means the variable costs must be $760,000 ($1,560,000 – $800,000 fixed costs). This is a variable cost per occupied room of $95 which is an increase of $35. This reflects the variable costs of the restaurant.

As a result of these changes, the breakeven point has increased from 5,000 to 5,161 occupied rooms so the hotel needs to sell more room nights to cover costs.

However, budgeted occupancy is now 7,300 occupied room nights which gives 80% occupancy (7,300/9,125). This gives a margin of safety of 2,139 occupied room nights or 29%. This is an increase on the current position and the hotel's position appears safer. At 7,300 occupied room nights the Alka Hotel's budgeted profit is $331,500 (7,300 × ($250 – $95) –$800,000.

Marking scheme

		Marks
(a)	Contribution	0.5
	BEP	1.0
	Total rooms available	1.0
	Budget occupancy	0.5
	Margin of safety %	1
(b)	Profit/loss	1.5
	Recommendation	0.5
	Explanation	2.0
(c)	C/S ratio	1.0
	BEP $ revenue	0.5
	Recommendation	0.5
	Explanation	2.0
(d)	Calculations	4.0
	Commentary	4.0
Total		**20**

278 BELTON PARK RESORT (MARCH 2019)

(a) (i) Hotel

Incremental revenue and contribution

Room revenue		
Number of rooms	**120**	
Number of nights	**31**	
Total room nights	**3,720**	
Occupancy rate	**50%**	
Total nights occupied	**1,860**	
Rate per night	**$70**	
Total room revenue		**$130,200**
Extras contribution		
Total nights occupied	**1,860**	
Contribution per night	**$12.00**	
Total 'extras' contribution		**22,320**
Total cash inflows		**152,520**

Incremental running costs

Staff costs	$120,000	
Less: manager's salary	($2,500)	
Less: chef's salary	($2,000)	
	$115,500	
50% normal hours		57,750
50% at reduced hours × 50/90		32,083
Maintenance costs:		
If open	$14,600	
If closed	$4,000	
Incremental cost		10,600
Power costs:		
Electric	$0	
Gas – fixed charge	$0	
Gas – variable ($20,000 – $10,200) × 1.5		14,700
Security		0
Water		6,450
Total cash outflows		**121,583**
Total incremental cash flows		**30,937**

Tutorial note

Note how 'nil' values, such as the one for 'security' in the table above, are listed regardless, so that the marker knows you have understood this cost has no incremental value.

(ii) Water park

Incremental revenue and contribution

Visitor revenue		$
Number of visitors	5,760	
Admission cost	$16.80	
Admission revenue		96,768
Extras contribution		
Number of visitors	5,760	
Contribution per visitor	$7.20	
Total contribution		41,472
Total cash inflows		138,240

Incremental running costs

Staff costs		$
Manager	$0	
Other staff ($75,600 – $2,000) × 48%		35,328
Maintenance costs:		
If open	$6,000	
If closed	($2,000)	
		$4,000
Incremental cost		
Power costs:		
Electric	$0	
Gas – fixed charge	$0	
Gas – variable ($18,000 – $8,500) × 1.5		14,250
Security		0
Water		12,100
Total cash outflows		**65,678**
Total incremental cash flows		**72,562**

Conclusion: Based on these figures, both of them should stay open because the incremental cash flows are both positive.

(b)

Tutorial note

There are many factors which could have been discussed here and would be given credit.

As regards the estimates calculated, these have been based on very limited data and should be approached with caution. The calculations are based on the first two months' of opening only and, consequently, it is difficult to say how accurate they are likely to be. In addition, the basis of estimating the revised occupancy rates for the hotel, for example, has not been given. If these estimates are too optimistic, the actual results could be far worse.

The figures suggest that both the water park and the hotel should stay open. Given that this is a new business and therefore it is still building up its customer base, this would seem like a wise decision anyway, even if the calculations had shown that the estimated incremental cash flows were not as positive as this.

Similarly, if Belton Park were to close either the hotel or the water park, they would invariably lose some valuable staff who might seek out other jobs after the closure. These staff might not be available again when the hotel and water park reopened in February.

The interdependency of the two sets of projections has not been taken into account in the calculations either. Since the incremental cash flows suggest that both the hotel and the water park should stay open, it is not a big problem. However, if they had shown, for example, that the water park alone should close, the effect that this could have on the number of hotel visitors would also need to be taken into account. Many visitors may be attracted to the hotel because it has a water park.

ACCA Marking scheme

			Marks
(a)	**(i)**	Hotel revenue	1.5
		Extras contribution	1
		Staff costs	2.5
		Maintenance cost	1
		Gas variable costs	1
		Water not security	0.5
		Net cash flow	0.5
		Conclusion: hotel	0.5
	(ii)	Admission revenue	1.5
		Extras contribution	1
		Staff costs	0.5
		Maintenance costs	1
		Gas variable costs	1
		Water not security	0.5
		Net cash flow	0.5
		Conclusion: water park	0.5
			15
(b)	Discussion		**5**
Total			**20**

279 GLOBAL SCAN CO (SEPTEMBER/DECEMBER 2024)

(a)

	Darby	Leek	Nott
	$	$	$
Sales revenue (W1)			
Pregnancy	281,600	339,200	874,016
Men's health	102,400	138,400	280,280
Women's health	395,360	253,120	796,796
	779,360	**730,720**	**1,951,092**
Less expenses (W2)			
Junior sonographer costs	(75,936)	(37,968)	(75,936)
Senior sonographer costs	(104,412)	(104,412)	(156,618)
Other staff costs	(170,856)	(128,142)	(213,570)
Machine lease costs	(48,000)	(36,000)	(90,000)
Clinic specific overhead costs	(432,000)	(360,000)	(444,000)
Contribution	**(51,844)**	**64,198**	**970,968**
Head Office costs	(240,000)	(180,000)	(300,000)
Profit/(loss)	**(291,844)**	**(115,802)**	**670,968**

The basis of the shut-down decision should be whether each clinic makes a contribution to Head Office (HO) costs, since these costs will be incurred by the company irrespective of the shut-down of any of the clinics. Since Darby makes a negative contribution to HO costs, only this clinic should be shut down.

Workings

(W1) Sales revenue

	Darby	Leek	Nott
Number of scans			
Pregnancy	1,760	2,120	4,966
Men's health	512	692	1,274
Women's health	1,412	904	2,587
Price per scan ($)			
Pregnancy	160	160	176
Men's health	200	200	220
Women's health	280	280	308
Pregnancy ($)	281,600	339,200	874,016
Men's health ($)	102,400	138,400	280,280
Women's health ($)	395,360	253,120	796,796
	779,360	**730,720**	**1,951,092**

(W2) Expenses

Sonographer costs

	Darby	**Leek**	**Nott**
Junior sonographers employed	2	1	2
Junior salary ($)	32,000	32,000	32,000
Total salaries ($)	64,000	32,000	64,000
Including pay rise (5%) and 13% costs ($)	**75,936**	**37,968**	**75,936**
Senior sonographers employed	2	2	3
Senior salary ($)	44,000	44,000	44,000
Total salaries ($)	88,000	88,000	132,000
Including pay rise (5%) and 13% costs ($)	**104,412**	**104,412**	**156,618**
Other staff employed	8	6	10
Other staff salary ($)	18,000	18,000	18,000
Total salaries ($)	144,000	108,000	180,000
Including pay rise (5%) and 13% costs ($)	**170,856**	**128,142**	**213,570**

	Darby	**Leek**	**Nott**	
Number of machines	4	3	5	
Cost per month ($)	1,000	1,000	1,500	
Total cost per year ($)	**48,000**	**36,000**	**90,000**	
Other costs ($)				
Total employees per clinic	12	9	15	
Total employees for GSC				150
Total HO costs ($)				3,000,000
Cost per employee ($)				20,000
HO costs per clinic for the year ($)	240,000	180,000	300,000	
Total other costs per annum ($)	672,000	540,000	744,000	
Clinic specific overhead costs (Total other costs less HO apportioned costs)	**432,000**	**360,000**	**444,000**	

(b) Other factors

The Darby clinic is making a loss before HO costs, thus negatively impacting the profit of the company by $51,844, hence it would appear that it should be closed.

However, this decision does not consider factors such as:

- There will be a substantial penalty involved in terminating the leases for the ultrasound machines at Darby, so the $48,000 lease costs will be replaced with another cost unless some of these machines can be used at other clinics instead.
- There may be large costs associated with making staff redundant at Darby, although some of the staff may be used at other clinics instead.
- Closing down one clinic could have a negative impact on the morale of staff at other clinics.
- The closure could cause the general public to think that the business is struggling, and this could put them off using the other clinics.
- The closing of the Darby clinic may mean that potential Darby patients may attend one of the other clinics instead, such that this business is not lost altogether.
- The Darby clinic's own overhead costs have been treated as if they are entirely avoidable if the clinic closes down, but this might not be the case; there could be, for example, rental costs for the building which are not avoidable.

Tutorial note

Other valid points would be given credit.

ACCA marking scheme		
		Marks
(a)	Calculations/recommendation	13
	Recommendation	1
		14
(b)	Discussion (1 mark per valid point)	**6**
	Total	**20**

BUDGETING AND CONTROL

280 STATIC CO (DECEMBER 2016)

(a) **Workings**

From budgeted figures: need to work out what the compound growth rate is and the distribution costs as a percentage of revenue.

Compound sales growth: $13,694/13,425 or $13,967/13,694 = 2% Distribution costs: $671/$13,425 = 5%

From actual figures: GPM = $5,356/14,096 = 38%

Distribution costs: $705/14,096 = still 5%.

Starting point for revenue now $14,096 but compound growth rate still 2%.

Rolling budget for the 12 months ending 30 November 20X7

	Q2	**Q3**	**Q4**	**Q1**
	$000	$000	$000	$000
Revenue	14,378	14,666	14,959	15,258
Cost of sales	(8,914)	(9,093)	(9,275)	(9,460)
Gross profit	5,464	5,573	5,684	5,798
Distribution costs	(719)	(733)	(748)	(763)
Administration costs	(2,020)	(2,020)	(2,020)	(2,020)
Operating profit	2,725	2,820	2,916	3,015

Tutorial note

The question made it clear that the assumptions of the original budget were accurate but incorrect prices had been used in the first place. This meant that, before the rolling budget could be prepared, the actual gross profit margin (GPM) from the quarter that had just ended needed to be calculated and this percentage then needed to be applied when calculating the cost of sales and gross profit figures for the rolling budget. If you simply calculate the GPM from the original budget and ignore the actual quarter 1 figures, the cost of sales and gross profit figures will be incorrect in their rolling budget.

Another mistake to avoid would be to start the rolling budget with the actual quarter 1 figures that had been given in the question and then only produce three further quarters. This would show a lack of understanding of how rolling budgets work.

(b) Problems

The use of fixed budgeting has caused serious problems at Static Co. The fact they were using inaccurate sales forecast figures led them to invest in a production line which was not actually needed, even though they knew they were inaccurate. This unnecessary investment cost them $6m and caused the return on investment to halve. Had rolling budgets been used at the time, and used properly, the sales forecasts for the remaining quarters would have been adjusted to reflect a fall in demand and the investment would not have been made.

Presumably, inaccurate sales forecasts would have led the business to get their staffing levels and materials purchases wrong as well. This too will have cost the business money. They were forced to heavily discount their goods in order to try to reach their targets at the end of the year, which was simply unrealistic. It can often be difficult to put prices back up again once they have been discounted. However, the actual results from the first quarter suggest that prices have increased again, which is fortunate.

Improvements

The use of rolling budgets should mean that a downturn in demand is adjusted for in future quarters, rather than sales simply being pushed into the last quarter, which is not a realistic adjustment. Management is forced to reassess the budget regularly and produce up to date information. This means that accurate management decisions can then be made and mistakes like investing in a new production line which is not needed should not happen again. Planning and control will be more accurate.

Tutorial note

Do not make the mistake to simply copy out parts of the scenario without adding any value to them. For example, it was not enough to say that a problem of the previous system was that many product lines had to be heavily discounted in the last quarter. Answers needed to go on and say that this discounting was a problem because it led to reduced sales revenues for the company and made it difficult to subsequently increase prices to their original level in later quarters.

(c) Problems trying to implement new budgeting system

The first problem may be trying to obtain the right information needed to update the budget. The FD has been sacked and two other key finance personnel are off work due to stress. This could make it very difficult to obtain information if the department is understaffed and lacking the direction given by the FD. Staff in the finance department may not have the skills to update the budget and roll it forward, having never done it before. Similarly, the sales department is without a SD and they would usually have played a key part in reviewing figures for the sales forecasts. Hence, it may be difficult to obtain reliable sales data.

Even without this staffing issue, obtaining the correct information could be difficult as actually preparing rolling budgets is new for Static Co. Staff will need training. They are only used to preparing fixed budgets, although these have often been revised in the past to move sales into later periods. Staff are not familiar with the process of updating all of their financial information again: reviewing sales demand to realistically reforecast, updating costs, etc. This process takes time and staff may feel resentful about having to do this again so soon after the annual budgeting process which would recently have been undertaken.

The new MD is new to this industry and therefore lacks experience of how it works. Whilst they are confident that the assumptions of the original fixed budget still stand true, they are not in a good position to know that this is in fact the case. The assumptions may be wrong and, if they are, the new rolling budget will be unreliable.

Tutorial note

Make double sure that you read the requirement carefully. On the whole, the problems of implementing rolling budgeting are different from the problems of using rolling budgets on an ongoing basis, apart from the fact that both implementation and ongoing use of rolling budgets are time consuming and therefore expensive. Please carefully review this suggested answer for this part of the question, because answers on exam day were fairly weak here and many opportunities to gain marks were lost.

Marking scheme

			Marks
(a)	Growth rate		1
	Actual distribution cost %		0.5
	Actual GPM %		0.5
	Use of Q1 actuals		1
	Rolling budget: sales		1
	COS		1
	GPM		0.5
	Distribution costs		1
	Administration costs		1
	Operating profit		0.5
		Maximum	**8**
(b)	Problems and improvements		**6**
(c)	Implementation problems		**6**
Total			**20**

281 YUMI CO (SEPTEMBER 2019)

(a) (i) Flexed budget for Cowly restaurant

	Original budgeted	**Flexed budget**
Number of customers	1,500	1,800
	$	$
Revenue	75,000	90,000
Food and drink costs	(22,500)	(27,000)
Staff costs	(31,500)	(37,800)
Heat, light and power	(7,500)	(9,000)
Rent, rates and overheads	(12,000)	(12,000)
	–––––	–––––
Profit	1,500	4,200
	–––––	–––––

Notes:

Revenue: $75,000/1,500 = $50 per customer: $50 × 1,800 = $90,000

Food and drink: $22,500/1,500 = $15 per customer: $15 × 1,800 = $27,000

Staff costs: $31,500/1,500 = $21 per customer: $21 × 1,800 = $37,800

Heat, light and power: $7,500/1,500 = $5 per customer: $5 × 1,800 = $9,000

(ii) The most significant weakness in the current performance report is that the original budget is not flexed to adjust for the actual numbers of customers served.

The existing report shows that the Cowly restaurant has overspent on all its costs which could be a concern given the importance of cost control in Yumi Co. However, the main reason for the revenue variance and the costs variances is the fact that the number of customers the restaurant served was 20% higher than budgeted (1,800 v 1,500).

If the budget is flexed for the actual number of customers, this allows a more meaningful assessment of the restaurant's performance to be made.

Once the flexed budget is prepared, it can be seen that revenues were actually lower than would have been expected, given the number of customers served with average spend per head being $48.50 instead of $50. Food and drink costs were also less than budget. Taken together with the reduction in average customer spending, this might suggest that some of the items on the menu had been changed since the budget was originally set.

Another weakness in Yumi Co's budgetary control report is the fact that staff costs and heat, light and power costs are assumed to be purely variable costs – dependent on the number of customers. However, although the restaurant may recruit some temporary staff in busy periods, it is likely that at least some of the staff will be permanent, meaning that it would be more appropriate to treat staff costs as semi-variable rather than variable.

Similarly, it seems likely that there will be a significant fixed element within heat, light and power costs, so treating these as wholly variable costs does not seem appropriate.

(b) Under an incremental budgeting approach, the current year's budget and results are taken as the starting point for preparing the next year's budget. The budget is then adjusted for any expected changes, such as the impact of inflation on costs and prices, and sales growth or decline.

The main advantage of the incremental approach is that it is a relatively straightforward way of preparing a budget, appropriate for organisations which are operating in relatively stable environments. The locations of Yumi Co's restaurants, away from significant competition, suggest that the operating environment is relatively stable, meaning incremental budgeting is appropriate.

Similarly, the fact that Yumi Co appears to have a relatively well-established brand and customer base suggests that using an incremental approach to budgeting future revenues appears reasonable, even if it is difficult to identify some changes which need to be adjusted for in the next year's budget.

However, one of the major disadvantages of incremental budgeting is that it does not provide any incentive to make operations more efficient or economical. If the current year figures include slack or inefficiencies, then using them as the start-point for the next year's figures means that inefficiency is automatically perpetuated into the next year.

Such an approach seems somewhat inconsistent with the focus on cost control within Yumi Co. If the company is worried about its relatively low margins, then an approach to budgeting which challenges costs more critically (such as zero-based budgeting or activity-based budgeting) might be more suitable for helping to drive down costs. For example, the highest cost is staff wages which could be analysed and Yumi Co could investigate making changes to its staffing model to reduce costs and/or improve efficiency.

As mentioned in part (a), whether labour costs and heat, light and power vary proportionately with the number of customers appears debatable. If Yumi Co's incremental budgets ignore the relationship between activities and costs, then ultimately the budgets will provide Yumi Co's management with little relevant information for managing costs. This could become an increasingly important issue if competition in Yumi Co's markets intensifies.

(c) The current budget process is a centralised, top-down process, meaning that the managers from Yumi Co's restaurants do not have any opportunity to influence the budgets for their restaurants.

By contrast, in a participative approach, the managers of each restaurant would be able to influence the figures for their restaurant, rather than having budget targets simply imposed on them. Involving the managers in the budgeting process should help to make the budgets more effective and realistic.

The local managers should have a greater understanding of the environmental factors and operational constraints which will influence the performance of their restaurants. For example, the manager of the Cowly restaurant will have a better understanding of their customers and market conditions and thus provide a greater insight into the potential impact of the new restaurant than a member of the finance team at Yumi Co's head office would have. Similarly, managers are more likely to be committed to achieving a budget if they have been involved in creating it – not least because their involvement in the preparing the budget should help to ensure that they feel the budget figures are realistic. However, involving the restaurant managers in the budgeting process is likely to make it more time-consuming. For example, instead of running their restaurants, managers will have to spend time in meetings with head office staff planning and preparing their budgets. In this respect, it may be more appropriate for Yumi Co to maintain the current, top-down process for restaurants which are operating in a stable environment (and where the insights from local managers will add little value), but introduce a more participative approach for restaurants like Cowly which are facing a period of change.

Another potential disadvantage of participative budgeting is that managers may try to influence the budgets so that their targets can be achieved easily. By doing this, a restaurant's performance, compared to budget, will appear to improve, but this would actually be an illusion. One of the main issues Yumi Co could face in this respect is that, given the range of different locations of its restaurants, it will be difficult for head office staff to know whether individual managers are setting targets which are easy or challenging. If the restaurants were all similar, or in similar locations, it would be easier to compare the figures suggested by individual managers to assess how challenging, or not, they are.

Similarly, managers are more likely to highlight issues which will lead to a reduction in their budget targets, rather than ones which increase their targets. For example, the manager at Cowly has highlighted that the new competitor will make it more difficult for them to achieve budget. However, the manager does not appear to have made a corresponding acknowledgement that the increased numbers of visitors to Cowly could support an increased revenue target. There is a danger that the managers' participation in the budgets could lead to the targets becoming less challenging, which in turn could affect Yumi Co's competitiveness and profitability.

ACCA Marking scheme

			Marks
(a)	**(i)**	Flexed budget	
		Revenue	0.5
		Food and drink	0.5
		Staff	0.5
		Heat, light and power	0.5
		Rent and rates	0.5
		Profit	0.5
			3
	(ii)	Weaknesses	**4**
(b)	Discussion		**6**
(c)	Definition of participative budgeting		1
	Advantages and disadvantages		6
			7
Total			**20**

282 TREAD CO (MARCH/JUNE 2022)

(a) The aim of activity-based budgeting (ABB) is to ensure that the amount of resources available accurately reflects the activities required by an organisation's expected production and sales volumes.

By focusing on the relationship between the level of resources available and the activities required, ABB tries to identify two key issues:

- the resources which are under utilised (for example, because there is spare capacity, or because current processes are inefficient)

and

- the areas where the level of resources available is insufficient to meet production and sales requirements.

Having identified these issues, ABB then requires an organisation to take action to adjust the level of resources available to match the projected production and sales requirements.

ABB also aims to eliminate activities which are not value-adding. This is an important area of difference between ABB and incremental budgeting, because looking to remove activities which do not add value means ABB has an inherent focus on increasing efficiency which incremental budgeting does not have.

Another key principle of ABB is that organisations should control the causes of costs (cost drivers), rather than the costs themselves. The logic for this is that activities drive costs. Therefore, if an organisation understands and manages the activities better, this should help it to reduce the costs resulting from those processes.

However, this understanding is not fully exploited unless management can use it to make changes in the way the organisation goes about its business. The most significant of the cost-beneficial changes can only be made if incorporated into budgets through discussion and performance reviews.

(b) **Calculation of spare capacity/shortage**

	Deluxe	**Standard**	**Total**	**Available**	**Spare/ (shortage)**
Monthly demand	22,500	24,000			
Pairs produced per machine hour	250	300			
Production machine hours required	90	80	**170**	175	5
Production batch sizes	300	400			
Number of batches produced	75	60			
Quality control time per batch (hours)	2.5	2.5			
Quality control time per month (hours)	187.5	150	**337.5**	300	(37.5)
Shipment batch sizes	125	150			
Number of batches shipped	180	160			
Shipping admin time per batch (hours)	0.75	0.75			
Shipping admin time per month (hours)	135	120	**255**	300	45

(c) **Production machine time**

The production line appears to be operating close to its current capacity, with only five production machine hours 'spare' each month.

Having a small amount of spare capacity each month would appear to be prudent, in case there are any unexpected disruptions (for example, defects in the process which require production to be halted whilst they are fixed).

As such, the balance between demand and capacity appears to be well-matched, with little scope to make any further efficiencies.

Quality control inspectors

The 'budgeted' resource requirements identify an important resource shortage in relation to quality control inspections, because having only two quality control inspectors does not appear sufficient to carry out the level of checks required. The resource budget suggests there is a shortage of 37.5 hours per month, equivalent to 25% of one full-time inspector's monthly hours.

If the inspectors have to rush to try to complete inspections in less than the 2.5 hours that each should take, this is likely to mean that the inspections are not as thorough as they should be. If inspectors are rushing their inspections and consequently fail to identify sub-standard shoes, this could be a factor in the recent increase in the number of complaints.

However, the extent of the shortage does not seem to be large enough to justify recruiting an additional inspector on a full-time basis. Therefore, the division should consider other alternatives, which could include:

- Employing an additional inspector on a part-time basis. However, this would increase cost, which would seem to contradict the FD's desire to increase profitability.
- Using inspectors from other parts of the business if they have any spare capacity.
- Assessing if the checking process itself can be re-designed, to make it quicker, without compromising quality.

Shipping administrators

By contrast, there appears to be a significant level of spare capacity among the shipping administrators. 45 hours per month is almost one-third of one administrator's monthly hours.

This level of spare capacity or idle time indicates inefficiency. If there are similar activities with spare capacity across the company, this would support the FD's belief that the company is not operating as efficiently as it could.

However, the surplus capacity does not appear so high that the division could afford to only have one shipping administrator. It is possible one of the administrators would be prepared to work part time thereby reducing wage costs. Alternatively, it may be possible for the administrators to assist other areas of the business.

ACCA marking scheme		
		Marks
(a)	Principles of activity-based budgeting – one mark per relevant point	
	Maximum	**5**
(b)	Calculation of spare capacity in production machine hours (0.5 mark for machine hours for each product/1 mark for calculation of spare capacity)	2
	Calculation of shortage in quality control inspector hours (0.5 mark for number of production batches for each product/0.5 mark for quality control time per month for each product/1 mark for calculation of shortage)	3
	Calculation of spare capacity in shipping administrator hours (0.5 mark for number of shipping batches for each product/0.5 mark for shipping administrator time per month for each product/1 mark for calculation of spare capacity)	3
	Maximum	**8**
(c)	Discussion of the impact of spare capacity/shortage on production – one mark per relevant point	
	Maximum	**7**
Total		**20**

283 QUALITY TYRE CO (MARCH/JUNE 2025)

(a) Overheads budget

	Basic	**Sport**	**Total**
	$	**$**	**$**
Material ordering costs	113,400	91,980	205,380
Store requisition costs	94,080	62,328	156,408
Machine set up costs	38,682	12,978	51,660
Quality inspection costs	335,244	253,071	588,315
Sales order costs	72,450	54,338	126,788
Delivery costs	241,500	181,125	422,625
Total budgeted overheads	895,356	655,820	1,551,176

Workings:

W1 – Production budget

	Basic	**Sport**
Sales (tyres)	60,000	45,000
Less opening inventory	(3,600)	(2,400)
Add closing inventory	5,000	3,750
Production (units)	61,400	46,350
Units per batch	200	450
Number of batches	**307**	**103**

W2 – Material ordering costs

	Basic	Sport	Total
Order numbers for the prior year	1,800	1,460	
Less decrease	(450)	(365)	
Order numbers for 20X1	1,350	1,095	
Cost per order (80 × 1.05)	84	84	
Total costs ($)	**113,400**	**91,980**	**205,380**

W3 – Store requisition costs

	Basic	Sport	Total
Number of store requisitions	6,400	4,240	
Cost per store requisition ($14 × 1.05)	14.70	14.70	
Total costs ($)	**94,080**	**62,328**	**156,408**

W4 – Machine set up costs

	Basic	Sport	Total
Number of batches	307	103	
Number of set ups	307	103	
Cost per set up ($120 × 1.05)	126	126	
Total costs ($)	**38,682**	**12,978**	**51,660**

W5 – Costs per QC inspection

	Basic	Sport	Total
Number of batches	307	103	
Number of inspections	1,228	927	
Cost per QC inspection ($260 × 1.05)	273	273	
Total costs ($)	**335,244**	**253,071**	**588,315**

W6 – Costs per sales order

	Basic	Sport	Total
Sales (tyres)	60,000	45,000	
Tyres per order	40	40	
Total orders	**1,500**	**1,125**	
Cost per sales order ($46 × 1.05)	48.30	48.30	
Total costs ($)	**72,450**	**54,338**	**126,788**

W7 – Cost per delivery order

High-low method to separate VC and FC:

VC: ($301,000 – $266,000) / (1,300 – 800) = $70 per unit

FC: $301,000 – (1,300 × $70) = $210,000

Increase in FC: ($210,000 × 1.05) = $220,500

	Basic	**Sport**	**Total**
Total deliveries (same as orders)	1,500	1,125	2,625
Variable cost per delivery ($70 × 1.10)	77	77	
Total variable cost ($)	**115,500**	**86,625**	
Cost per sales order ($)	126,000	94,500	220,500
($220,500 split by deliveries)			
Total costs ($)	**241,500**	**181,125**	**422,625**

(b) Costs of implementing new system

All new systems have cost implications and the saving envisaged by the new budgeting system must justify the costs incurred to implement it. A cost/benefit analysis is usually performed.

Staff training

Staff will need to be trained to prepare the activity-based budgets (ABB). This will take some time and could distract from other activities happening in the organisation.

Availability of information

The information which is necessary to implement ABB needs to be available. For a business already using activity-based costing (ABC), this should be less of a problem but generally it can be difficult to gather all the information about costs and cost drivers.

Resistance by employees

Employees are generally resistant to change. Variances will have to be calculated based on the new budget and employees are likely to be appraised on this basis. Some will be concerned that this could impact negatively on their performance.

The reliability of cost driver rates

ABC assumes that all costs vary with cost driver activity. In reality, many overhead costs are fixed/stepped/semi variable in the short run and budgets could be unrealistic.

Tutorial note

Other valid points could be made that would also score marks.

ACCA marking scheme

		Marks
(a)	2 marks per working	14
(b)	Up to 2 marks per point explained	6
Total		**20**

284 VENHOSP (MARCH/JUNE 2024)

(a) **(i)** Staff days: (given x = 114)

Y = a + bx

$$a = \frac{\sum y}{n} - \frac{b\sum x}{n}$$

$$b = \frac{n\sum xy - \sum x \sum y}{n\sum x^2 - (\sum x)^2}$$

Rounded to the nearest day = **26,515 days**

	A	B	C	D	E	F	G
1	**Total number of events (x)**	**Staff days (y)**	**Σx²**	**Σy²**	**Σxy**		
2	1,757	404,410	196,615	10,724,385,113	45,496,648		
3							
4	(n=16)						
5							
6				**Workings**			
7				n=16; x=114			
8							
9	b=	295.93	b=	((16*E2)-(A2*B2))/((16*C2)-A2^2)			
10			b=	((16*45,496,648)-(1,757*404,410))/((16*196,615)-1,757^2)			
11							
12	a=	7,221.15	a=	(B2/16)-(B9*A2/16)			
13			a=	(404,410/16)-(295.93*1,757/16)			
14							
15	y=	26,514.83	y=	B12+(B9*114)			
16			y=	−7,221.15+(295.93*114)			

(ii) **Forecast for Quarter 4 20X6**

Assume staff days to be 30,000.

		$
Revenue	Staff days * $16 per hour * 8 hrs per day	3,840,000
Wages to staff	Staff days * $11.25 per hour * 8 hrs per day	2,700,000
Additional contribution to government	10% of wages to staff	270,000
Staff costs		2,970,000
Gross profit		**870,000**

(iii) $r = \dfrac{n\sum xy - \sum x \sum y}{\sqrt{(n\sum x^2 - (\sum x)^2)(n\sum y^2 - (\sum y)^2)}}$

	A	B	C	D	E	F	G	H	I	J	K
1	**Total number of events (x)**	**Staff days(y)**	**Σx²**	**Σy²**	**Σxy**						
2	1,757	404,410	196,615	10,724,385,113	45,496,648						
3											
4	**(n=16)**										
5											
6				**Workings**							
7				n=16;							
8											
9	r=	0.80		=((16*E2)-(A2*B2))/(((16*C2)-(A2^2))*((16*D2)-B2^2))^0.5							
10				= ((16*45,496,648)-(1, 757*404,410))/ (((16*196,615)-1,757 ^ 2)*((16*10,724,385,113)-404,410^ 2)) ^ 0.5							
11											

(b) **Assumes a linear relationship** – Linear regression, by definition, assumes there is a linear (straight line) relationship between the independent variable ('x') and the dependent variable ('y'). However, in reality, the relationship between the variables may not be linear.

Other variables – Regression analysis, and correlation, can suggest a relationship exists between two variables, but this does not prove the relationship. There could be other factors involved in the changes in the variables which may not have been considered. In other words, 'y' could be influenced by other factors apart from 'x'.

Extrapolation – Regression analysis uses past observations to attempt to predict what will happen in the future. However, the assumption that what has happened in the past is a good indicator of what will happen in the future is a simplistic one. Changes in the business environment can create uncertainty, which could make forecasts based on past observations unrealistic. (For example, if a new agency entered the market, or if a stadium decided to employ its own, in-house catering and hospitality staff, these changes could affect the relationship between the number of events and Venhosp's staff days.)

Outliers – Regression analysis could be distorted by outliers, which could make the regression line less accurate in predicting other data.

Tutorial note

This answer is longer than that required to score the three marks available, but is intended to show a range of relevant points candidates could have included in their answers.

(c) **Financial** – Due to the price competition in the industry, it seems unlikely that Venhosp will be able to increase the rates it charges the stadiums for the staff it provides them with. Therefore, increasing the wage rates it pays to staff will have a direct impact on Venhosp's gross profit.

If the proposed increase were applied to the forecast figures for Quarter 4, it would lead to a 15% reduction in gross profit, which is quite a large reduction.

		Existing forecast from (a) (ii)	Revised	Impact
		$	$	$
Revenue	Staff days * $16 per hour * 8 hrs per day	3,840,000	3,840,000	–
Wages to staff	Staff days * $11.25 per hour * 8 hrs per day	2,700,000	2,820,000	120,000
Additional contribution to government	10% of wages to staff	270,000	282,000	12,000
Staff costs		2,970,000	3,102,000	132,000
Gross profit		**870,000**	**738,000**	**(132,000)**
% reduction gross profit				–15.2%

Nothing is known about the size of Venhosp's administrative expenses, but an important factor to consider will be whether the business would still be profitable if this wage increase was given to staff.

Ethical – Although Venhosp's existing hourly wage rate is still above the revised minimum wage rate in Deeland ($11.25 v $11), it is only marginally above the minimum. Catering and hospitality work is acknowledged as being physically demanding yet is still poorly paid. Therefore, from an ethical perspective, there could be questions about whether Venhosp is paying its staff fairly. Also, the fact that the minimum wage in Deeland has risen could suggest that living costs in the country are rising. However, if Venhosp does not offer its staff any wage increase, they will – in effect – be worse off.

Attracting and retaining staff – Another important consideration will be to compare Venhosp's pay rates against other similar roles — – particularly those offered by its competitors. To an extent, this could be helpful in identifying whether Venhosp is paying its staff fairly. However, the more significant implications could be in Venhosp's ability to attract staff.

There is a shortage of staff in the industry, and if agency firms are unable to attract staff, this will limit their ability to provide services to their clients. If Venhosp is seen as being a more attractive company to work for than its competitors, that could help it attract staff. Conversely, if Venhosp is seen as less attractive than its rivals, that will threaten its ability to find staff.

Nothing is known about the pay rates offered by Venhosp's competitors, but that should be a key factor for the board to identify. In particular, if competitors are increasing their rates – such that they become higher than Venhosp's – it would seem almost inevitable that Venhosp will need to do likewise. Otherwise, it will risk losing staff who choose to go and work for rival agencies and earn more per hour.

ACCA marking scheme			
			Marks
(a)	**(i)**	Calculation of a	2
		Calculation of b	2
		Calculation of y	1
	(ii)	Revenue	1
		Wages	1
		Additional contribution	1
		Gross profit	1
	(iii)	Calculation of r	2
		Maximum	**11**
(b)	Discussion (1 mark per well explained point)		3
(c)	Discussion (1 mark per well explained point)		6
Total			**20**

285 HENRY COMPANY (DECEMBER 2008)

(a) There are various issues that HC should consider in making the bid. (Only five are required for two marks each.)

Contingency allowance. HC should consider the extent to which its estimates are accurate and hence the degree of uncertainty it is subjected to. It may be sensible to allow for these uncertainties by adding a contingency to the bid.

Competition. HC must consider which other businesses are likely to bid and recognise that the builder may be able to choose between suppliers. Moreover HC has not worked for this builder before and so they will probably find the competition stiff and the lack of reputation a problem.

Inclusion of fixed overhead. In the long run fixed overhead must be covered by sales revenue in order to make a profit. In the short run it is often correctly argued that the level of fixed cost in a business may not be affected by a new contract and therefore could be ignored in bid calculation. HC needs to consider to what extent the fixed costs of its business will change if it wins this new contract. It is these incremental fixed costs that are relevant to a bid calculation.

Materials and loose tools. No allowance has been made for the use of tools and the various fixings (screws etc.) that will be needed to assemble and fit the kitchens. It is possible that most fixings would be provided with the kitchen units but HC should at least consider this.

Supervision of labour. The time given in the question is 24 hours to 'fit' the first kitchen. There seems no allowance for supervision of the labour force. It could of course be included within the overhead figures but no detail is shown.

Idle time. It is common for building works to be delayed by lack of materials for example. The labour time figure needs to reflect this.

Likelihood of repeat business. Some businesses consider it worthwhile to accept a low price for a new contract if it establishes a reputation with a new buyer. HC could offer to do this work cheaper in the hope of more profitable work later on.

The risk of non-payment. HC may decide not to bid at all if it feels that the builder may struggle to pay.

Opportunity costs of alternative work.

Possibility of working in overtime.

Key answer tips

Easy marks were available here for discussing any sensible and relevant factors that should be taken into account. Good candidates related their discussion back to the information provided in the scenario and used short paragraphs to explain each factor, with the aim of scoring one mark for each of the factors explained.

(b) Bid calculations for HC to use as a basis for the apartment contract.

Cost	**Hours**	**Rate per hour**	**Total ($)**
Labour	9,247 (W1)	$15	138,705
Variable overhead	9,247	$8 (W2)	73,976
Fixed overhead	9,247	$4 (W2)	36,988
Total cost			249,669

Workings

(W1) Need to calculate the time for the 200th kitchen by taking the total time for the 199 kitchens from the total time for 200 kitchens.

For the 199 Kitchens

Using

$y = ax^b$	OR	$y = ax^b$
$y = 24 \times 199^{-0.074}$		$y = (24 \times 15) \times 199^{-0.074}$
y = 16.22169061 hours		y = 243.32536
Total time = 16.22169061 × 199		Total cost = $48,421.75
Total time = 3,228.12 hours		

For the 200 Kitchens

$y = ax^b$	OR	$y = ax^b$
$y = 24 \times 200^{-0.074}$		$y = (24 \times 15) \times 200^{-0.074}$
y = 16.21567465 hours		Total cost = $48,647.02
Total time = 16.21567465 × 200		200th cost = $225.27
Total time = 3,243.13 hours		

The 200th Kitchen took 3,243.13 – 3,228.12 = 15.01 hours

Total time is therefore:

For first 200	3,243.13 hours
For next 400 (15.01 hours × 400)	6,004.00 hours
Total	9,247.13 hours (9,247 hours)

(W2) The overheads need to be analysed between variable and fixed cost elements.

Taking the highest and lowest figures from the information given:

	Hours	**Cost $**
Highest	9,600	116,800
Lowest	9,200	113,600
Difference	400	3,200

Variable cost per hours is $3,200/400 hours = $8 per hour

Total cost = variable cost + fixed cost

116,800 = 9,600 × 8 + fixed cost

Fixed cost = $40,000 per month

Annual fixed cost = $40,000 × 12 = $480,000

Fixed absorption rate is $480,000/120,000 hours = $4 per hour

(c) A table is useful to show how the learning rate has been calculated.

Number of Kitchens	**Time for Kitchen (hours)**	**Cumulative time (hours)**	**Average time (hours)**
1	24.00	24.00	24.00
2	21.60	45.60	22.80

The learning rate is calculated by measuring the reduction in the average time per kitchen as cumulative production doubles (in this case from 1 to 2).

The learning rate is therefore 22.80/24.00 or 95%.

Marking scheme

			Marks
(a)	1 mark for each description	**Maximum**	**5**
(b)	Average time for the 199th kitchen		1.0
	Total time for 199 kitchens		1.0
	Average time for the 200th kitchen		1.0
	Total time for 200 kitchens		1.0
	200th kitchen time		1.0
	Cost for the first 200		1.0
	Cost for the next 400		1.0
	Variable cost per hour		2.0
	Fixed cost per month		1.0
	Fixed cost per hour		1.0
	Cost for variable overhead		1.0
	Cost for fixed overhead		1.0
		Maximum	**13**
(c)	Average time per unit and explanation		**2**
Total			**20**

Examiner's comments (extract)

Part (a) was not done well by many. All that was required was sensible ideas about figures that might have to be included in the bid (without calculations). The marking scheme was generously applied and marks were given if candidates included factors relating whether or not to bid instead of factors concerning the amount of the bid. Some marks were also given for a more theoretical approach (opportunity costs should be allowed for...). Despite this the average mark struggled to reach half marks. Perhaps candidates were looking for something more difficult than is there or grasping at the text book hoping for a text book answer to fit.

Part (b) was well done by many candidates despite it being a fairly demanding aspect of learning curves (the steady state).

Part (c) was reasonably attempted by most.

286 MEDICAL TEMP CO (MARCH/JUNE 2021)

(a) The market size and market share variances are a breakdown of the sales volume variance. The sales volume variance shows the effect on profit of the actual sales level being different from the budgeted sales level. However, without considering how the market itself has changed, it is difficult to draw conclusions about performance from the sales volume variance. Therefore, the sales volume variance is broken down into its two components. By doing this, it is possible to assess the extent to which changes in profit are as a result of:

(i) A change in the size of the market as a whole, which is beyond the control of the sales manager; and

(ii) A change in the share of the market which the company holds, which is deemed to be within the control of the sales manager.

Consequently, the variances become far more meaningful for performance management as businesses can identify external and internal factors which can influence the results and what was controllable and uncontrollable.

(b) **Quarter 2 original budgeted sales volumes and contribution**

	Nurses	**Doctors**
National Q1 sales volume (no. of weekly contracts)	14,000	4,000
Percentage of market	30%	40%
Budgeted Sales Volume	4,200	1,600
	$000	$000
Budgeted Revenue for MTC	4,200	3,200
Standard Contribution	80%	80%
Budgeted Standard Contribution	3,360	2,560

Quarter 2 revised budgeted sales volumes and contribution

	Nurses	Doctors
National Q2 sales volume (no. of weekly contracts)	18,900	4,100
Percentage of market	30%	40%
Budgeted Sales Volume	5,670	1,640
	$000	$000
Budgeted Revenue for MTC	5,670	3,280
Standard Contribution	80%	80%
Budgeted Standard Contribution	4,536	2,624

Quarter 2 Actual Results

	$000	$000
Actual Revenue in quarter 2	5,300	3,600
Standard Contribution	80%	80%
Budgeted Standard Contribution	4,240	2,880

Market size variance (planning)

(Budgeted vs revised contribution)

	Nurses		Doctors		Total	
	$000		$000		$000	
Budget contribution for MTC	3,360		2,560			
Revised budget contribution for MTC	4,536		2,624			
Variance	**1,176**	**F**	**64**	**F**	**1,240**	**F**

Market share variance (operational)

(Revised contribution vs actual)

	Nurses		Doctors		Total	
	$000		$000		$000	
Revised budget contribution for MTC	4,536		2,624			
Actual sales volume at standard contribution	4,240		2,880			
Variance	**(296)**	**A**	**256**	**F**	(40)	**A**

(c) The sales director at Cheat Co has deliberately manipulated the market size figures to make the market for doctors and nurses look smaller. Now, instead of being the actual market size of 18,900 weekly contracts ($18.9m/$1,000) and 4,100 weekly contracts ($8.2m/$2,000), they will be much lower at 13,230 and 2,870 respectively. This means that the revised budgeted sales volume figures used to calculate Cheat Co's variances were far lower. This behaviour is unethical and may well lead to the sales director getting a bonus which they do not deserve.

As a consequence of this, the market size variances are highly adverse, so it looks like Cheat Co's original budgets are very wrong. The sales director will not care about this since they will not be held accountable for that variance; instead they will be responsible for the favourable market share variance of over $2m. This makes the sales director's performance look really good, but the reality is that it only looks this high because the budgeted sales figures include revenue for maternity units and the revised budgeted figures do not. This does not reflect the sales director's real performance for the quarter.

ACCA marking scheme

		Marks
(a)	Market size and share variances are breakdown of sales volume variance/need to consider change in size of market	1
	Description of market size/market share variances/reference to controllability	3
		4
(b)	Original budget (1 mark each doctors and nurses)	2
	Revised budget (1 mark each doctors and nurses)	2
	Actual sales volume at standard contribution (0.5 each doctors and nurses)	1
	Market size variance – doctors	1
	Market size variance – nurses	1
	Total market size variance	0.5
	Market share variance – doctors	1
	Market share variance – nurses	1
	Total market share variance	0.5
		10
(c)	Discussion – up to 2 for each well discussed point. Must address both parts of the requirement	6
Total		**20**

287 CLEAR CO (MARCH/JULY 2020 SAMPLE EXAM)

Tutorial note

Previous question practice should hopefully help students identify that the first thing to calculate (in a separate working, for example) is the budgeted (=standard) contribution per type of lens treatment. It amounts to $2,400 per RLE treatment and $2,500 per ICL treatment.

(a) Variance calculations

	RLE	ICL	Total
AQAM	4,130	960	5,090
AQBM	3,764.79	1,325.21	5,090
BQBM	3,750	1,320	5,070
Standard contribution (W1)	$2,400	$2,500	
Mix variance	$876,504 F	$913,025 A	$36,521 A
Quantity variance	$35,496 F	$13,025 F	$48,521 F

Alternative quantity variance calculation:

Total contribution ($)	12,300,000
Budgeted total sales quantity	5,070
Weighted average contribution ($)	2,426.04
Quantity variance ($)	48,521F

(W1) Standard contribution

	RLE	ICL
	$	$
Selling price	3,000	3,650
Variable costs	600	1,150
	2,400	2,500

(b) The sales mix contribution variance measures the effect on contribution of changing the mix of actual sales from the budgeted sales mix.

The sales quantity contribution variance measures the effect on contribution of selling a different total quantity from the budgeted total quantity.

(c) Possible additional calculations

Actual compared to budgeted revenue	**RLE**	**ICL**	**Total**
	$	$	$
Actual sales revenue	11,977,000	3,264,000	15,241,000
Budgeted sales revenue	11,250,000	4,818,000	16,068,000
Difference in revenue	**727,000**	**–1,554,000**	**–827,000**
Percentage terms	**6.46%**	**–32.25%**	**–5.15%**
Sales volume variance	$	$	$
(AQ–BQ) × standard contribution	**912,000 F**	**900,000 A**	**12,000 F**
Selling price variance			
(AP–SP) × AQ	**413,000 A**	**240,000 A**	**653,000 A**

Total sales variance

(AP – standard variable costs) × AQ	9,499,000	2,160,000	11,659,000	Actually received
Budgeted units × standard contribution	9,000,000	3,300,000	12,300,000	Expect to receive
	499,000 F	**1,140,000 A**	**641,000 A**	

Sales performance

When comparing budgeted revenues to actual revenues, it can be seen that ICL has under-performed this year, with revenues being 32.25% lower than budgeted. This is a result of both lower sales volumes and a lower selling price for ICL, which has resulted in an adverse sales volume variance of $900,000 and an adverse sales price variance of $240,000. The main reason for this is probably the merger that took place during the year, which resulted in Clear Co's now biggest competitor subsequently reducing prices for ICL and presumably capturing a bigger slice of the market as a result. Even though Clear Co's actual price for ICL was $250 less than budgeted, its sales volumes still fell by 27% so it was apparently unable to match the competition.

Looking at the mix of sales between RLE and ICL at Clear Co, there is an adverse mix variance of $36,521. This is because, whilst the sales of ICL were lower than budgeted, the sales of RLE were higher than budgeted. Since RLE has a lower standard contribution than ICL, this produced an adverse mix variance. This shift in sales mix could be partly attributable to the fact that the RLE procedure is for people aged over 40 and there is an increasingly ageing population in Zeeland. Clear Co has had to lower its price to take these sales of RLE but again, this is probably due to increased pressure to reduce prices resulting from the merger.

Another factor which it is not possible to quantify from the information provided, but which will invariably have had an impact on sales of lens treatments overall, is the increased availability of laser treatments to customers. Given that 90% of customers are now eligible for the less complex laser treatment, this side of the business may well have grown at Clear Co.

Overall, the sales volume variance is favourable for Clear Co because of the increased sales of RLE. However, to achieve this, prices have been reduced, resulting in a significant adverse sales price variance of $653,000. These results are disappointing and Clear Co may have to rethink its strategy moving forwards.

ACCA Marking scheme			
			Marks
(a)	(i)	Calculation of sales mix contribution variance	4
	(ii)	Calculation of sales quantity contribution variance	4
(b)		Explanation of what sales mix contribution variance measures	1
		Explanation of what sales quantity contribution variance measures	1
(c)		Calculations	4
		Discussion of sales performance	6
Total			**20**

288 THE SCHOOL UNIFORM COMPANY (MARCH/JUNE 2017)

Tutorial note

In the first requirement it is clear that we need to know material variances. The question is not specific however, and we don't know which variances are required – this is one of the key skills that are being tested. There are several variances we might be able to calculate here – the "basic" price and usage variances and the more advanced planning and operational variances or mix and yield.

Reading the scenario very carefully, and being on the lookout for information about both standard and actual usage and prices for material, will help. The second paragraph provides information – firstly that the design has changed, and now requires more material than previously – the standard cost card will need to be revised to allow for this, and any usage variance should be analysed between the planning variance caused by the change in design, and the operational variance which we can use to assess the production manager. Secondly, a new material is being used, which is cheaper than the previous material. It is worth noting here that the new material was chosen by GPST – a customer of SU, therefore this decision was not made by the production manager. This is crucial for two reasons – firstly this cannot be used to assess the production manager's performance for part (c) and secondly an uncontrollable change from the original standard means that we should split our materials price variance into planning and operational components – the 5% reduction in price constitutes the planning variance.

There are 12 marks available in total – for 6 variances – materials price (planning and operational), materials usage (planning and operational) and labour efficiency (planning and operational). Calculating just the 3 basic variances would not score a passing mark.

(a) SP (standard price per metre: $2.85/0.95) $3.00

SQ (standard quantity per dress: 2.2 metres/1.1) 2 metres

From scenario the revised price per metre (RP) is $2.85, the actual price per metre (AP) is $2.85 and the revised quantity per dress (RQ) is 2.2 metres.

SQAP (standard quantity for actual production: 2 metres × 24,000) 48,000 metres
RQAP (revised quantity for actual production: 2.2 metres × 24,000) 52,800 metres.

From the scenario the actual production level (AP) is 24,000 dresses and actual quantity of material bought and used (AQ) is 54,560 metres.

Material price variances

Planning variance (SP – RP) × AQ: ($3.00 – $2.85) × 54,560	8,184F
Operational variance (RP – AP) × AQ: ($2.85 – $2.85) × 54,560	0
Total price variance	8,184 F

Material usage variances

Planning variance (SQAP – RQAP) × SP: (48,000 – 52,800) × $3.00	14,400 A
Operational variance (RQAP – AQ) × SP: (52,800 – 54,560) × $3.00	5,280 A
Total usage variance	19,680 A
Total material variance	11,496 A

Tutorial note

The most common error when calculating variances of this type is to use budgeted production to calculate standard usage. For example, taking the basic materials usage variance –many candidates write this as the difference between the actual quantity of material at the standard price, and the standard quantity of material at the standard price. It is the SQ that causes the problems – it means the standard (expected) quantity of material to make ACTUAL production.

*So in our case, actual production was 24,000 units – the original standard amount per unit was 2m, so SQ would be 2m*24,000 = 48,000m. Similarly, the revised standard quantity would be 2.2*24,000 = 52,800m. You would never use the budgeted quantity to calculate standard usage, as you're comparing it to the actual quantity of material used to make ACTUAL production.*

Tutorial note: *These variances could have been calculated using the alternative approach as below:*

Material price variances

Planning variance

(AP × RQ) × (SP – RP): 24,000 × 2.2 metres × ($3.00 – $2.85)	*7,920 F*

Operational variance

(RP – AP) × AQ: 54,560 metres × ($2.85 – $2.85)

Material usage variances

Planning variance

(SQ – RQ) × AP × SP: 24,000 × (2 metres – 2.2 metres) × $3.00	*14,400 A*

Operational variance

((AP × RQ) – AQ) × RP: 24,000 × 2.2 metres – 54,560 × $2.85	*5,016 A*
Total material variance	*11,496 A*

(b)

AH (actual hours worked and paid): 24 × 160 hours	3,840 hours
SHAP (standard hours for actual production): (24,000 × 8)/60	3,200 hours RHAP
(revised hours for actual production): (24,000 × 10)/60	4,000 hours

From the scenario the standard rate per hour (SR) is $12, the standard time per dress is eight minutes and the revised time per dress is 10 minutes.

Labour efficiency variances

Planning variance (SHAP – RHAP) × SR: (3,200 – 4,000) × $12	9,600 A
Operational variance (RHAP – AH) × SR: (4,000 – 3,840) × $12	1,920 F
Total labour efficiency variance	7,680 A

Tutorial note

We know we will need details about labour time to calculate our efficiency variance. Again, the change in design has had an effect on time taken – the new design will take 2 minutes longer to make. Again, this will cause a planning variance – the original standard will need to be revised to allow for this extra time, as the production manager should not be criticised for the change in design, which was not their decision. We are also told that there was no idle time, ruling out any idle time variances.

Next we are given budgeted and actual production. Actual production levels are essential in working out variances, as they compare actual figures to the flexed budget (based on actual production). The budgeted production figure is less important here, although it could be noted that actual production was 20% under budget, which may have a knock-on effect on profits.

(c)

Tutorial note

In the final paragraph, we are told that the production manager is responsible for purchasing and production issues. This means that they can be have some control over the materials price variance, as well as materials usage and labour efficiency variances, so we can use these to assess their performance.

The production manager did not have any control over the change in the design of the dress as this change was requested by the client. Similarly, it was not their fault that the company accountant responsible for updating standard costs was off sick and therefore unable to update the standards. Therefore, the production manager should be judged only by those variances over which they have control, which are the operational variances.

Materials

No operational variance arose in relation to materials price, since the actual price paid was the same as the revised price. A planning variance of $8,184F does arise but the production manager cannot take the credit for this, as the material chosen by GPST for the new dresses just happens to be cheaper. As regards usage, an adverse variance of $5,280 arose. This suggests that, even with the revised quantity of material being taken into account, staff still used more than 2.2 metres on average to produce each dress. This is probably because they had to learn a new sewing technique and they probably made some mistakes, resulting in some wastage. The manager is responsible for this as it may have been caused by insufficient training. However, the labour efficiency variances below shed some more light on this.

Tutorial note

It was much easier to score well on part (c) if you had already determined what was controllable and what was not. Easy marks could be gained here for explaining that the materials usage was due to the change in design, and therefore not controllable, and the materials price planning variance was due to GPST's decision to change the material – again, not controllable. You could then look at the operational variances and, based on whether they were adverse or favourable, decide whether the production manager had performed well or not.

Labour

Tutorial note

Easy marks could be gained here for explaining that labour efficiency planning variances were due to the change in design, and therefore not controllable, You could then look at the operational variances and, based on whether they were adverse or favourable, decide whether the production manager had performed well or not.

Remember that in many cases the variances have some interconnectivity. For example here, the operational labour efficiency variance was favourable, showing that the workers worked faster than expected. However the operational material usage variance was adverse, meaning that more material was used to make the actual production of 24,000 dresses than expected. This could have been because the workers were rushing, and therefore more material was wasted. Identifying possible cause and effect relationships like this will lead to a lot of credit being given.

The labour efficiency operational variance was favourable, which suggests good performance by the production manager. Staff took less than the expected revised 10 minutes per dress. However, when looked at in combination with the material usage operational variance above, it could be inferred that staff may have rushed a little and consequently used more material than necessary.

Tutorial note

When assessing performance it is also useful to give a conclusion. This should be in line with your previous findings – using total operational variance here would be a useful yardstick.

When both of the operational variances are looked at together, the adverse materials usage \$5,280 far outweighs the favourable labour efficiency variance of \$1,920. Consequently, it could be concluded that, overall, the manager's performance was somewhat disappointing.

ACCA Marking scheme

			Marks
(a)	Standard price		1
	Standard quantity		0.5
	SQAP		0.5
	RQAP		0.5
	Price planning variance		1.5
	Usage planning variance		1.5
	Usage op variance		1.5
		Maximum	**7**
(b)	Actual hours		1
	SHAP		0.5
	RHAP		0.5
	Planning variance		1.5
	Operating variance		1.5
		Maximum	**5**
(c)	Controllability		1
	Variances/performance		6
	Other/conclusion		1
		Maximum	**8**
Total			**20**

289 KAPPA CO (SEPTEMBER 2018)

(a) (i) Usage variance

	Should use	**Did use**	**Difference**	**Std cost/kg**	**Variance**
	kg	kg	kg	$	$
Alpha	1,840	2,200	360 A	2.00	720 A
Beta	2,760	2,500	260 F	5.00	1,300 F
Gamma	920	920	1.00		
	5,520	5,620			580 F

(ii) Mix variance

	AQSM	**AQAM**	**Difference**	**Std cost/kg**	**Variance**
	kg	kg	kg	$	$
Alpha	1,873.33	2,200	326.67 A	2.00	653.34 A
Beta	2,810.00	2,500	310.00 F	5.00	1,550.00 F
Gamma	936.67	920	16.67 F	1.00	16.67 F
	5,620	5,620			913.33 F

(iii) Yield variance

	SQSM	AQSM	Difference	Std cost/kg	Variance
	kg	kg	kg	$	$
Alpha	1,840	1,873.33	33.33 A	2.00	66.66 A
Beta	2,760	2,810.00	50.00 A	5.00	250.00 A
Gamma	920	936.67	16.67 A	1.00	16.67 A
	5,520	5,620			333.33 A

Alternative solution

5,620 kg input should produce 4,683.33 kg of Omega

5,620 kg input did produce 4,600 kg of Omega

Difference = 83.33 kg × $4 per kg ($400/100 kg) = $333.32 A

(b) The raw material price variances included in the report are probably outside the production manager's control, and are more the responsibility of the purchasing manager. Furthermore, the production manager has no participation in setting the standard mix. Holding managers accountable for variances they cannot control is demotivating.

There appears to be no use of planning variances. Prices and quality of the three materials are volatile and using ex ante prices and usage standards can give a distorted view of mix and yield variances. Failing to isolate non-controllable planning variances can be demotivating.

The standard mix for the product has not changed in five years despite changes in the quality and price of ingredients. It can also lead the production manager to attempt control action based on variances which are calculated based on standards which are out of date.

As Kappa Co does not currently give feedback or commentary, a true picture is lacking as to the production manager's performance. There is also no follow up on the variances calculated. As Kappa Co does not appear to place much importance on the variances, the production manager will not be motivated to control costs and could become complacent which could adversely impact Kappa Co overall.

This can be illustrated by looking at the overall usage variance reported which shows a $580 favourable variance, so the production manager could assume good performance. However, if the usage variance is considered in more detail, through the mix and yield calculations, it can be seen that it was driven by a change in the mix. There is a direct relationship between the materials mix variance and the materials yield variance and by using a mix of materials which was different from standard, it has resulted in a saving of $913.33; however, it has led to a significantly lower yield than Kappa Co would have got had the standard mix of materials been adhered to. Also changing the mix could impact quality and as a result sales and there is no information about this.

ACCA marking scheme

			Marks
(a)	**(i)**	Alpha usage variance	1
		Beta usage variance	1
		Gamma usage variance	1
		Total usage variance	1
			4
	(ii)	AQSM figures	1.5
		Variance quantities	0.5
		Variance in $	1.5
		Total mix variance	0.5
			4
	(iii)	SQSM or $4,683.33 kg (depending on method used)	1
		Variance quantity or 83.33 kg (depending on method used)	0.5
		Variance in $ or calculation of $4 (depending on method used)	1
		Total yield variance	0.5
			3
(b)		Controllability issues	5
		Other relevant points relating to performance	4
			9
Total			**20**

290 VEGAN CO (MARCH/JUNE 2023)

(a) Soybeans

			$
(i)	Price planning	(standard price – revised price) × actual quantity	
		(5.90 – 5.31) × 94,000	55,460 F
(ii)	Price operational	(revised price – actual price) × actual quantity	
		(5.31 – 5.70) × 94,000	(36,660) A
(iii)	Usage planning	(standard quantity for actual production – revised quantity) × standard price	
		(96,000 – 91,200) × 5.90	28,320 F
(iv)	Usage operational	(revised quantity for actual production – actual quantity) × standard price	
		(91,200 – 94,000) × 5.90	(16,520) A

Sugar

			$
(i)	Price planning	(standard price – revised price) × actual quantity (1.80 – 2.16) × 5,280	(1,900.80) A
(ii)	Price operational	(revised price – actual price) × actual quantity (2.16 – 1.90) × 5,280	1,372.80 F
(iii)	Usage planning	(standard quantity for actual production – revised quantity) × standard price (5,760 – 4,800) × 1.80	1,728.00 F
(iv)	Usage operational	(revised quantity for actual production – actual quantity) × standard price (4,800 – 5,280) × 1.80	(864.00) A

The alternative method of using revised quantity for the price planning variance and revised price for the usage operational variance is also acceptable:

Soybeans

			$
(i)	Price planning	(standard price – revised price) × revised quantity (5.90 – 5.31) × 91,200	53,808 F
(ii)	Price operational	(revised price – actual price) × actual quantity (5.31 – 5.70) × 94,000	(36,660) A
(iii)	Usage planning	(standard quantity for actual production – revised quantity) × standard price (96,000 – 91,200) × 5.90	28,320 F
(iv)	Usage operational	(revised quantity for actual production – actual quantity) × revised price (91,200 – 94,000) × 5.31	(14,868) A

Sugar

			$
(i)	Price planning	(standard price – revised price) × revised quantity (1.80 – 2.16) × 4,800	(1,728.00) A
(ii)	Price operational	(revised price – actual price) × actual quantity (2.16 – 1.90) × 5,280	1,372.80 F
(iii)	Usage planning	(standard quantity for actual production – revised quantity) × standard price (5,760 – 4,800) × 1.80	1,728.00 F
(iv)	Usage operational	(revised quantity for actual production – actual quantity) × revised price (4,800 – 5,280) × 2.16	336.00 F

(b) Purchasing manager's performance

The purchasing manager is responsible for negotiating prices with suppliers. However, they are not responsible for the prices being used in the standard cost cards, which, as they have already stated, are not updated frequently enough. Consequently, their performance should only be assessed based on the materials price operational variances (MPOVs).

For soybeans, the MPOV is $36,660 adverse. This shows that the price they negotiated was significantly higher than the market price. However, Vegan Co has committed to use suppliers within a 50 km distance only, so the purchasing manager does not have access to all of the suppliers in Zeeland. Consequently, their ability to negotiate prices is restricted and their performance needs to be reviewed in light of this.

As regards sugar, the MPOV was $1,373 favourable. Whilst this is only a relatively small amount, due to the fact that the quantity of sugar used in production is much lower than soybeans, it still shows that the purchasing manager managed to achieve a good price for sugar relative to the market price.

Production manager's performance

The production manager is responsible for the quantities of soybeans and sugar used in the production of soya milk. However, like the purchasing manager, they have no control over the standard cost cards, which are out of date. Consequently, they should only be assessed on the materials usage operational variances (MUOVs).

For soybeans, the MUOV is $16,520 adverse, which shows that more soybeans were used in production than would have been expected given the revised quantity of 190 grams per unit. Given that 94,000 kg were used to produce 480,000 units, this means that the average content of soybeans per unit was 195.83 grams. This must be looked at together with the MUOV for sugar, which is also $864 adverse, an average sugar content of 11 grams per unit (5,280 kg of sugar/480,000 units). This means that, as well as costing the business more money, the soya milk now produced in November has too high a sugar content and is therefore not compliant with the new government legislation. More soybeans presumably had to be used because the sugar content was not reduced as much as it should have been. All of this reflects as poor performance of the production manager and should be investigated.

Marking scheme				
				Marks
(a)	(i)	MPPV		3
	(ii)	MPOV		3
	(iii)	MUPV		3
	(iv)	MUOV		3
			Maximum	**12**
(b)	Discussion of purchasing manager performance			4
	Discussion of production manager performance			4
			Maximum	**8**
Total				**20**

PERFORMANCE MEASUREMENT AND CONTROL

291 MAN CO (JUNE 2016)

(a) Maximising group profit

Division L has enough capacity to supply both Division M and its external customers with component L. Therefore, incremental cost of Division M buying externally is as follows:

Cost per unit of component L when bought from external supplier: $37 Cost per unit for Division L of making component L: $20.

Therefore incremental cost to group of each unit of component L being bought in by Division M rather than transferred internally: $17 ($37 – 20).

From the group's point of view, the most profitable course of action is therefore that all 120,000 units of component L should be transferred internally.

(b) Calculating total group profit

Total group profits will be as follows:

Division L:

Contribution earned per transferred component = $40 – $20 = $20 Profit earned per component sold externally = $40 – $24 = $16.

	$
120,000 × $20	2,400,000
160,000 × $16	2,560,000
	4,960,000
Less fixed costs	(500,000)
Profit	4,460,000

Division M:

Profit earned per component sold externally = $27 – $1 = $26

	$
120,000 × $26	3,120,000
Less fixed costs	(200,000)
Profit	2,920,000
Total profit	7,380,000

(c) Problems with current transfer price and suggested alternative

The problem is that the current transfer price of $40 per unit is now too high. Whilst this has not been a problem before since external suppliers were charging $42 per unit, it is a problem now that Division M has been offered component L for $37 per unit. If Division M now acts in its own interests rather than the interests of the group as a whole, it will buy component L from the external supplier rather than from Division L. This will mean that the profits of the group will fall substantially and Division L will have significant unused capacity.

Consequently, Division L needs to reduce its price. The current price does not reflect the fact that there are no selling and distribution costs associated with transferring internally, i.e. the cost of selling internally is $4 less for Division L than selling externally. So, it could reduce the price to $36 and still make the same profit on these sales as on its external sales. This would therefore be the suggested transfer price so that Division M is still saving $1 per unit compared to the external price. A transfer price of $37 would also presumably be acceptable to Division M since this is the same as the external supplier is offering.

Marking scheme

			Marks
(a)	Maximising group profits		
	Calculating incremental cost per unit		2
	Recommendation		1
		Maximum	**3**
(b)	Profit		
	Profit of L		3
	Profit of M		2
	Total profit		1
		Maximum	**6**
(c)	Discussion		
	Transfer price is too high		2
	Division M will not buy		1
	Profits for group will fall		1
	S/D costs should mean lower TP anyway		2
	Suggested transfer price		1
		Maximum	**6**
Total			**15**

292 BEST NIGHT CO (MARCH 2019)

Performance for year ended 30 June 20X7

Gross room revenue – Best Night's 'gross' room revenue based on standard room rates has increased by 6.6% in 20X7, which reflects the higher occupancy rates (74% v 72%) and the increase in standard room rates ($140 v $135 per night).

However, this gives a rather misleading impression of how well the hotels have performed in the year to 20X7.

Revenue after discounts – Revenue from room sales, adjusted for discounts or rate reductions offered, has actually only increased 1.8%, and that reflects the significant 45% increase in discounts or reductions offered:

	20X7	20X6	% change
	$000	$000	
Standard revenue	111,890	104,976	6.6%
Discounts/reductions	16,783	11,540	45.4%
Room revenue net of discounts	95,107	93,436	1.8%

Faced with the declining number of business customers, and consequently the prospect of lower occupancy rates, managers may have decided to offer lower room rates to try to retain as many of their existing business customers as possible, or to try to attract additional leisure customers.

Although occupancy rates increased by 2.8% (from 72% to 74% which now exceeds the budgeted level), revenue, net of discounts, only increased by 1.8%. This means that revenue per room per night after discounts in 20X7 was lower than in 20X6, despite the standard rate being higher ($140 v $135).

In the context of tough market conditions, the decision to increase the standard room rate for 20X7 appears rather optimistic. Although the hotel managers have managed to achieve occupancy rates higher than budget, they have only managed to do so by reducing room rates.

Additional revenue – One of the potential benefits of increased occupancy rates, even if guests are paying less per room per night, is that they will generate additional revenue from food and drink sales. This appears to be the case because additional revenues have increased by approximately 5%.

Total revenue – In total, revenue (net of discounts) has increased 2.4% in 20X7 v 20X6. Given the tough competitive environment, Best Night Co could view any increase in revenues as positive. Moreover, provided the revenue achieved from selling the room is greater than the variable cost of providing it, then increasing occupancy levels should increase the hotels' contribution to profit.

Operating profit – However, despite the increase in revenue, operating profits have fallen by $0.3m (1.3%) between 20X7 and 20X6, due to a sizeable increase in operating costs. There is no detail about Best Night Co's operating costs, for example, the split between fixed and variable costs. However, in an increasingly competitive market, cost control is likely to be very important. As such, the $3 million (3.3%) increase in operating costs between 20X6 and 20X7 is potentially a cause for concern, and the reasons for the increase should be investigated further. However, when looking to reduce costs, it will be very important to do so in a way which does not compromise customer satisfaction. More generally, Best Night Co needs to avoid cutting expenditure in areas which will have a detrimental impact on customer satisfaction ratings, for example, not replacing mattresses even though they are becoming uncomfortable to sleep on.

Operating profit margin – The increase in costs has also led to a fall in operating profit margin from 20.8% to 20.0%. It is perhaps more instructive to look at the margin based on standard room rates per night, thereby reflecting the impact of the discounts offered as well as the increase in costs. On this basis, the margin falls slightly more: from 18.9% to 17.6%.

	20X7	**20X6**
	$000	$000
Total revenue	119,377	116,621
Discounts offered	16,783	11,540
	————	————
Gross revenue	136,160	128,161
	————	————
Operating profit	23,915	24,242
Operating profit margin	17.6%	18.9%

ROCE – This reduced profitability is also reflected in the company's return on capital employed which has fallen slightly from 62% ($24.2m/$39.1m) to 60.5% ($23.9m/$39.5m). This suggests that the value which Best Night Co is generating from its assets is falling. The decline in ROCE could be a particular concern given the relative lack of capital investment in the hotels recently. Capital investment will increase the cost of Best Night Co's non-current assets, thereby reducing ROCE for any given level of profit.

Customer satisfaction scores

Although the reduction in profitability should be a concern for Best Night Co, the reduction in customer satisfaction scores should potentially be seen as a greater cause for concern. The scores suggest that, in the space of one year, Best Night Co hotels have gone from being in the top 10% of hotels to only just being in the top 25%. This is a significant decline in one year, and one which Best Night Co cannot afford to continue.

Best Night Co prides itself on the comfort of its rooms and the level of service it offers its guests. Both of these factors are likely to be important considerations for people when considering whether or not to stay in a Best Night Co hotel. Therefore, falling customer satisfactions levels could be seen as an indication that fewer existing customers will stay at a Best Night Co hotel in future – thereby threatening occupancy rates, and prices, in future.

Moreover, the scores suggest that the decision to defer the refurbishment programme is likely to have a detrimental impact on future performance.

ACCA marking scheme	
	Marks
Calculations	5
Revenue	4
Operating profit	2
ROCE	2
Customer satisfaction	3
Other valid point	4
	——
Total	**20**
	——

293 YETGO CO (SEPTEMBER/DECEMBER 2024)

(a)

	Yuri	Lux
Receivables collection period		
(Receivables/sales revenue) × 365	(90,000/350,000) × 365	(70,000/420,000) × 365
	94 days	61 days
Operating profit margin		
(Operating profit (excl. dep)/sales revenue) × 100	(124,000/350,000) × 100 35%	(160,000/420,000) × 100 38%
Current ratio		
Current assets/current liabilities	180,000/40,000	110,000/40,000
	4.5	2.75

The ratios show that the Lux resort is outperforming the Yuri resort in every case.

The receivables collection period indicates that the guests at Yuri are paying very late, perhaps indicating inefficiency in the debt collecting process. Given that Yuri is a fashionable area and Lux an area considered to be in decline, it should be easier to collect the Yuri debt.

The operating profit margin for Lux is clearly above the Yetgo Co average level. Once again, this is an excellent achievement in a declining area. The poorer performance of Yuri could be due to an unexpected fall in sales revenue and a high proportion of fixed costs which are difficult to reduce in the short term, poor cost management, or lower vacation prices at Yuri reflecting the lack of investment in the resort.

The current ratio indicates that both vacation resorts have a high degree of liquidity. However, to have a current ratio of 4.5 shows that the Yuri resort is not using the assets efficiently, whereas the Lux resort is.

(b) (i)

	Yuri	Lux
	$	$
PBIT	124,000	160,000
Net assets	490,000	770,000
ROI	25.3%	20.8%

As the threshold ROI is 22%, the manager of Yuri will receive a bonus but the manager of Lux will not.

(ii) Yetgo Co's bonus system appears to neither fair to the resort managers nor beneficial to Yetgo Co. By most measures Lux appears to have performed well, despite being situated in a declining area. Yuri appears to manage working capital badly and has an operating margin below both Lux and the Yetgo Co average.

Despite this, the Yuri manager will receive a bonus as the Yuri resort's controllable ROI exceeds the bonus threshold of 22%. As the Lux resort's controllable ROI is below 22%, its manager will not receive a bonus.

The main reason Yuri has produced a better ROI is that the investment in controllable non-current assets is half that of Lux. This is possible evidence of short-termism and manipulation. A failure to invest in new assets will see a good ROI in the short term but at the possible expense of the longer term health of the business. The fact that the sales revenue is significantly lower in Yuri as compared to the Lux resort may indicate that the lack of facilities or presentation of the resort is not attracting guests even in this fashionable location.

The use of residual income as a basis for bonus payments would not necessarily rectify this problem. A failure to invest in new assets can similarly boost short-term residual income at the expense of the longer term health of the business.

ROI can cause managers to manipulate results. This could be the case here. The Yuri manager has enjoyed 'large bonuses' for the last five years and may now be withholding the investment needed in order to continue enjoying them. In short, the manager is acting in self-interest rather than in the interest of the company as a whole. The best way to prevent this behaviour is to use performance measurement systems which cover both long and short-term performance, such as the balanced scorecard.

Yuri also has a built-in advantage as asset values do not represent up to date property values in the area. Yuri's ROI does not reflect the huge capital gain on the property.

(c) Existing Yuri ROI = 25.3%

Yuri + new investment ROI = ($124,000 + $3,000)/($490,000 + $20,000) = 24.9%

This leads to a dilution of Yuri's ROI and will not be acceptable to the manager of Yuri.

On the basis of ROI, the manager of the Yuri resort will not invest in the solarium as it will dilute the overall ROI of his division.

The ROI is below Yetgo Co's 22% threshold too but, as the investment has a positive RI (RI = $3,000 – ($20,000 × 10%) = $1,000), then it should most likely be adopted and it can be concluded that the manager will not be acting in the best interest of Yetgo Co if the investment is rejected.

Alternative approach

ROI of new investment

	$
Net annual cash inflow	8,000
Less annual depreciation ($20,000 – $5,000)/3	(5,000)
Annual return	**3,000**

ROI= $3,000/$20,000 = **15%**

The ROI is below the Yetgo Co's 22% threshold too but as the investment has a positive RI, then it should most likely be adopted and we can conclude that the manager will not be acting in the best interest of Yetgo Co if the investment is rejected.

Note: It is possible that candidates will calculate the project's NPV as a measure of its attractiveness as an alternative to residual income.

= –$20,000 – ((AF 3 years at 10% × $8,000) + (PVF 3 years at 10% × $5,000))

= –$20,000 – ((2.487 × $8,000) + (0.751 × $5,000))

= $3,651

As the project's NPV is positive it would be in the best interests of the company to accept it.

ACCA marking scheme			
			Marks
(a)	Ratios		3
	Comments		4
			7
(b)	**(i)**	Calculations/bonus comment	3
	(ii)	Problems	6
			9
(c)	Calculations		2
	Explanations		2
			4
Total			**20**

294 SPORTS CO (SEPTEMBER/DECEMBER 2017)

(a) (i)

Tutorial note

In (a) (i), calculating the ROI should have been very straightforward indeed for the well prepared candidate. The areas to watch out for, or pitfalls to avoid, centred around the controllability of some of the fixed costs. The skill tested here is the ability to adjust profit calculations by discarding uncontrollable fixed costs.

Return on investment = controllable profit/average divisional net assets

Controllable profit

	C	E
	$000	$000
Net profit	1,455	3,950
Add back depreciation on non-controllable assets	49.5	138
Add back Head Office costs	620	700
Controllable profit	2,124.50	4,788

Average divisional net assets

	$000	$000
Opening assets	13,000	24,000
Closing assets	9,000	30,000
Average assets	11,000	27,000
ROI	19.3%	17.7%

(ii)

Tutorial note

The discursive aspects of questions very often drive candidates to focus on the irrelevant or the unnecessary. In here, once the ROI difference between the divisions had been established, time should be spent establishing the impact of that difference as part of the discussion.

Other narrative marks worth harvesting centred around behavioural considerations such as how a demotivated manager would be tempted to try and manipulate figures by not investing and thereby improving ROI artificially.

Whilst Division C has exceeded the target ROI, Division E has not. If controllable profit in relation to revenue is considered, Division C's margin is 56% compared to Division E's margin of 57%, so Division E is actually performing slightly better.

However, Division E has a larger asset base than Division C too, hence the fact that Division C has a higher ROI.

Since Division E appears to be a much larger division and is involved in sports equipment manufacturing, then it could be expected to have more assets. Division E's assets have gone up partly because it made substantial additions to plant and machinery. This means that as well as increasing the average assets figure, the additions will have been depreciated during the year, thus leading to lower profits. This may potentially have had a large impact on profits since Division E uses the reducing balance method of depreciation, meaning that more depreciation is charged in the early years.

Based on the ROI results, the manager of Division C will get a bonus and the manager of Division E will not. This will have a negative impact on the motivation level of the manager of Division E and may discourage them from making future investments, unless a change in the performance measure used is adopted.

(b) (i)

	C	E
	$000	$000
Controllable profit	2,124.50	4,788
Less: imputed charge on assets at 12%	(1,320)	(3,240)
Residual income	804.50	1,548

From the residual income results, it can clearly be seen that both divisions have performed well, with healthy RI figures of between $0.8m and $1.55m. The cost of capital of Sports Co is significantly lower than the target return on investment which the company seeks, making the residual income figure show a more positive position.

(ii)

Tutorial note

Don't simply state the pros and cons of the RI measure – explain in as much detail as necessary. A tip to candidates: the use of the word 'because' often helps to grasp the last remaining marks. For example, simply stating that 'RI reduces dysfunctional decision making' is not enough; explaining that 'RI reduces dysfunctional decision making because it uses the whole company's cost of capital, so positive RI projects for the company would also be accepted by the division' is more likely to maximise marks.

Advantages

The use of RI should encourage managers to make new investments, if the investment adds to the RI figure. A new investment can add to RI but reduce ROI and in such a situation measuring performance with RI would not result in the dysfunctional behaviour which has already been seen at Sports Co. Instead, RI will lead to decisions which are in the best interests of the company as a whole being made.

RI reduces dysfunctional decision making **because** it uses the whole company's cost of capital, so positive RI projects for the company would also be accepted by the division.

Since an imputed interest charge is deducted from profits when measuring the performance of the division, managers are made more aware of the cost of assets under their control. This is a benefit as it can discourage wasteful spending.

Alternative costs of capital can be applied to divisions and investments to account for different levels of risk. This can allow more informed decision-making.

Disadvantages

RI does not facilitate comparisons between divisions since the RI is driven by the size of divisions and their investments. This can clearly be seen in Sports Co where the RI of Division E is almost twice that of Division C, which will be related to Division E being a much larger division.

RI is also based on accounting measures of profit and capital employed which may be subject to manipulation so as, for example, to obtain a bonus payment. In this way it suffers from the same problems as ROI.

Marking scheme

				Marks
(a)	**(i)**	Net profit		1
		Add back depreciation		1
		Add back HO costs		1
		Controllable profits		1
		Average assets		1
		ROI		1
			Maximum	**6**
	(ii)	Discussion		**6**
(b)	**(i)**	Controllable profit		1
		Imputed interest		1
		RI		1
		Comment		1
			Maximum	**4**
	(ii)		**Maximum**	**4**
Total				**20**

295 THE PORTABLE GARAGE COMPANY (JUNE 2018)

Tutorial note

Check out this link to an excellent technical article on Transfer Pricing from the ACCA website:

https://www.accaglobal.com/my/en/student/exam-support-resources/fundamentals-exams-study-resources/f5/technical-articles/trans-pricing.html.

(a) Profit statement for current position:

	Division B	**Division A**	**PGC Co**
	$000	$000	$000
Sales revenue:			
External sales (150,000 × $180/200,000 × $15)	27,000	3,000	30,000
Internal transferred sales (150,000 × $13)		1,950	
Total revenue	27,000	4,950	30,000
Variable costs:			
External material costs	6,750	1,050	7,800
Internal transferred costs	1,950		
Labour costs	5,250	1,400	6,650
Other costs of external sales		200	200
Total variable costs	13,950	2,650	14,650
Contribution	13,050	2,300	15,350
Less fixed costs	5,460	2,200	7,660
Profit	7,590	100	7,690

(b) If Division B can buy adaptors from outside the group at $13 per unit, then the optimum position is for Division A to sell as many adaptors as possible to external customers at $15 each and then sell the remainder to Division B at a price to be agreed between them.

This would mean that Division A continues to sell Division B 150,000 adaptors but Division B then buys the remaining 30,000 adaptors from an external supplier. This is because the contribution per unit for Division A's external sales is $7 ($15 – $3 – $4 – $1). This means that for every external sale it loses, it forfeits $7 for the group. However, the incremental cost for the group of Division B buying adaptors from outside the group is only $6 ($13 external cost less the $7 cost of making them in-house). So, it makes sense for Division A to satisfy its external sales first before selling internally.

(c) In order for Division A to supply Division B with 180,000 adaptors, it would have to reduce its external sales from 200,000 units to 170,000. This is because it only has enough spare capacity to supply Division B with 150,000 units at present after it has supplied adaptors to its external customers.

The minimum transfer price in situations where there is no spare capacity is marginal cost plus opportunity cost. In this case, contribution is lost by not selling 30,000 units to the external customers. As the marginal cost for Division A's internal sales is $7 ($4 + $3) and the contribution per unit for external sales is $7 per unit ($15 – $3 – $4 – $1), the transfer price for the additional 30,000 units would need to be $14.

ACCA marking scheme

			Marks
(a)	External sales – A/B		1
	Internal sales – A		0.5
	External materials – A/B		1
	Internal costs – B		0.5
	Labour costs – A/B		1
	Other costs – A		1
	Fixed costs		0.5
	Profit – A/B		1
	PGC Co figures		2.5
		Maximum	**9**
(b)	External cont of $7 – A		1
	Incremental cost of $6		1
	External sales first – A		1
	150,000 from A/30,000 externally		1
	Approach		2
		Maximum	**6**
(c)	Minimum transfer price (marginal cost + opportunity cost)		1
	Opportunity cost – lost contribution $7		1
	Add marginal cost for transfer price of $14		1
	Approach		2
		Maximum	**5**
Total			**20**

296 CTD

(a) The current transfer price is ($40 + $20)) × 1.1 = $66.

		FD		TM	
		$000	$000	$000	$000
Internal sales	15,000 × $66		990		
External sales	5,000 × $80		400		
	15,000 × $500				7,500
			1,390		7,500
Production – variable costs	20,000 × $40	(800)			
	15,000 × $366			(5,490)	
Selling/distribution – variable costs	5,000 × $4	(20)			
	15,000 × $25			(375)	
			(820)		(5,865)
			570		1,635
Production overheads	20,000 × $20		(400)		
	15,000 × $60				(900)
Administration overheads	20,000 × $4		(80)		
	15,000 × $25				(375)
Net profit			90		360
Interest charge	$750,000\$1,500,000 × 12%		(90)		(180)
Residual income (RI)			0		180
Target RI			85		105
Bonus	$180,000 × 5%		0		9

Implications of the current reward system

While the TM manager has received a bonus and presumably will be pleased about it, the FD manager has received nothing. This will not be very motivating and may lead to problems within the division as a whole, such as inefficiency, staff turnover and unreliability. Since the TM division relies so completely on the FD division, this situation is clearly unacceptable.

Key answer tips

The calculations involved in this question are very straightforward, but don't be deceived – the real thrust of this question is to make sure that you both understand the principles of different transfer pricing methods, and can apply them to a situation.

(b) **(i)** In order to achieve a 5% bonus, the manager of TM division will be willing to accept a decrease in residual income of $(180,000 – 105,000) = $75,000. This is an increase in transfer price of the 15,000 units transferred of $75,000/15,000 = $5. Thus the transfer price would rise to $66 + $5 = $71.

(ii) In order to achieve a 5% bonus, the manager of FD division will want an increase in residual income of $85,000. This is an increase in transfer price of the 15,000 units transferred of $85,000/15,000 = $5.67. Thus the transfer price would have to rise to $66 + $5.67 = $71.67.

297 ROTECH (JUNE 2014)

(a) **Ratios**

(i) **ROCE = operating profit/capital employed × 100%**

		$000	ROCE
W Co	Design Division	6,000/23,540	25.49%
	Gearbox division	3,875/32,320	11.99%
C Co		7,010/82,975	8.45%

(ii) **Asset turnover = sales/capital employed × 100%**

		$000	Asset turnover
W Co	Design Division	14,300/23,540	0.61
	Gearbox division	25,535/32,320	0.79
C Co		15,560/82,975	0.19

(iii) **Operating profit margin = operating profit/sales × 100%**

		$000	Operating profit
W Co	Design Division	6,000/14,300	41.96%
	Gearbox division	3,875/25,535	15.18%
C Co		7,010/15,560	45.05%

Both companies and both divisions within W Co are clearly profitable. In terms of what the different ratios tell us, ROCE tells us the return which a company is making from its capital.

The Design division of W Co is making the highest return at over 25%, more than twice that of the Gearbox division and nearly three times that of C Co. This is because the nature of a design business is such that profits are largely derived from the people making the designs rather than from the assets. Certain assets will obviously be necessary in order to produce the designs but it is the employees who are mostly responsible for generating profit.

The Gearbox division and C Co's ROCE are fairly similar compared to the Design division, although when comparing the two in isolation, the Gearbox division's ROCE is actually over three percentage points higher than C Co's (11.99% compared to 8.45%).

This is because C Co has a substantially larger asset base than the Gearbox division. From the asset turnover ratio, it can be seen that the Gearbox division's assets generate a very high proportion of sales per $ of assets (79%) compared to C Co (19%).

This is partly because the Gearbox division buys its components in from C Co and therefore does not need to have the large asset base which C Co has in order to make the components. When the unit profitability of those sales is considered by looking at the operating profit margin, C Co's unit profitability is much higher than the Gearbox division (45% operating profit margin as compared to 15%).

The Design division, like the Gearbox division, is also using its assets well to generate sales (asset turnover of 61%) but then, like C Co, its unit profitability is high too (42% operating profit margin.) This is why, when the two ratios (operating profit margin and asset turnover) are combined to make ROCE, the Design division comes out top overall – because it has both high unit profitability and generates sales at a high level compared to its asset base.

It should be noted that any comparisons between such different types of business are of limited use. It would be more useful to have prior year figures for comparison and/or industry averages for similar businesses. This would make performance review much more meaningful.

(b) Transfer prices

From C Co's perspective

C Co transfers components to the Gearbox division at the same price as it sells components to the external market. However, if C Co were not making internal sales then, given that it already satisfies 60% of external demand, it would not be able to sell all of its current production to the external market.

External sales are $8,010,000, therefore unsatisfied external demand is ([$8,010,000/0.6] – $8,010,000) = $5,340,000. From C Co's perspective, of the current internal sales of $7,550,000, $5,340,000 could be sold externally if they were not sold to the Gearbox division.

Therefore, in order for C Co not to be any worse off from selling internally, these sales should be made at the current price of $5,340,000, less any reduction in costs which C Co saves from not having to sell outside the group (perhaps lower administrative and distribution costs). As regards the remaining internal sales of $2,210,000 ($7,550,000 – $5,340,000), C Co effectively has spare capacity to meet these sales.

Therefore, the minimum transfer price should be the marginal cost of producing these goods. Given that variable costs represent 40% of revenue, this means that the marginal cost for these sales is $884,000. This is therefore the minimum price which C Co should charge for these sales. In total, therefore, C Co will want to charge at least $6,224,000 for its sales to the Gearbox division.

From the Gearbox division's perspective

The Gearbox division will not want to pay more for the components than it could purchase them for externally. Given that it can purchase them all for 95% of the current price, this means a maximum purchase price of $7,172,500.

Overall

Taking into account all of the above, the transfer price for the sales should be somewhere between $6,224,000 and $7,172,500.

298 KLEN CO (SEPTEMBER/DECEMBER 2025)

(a)

	A	B	C
1	**Klen Co – Balanced Scorecard**		
2			
3	**Measures**	**20X5**	**20X4**
4	**Financial**		
5	Revenue growth (%)	-9.10%	n/a
6	Operating profit ($m)	**8,150**	**8,628**
7	**Customer**		
8	Market share (%)	**6.7%**	**6.5%**
9	% of customers who recommend Klen	59.0%	56.0%
10	**Internal business process**		
11	Downtime (hours)	5,956	6,354
12	% of manufactured machines with defects	**0.64%**	**0.69%**
13	**Innovation and learning**		
14	Average output (machines per employee)	**60.8**	**59.7**
15	ECO10 machines as % of machines produced	**46.5%**	**40.8%**

Workings

	20X5	20X4	% change
Financial			
Revenue ($m)	107,209	117,995	
Operating costs ($m)	-88,669	-99,528	
Depreciation ($m)	-10,390	-9,785	
Operating profit ($m)	**8,150**	**8,682**	**-6.10%**
Market Share			
Global revenue ($m)	1,600,134	1,815,308	
Market share (%)	**6.70%**	**6.50%**	
Quality & Operations			
Machines manufactured	3,763,400	4,249,600	
Machines with defects	24,086	29,322	
Defect rate (%)	**0.64%**	**0.69%**	
Number of employees	61,860	71,200	
Output per employee	**60.8**	**59.7**	
Product Innovation			
Traditional machines	2,012,236	2,517,264	
ECO10 machines	1,751,164	1,732,336	
ECO10 % of total	**46.50%**	**40.80%**	

(b) **Revenue growth**

Klen's revenue declined significantly (9.1%) in the year to 30 June 20X5, so, in this respect, Klen has not achieved its objective of sustaining growth.

Similarly, the decline in Klen's revenue is likely to reflect the significant fall in the total number of machines it produced in the year (–11.4%). This again indicates that Klen did not achieve its objective of sustaining growth.

However, Klen's performance needs to be viewed in the context of the economic downturn, and the global decline in sales of new machines. Global revenues from the sale of new machines fell by 11.9%, which gives an indication of the impact of the economic downturn on the industry as a whole. Moreover, the overall global decline in revenues (11.9%) is greater than the decline in Klen's revenue (9.1%).

Market position

Despite the fall in its revenue, Klen's market share actually increased in the year to 30 June 20X5. This could help to justify the CEO's confidence in Klen's ability to strengthen its market position as the global economy recovers.

Operating profit

Klen's operating profit fell by 6.1% compared to the year to 30 June 20X4 ($8,150m v $8,682m), but a decline in operating profit was almost inevitable given the economic downturn and the corresponding decline in revenue.

However, the overall decline in operating profit was less than the fall in revenue, which suggests that Klen has been effective in controlling its operating costs, as evidenced by operating costs (excluding depreciation) decreasing by more than the decrease in revenue (10.9% v 9.1%). This has enabled Klen to increase its operating profit margin slightly (from 7.4% to 7.6%), despite a significant increase in depreciation charges.

However, the increase in depreciation charges is potentially also instructive because it suggests that, despite the downturn, Klen has continued to invest in new assets, which again should help to strengthen its competitiveness in the future.

% of customers who recommend Klen

The proportion of customers who would recommend Klen's machines is a useful indicator of customer satisfaction, because customers are only likely to recommend Klen's machines if they are satisfied with their own machines. Therefore, the increase in the number of people who would recommend Klen's machines is a positive sign.

However, although 59% of people would recommend Klen's machines, this means 41% would not. It would be useful to know how the proportion of people who recommend Klen's machines compares to the proportions of customers who would recommend other makes of machines, to get an indication of how Klen's customer satisfaction levels compare to those of its competitors.

Machine downtime

Given that Klen's production process is highly automated, minimising downtime is likely to be critical to the efficiency of the production process. Therefore, the decline in the number of downtime hours is a positive indicator, particularly if it is linked to capital investment in new machines and technologies, as implied by the higher depreciation charges, which are more reliable than older ones.

% of machines with defects

If customers experience problems or defects with their machines, this could affect how satisfied they are, and therefore how likely they would be to buy another Klen machine in future, or to recommend Klen machines to other people. As the CEO has highlighted, quality (and minimising the number of defects) will be important in helping Klen become more competitive and strengthen its market position.

In this respect, the reduction in the proportion of machines with defects reported (from 0.69% to 0.64%) is a favourable indicator.

However, perhaps more importantly, the proportion of Klen's machines which had defects reported in them is less than half that of the industry average (0.64% v 1.33%). This suggests that Klen does have a competitive advantage over a number of other manufacturers in relation to quality and could use this to help strengthen its market position further.

Productivity

Despite the number of machines Klen produced falling significantly in the year, average output per employee increased slightly (60.8 v 59.7), suggesting an increase in efficiency.

At the same time, the number of Klen's employees has fallen significantly (–13.1%.) It is not clear how far this is a temporary decline, in response to falling production in the economic downturn, or a more structural change reflecting the continued automation of the production process. However, it would be expected that investing in new machinery and the increasing automation of the production process will lead to an increase in output per employee.

ECO10 machines produced as a proportion of total machines produced

The change in product mix (energy efficient machines v traditional machines) between 20X4 and 20X5 has been significant, with the proportion of ECO10 machines increasing from 40.8% to 46.5%; an increase of 14% in one year. Significantly, despite the overall reduction in machine sales, the number of ECO10 machines Klen sold in the year to 30 June 20X5 actually increased slightly compared to the previous year. This suggests that Klen is not only embracing new technologies in developing environmentally friendly machines, but also demonstrating its goal of respecting the planet (by reducing the number of traditional machines it produces in favour of ones which are more environmentally friendly).

Overall comments

Although Klen's revenue declined sharply in the year to 30 June 20X5 compared to 20X4, due to the global economic downturn, its performance against all the non-financial metrics in its balanced scorecard improved. If its performance in the key non-financial areas continues to improve, this should help to strengthen Klen's competitive and market position going forward, as the CEO has suggested, and then, in turn, help to strengthen its financial performance.

Key answer tips

The first not of importance, is that you could gain additional marks for further calculations. If this is explicitly stated in a note to the question, it is worthwhile considering what additional calculations would provide valuable insight into performance. However, it is also important to recognise that only relevant figures which had not already been provided, would be awarded the marks. If figures are specifically provided in the scenario, marks will not be earned by recalculating those values.

To earn written analysis marks candidates needed to provide some element of analysis or insight, which adds value in helping assess Klen's performance. For example, "The percentage of machines with defects has fallen from 0.69% in 20X4, to 0.64% in 20X5" would not earn a mark in (b), because it is simply restating the calculations required in (a). Some candidates took this approach and therefore did not perform well on this question requirement. To earn written analysis marks, candidates needed to include some comment on the significance of these figures.

Strong answers would take either a new calculation, or one calculated in part (a) and use it to develop an answer which provides insight into the performance of Klen. For example, it was possible to calculate the decline in industry sales, which would make an excellent comparator for the decline in Klen's revenue. Consider, therefore, the difference between a weaker answer, suggesting that "Klen has done badly against its growth objective due to a decline in revenue" with a stronger one that suggests "although Klen has seen a decline in revenue of 9.1%, and therefore is not meeting its objective for growth, the market has declined by 11.9% and therefore Klen is beating the market. This is further supported by the increase in market share".

ACCA Marking scheme		
		Marks
(a)	Calculations – half mark per correct figure	5
(b)	Analysis – up to 2 for each well discussed point	15
Total		**20**

299 MEDCOMP (MARCH/JUNE 2021)

(a)

FINANCIAL	**CSF:** The critical success factor identified for this perspective is most likely to be positive cash flow.
	KPI: The most appropriate performance indicator is total donations less operating costs.
	Performance Analysis: Total donations in 20X8, 20X7 and 20X6 are \$1,710,000, \$1,605,000 and \$1,475,000 respectively and when the operating costs are deducted, the net cash flows are \$(20,000), \$55,000 and \$45,000 respectively. This shows that for the current year Medcomp is not achieving a positive cash flow. However, this is a relatively small cash deficit for the year and does not suggest that the charity has any real problems. The size of the donations has risen considerably over the years and the number of businesses donating has fallen. This could indicate that the fundraisers have focused their efforts on a smaller number of more affluent businesses.

CUSTOMER	**CSF:** The critical success factor identified for this perspective is most likely to be medical effectiveness.
	KPI: The best performance indicator for this perspective is the percentage of successful treatments.
	Performance Analysis: For the years 20X8, 20X7 and 20X6 these are 77%, 86% and 87% respectively. As treatment for cataracts is a relatively simple procedure, a high success rate would be expected but the results in 20X8 show a significant deterioration. The reasons for the recent fall in effectiveness could be the result of factors outside the control of Medcomp, such as variations in the disease or the advanced condition of the disease when presented. However, it could be also linked to the lack of efficiency of the new treatments.
INTERNAL BUSINESS PROCESS	**CSF:** The critical success factor identified for this perspective is most likely to be functional efficiency.
	KPI: The performance indicator for this perspective could be: 'average number of days to deliver drugs and equipment to treatment centres'.
	Performance Analysis: This has remained at seven days since 20X6 and in some ways this can be expected as the 12 treatment centres have been at the same location for many years and the logistics of the delivery well established. It should be noted that this measure is an average lead time and will also vary on location. However, as Medcomp rarely experiences shortages at the treatment centres, it can be surmised that transport costs are managed as efficiently as possible and this means an average seven-day lead time.
LEARNING AND GROWTH	**CSF:** The critical success factor identified for this perspective is most likely to be innovation.
	KPI: The performance indicator for this perspective is the new procedures as a percentage of total procedures from the table.
	Performance Analysis: It is clear that Medcomp has made several changes to the existing protocol in 20X8. One in five procedures administered are new and have been introduced within the past 12 months. This is a clear improvement on 20X7 and 20X6 as the CSF is for new treatments. However, the new treatments have not improved the efficiency of the treatment, as evidenced by the percentage of successful treatments, and this will need to be monitored.

(b) The benefits to an organisation of using the balanced scorecard to assess performance instead of relying solely on financial measures are as follows:

Not all organisations have profit or financial return as the main objective. In an altruistic not-for-profit charity such as Medcomp, the objectives are based on delivering a service which can be measured in benefit to people who are unable to pay for the service. Therefore, it is necessary to have measures which are not purely financial to reflect the different emphasis of the mission and supporting objectives.

Financial performance indicators are 'lagging' indicators. This means that the events and decisions which caused these indicators occurred long ago. The balanced scorecard includes 'leading' indicators. For example, the learning and growth perspective may encourage spending on training or techniques which will depress profits or increase costs in the short term, but will have much greater benefits in the future.

The balanced scorecard helps to align key performance measures with strategy at all levels. This means that all employees will be able to link their individual goals to those of the organisation as a whole. The benefit of this is that it ensures that what gets measured is important to the organisation.

Financial measures used in isolation are relatively easy to manipulate in the short term. For example, a high return on investment figure may be considered an indicator of good performance whereas it may have been caused by a manager delaying the purchase of a necessary asset. The balanced scorecard provided a range of indicators which makes this type of manipulation more difficult to conceal.

ACCA Marking scheme		
		Marks
(a)	Identification of CSF for each perspective (0.5 each)	2
	Identification of KPI for each perspective (1 each)	4
	Analysis of performance using the KPIs (max 4 for any perspective)	10
		16
(b)	Benefits of balanced scorecard – up to 2 for each well discussed point	4
Total		**20**

300 HAMMOCK CO (MARCH/JULY 2020 SAMPLE EXAM)

(a) To make a profit long-term

In order to make a profit the long term revenues need to be higher than the long term costs.

The weekly revenue per guest is $2,000 in the 20X7 budget, the 20X7 actual results and the 20X6 actual results which is not in line with inflation. This means that revenues per guest are falling in real terms.

However, all staff costs have increased by 2% which is caused by inflation.

Overall this means that the profit per guest, based on the limited figures available is falling.

The repair costs, allowing for inflation have been set at the same level as 20X6. The actual for 20X7 appears to be better than budget, but as repairs are likely to be incurred on an ad hoc basis, this does not necessarily indicate an improvement. The 20X6 repair costs are higher than the competitor's but it is difficult to compare because Hammocks Co have more rooms so we are not comparing like with like. On a repair per room basis Hammocks has slightly lower cost at $163 per room compared to the competition's $164 per room.

Due to the secure long-term contracts which Hammocks Co offers its staff, staff costs are fixed costs in the management accounts. This means that in order to be profitable, these costs need to be covered by the contribution per guest. Although there is not the data to calculate the contribution per guest per week, the higher level of guest occupancy level in 20X7 (both budgeted and actual) is a positive indication. Hammocks' occupancy level per room was 81% compared to the competitor's 77% (all based on double occupancy) indicating that performance is good.

To create customer loyalty

There are a number of indicators to show that Hammocks Co have created a loyal customer base.

Firstly, compared to their main competitor Hammocks Co receive more revenue, charge a higher price per guest per week and have better occupancy rates. This indicates good customer satisfaction.

Secondly the ratio of staff to guest is higher than the competition; 1.5 compared to 1.3 in 20X6 (actual in 20X7 is slightly higher due to a lower occupancy rate than budgeted and the fact that staff numbers are fixed). As this is a seasonal business this is may simply be a blip.

Finally, the comments on TripEvent are very positive about the level of service and standard of cleanliness and maintenance. However it should be noted that the entire customer experience is not positive. Complaints like the administrative errors and unchanging menus could be a warning sign of possible erosion of customer loyalty.

(b) **(i)** A balanced scorecard approach to performance management is important to Hammocks Co because it will provide management with a set of information which covers all relevant areas of business performance. At present Hammocks Co considers performance from a financial and customer perspective. These perspectives are important but they do not allow a wide enough consideration of all of the factors that should be considered in this business.

Introducing the balanced scorecard will:

- Ensure that all internal systems and processes support the customer and financial objectives. For example, in decision-making there is little point in buying a new IT system that does not either improve customer experience or reduce processing costs.
- Encourage full integration between all departments. Errors in invoicing or sending specific requirements are system or internal process errors. While a customer might not choose a holiday resort for its excellent administration, they may refuse to use a company again if they receive poor service. Thus neglecting one aspect of the scorecard can impact on customer satisfaction and longer term financial performance.
- Make sure important elements are assessed and expected performance levels quantified and/or qualified. This this means that performance can be measured, explained, compared and where necessary, control action can be taken. The errors that occur at Hammocks Co are spoiling the company's reputation, but there is no evidence that any action is being taken.

(Note: Only TWO were required)

(ii) **Internal business process**

Goal: To have an effective and efficient administration.

The feedback on TripEvent indicates that the only guest complaints relate to administrative issues prior to the guest arrival and not operational issues at the resort. In fact the actions of the resort staff with the speedy resolution of bedding issues and the organising of a complimentary transfer seems to have diverted trouble. Therefore measures need to be focused on the weaker area which is the administration.

Measures:

1 Number of times that a guest request is not received at resort prior to their arrival/number of requests made.

This will measure the number of times the guest experience is not seamless from booking to arrival.

2 Average number of corrections to booking due to an administrative error.

This measures inefficient use of staff time and potentially increased customer frustration.

Innovation and Learning

Goal: To match leading competitor's facilities

The comment on TripEvent shows that even loyal customers are noticing that rivals are including more innovative facilities at their resorts. Although the true strength of Hammocks Co lies in the quality of the service it is important that the facilities' appliances and service offerings are updated to compare favourably with that of its rivals.

Measures:

1 Number of in-room appliances offered by rivals but not by Hammocks Co.

The measure will ensure that Hammocks Co consider what is included within the guest rooms by comparing to external factors.

2 Number of new items offered on the menu each month.

This should ensure that the chefs consider the latest trends in fine dining and do not ever appear stagnant from the point of view of the customer.

ACCA Marking scheme				
				Marks
(a)	Discuss the performance of Hammocks			8
(b)	(i)	Two advantages of using the Balanced Scorecard		3
	(ii)	One goal, two performance measures for:		
		–	Internal business processes	4.5
		–	Innovation and growth	4.5
Total				**20**

301 LEMIC AIR CO (SEPTEMBER/DECEMBER 2023)

(a) Dimension: Financial performance

Objective: To increase additional revenues from sale of pre-allocated seat bookings.

Performance indicator: Percentage increase in revenue from pre-allocated seats.

Justification: Lemic Air charges low prices for flights so it relies on extras such as pre-allocated seat bookings to enhance revenues. Its current seat bookings are below industry average.

Dimension: Competition

Objective: To increase market share and become the leading low-cost airline in Surland.

Performance indicator: Percentage of market share compared to prior year/ competitors.

Justification: Lemic Air is already only 5 percentage points away from its largest competitor, increasing market share will increase revenues.

Dimension: Quality

Objective: To improve customer satisfaction with the cleanliness of Lemic Air's planes by improving the cleaning.

Performance indicator: Reduction in the percentage of customers complaining about dirty planes/increase in customer satisfaction on cleanliness in the questionnaire.

Justification: Customers have historically complained about the cleanliness of planes, and the company has introduced measures to improve this by using cabin crew to clean the planes.

Dimension: Innovation

Objective: To reduce the queuing time for customers by investing in machines for customers to use for checking in/bag drop off.

Performance indicator: Reduction in average queue time per customer.

Justification: It is important that Lemic Air invests in innovative processes to reduce queue times for customers as this has caused complaints in the past and may lead to lack of returning customers in the future.

Dimension: Flexibility

Objective: To increase the extent of cross-training of staff so that they have the ability to move fluidly between aircraft and airport roles hence reducing cancellations due to staffing issues.

Performance indicator: Increase in the number of staff who are cross-trained/increase in the percentage of staff who are cross-trained.

Justification: Lemic Air has had to cancel flights because of staff absence and cross-training has the potential to reduce cancellations and increase satisfaction of staff members.

Dimension: Resource utilisation

Objective: To increase the average flight occupancy rate.

Performance indicator: Increase in the average occupancy rate compared to previous year.

Justification: Lemic Air's low-cost strategy relies on planes being as full as possible.

(b) It is clear from the scenario that there are particular environmental costs associated with the airline industry. The largest of these is the effect of carbon emissions on the planet and consequently those who inhabit it. In particular, the scenario refers to the fact that Lemic Air uses cheaper but more polluting fuel on its planes. It also uses the cheaper ground boarding rather than passenger loading bridges which results in a greater environmental impact as buses have engines running for some time on the tarmac. So, the costs associated with these are purely what would be classed as 'external environment costs' because it is the planet and the public at large who are bearing the costs of these actions, not Lemic Air.

Managing environmental costs by keeping them to a minimum is a particular challenge for a company with a low-cost pricing approach, such as Lemic Air, because profit margins are usually low in such businesses. Hence, it cannot afford to make decisions which would reduce these external costs, e.g. using less polluting fuel without increasing its costs.

However, external costs can often be converted to internal costs for the company by the imposition of fines. Although the scenario does not mention it, Lemic Air may well be facing fines as a result of its decisions. It is important, when managing environmental costs, to balance the cost of these fines with the benefits of using cheap fuel, for example. In addition, although it is more difficult to quantify it, the general public are becoming increasingly aware about the impact of climate change and the need for companies to be more sustainable, so there could be an unknown cost of lost revenues from customers who choose to boycott Lemic Air because of this. Given the difficulty of identifying such costs, it is even more difficult to manage them.

ACCA Marking scheme		
		Marks
(a)	Each dimension (2.5 marks each)	15
(b)	Discussion	5
Total		**20**

302 CAROLINE CO (MARCH/JUNE 2024)

(a) Profit statement for the current position

	Packaging Division	Radio Division	Caroline Co
	$000	$000	$000
External sales		4,400	4,400
Internal sales	120		
Variable cost	(20)	(2,400)	(2,420)
Internal costs		(120)	
Contribution	**100**	**1,880**	**1,980**
Fixed costs	(80)	(500)	(580)
Profit	**20**	**1,380**	**1,400**

External sales = $220,000 × 20,000 = $4,400,000

Current transfer price = $1 + ($80,000/20,000 boxes) + 20% mark-up = $6 per box

Internal sales/costs = $6 × 20,000 boxes = $120,000

Variable costs: Packaging = $1 × 20,000 = $20,000

Radio = $120 × 20,000 = $2,400,000

(b) **(i)** This calculation can be performed on an incremental basis as follows:

The Packaging Division's profit will decrease by $40,000 (20,000 boxes × the $2 reduction in transfer price). This will result in a loss of $20,000 in the Packaging Division.

The Radio Division's profit will increase by $40,000 (20,000 boxes × the $2 reduction in transfer price). This will result in a new profit of $1,420,000.

Overall, Caroline Co's profit will be unchanged at $1,400,000 as the transfer price decrease of $2 is a loss to one division but a gain to the other.

Alternatively, the profit statement could be redrafted as follows:

Profit statement if the transfer price is $4 per box

	Packaging Division	**Radio Division**	**Caroline Co**
	$000	$000	$000
External sales		4,400	4,400
Internal sales	80		
Variable cost	(20)	(2,400)	(2,420)
Internal costs		(80)	
Contribution	**60**	**1,920**	**1,980**
Fixed costs	(80)	(500)	(580)
Profit/(loss)	**(20)**	**1,420**	**1,400**

(ii) This calculation can be performed on an incremental basis as follows:

The closure of the Packaging Division will save $20,000 in fixed costs but cause Caroline Co to incur extra variable costs of $60,000 (20,000 boxes × ($4 – $1)). The extra variable cost is the difference between the Packaging Division's variable cost and the price offered by the external supplier.

This will result in a reduction in Caroline Co's profit of $40,000 reducing the profit to $1,360,000.

Alternatively, the profit statement could be redrafted as follows:

Profit statement if the Packaging Division is shut down

	Packaging Division	**Radio Division**	**Caroline Co**
	$000	$000	$000
External sales		4,400	4,400
Internal sales			
Variable cost		(2,400)	(2,400)
External costs		(80)	(80)
Contribution	**0**	**1,920**	**1,920**
Fixed costs	(60)	(500)	(560)
Profit/(loss)	**(60)**	**1,420**	**1,360**

(c) The advantages and disadvantages to Caroline Co of a transfer price of $4 per box are:

It ensures that corporate profits are maximised. The Radio Division will buy internally, and closure of the Packaging Division will be avoided, saving the company $40,000. It will also continue to allow the company to control the supply and quality of the boxes which the radios are packaged in.

It ensures that the performance of both divisions is measured fairly as it is a market-based price. In this way, both divisions will face the 'test of the market place'.

It maintains the autonomy of the Radio Division as it will not need to be forced to buy internally. However, the autonomy of the Packaging Division may be compromised as the $4 transfer price per box will result in a loss and it may no longer be motivated to produce the boxes.

Using a transfer price of $4 per box continues to assume that the Packaging Division operates as a profit centre, but this could be questioned as it has no external market. It may be better to operate it as a cost centre.

ACCA marking scheme				
				Marks
(a)	Statement of profits			6
(b)	**(i)**	Effect of transfer price		4
	(ii)	Effect on profit		4
			Maximum	8
(c)	Advantages/disadvantages			6
Total				**20**

303 ROBINHOLT UNIVERSITY (SEPTEMBER 2019)

1 To provide education which promotes intellectual initiative and produces confident and ambitious graduates who have reached the highest academic standards to prepare them for success in life and the workplace

There are various performance indicators which can be looked at to ascertain whether RU is meeting this strategic aim. First, question 1 of the survey shows that 83% of students think that the course is intellectually stimulating and the quality of teaching is high. This has gone down by three percentage points since 20X5, which is not good.

In the NOS survey, the percentage of graduates agreeing that the course has developed them as a person has increased from 80% in 20X5 to 82% in 20X6. This would indicate that RU is indeed developing confident and ambitious graduates.

However, the number of graduates achieving first class degrees in 20X6 has fallen vastly from 28% to 20%. Given that the entry requirements were only relaxed in 20X6, this should not have had any impact on results. This infers that the quality of teaching may have declined and the ratio of students to academic staff has increased from 35:1 to 40:1. It appears that, although many new students were recruited in 20X6, there were not enough new academic staff recruited to deal with the influx of students. This is shown by the fact that student numbers increased by 13% but academic staff costs only increased by 6%.

As there was presumably a pay rise in the year too, it is clear that a proportionate amount of new staff were not recruited. This failing is also reflected by the fall in the answer to question 2 from 86% to 82%, with students being less satisfied in 20X6 with the advice and support they have received. Also, the staff retention rate has gone down in 20X6, meaning that staff are less familiar with RU and therefore more likely to provide a fragmented service.

However, in 20X5 75% of employers were happy with the graduates they recruited, in 20X6 this dropped to 72%. In addition, in 20X5 only 65% of students have managed to obtain graduate jobs within a year compared to previous years. Given that RU has relaxed the entry requirements for students in 20X6, this may mean that its 20X6 recruits are not as well qualified as its 20X5. This could mean that in the future the number of graduates obtaining graduate jobs within a year and the satisfaction percentages of employers could fall further. This decision has meant that there has been a 9% increase in fee income, but it compromises RU's ability to meet its first strategic aim.

2 To provide an organised, efficient learning environment with access to cutting edge technology and facilities

As regards premises, the money spent on maintaining these has decreased by 10% in 20X6, despite the increased student numbers. In the NOS survey, the percentage of students satisfied with these facilities has gone down nine percentage points from 92% to 83%. This suggests that this particular strategic aim has been neglected. Students seem far less satisfied with the way that the courses are run and administered now, with a fall of nine percentage points. Administration staff costs have only increased by 5% despite a 13% increase in student numbers and, presumably, a pay rise during the year. It can be inferred that staff are under increasing pressure and unable to cope with the increased numbers. This is again reflected by the fall in the staff retention rate from 90% in 20X5 to 75% in 20X6.

3 To be a leader in sustainable business practices which protect the environment and support local people

As with the above strategic aim, this one also seems to have been a little forgotten in 20X6. In 20X5, RU won an environmental award for its campuses. It also took part in a food sharing initiative which helped the local community. It has now got rid of its recycling bins and ceased to be involved in the food share project. RU's spending on sustainability and community assistance has actually halved in 20X6. This decline in activity is partly attributable to staff shortages. All in all, this is not very good as RU is now failing to meet one of its main strategic aims.

4 To provide attractive, innovative conference and event facilities, attracting clients both nationally and internationally

Conference and event income has gone up by 13% in 20X6, which is a good increase for RU. It has managed to control its costs relating to these events well too, since these have only increased by 4%. RU has also won an award for its conference facility and attracted a number of new clients. RU therefore appears to be focusing well on this strategic aim.

5 To be recognised both nationally and internationally for the scope and relevance of their research

Income from research at RU has actually gone down by 22% this year, as have the associated costs. Whilst a local university has won an award for their contribution to research, RU has not been successful in this regard. The suggestion is that this aim has not been focused on in 20X6.

Overall satisfaction

In addition to the above, it should be considered that the overall satisfaction percentage for students has decreased from 83% to 81%. This could have serious implications for RU as it is the main performance indicator used both internally and externally to assess how RU is performing. As well as meaning that RU may well now attract fewer students, it will also have an impact on the fees which can be charged to students in future years. The university needs to consider how it can improve the service it is providing in order to improve overall satisfaction.

Calculations

	20X6 $m	**20X5** $m	**% increase/ decrease**
Income			
Tuition fees	148	135.6	9%
Research grants	3.5	4.5	(22%)
Conferences and other events	18	16	13%
	———	———	———
Total income	169.5	156.1	9%
	———	———	———
Expenditure			
Academic staff costs	80.8	76.2	6%
Administration staff costs	50.4	48	5%
Premises, facilities and technology costs	7.6	8.4	(10%)
Event and conference costs	8.3	8	4%
Research grants	3.1	4	(23%)
Sustainability and community assistance	1.2	2.4	(50%)
	———	———	———
Total expenditure	151.4	147	3%
	———	———	———
Surplus	18.1	9.1	99%
Student numbers	27,000	24,000	13%

ACCA Marking scheme	
	Marks
Calculations	4
Strategic aims discussion	16
	——
Total	**20**
	——

304 TONFORD SCHOOL (SEPTEMBER/DECEMBER 2020)

(a) The primary objective of commercial organisations is to maximise the wealth they generate for their owners (shareholders). In contrast, the objectives of NFPO's are often non-financial and reflect the interests which the various stakeholders have in an organisation. These stakeholders often have varying interests in the organisation, meaning that the organisation will also have a number of different objectives.

These conflicts may make it difficult to set clear objectives on which all stakeholders agree. Consequently, the organisation's management will face a dilemma when trying to decide which objectives are most important and therefore prioritised in the course of strategic planning and decision-making. This can be a particular problem when different objectives make different demands on resources or require different courses of action.

Another problem is that these organisations often do not generate revenue but simply have a fixed budget for spending which they have to keep to and are often subject to strong external influences which will influence the setting of objectives e.g. political factors.

(b)

Tutorial note

This solution is longer than one which candidates would need to produce to score the marks available. However, it is intended to illustrate the range of relevant points candidates could have identified from the scenario, and therefore the number of marks potentially available in this question.

Objective 1 – Strive for continuous improvement in performance standards.

The percentage of pupils achieving the target grades is not only below the national target, it is also lower than Tonford School achieved five years ago. As such, the school's does not appear to be achieving continuous improvement.

However, exam results alone are not necessarily an accurate indicator of a school's performance. For example, exam results will reflect the underlying ability of the pupils, as well as the quality of the teaching they receive.

There is a danger that if Tonford School focuses only on exam results it will become 'selective' and will only accept the most academically gifted pupils. However, such an approach would contradict the objective to provide 'all children' with access to high quality education, regardless of their background.

Pupil progress may be a more valuable measure than exam results, because the extent to which pupils' performance improves provides an indication of the value added by the school, rather than pupils' inherent ability.

Given the typical range of scores, Tonford School's performance in this respect (+0.4) is significantly above the national target (+0.25) and is at the upper end of the range.

The fact that pupil numbers have increased seems likely to suggest that the school is becoming more popular with parents. Given that parents can choose which school to select for their children, the increase in pupil numbers is likely to reflect a perception among parents that the school is performing well.

The results of the recent inspection visit would seem likely to reinforce this perception.

Note: An alternative interpretation could be that all the other schools in the area are already full, and Tonford has spare capacity, which is why its pupil numbers increased. However, such an explanation seems less likely given the context of the other performance indicators.

Objective 2 – Provide a supportive learning environment, which encourages a high standard of pupil achievement.

The 'pupil progress' score suggests the school is providing children with a high quality education and a learning environment which encourages a high standard of pupil achievement. The fact that Tonford School's 20X7 score is higher than its 20X2 score also suggests an improvement in the learning environment (although here again, to some extent the scores may reflect pupils' aptitude for learning as well as the efforts of the school).

The school's inspection grade is higher than five years ago, and is above the national target, which suggests the school is improving, and is performing relatively well. Although there is no indication that the DoE gives any more weighting to any single aspect of the performance data compared to other areas, the inspection grades could potentially be the most important indicator of how well as school is performing.

However, although Tonford School's grading is 'Very good' this suggests there is still room for further improvement, because the school did not achieve the top grade: 'Excellent'.

Tonford School's teacher/pupil ratio has remained essentially the same over the last five years – at 19 pupils per teacher, which is favourable compared to the national target of 22 pupils per teacher.

20X7: 662 pupils/35 members of teaching staff = 18.9 pupils per member of staff

20X2: 627 pupils/33 members of teaching staff = 19 pupils per member of staff

Having a low teacher pupil ratio is likely to be beneficial because it will allow teachers to give more time to each pupil, thereby providing a supportive learning environment.

Given that the school is funded by the DoE, it seems likely that the DoE would have had to authorise the budget needed to recruit the additional teachers. On this basis, the fact that Tonford School has been able to increase the number of teachers it employs suggests that the DoE is pleased with the way it is performing, and therefore authorised the additional budget.

Objective 3 – Ensure pupils are prepared for adult life and have the skills and character necessary to contribute to society and the economy.
The inspector has highlighted Tonford School's 'strong sense of community values and citizenship'. This suggests the school is performing well in relation to the objective of preparing students for adult life, and developing their social skills. Exam results and the 'pupil progress' scores in compulsory subjects indicate that the school is making a significant contribution in providing pupils with core knowledge and skills necessary for adulthood.
Objective 4 – Provide all children with access to high quality education, regardless of their location or background.
The inspector's report has highlighted that pupils at Tonford School come from diverse backgrounds' and awarded the school an improved grading over the last five years. Coupled with 'pupil progress' scores, this indicates that the school is fulfilling the objective to provide children which access to high quality education, regardless of their background.

(c) In order to assess any organisation's performance against its objectives, performance information needs to be available, and, in many cases, this information is obtained by measuring aspects of performance relevant to the objectives.

Difficulties of measurement

However, one of the inherent difficulties with qualitative objectives compared to quantifiable objectives is how to measure them.

For example, exam success rate (% of pupils achieving 5 grades A-C) is quantifiable, and relatively easy to measure, using exam results data. However, trying to measure the overall quality of education in a school or whether a school provides a 'supportive learning environment' is potentially much more difficult, because there aren't any specific outputs (e.g. results) which can be measured.

So, while exam results and pupil progress metrics are indicators of pupil achievement in schools – which can be measured – assessing them only provides a partial assessment of whether schools are providing children with 'access to high quality education' or whether they are providing 'supportive learning environment which encourages a high standard of pupil achievement.'

A related problem is that the aspects of performance which are monitored end up being the ones where performance can most easily be measured, rather than those which are most important in ensuring that the objectives are achieved.

The DoE has recognised these issues though and acknowledged the need for inspectors to visit schools on a regular basis, to gain an insight into the aspects of performance which cannot be reflected in statistical measures.

Subjectivity

Another major problem with assessing qualitative aspects of performance is that they tend to be subjective. For example, people are likely to have different expectations of what constitutes a high quality of education, a supportive learning environment, or the extent to which students are prepared for adult life.

In this respect, one of the key things the DoE has to ensure is that its inspectors are consistent in their grading of schools. For example, if one inspector rates a school as 'Good', but another inspector would have rated the same school as 'Excellent', this inconsistency would significantly reduce the validity of the performance data which is produced.

ACCA Marking scheme		
		Marks
(a)	Explain problems of multiple objectives for NFPs.	4
(b)	Performance assessment of Tonford School	12
(c)	Explanation of difficulties in qualitative objectives	4
Total		**20**

305 MOBE (JUNE 2015 ADAPTED)

(a) **From the group's perspective**

For every motor sold externally, Division M generates a profit of $80 ($850 – $770) for the group as a whole. For every motor which Division S has to buy from outside of the group, there is an incremental cost of $60 per unit ($800 – ($770 – $30)). Therefore, from a group perspective, as many external sales should be made as possible before any internal sales are made. Consequently, the group's current policy will need to be changed. This does, however, assume that the quality of the motors bought from outside the group is the same as the quality of the motors made by Division M.

Division M's total capacity is 60,000 units. Given that it can make external sales of 30,000 units, it can only supply 30,000 of Division S's demand for 35,000 motors. These 30,000 units should be bought from Division M since. from a group perspective, the cost of supplying these internally is $60 per unit cheaper than buying externally. The remaining 5,000 motors required by Division S should then be bought in from the external supplier at $800 per unit.

In order to work out the transfer price which should be set for the internal sales of 30,000 motors, the perspective of both divisions must be considered.

From Division M's perspective

Division M's only buyer for these 30,000 motors (once external demand is exhausted) is Division S, so the lowest price it would be prepared to charge is the marginal cost of making these units and selling them internally, which is $740 per unit. However, it would ideally want to make some profit on these motors too and would consequently expect a significantly higher price than this.

From Division S's perspective

Division S knows that it can buy as many external motors as it needs from outside the group at a price of $800 per unit. Therefore, this will be the maximum price which it is prepared to pay.

Overall

Therefore, the transfer price should be set somewhere between $740 and $800. From the perspective of the group, the total group profit will be the same irrespective of where in this range the transfer price is set. However, it is important that divisional and staff remain motivated. Given the external sales price which Division M can achieve and the fact that Division S would have to pay $800 for each motor bought from outside the group, the transfer price should probably be at the higher end of the range.

(b) (i) Return on investment

Division S

Net Profit = $44,600 × 28% = $12,488

ROI = $12,488 ÷ $82,800 = 15.08%

Division M

Net Profit = $21,800 × 33% = $7,194

ROI = $7,194 ÷ $40,600 = 17.72%

(ii) Residual income

Division S

Divisional Profit = $12,488

Capital employed = $82,800

Imputed interest charge = $82,800 × 12% = $2,552

Residual income = $12,488 – $9,936 = $2,552

Division M

Divisional Profit = $7,194

Capital employed = $40,600

Imputed interest charge = $40,600 × 12% = $4,872

Residual income = $7,194 – $4,872 = $2,322

(iii) Comments

If a decision about whether to proceed with the investments is made based on ROI, it is possible that the Division S will reject the proposal whereas the of Division M will accept the proposal. This is because each division currently has a ROI of 16% and since the Division S investment only has a ROI of 15.08%, it would bring the division's overall ROI down to less than its current level. On the other hand, since the Division M investment is higher than its current 16%, the investment would bring the division's overall ROI up.

When you consider what would actually be best for the company as a whole, you come to the conclusion that, since both investments have a healthy return (as shown by the residual income), so they should both be accepted. Hence, the fact that ROI had been used as a decision-making tool has led to a lack of congruence between Division S and the company as whole. This backs up what the new manager of Division S is saying. If they used residual income in order to aid the decision-making process, both proposals would be accepted by the divisions since both have a healthy RI. In this case, RI helps the divisions to make decisions which are in line with the best interests of the company. Once again, this backs up the new manager's viewpoint.

It is important to note, however, that each of the methods has numerous advantages and disadvantages which have not been considered here.

306 FLAG CO (SEPTEMBER/DECEMBER 2021)

(a) Profitability

	Flag Co	Budget Co
ROCE	12.8%	13.7%
Operating margin	10.93%	6.07%
Asset turnover	1.17	2.26

Budget Co has a better return on capital employed and is therefore making better returns for its investors. The main cause of this is Budget Co's ability to generate sales. For every $ of capital employed, it generates $2.26 of sales revenue as compared to only $1.17 in the case of Flag Co. Budget Co has much shorter flight times than Flag Co and therefore could be making more journeys and spending less time parked at airports.

Budget Co earns a lower operating margin than Flag Co, as Budget Co's operating costs as a percentage of revenue are 94% compared to Flag Co at 89%. This is probably due to Budget Co's pricing strategy. The lower operating margin is more than offset by Budget Co's higher asset turnover, resulting in a higher capital employed (asset turnover × operating margin = ROCE, therefore 6.07% × 2.26 = 13.7%).

Analysis of the other information provided shows that Budget Co has a much higher seat occupancy rate.

	Flag Co	Budget Co
Seat occupancy rate	66.29%	95.00%

This is probably a consequence of its low fares policy resulting in higher sales of seats relative to Flag Co and therefore a higher asset turnover.

Budget Co also appears more fuel efficient than Flag Co.

	Flag Co	Budget Co
Available seat kilometre per litre of fuel	8,802	12,001

The better fuel economy is probably related to Budget Co's newer fleet of aircraft. Better fuel economy would tend to improve Budget Co's operating margin, however, it is still lower than Flag Co's.

Liquidity

	Flag Co	Budget Co
Current ratio	0.60	0.79

The current ratios of the two businesses are below the text book norm of 2:1, however, they are both service companies which carry little inventory, so this is not surprising or worrying. There is no apparent reason for the difference between the two companies.

Risk

	Flag Co	Budget Co
Capital gearing (debt:equity)	110.44%	51.47%
Interest cover	4.96 times	8.08 times
Operating gearing	950%	820%

Flag Co has a relatively high level of long-term borrowings. This adds to the risks of the business as interest on these borrowings has to be paid no matter the company's operating profit. At present, its operating profit is nearly five times larger than its interest bill and it appears to be able to comfortably pay its commitments. Its operating gearing is 950%, indicating that if sales volume fell by 10%, then its profit before interest and tax would fall by 95% (that is 950% or 9.5 times more). This would cause Flag Co difficulty in covering its interest payments. As demand for business travel is very sensitive to economic conditions, there is a strong probability that at some point Flag Co will experience a fall in sales volume.

As a result of its owner's equity investment, Budget Co carries less financial gearing than Flag Co and has better interest cover. Its operating gearing is slightly lower and given its relative insensitivity to economic conditions, it can be considered a safer company than Flag Co.

(b) Fitzgerald and Moon's building block model provides a framework for service companies to design performance measurement systems which are linked to management rewards. It provides a system of targets (standards) which will motivate managers to improve business performance.

There are three building blocks in the model. The first block gives **six dimensions**, meaning the aspects of performance which must be measured in a service business. These are:

- Financial performance, for example, profitability and growth.
- Competitiveness which measures an organisation's standing against its competition.
- Quality of the service offered.
- Flexibility of the organisation in providing the service.
- Innovation which addresses the ability to introduce new processes and services.
- Resource utilisation which measures productivity and efficiency.

These six dimensions should be split into results (financial performance and competitiveness) which are the outcomes of past decisions and determinants (quality, flexibility, innovation and resource utilisation) which drive future performance and results.

The second block relates to setting **standards**. To motivate managers, it is important that they take ownership of standards (that is accept or internalise them) and the standards appear achievable and equitable (fair).

The third block relates to the **rewards** managers are offered for achieving the standards. These must have clarity (the performance measurement scheme must be understood by managers), they must be motivating (rewards must be attractive) and controllable (not subject to influences outside the manager's control).

ACCA Marking scheme

		Marks
(a)	Calculations	6
	Discussion	8
		14
(b)	Explanation	6
Total		**20**

307 CLEAN FEET CO (MARCH/JUNE 2022)

(a) (i) Calculation of return on investment (ROI)

	Division HG	Division PC
	$000	$000
Sales	12,655	22,834
Less direct costs	(5,796)	(11,134)
Less indirect costs	(4,023)	(6,078)
Net profit	2,836	5,622
Non-current assets	14,570	20,698
Inventory	1,286	1,984
Cash	650	–
Trade receivables	1,040	3,753
Less trade payables	(800)	(2,230)
Less overdraft	–	(1,650)
Capital employed	16,746	22,555
ROI	16.94%	24.93%

(ii) Calculation of bonuses

Bonus	**Division HG**	**Division PC**
(3% × $180,000)	**$5,400**	
(10% × $180,000) Max		**$18,000**

(b) Calculations

	Division HG	**Division PC**
Gross profit margin	54.20%	51.24%
Net profit margin	22.41%	24.62%
Current ratio	3.72:1	1.48:1
Quick ratio	2.11:1	0.97:1
Asset turnover	0.76	1.01
Receivables collection period (days)	30.00	59.99
Payables payment period (days)	50.38	73.10
Inventory holding period (days)	80.99	65.04

Discussion

Note: Division PC is referred to simply as 'PC' throughout and Division HG is referred to simply as 'HG'.

ROI and margins

When looking purely at the ROI for each division, it appears that PC has performed better than HG, since its ROI is almost eight percentage points higher. Similarly, whilst HG's gross profit margin (GPM) is higher than PC's, its net profit margin (NPM) is over two percentage points lower.

However, these figures must be viewed with a degree of scepticism because, first, the net profit margin is after the deduction of head office (HO) costs and second, HO made a decision to invest in a computer system which cost a lot of money and was not very good.

As regards the HO costs, each division apparently bears an equal share. However, the divisions have no control over these costs and also, given that PC is a significantly larger division, it would be expected that it would bear more of the costs.

Therefore, when looking at the profit margins, it would seem wise to assess performance by looking at the GPM rather than the NPM, and in this regard, HG has performed better.

New computer system and complaints

As regards the ROI, HG's assets have increased by at least $2m this year because of the new IT system. This means that its ROI looks lower than it otherwise would, as does its asset turnover. Given the problems which have arisen from the system's introduction, it is likely to have affected HG's costs and sales figures too, yet it was introduced against the advice of HG. It is clear from the year-on-year increase in HG's customer complaints and the reduction in the number of orders completed in seven days that the IT system has affected its results.

Whilst PC's comparative data for 20X9 for the seven days and the customer complaints looks better than HG's, these measures actually show a deterioration in its performance here from one year to the next, with no explanation being given for this.

Working capital management

From the working capital ratios it is clear that, despite all the problems, HG has actually managed to collect cash from customers within the 30-day limit, although it is late in paying its suppliers. PC, on the other hand, has performed worse here, taking almost 60 days to collect its debts and 73 days to pay its liabilities.

PC seems to have better control of its inventory, but this may be because of the delays caused by the IT system at HG.

Both divisions have apparently healthy current and quick ratios, although no industry norm is given against which they could be compared. However, it is noticeable that HG has a healthy cash balance compared to PC's overdraft, so it would appear to be managing its cash better.

Staff turnover

HG has a low staff turnover rate which has stayed the same year on year, unlike that of PC, which has increased from 8% to 18%. It is impressive that HG has such an apparently loyal workforce compared to PC, particularly given the problems which have arisen during the year.

To conclude, although at a glance it would appear that PC is performing better than HG, when the introduction of the new computer system is taken into account, a different picture emerges.

Tutorial note

This solution contains more points than would be required to score full marks.

(c) Given the fact that the two divisions can only control capital expenditure of up to $50,000, it is inappropriate to use ROI to assess their performance. ROI measures the effectiveness of assets in generating profit, but the managers of the divisions do not have total control over asset purchases, so this goes against the controllability principle. Furthermore, ROI is currently calculated based on net profit rather than controllable profit, so the HO costs recharged have been deducted before the ROI is calculated. This means that the managers are both being held accountable for further costs which they cannot control.

Using ROI as a basis for the bonus means that, for the year ending 31 August 20X9, the manager of HG is earning a bonus of only $5,400 because the ROI is only one whole percentage point above 15%. The manager of PC, on the other hand, is earning the maximum bonus of $18,000. This is not fair and will demotivate the manager of HG. This may lead the manager to minimise the capital expenditure which they control in future, maybe cut costs inappropriately or simply cause them to lose interest in generating sales for the business.

ACCA marking scheme				
				Marks
(a)	**(i)**	Calculation of ROI (0.5 mark for net profit of each division/0.5 mark for capital employed of each division/0.5 mark for calculation of ROI for each division)		3
	(ii)	Calculation of bonus (0.5 mark for each division)		1
			Maximum	**4**
(b)	Calculations (0.5 mark per pair of calculations)			4
	Discussion of the performance of each division – 1 mark per relevant point (max 5 marks if no mention of working capital)			8
			Maximum	**12**
(c)	Discussion of use of ROI and any issues it causes –– one mark per relevant point (max 3 marks if no mention of issues)			
			Maximum	4
Total				**20**

308 WYELAND (SEPTEMBER/DECEMBER 2022)

(a) Value for money

Value for money identifies three aspects of performance – economy, efficiency and effectiveness.

Economy assesses the extent to which services of an acceptable quality are provided at the cheapest cost possible. Funding constraints often emphasise the importance of economy.

Efficiency looks at outputs achieved in relation to the resources available; for example, in this case, how well the police forces are using the resources available to them. Maximising the results achieved from a given level of resources will be critical for maintaining performance levels.

Effectiveness assesses the extent to which an organisation achieves its aims and objectives; for example, how well the police forces are ensuring the safety and security of communities across Wyeland.

(b) Performance indicators

	Northern	Central	Southern
Crimes reported per 1,000 residents	49.9	44.4	42.6
Number of police staff per 1,000 residents	4.90	5.42	5.32
% of crimes solved within 12 months	50.7	57.6	52.7
Crimes solved per member of the police force	5.17	4.71	4.23
Cost of police force per member of the population ($)	326.7	360.5	343.8

Northern region

Economy — The Northern force appears to be the most 'economical' since the cost of its police force per member of the population is the lowest of the three regions. This also reflects the fact it has the fewest police staff per head of population.

Efficiency — Although the Northern force has the lowest crime solving rate, its number of crimes solved per member of the force is the highest of the three regions. This suggests that the relatively low proportion of crimes being solved within 12 months is due, at least in part, to the low numbers of staff, rather than any lack of competence or effect on their part. As such, this again appears to reinforce the chief police officer's comments about the impact of cutting staff numbers.

Effectiveness — The Northern region has the highest number of crimes reported (per head of population), and the lowest proportion of crimes solved within 12 months. Therefore, in contrast to its economy, the Northern force appears to be the least effective. Although there might be wider social factors which influence crime rates in the regions, the fact that the region with the lowest funding per head of population has the highest crime rate would appear to support the chief police officer's argument that reducing funding will reduce the service police forces can provide to their local communities.

Under the current budgets, the Northern region is only just achieving the target of solving 50% of crimes within 12 months, so further reductions in funding and staffing could lead to this target being missed.

Central region

Economy	The Central region's force appears to be the least 'economical', because it has the highest cost per member of the population, and the highest number of staff per member of the population. As such, of the three forces, the Central region potentially has the most scope to absorb cuts to its budget.
Efficiency	Although, overall, the Central region solves the highest proportion of cases within 12 months, the number of crimes solved per member of the police force in this region is lower than in the Northern region. This suggests that the Central region force is less efficient than the Northern region's force, although it is more effective.
Effectiveness	Possibly as a result of having a relatively high number of staff per member of the population, the Central region's force solves the highest proportion of crimes within 12 months. However, although the region has a lower crime rate than the Northern region, its crime rate is higher than in the Southern region. This suggests there is not necessarily a correlation between the number of police and the level of crime in a region. One of the difficulties when assessing performance in relation to crime rates is that regional variations in the rates are likely to be influenced by other factors and not simply police forces numbers. For example, socio-economic differences between the regions mean that crime rates are inherently higher in some regions than others.

Southern region

Economy	The number of police and policing costs per head of population are lower than in the Central region, but higher than in the Northern region. This suggests that there might be some scope to make budget cuts in the Southern region, alongside initiatives to try to improve the force's efficiency.
Efficiency	The Southern region's relatively low detection rate is also reflected in the fact that their number of crimes solved per employee is the lowest of the three regions, suggesting the Southern force is the least efficient of the three.
Effectiveness	The Southern region has the lowest reported crime rate of the three, and so, in terms of the overall aim of providing safety and security, the Southern force could be seen as the most effective. However, although the region has the lowest crime rate, the Southern police force appears less effective at solving crimes than the Central region, because their detection rate (% of crimes solved in less than 12 months) is significantly lower.

Overall

None of the regions performs consistently better or worse than the others across all three aspects of value for money. This suggests there are potentially trade-offs between the different elements, and, as the chief police officer has intimated, highlights the problems the police forces will face in trying to reduce costs without compromising their effectiveness.

Marking scheme		
		Marks
Wyeland Police Forces		
(a)	3 Es	**3**
(b)	Calculations	5
	3 Es assessment	12
		17
Total		**20**

309 TROT CO (MARCH/JUNE 2023)

Calculations

	20X7	**20X6**
Percentage fall in European sales	20.0%	
Percentage increase in total sales	20.0%	
Gross profit margin	19.5%	30.0%
Net profit margin	–1.6%	12.1%
Increase in cost of sales	38.0%	
Flight cost as a percentage of sales	18.0%	20.0%
Accommodation cost as a percentage of sales	50.0%	40.0%
Transfer fees as a percentage of sales	12.5%	10.0%
Increase in flights costs	8.0%	
Increase in accommodation costs	50.0%	
Increase in transfer costs	50.0%	
Increase in rent	2.0%	
Increase in salaries	5.0%	
Increase in advertising	50.0%	
Total cost of new adverts (12 × V$600)	V$7,200	
Other advertising costs (V$15,300 – V$7,200)	V$8,100	
Amount saved by reducing university advertising (V$10,200 – V$8,100)	V$2,100	
Decrease in administration costs	–10.0%	
Increase in finance costs	60.0%	
Increase in finance costs excluding V$3,000 loan	23.0%	
Increase in miscellaneous costs	300.0%	
Increase in miscellaneous costs excluding V$22,000 compensation cost	116.7%	

Sales performance and advertising

Overall, sales have increased from one period to the next by 20%. This is purely because of the expansion of the business into North America. In terms of revenue growth, the expansion into North America should definitely be seen as a success rather than a failure.

As regards European sales, however, these have decreased by 20% from one period to the next. Given that the European holiday market has only decreased by 5% in the year, this means that Trot Co has underperformed. Given that all customers pay in V$, the sales figures are unaffected by the currency's decline in Veeland.

Trot Co has changed its advertising strategy this year. It has started advertising on a North American television station and, given the level of new sales, this advertising seems to have been fairly successful. However, Trot Co also decided to stop its advertising in Veeland.

Given the drop in European sales, this seems to have been a bad decision, especially since it only saved costs of V$2,100. It could be that the fall in the V$ has made customers more reticent to go abroad but this does not explain why Trot Co's European sales have fallen by such a large amount.

Cost of sales/gross profit margin

Cost of sales has increased by 38% in total. This percentage increase is almost twice the increase in revenue and the reduction in gross profit margin from 30% to 19% reflects this. In order to understand what has happened, it is necessary to look at each of the costs individually.

Flight costs as a percentage of sales have actually fallen from 20% to 18%. As then expected, the increase in flight costs from one year to the next is less than the increase in revenue and is actually only 8%. So, these costs have not increased in line with revenue. This suggests that the price of flights has fallen, probably as a result of using the new booking agent who promised more competitive prices. This is good news for Trot Co.

Accommodation costs, on the other hand, have increased by 50% this year compared to the 20% increase in revenue. Further information about the cause of this can be established from seeing that accommodation costs as a percentage of sales have gone up from 40% to 50%. This must be a direct result of the effect of the decline in the V$. Since accommodation is paid for in the visiting country's currency and the V$ is now worth 25% less than six months ago, the accommodation has become much more expensive. Given that customers pay six months in advance, Trot Co suffered the effects of the decline in the value of the currency and was not able to pass the cost on to the customer. This is exactly the same for transfer costs which now constitute 12.5% of sales value rather than the previous 10% and have gone up by 50% from one year to the next. The company has been very exposed to exchange rate fluctuations and should have hedged against them.

Other expenses/net profit margin

The company's net profit margin has fallen from 12.1% to –1.6%, which is a drastic fall. Whilst this is largely attributable to the 11% fall in the gross profit margin, the remaining 2.7% decrease is due to an increase in indirect costs. The main changes are discussed in turn below.

Rent has increased by 2%, which is probably to be expected and may just reflect inflation rates. Salaries have increased by 5% in the year due to the 10% pay rise given to staff members half way through the year. Advertising costs have increased by 50%, driven by the new advertising taken out to promote North America sales which has increased revenues. Administration costs have actually decreased by 10% which is presumably as a result of the new system introduced three months before the year end. This is promising for the future as administration costs should be even lower next year when a whole year's benefit will be gained.

Finance costs have increased by 60% but this is partly due to the fact that professional costs were incurred in relation to the loan of V$3,000. When these are taken out, the increase falls to 23%. This is still high, especially given the fact that the new loan has only been running for three months. This indicates that the new interest rate is very high and could have a particularly big impact next year when a full year's interest will be charged.

Finally, miscellaneous costs have increased by 300%, far more than any other costs. Presumably the compensation payment of V$22,000 for unfair dismissal is in here and has had a huge effect on the increase. However, even without this, this category of costs has increased by 116.7%. Further information is needed as to why this is the case.

To conclude, the performance for the year is disappointing and the owner is right to be concerned. However, it is not the expansion into North America which appears to be causing the problems but other factors, as discussed above.

ACCA Marking scheme	
	Marks
Calculations	6
Discussion	14
Total	**20**

Key answer tips

The examiner's suggested approach to this type of question:

1 **Identify the verb** – the verbs used in the requirements not only indicate what to do but often how much detail to go into. Here the requirement is asking for a discussion.

Discuss is defined: 'Consider and debate/argue about the pros and cons of an issue. Examine in detail by using arguments in favour or against.'

Therefore, thought needs to be given to any conflict, comparison and contrast that can be discussed and how information in the scenario can add depth and reasoning to any points made.

2 **Look for extra requirements** – a note is given that marks are available for calculations. It is important that calculations in a performance analysis question add value to the discussion, they should be calculations which are relevant to the numerical information provided AND they must be calculations of interest based on the other information in the scenario.

3 **Look at the number of marks** – there is one 20-mark requirement, but it is broken down into 6 marks for calculations and 14 marks for discussion. This should give an indication of the number of calculations to perform and the time to spend on these and on the discussion. More time needs to be spent on the discussion, so it is important not to get carried away with too many calculations. For 6 marks, 12 calculations could gain full marks here.

4 **Presentation** – Headings and tables – split the answer up wherever possible. With just one requirement a clear structure is needed. The information provided in the scenario will help decide what these headings should be so thought can be given to this whilst reading through the scenario. Calculations can be prepared in a table to give clear space for showing workings and any results which can be compared.

310 EASTERN HOSPITALS TRUST (MARCH/JUNE 2025)

(a) **(i)** **Value for money**

Value for money identifies three aspects of performance which need to be measured: economy, efficiency and effectiveness.

Economy in the context of service organisations (such as hospitals) assesses the extent to which services of an acceptable quantity and quality are provided at lowest cost possible.

Efficiency considers the way the organisations are organised to maximise the benefits and outputs they can obtain from their resources. It is usually defined as the relationship of inputs to outputs.

Effectiveness describes the extent to which an organisation achieves its objectives.

(ii) It is important to have a balanced mix of performance measures looking at the three elements of economy, efficiency and effectiveness as there are clearly relationships between the three measures. It should help to reduce the risk that EHT's managers prioritise one element of performance to the detriment of others. For example, cutting costs could help to improve measures of economy, but making any such cuts will need to be done in a way which does not threaten the quality of medical services and care which the hospitals provide to their patients.

The chief executive has already identified this issue in relation to the funding cuts which the government have and the impact these cuts will have on the number of staff the hospitals can employ and the quality of care they can provide to their patients. Similarly, reducing staff numbers could lead to longer waiting times to receive treatment. It therefore important that the 3Es are managed in conjunction with each other.

(b) **Economy**

A hospital's spending against budget could be used an indicator for measuring how economically it operates. In this case, Mid-East and North-East would appear to be more economical than South-East, and therefore the need to make economy savings is most urgent at South-East hospital. However, all three of the hospitals have spent more than their initial budget allocations, so – given the government's focus on funding cuts and cost reduction – this is still an important issue for each of them.

The focus on economy should encourage EHT's management to investigate which areas of their spending caused the hospitals to exceed their budgets, and in turn to try to identify ways of making cost savings, for example, whether they can reduce the number of staff they employ.

The measure of cost per patient could be viewed as either a measure of economy or a measure of efficiency, although there are potential problems with it when comparing performance between the different hospitals if there are variations in the different types of treatment patients need, or length of hospital stay. North-East hospital performed least well in relation to cost per patient. This could be because treatments are taking longer, thereby increasing the cost per patient as well as waiting times.

Efficiency

Whereas 'economy' looks at the amounts the hospitals are spending to obtain resources, 'efficiency' looks at how efficiently the hospitals are using those resources in order to provide medical care and services for their patients. Cost per patient could be considered here but has instead been considered above.

The proportion of emergency patients who are treated within four hours and the proportion of non-emergency patients who have appointments scheduled within 12 weeks can be used an indicators of efficiency.

North-East hospital performed least well in relation to target times, which suggests it is the least efficient of the three hospitals. This could mean that treatments are taking longer at North-East than the other two hospitals, thereby increasing waiting times (and cost per patient).

The reasons for the variations in performance are something which EHT would need to investigate further. EHT's management then needs to identify if there are any ways of improving efficiency at North-East hospital, whilst at the same time not increasing costs (the 'economy' aspect of VFM) or reducing the quality of medical care it provides (the 'effectiveness' aspect).

Tutorial note

The proportion of patients who are seen within the target time scales could be viewed as a measure of effectiveness, given the Trust's objective to provide services which are quick to access.

Effectiveness

Given the trust's objectives, the patients' scores and the quality rating score can both be used as indicators of how effectively the hospitals are operating. These indicators help to illustrate whether the hospitals are providing the top-quality medical services and the excellent patient care they aim to achieve.

In this respect, Mid-East is the hospital which performs least well (although it is the one which appeared to have performed best in relation to 'economy' and 'efficiency'). By contrast, North-East, which spends the most per patient, performed the best in relation to the quality of medical services and patient care.

(c)

Key answer tips – Requirement (c)

The focus of this question is on the measuring of performance NOT on the performance of EHT.

Firstly, consider challenges which may occur in measuring performance:

- Data accuracy
- Data quality
- Qualitative vs quantitative

- Multiple key performance indicators
- Systems available/integration of systems between different departments
- Bias and subjectivity
- Employee resistance to gathering or recording data
- Customer resistance to providing data
- Time and effort required to collect/clean data

Secondly, given the information provided in the scenario, identify which of these challenges are relevant to EHT, to be discussed:

- Data accuracy – Quality rating scores are based on a sample of medical procedures
- Subjectivity – Patients asked to rate their quality of care which could differ depending on the perspective of the individual
- Customer resistance – Relatives may rate the quality of care rather than the patient and they may have different requirement to the patient from the hospital service
- Data quality – Treatment within 4 hours will depend on the type of emergency and the treatment which is required
- Subjectivity – Quality can be difficult to identify a measure for and subjective in response
- Time and effort to collect/clean data – funding constraints and reduced staffing can make it more challenging to dedicate the time to collecting the data

A good response correctly identified two challenges and provided relevant application to the challenge faced by EHT.

Challenges:

Availability of information

The underlying focus of EHT's objectives is the patients and the quality of the treatment they receive from EHT's hospitals. EHT's management need performance information to measure how well they are performing in relation to these objectives, and, where necessary, to take action to try to improve performance. Since the objectives are non-financial, this means that non-financial data will be very important to performance management at EHT.

By contrast, the government's primary interest appears to be one of reducing expenditure. So, as well as looking at non-financial information linked to its own objectives, EHT's managers will also have to monitor financial information to ensure that their spending remains within budget, and again, where necessary, to find ways of cutting costs.

Subjectivity

EHT's objectives highlight three key areas for which performance will need to be measured: the quality of medical services provided; the quality of patient care; and the speed with which patients can be treated.

A major difficulty in measuring the quality of medical services and patient care is that these are inherently non-quantifiable. The length of time it takes between an emergency patient arriving at hospital and then starting to receive treatment can be measured, but quality cannot be measured in the same way, because it is inherently subjective.

The key performance indicators have tried to make the data more measurable and comparable by assigning values to the Quality Rating score, and analysing the proportion of patients who rate services as 'Excellent', however, this cannot entirely remove the subjectivity from these indicators. For example, the level of care which one patient might rate as 'Excellent', another might only rate as 'Good'.

Systems

A further issue for EHT to consider is how performance information will be recorded and stored in the hospitals' information systems. Again, the hospitals may not have systems in place to record patient feedback scores in the same way that they have medical systems or financial systems in place.

Tutorial note

Other valid points could be made that would also score marks.

ACCA marking scheme

				Marks
(a)	**(i)**	3 Es		3
	(ii)	Explanation		4
			Maximum	**7**
(b)		Discussion (3-4 marks per heading)		9
(c)		Discussion of challenges		4
Total				**20**

Section 7

SPECIMEN EXAM QUESTIONS

SECTION A

1 A company manufactures two products, C and D, for which the following information is available:

	Product C	Product D	Total
Budgeted production (units)	1,000	4,000	5,000
Labour hours per unit/in total	8	10	48,000
Number of production runs required	13	15	28
Number of inspections during production	5	3	8

	$
Total production set up costs	140,000
Total inspection costs	80,000
Other overhead costs	96,000

Other overhead costs are absorbed on a labour hour basis.

Using activity-based costing, what is the budgeted overhead cost per unit of product D?

A $43.84

B $46.25

C $131.00

D $140.64

2 P Co makes two products, P1 and P2. The budgeted details for each product are as follows:

	P1	P2
	$	$
Selling price	10.00	8.00
Cost per unit:		
Direct materials	3.50	4.00
Direct labour	1.50	1.00
Variable overhead	0.60	0.40
Fixed overhead	1.20	1.00
Profit per unit	3.20	1.60

Budgeted production and sales for the year ended 30 November 20X5 are:

	Units
Product P1	10,000
Product P2	12,500

The fixed overhead costs included in P1 relate to apportionment of general overhead costs only. However, P2 also included specific fixed overheads totalling $2,500.

If only product P1 were to be made, how many units would need to be sold in order to achieve a profit of $60,000 each year (to the nearest whole unit)?

______________ **units**

3 **Which TWO of the following statements, regarding environmental cost accounting, are true?**

A The majority of environmental costs are already captured within a typical organisation's accounting system. The difficulty lies in identifying them

B Input/output analysis divides material flows within an organisation into three categories: material flows; system flows; and delivery and disposal flows

C One of the cost categories used in environmental activity-based costing is environment-driven costs which is used for costs which can be directly traced to a cost centre

D Environmental life-cycle costing enables environmental costs from the design stage of the product right through to decommissioning at the end of its life to be considered

4 To produce 19 litres of product X, a standard input mix of 8 litres of chemical A and 12 litres of chemical B is required.

Chemical A has a standard cost of $20 per litre and chemical B has a standard cost of $25 per litre.

During September, the actual results showed that 1,850 litres of product X were produced, using a total input of 900 litres of chemical A and 1,100 litres of chemical B.

The actual costs of chemicals A and B were at the standard cost of $20 and $25 per litre respectively.

Based on the above information, which of the following statements is true?

A Both variances were adverse

B Both variances were favourable

C The total mix variance was adverse and the total yield variance was favourable

D The total mix variance was favourable and the total yield variance was adverse

5 A leisure company owns a number of large health and fitness resorts, but one is suffering from declining sales and is predicted to make a loss in the next year. As a result management have identified a number of possible actions:

1 Shut down the resort and sell off the assets

2 Undertake a major upgrade to facilities costing $4.5m

3 Undertake a minor upgrade to facilities costing $2m

The upgrades are predicted to have variable results and the probability of good results after a major upgrade is 0.8, whereas the probability of good results after a minor upgrade is 0.7.

The company is risk neutral and has prepared the following decision tree.

Using the information below, identify, by clicking on the relevant branch of the decision tree, which action the company should take.

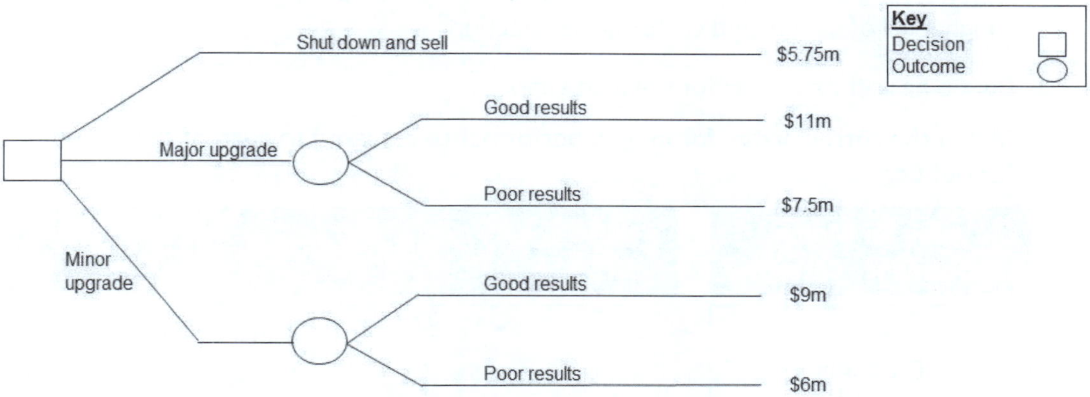

A Shut down and sell

B Major upgrade

C Minor upgrade

6 A company has the following production planned for the next four weeks. The figures reflect the full capacity level of operations. Planned output is equal to the maximum demand per product.

Product	**A**	**B**	**C**	**D**
	$ per unit	**$ per unit**	**$ per unit**	**$ per unit**
Selling price	160	214	100	140
Raw material cost	24	56	22	40
Direct labour cost	66	88	33	22
Variable overhead cost	24	18	24	18
Fixed overhead cost	16	10	8	12
Profit	30	42	13	48
Planned output	300	125	240	400
Direct labour hours per unit	6	8	3	2

It has now been identified that labour hours available in the next four weeks will be limited to 4,000 hours.

Rank the products in the order they should be manufactured, assuming that the company wants to maximise profits in the next four weeks.

Product	Ranking	
A	1st	
B	2nd	
C	3rd	
D	4th	

7 Def Co provides accounting services to government departments. On average, each staff member works six chargeable hours per day, with the rest of their working day being spent on non-chargeable administrative work. One of the company's main objectives is to produce a high level of quality and customer satisfaction.

Def Co has set its targets for the next year.

Match the correct value for money performance category to each of the following targets for Def Co.

Value for Money Performance Category	Performance targets	
Economy		Increasing the number of chargeable hours handled by advisors to 6.2 per day
Efficiency		Obtaining a score of 4.7 or above on customer satisfaction surveys
Effectiveness		Cutting departmental expenditure by 5%

8 Different types of information systems provide the information which organisations need for strategic planning, management and operational control.

Match the following characteristics to the relevant information systems

Characteristic	Management Information System	Transaction Processing System
Summaries internal data into periodic reports		
Can be set with extranet links to customers and suppliers	**Executive Information System**	**Enterprise Resource Planning System**
Utilities dashboard facilities and interactive graphics		
Facilities the immediate processing of data		

9 **Which TWO of the following statements regarding life-cycle costing are correct?**

A It can be applied not only to products but also to an organisation's customers

B Often between 70% to 90% of costs are determined early in the product life-cycle

C It includes any opportunity costs associated with production

D The maturity phase is characterised by a rapid build up in demand

10 A company manufactures a product which requires four hours per unit of machine time. Machine time is a bottleneck resource as there are only ten machines which are available for 12 hours per day, five days per week. The product has a selling price of $130 per unit, direct material costs of $50 per unit, labour costs of $40 per unit and factory overhead costs of $20 per unit. These costs are based on weekly production and sales of 150 units.

What is the throughput accounting ratio?

A 1.33

B 2.00

C 0.75

D 0.31

11 Ox Co has two divisions, A and B. Division A makes a component for air conditioning units which it can only sell to division B. It has no other outlet for sales.

Current information relating to division A is as follows:

Marginal cost per unit	$100
Transfer price of the component	$165
Total production and sales of the component each year	2,200 units
Specific fixed costs of division A per year	$10,000

Cold Co has offered to sell the component to division B for $140 per unit. If division B accepts this offer, division A will be closed.

If division B accepts Cold Co's offer, what will be the impact on profits per year for the group as a whole?

A Increase of $65,000

B Decrease of $78,000

C Decrease of $88,000

D Increase of $55,000

12 Identify, by clicking on the relevant box in the table below, whether each of the statements regarding Fitzgerald and Moon's Building Blocks model is true or false.

The determinants of performance are quality, innovation, resource utilisation and competitiveness	**TRUE**	**FALSE**
Standards are targets for performance and should be fair, achievable and controllable	**TRUE**	**FALSE**
Reward encourage staff to work towards the standards and should be clear, motivating and controllable	**TRUE**	**FALSE**
It is a performance measurement framework suitable for service organisations	**TRUE**	**FALSE**

13 A budget is a quantified plan of action for a forthcoming period. Budgets can be prepared using a variety of different approaches.

Match each of the following statements to the correct budgeting process.

Statements	Budgeting approach	
Builds in previous problems and inefficiencies		Beyond budgeting
Recognises different cost behaviour patterns		Incremental budgeting
Focuses employees on avoiding wasteful expenditure		Activity-based budgeting
Focuses on controlling the causes of costs		Rating budgeting
Always extends the budget one year into the future		Flexible budgeting
Uses adaptive management processes		Zero-based budgeting

14 LPM Co has identified the trend line relating to its sales revenue as 2,000 + 25X.

X denotes the quarter number, with the first quarter of 20X5 being 13, the second quarter of 20X5 being 14, etc.

LPM Co uses the multiplicative model and has calculated the following seasonal variations:

Quarter 1: –0.20

Quarter 2: –0.08

Quarter 3: +0.04

Quarter 4: +0.24

What is LPM CO's seasonally adjusted sales revenue forecast for the second quarter of 20X7?

$ ___________

15 Yoyo Co manufactures a single product, the Yog, which is made from a mix of two ingredients: X and Y. Yoyo Co accounts for environmental costs using input/output analysis.

Ingredient X costs $550 per tonne and ingredient Y costs $825 per tonne. Any ingredients which are wasted in the production process must be disposed of at a cost of $150 per tonne.

July's production run used 24 tonnes of ingredient X and 36 tonnes of ingredient Y, total output of Yog was 57 tonnes.

What is the environmental cost of July's production run?

A $450

B $1,695

C $2,145

D $2,595

SECTION B

QUESTIONS 16 TO 20 REFER TO THE FOLLOWING INFORMATION

Glam Co is a hairdressing salon which provides both 'cuts' and 'treatments' to clients. All cuts and treatments at the salon are carried out by one of the salon's three senior stylists. The salon also has two salon assistants and two junior stylists.

Every client attending the salon is first seen by a salon assistant, who washes their hair; next, by a senior stylist, who cuts or treats their hair depending on which service the client wants; then finally, a junior stylist who dries their hair. The average length of time spent with each member of staff is as follows:

	Cut (Hours)	Treatment (Hours)
Assistant	0.1	0.3
Senior stylist	1.0	1.5
Junior stylist	0.6	0.5

The salon is open for eight hours each day for six days per week. It is only closed for two weeks each year. Staff salaries are $40,000 each year for each senior stylist, $28,000 each year for each junior stylist and $12,000 each year for each of the assistants. The cost of cleaning products applied when washing clients' hair is $1.50 per client. The cost of all additional products applied during a 'treatment' is $7.40 per client. Other salon costs (excluding labour and raw materials) amount to $106,400 each year.

Glam Co charges $60 for each cut and $110 for each treatment.

The senior stylists' time has been correctly identified as the bottleneck activity.

16 What is the annual capacity of the bottleneck activity?

A 2,400 cuts or 1,600 treatments

B 4,800 cuts or 4,800 treatments

C 7,200 cuts or 4,800 treatments

D 9,600 cuts or 9,600 treatments

17 The salon has calculated the cost per hour to be $42.56.

Calculate the throughput accounting ratio (TPAR) for both services (to two decimal places).

Cuts ______________

Treatments ______________

18 Which THREE of the following activities could the salon use to improve the TPAR?

A Identify ways to reduce the material costs for the services

B Increase the time spent by the bottleneck activity on each service

C Improve the control of the salon's total operating expenses

D Increase the level of inventory to prevent stockouts

E Increase the productivity of the stage prior to the bottleneck

F Apply an increase to the selling price of the services

19 What would be the effect on the bottleneck if the salon employed another senior stylist?

A The senior stylists' time will be a bottleneck for cuts only

B The senior stylists' time will be a bottleneck for treatments only

C The senior stylists' time will remain the bottleneck for both cuts and treatments

D There will no longer be a bottleneck

20 Which of the following statements regarding the theory of constraints are correct?

(1) It focuses on identifying stages of congestion in a process when production arrives more quickly than the next stage can handle

(2) It is based on the concept that organisations manage three key factors -throughput, operating expenses and inventory

(3) It uses a sequence of focusing steps to overcome a single bottleneck, at which point the improvement process is complete

(4) It can be applied to the management of all limiting factors, both internal and external, which can affect an organisation

A (1) and (2) only

B (1), (2) and (3)

C (2), (3) and (4)

D (1), (3) and (4)

QUESTIONS 21 TO 25 REFER TO THE FOLLOWING INFORMATION

Chair Co has several new products in development. Information relating to three of these products is as follows:

Luxury car seat

The estimated labour time for the first unit is 12 hours but a learning curve of 75% (b = –0.415)is expected to apply for the first eight units produced. The cost of labour is $15 per hour.

The cost of materials and other variable overheads is expected to total $230 per unit. Chair Co plans on pricing the seat by adding a 50% mark-up to the total variable cost per seat, with the labour cost being based on the incremental time taken to produce the eighth unit.

High chair

Another product which Chair Co has in development is a new design of high chair for feeding young children. Based on previous experience of producing similar products, Chair Co had assumed that a learning rate of 85% would apply to the manufacture of this new design but after the first phase of production had been completed, management realised that a learning rate of 80% had been achieved.

Office chair

Chair Co has also developed a new type of office chair and management is trying to formulate a budget for this product. They have decided to match the production level to demand, however, demand for this chair is uncertain.

Management have collected the following information:

	Demand (units)	**Probability**
Worst possible outcome	10,000	0.3
Most likely outcome	22,000	0.5
Best possible outcome	35,000	0.2

The selling price per unit is $25. The variable cost per unit is $8 for any production level up to 25,000 units. If the production level is higher than 25,000 units then the variable cost per unit will decrease by 10% and this reduction will apply to all the units produced at that level.

Total fixed costs are estimated to be $75,000.

Chair Co uses cost-plus pricing when setting prices for its products.

21 In relation to the luxury car seat, what is the labour cost of the eighth unit?

A $45.65

B $75.94

C $4.32

D $3.04

22 The first phase of production has now been completed for the new car seat. The first unit actually took 12.5 hours to make and the total time for the first eight units was 34.3 hours, at which point the learning effect came to an end. Chair Co are planning on adjusting the price to reflect the actual time it took to complete the eighth unit.

What was the actual rate of learning which occurred (to two decimal places)?

___________ %

23 In relation to the new design of high chair, which THREE of the following statements could explain why the actual rate of learning differed from the rate which was expected?

A Staffing levels were stable during the first manufacturing phase B. There were machine breakdowns during production

B There were machine breakdowns during production

C Assembly of the chairs was manual and very repetitive

D There was high staff turnover during this period

E There were minimal stoppages in the production process

F The design of the chair was changed several times at this early phase

24 Using an expected value approach, what is the expected budgeted contribution of the office chairs (to the nearest whole $)?

$ ___________

25 Identify, by clicking on the relevant box in the table below, whether each of the statements regarding cost-plus pricing strategies is true or false.

Marginal cost plus pricing is easier where there is a readily identifiable variable cost	**TRUE**	**FALSE**
Full cost plus pricing requires the budgeted level of output to be determined at the outset	**TRUE**	**FALSE**
Cost-plus pricing is a strategically focused approach as it accounts for external factors	**TRUE**	**FALSE**
Cost-plus pricing requires that the profit mark-up applied by an organisation is fixed	**TRUE**	**FALSE**

QUESTIONS 26 TO 30 REFER TO THE FOLLOWING INFORMATION

The Hi Life Co makes sofas. It has recently received a request from a customer to provide a one-off order of sofas, in excess of normal budgeted production. The order would need to be completed within two weeks.

The following cost estimate has already been prepared:

		Note	$
Direct materials:			
Fabric	200 m^2 at \$17 per m^2	1	3,400
Wood	50 m^2 at \$8.20 per m^2	2	410
Direct labour:			
Skilled	200 hours at \$16 per hour	3	3,200
Semi-skilled	300 hours at \$12 per hour	4	3,600
Factory overheads	500 hours at \$3 per hour	5	1,500
Total production cost			**12,110**
General fixed overheads at 10% of total production cost			1,211
Total cost			**13,321**

Notes:

(1) The fabric is regularly used by Hi Life Co. There are currently 300 m^2 in inventory, which cost \$17 per m^2. The current purchase price of the fabric is \$17.50 per m^2.

(2) The wood is regularly used by Hi Life Co and usually costs \$8.20 per m^2. However, the company's current supplier's earliest delivery time for the wood is in three weeks' time. An alternative supplier could deliver immediately but they would charge \$8.50 per m^2. Hi Life Co already has 500 m^2 in inventory but 480 m^2 of this is needed to complete other existing orders in the next two weeks. The remaining 20 m^2 is not going to be needed until four weeks' time.

(3) The skilled labour force is employed under permanent contracts of employment under which they must be paid for 40 hours per week's labour, even if their time is idle due to absence of orders. Their rate of pay is \$16 per hour, although any overtime is paid at time and a half. In the next two weeks there is spare capacity of 150 labour hours.

(4) There is no spare capacity for semi-skilled workers. They are currently paid \$12 per hour or time and a half for overtime. However, a local agency can provide additional semi-skilled workers for \$14 per hour.

(5) Of the \$3 per hour factory overheads costs, \$1.50 per hour reflects the electricity costs of running the cutting machine which will be used to cut the fabric and wood for the sofas. The other \$1.50 per hour reflects the cost of the factory supervisor's salary. The supervisor is paid an annual salary and is also paid \$15 per hour for any overtime he works. The supervisor will need to work 20 hours' overtime if this order is accepted.

A quotation now needs to be prepared on a relevant cost basis so that Hi Life Co can offer as competitive a price as possible for the order.

26 **What is the cost of the fabric and the wood which should be included in the quotation (to the nearest whole $)?**

Fabric $ ____________

Wood $ ____________

27 **What cost should be included in the quotation for skilled labour and semi-skilled labour (to the nearest whole $)?**

Skilled $ ____________

Semi-skilled $ ____________

28 **What is the cost which should be included in the quotation for factory overheads (to the nearest whole $)?**

$ ____________

29 **Which statement correctly describes the treatment of the general fixed overheads when preparing the quotation?**

A The overheads should be excluded because they are a sunk cost

B The overheads should be excluded because they are not incremental costs

C The overheads should be included because they relate to production costs

D The overheads should be included because all expenses should be recovered

30 **Which FOUR of the following statements about relevant costing are true?**

A An opportunity cost will always be a relevant cost even if it is a past cost

B Fixed costs are always general in nature and are therefore never relevant

C Committed costs are never considered to be relevant costs

D An opportunity cost represents the cost of the best alternative forgone

E Notional costs are always relevant as they make the estimate more realistic

F Avoidable costs would be saved if an activity did not happen and so are relevant

G Common costs are only relevant if the viability of the whole process is being assessed

H Differential costs in a make or buy decision are not considered to be relevant

31 CARAD CO

Carad Co is an electronics company which makes two types of television -plasma screen TVs and LCD TVs. It operates within a highly competitive market and is constantly under pressure to reduce prices. Carad Co operates a standard costing system and performs a detailed variance analysis of both products on a monthly basis. Extracts from the management information for the month of November are shown below:

	Note	
Total number of units made and sold	1	1,400
Material price variance	2	$28,000 A
Total labour variance	3	$6,050 A

Notes:

(1) The budgeted total sales volume for TVs was 1,180 units, consisting of an equal mix of plasma screen TVs and LCD screen TVs. Actual sales volume was 750 plasma TVs and 650 LCD TVs. Standard sales prices are $350 per unit for the plasma TVs and $300 per unit for the LCD TVs. The actual sales prices achieved during November were $330 per unit for plasma TV and $290 per unit for LCD TVs. The standard contributions for plasma TVs and LCD TVs are $190 and $180 per unit respectively.

(2) The sole reason for this variance was an increase in the purchase price of one of its key components, X. Each plasma TV made and each LCD TV made requires one unit of component X, for which Carad Co's standard cost is $60 per unit. Due to a shortage of components in the market place, the market price for November went up to $85 per unit for X. Carad Co actually paid $80 per unit for it.

(3) Each plasma TV uses 2 standard hours of labour and each LCD TV uses 1.5 standard hours of labour. The standard cost for labour is $14 per hour and this also reflects the actual cost per labour hour for the company's permanent staff in November. However, because of the increase in sales and production volumes in November, the company also had to use temporary labour at the higher cost of $18 per hour. The total capacity of Carad Co's permanent workforce is 2,200 hours production per month, assuming full efficiency. In the month of November, the workforce were wholly efficient, taking exactly 2 hours to complete each plasma TV and exactly 1.5 hours to produce each LCD TV. The total labour variance therefore relates solely to the temporary workers, who took twice as long as the permanent workers to complete their production.

Required:

(a) Calculate the following for the month of November, showing all workings clearly:

(i) The sales price variance and sales volume contribution variance (4 marks)

(ii) The material price planning variance and material price operational variance (2 marks)

(iii) The labour rate variance and the labour efficiency variance. (5 marks)

(b) Explain the reasons why Carad Co would be interested in the material price planning variance and the material price operational variance.

(9 marks)

(Total: 20 marks)

32 THATCHER INTERNATIONAL PARK

Thatcher International Park (TIP) is a theme park and has for many years been a successful business, which has traded profitably. About three years ago the directors decided to capitalise on their success and reduced the expenditure made on new thrill rides, reduced routine maintenance where possible (deciding instead to repair equipment when it broke down) and made a commitment to regularly increase admission prices. Once an admission price is paid customers can use any of the facilities and rides for free.

These steps increased profits considerably, enabling good dividends to be paid to the owners and bonuses to the directors. An extract of financial results and performance information for the last years is shown below:

	20X4	**20X5**
	$	$
Sales	5,250,000	5,320,000
Wages	2,500,000	2,200,000
Maintenance – routine	80,000	70,000
Repairs	260,000	320,000
Directors' salaries	150,000	160,000
Directors' bonuses	15,000	18,000
Operating profit	1,045,000	1,372,000
Carrying amount of assets at start of year	13,000,000	12,000,000
Dividend paid	500,000	650,000
Number of visitors	150,000	140,000

TIP operates in a country where the average rate of inflation is around 1% per annum.

Required:

(a) Using the information provided, assess the financial performance of Thatcher International Park (TIP). (14 marks)

During the early part of 20X4 TIP employed a newly qualified management accountant. He quickly became concerned about the potential performance of TIP and to investigate his concerns, he started to gather data to measure some non-financial measures of success. The data he has gathered is shown below:

Table 1		
	20X4	**20X5**
Hours lost due to breakdown of rides (Note 1)	9,000 hours	32,000 hours
Average waiting time per ride	20 minutes	30 minutes

Note:

TIP has 50 rides of different types. It is open 360 days of the year for ten hours each day.

Required:

(b) Assess the QUALITY of the service which TIP provides to its customers using Table 1 and any other relevant data and indicate the RISKS it is likely to face if it continues with its current policies. (6 marks)

(Total: 20 marks)

Section 8

ANSWERS TO SPECIMEN EXAM QUESTIONS

SECTION A

1 B

Set-up costs per production run = $140,000/28 = $5,000

Cost per inspection = $80,000/8 = $10,000

Other overhead costs per labour hour = $96,000/$48,000 = $2

Overhead costs of product D:

	$
Set-up costs (15 × $5,000)	75,000
Inspection costs (3 × $10,000)	30,000
Other overheads (40,000 × $2)	80,000
	185,000

Overhead cost per unit = $185,000/4,000 units = $46.25

2 18,636 units

The number of units required to make a target profit = (fixed costs + target profit)/contribution per unit of P1.

Fixed costs = ($1.20 × 10,000) + ($1.00 × 12,500) – $2,500 = $22,000

Contribution per unit of P1 = $3.20 + $1.20 = $4.40

($22,000 + $60,000)/$4.40 = 18,636 units

3 A, D

Most organisations do collect data about environmental costs but find it difficult to split them out and categorise them effectively.

Life-cycle costing does allow the organisation to collect information about a product's environmental costs throughout its lifecycle.

The technique which divides material into three categories is material flow cost accounting, not input/output analysis.

ABC does categorise some costs as environment-driven costs, however, these are costs which are normally hidden within total overheads in a conventional costing system. It is environment-related costs which can be allocated directly to a cost centre.

4 D

Mix variance:

Material	AQAM (litres)	AQSM (litres)	Difference (litres)	Std cost ($ per litre)	Variance
A	900	800	100A	20	$2,000 A
B	1,100	1,200	100F	25	$2,500 F
	2,000	**2,000**	**0**		**$500 F**

Yield variance:

Material	AQSM (litres)	SQSM (litres)	Difference (litres)	Std cost ($ per litre)	Variance
A	800	779	21A	20	$420 A
B	1,200	1,168	32A	25	$800 A
	2,000	**1,947**	**0**		**$1,220 A**

5 C

EV for major upgrade = (0.8 × $11m) + (0.2 × $7.5m) = $10.3m

EV for major upgrade = (0.7 × $9m) + (0.3 × $6m) = $8.1m

Decision

Shutdown and sell	$5.75m
Major upgrade (10.3m – 4.5m)	$5.8m
Minor upgrade ($8.1m – S2m)	$6.1m

As the minor upgrade has the highest expected return that should be the option chosen.

6 1st D, 2nd A, 3rd C, 4th B

In a single limiting factor situation products should be ranked based on their contribution per unit of limiting factor. Which in this case is labour hours.

Material	**A**	**B**	**C**	**D**
Contribution per unit ($)	46	52	21	60
Number of labour hours per unit	6	8	3	2
Contribution per labour hour ($)	7.67	6.50	7.00	30.00
Ranking	**2nd**	**4th**	**3rd**	**1st**

7 **Efficiency** – Increasing the number of chargeable hours handled by advisors to 6.2 per day.

Effectiveness – Obtaining a score of 4.7 or above on customer satisfaction surveys.

Economy – Cutting departmental expenditure by 5%.

8 **MIS** – Summaries internal data into periodic reports.

TPS – Facilities the immediate processing of data.

EIS – Utilities dashboard facilities and interactive graphics.

EPRS – Can be set with extranet links to customers and suppliers.

9 A, B

Customer life-cycle costing can be used by organisations.

It has been reported that the majority of a products costs are determined early on, i.e., at the design phase.

Life-cycle costing does not include any opportunity costs associated with production.

The growth phase is characterised by a rapid increase in demand.

10 A

Return per factory hour = ($130 – $50)/4 hours = $20

Factory costs per hour = ($20/4) + ($40/4) = $15

TPAR = $20/$15 = 1.33

11 B

Increase in variable costs per unt from buying in ($140 – $100) = $40

Therefore total increase in variable costs (2,200 units × $40) = $88,000

Less the specific fixed costs saved if A is shut down = ($10,000)

Decrease in profit = $78,000

12 FALSE, FALSE, TRUE, TRUE

The determinants of performance are quality, innovation, resource utilisation and flexibility. Competitiveness is a result of the determinants.

Standards should be fair, achievable and staff should have ownership of them. Controllability is a feature of the rewards block.

Rewards should be clear, motivating and controllable.

It is a framework designed to attempt to overcome the problems associated with performance management in service companies.

13 **Beyond –** Uses adaptive management processes

Incremental – Builds in previous problems and inefficiencies

Activity – Focuses on controlling the causes of costs

Rolling – Always extends the budget one year into the future

Flexible – Recognises different cost behaviour patterns

Zero-based – Focuses employees on avoiding wasteful expenditure

14 2,346

If the first quarter of 20X5 is quarter 13, the second quarter of 20X7 is quarter 22.

The forecasted sales revenue using the trend line is 2,000 + (25 × 22) = 2,550.

The seasonal variation for quarter 2 is -8%, so the sales revenue forecast is 2,550 × (1 – 0.08) = $2,346

15 D

Tonnes wasted = (24 + 36) – 57 = 3 tonnes

Cost of wasted materials per tonne (assuming constant mix)

= ((24/60) × $550) + ((36/60) × $825)

= $715

Cost of disposal = $150 per tonne

So total cost of wasted materials = 3 tonnes × ($715 + $150) = $2,595

SECTION B

16 C

Total salon hours = 8 × 6 × 50 = 2,400 each year

There are three senior stylists, therefore total hours available = 7,200.

Based on the time taken for each activity, they can perform 7,200 cuts (7,200 hours/1 hour per cut) or 4,800 treatments(7,200 hours/1.5 hours per treatment).

17 Cuts: 1.37

Treatments: 1.58

Cuts

Return per hour = (Selling price – material cost)/time taken on the bottleneck = (60 – 1.50)/1 = 58.50

TPAR = Return per hour/cost per hour = 58.50/42.56 = 1.37 (to 2 decimal places)

Treatments

Return per hour = (Selling price – material cost)/time taken on the bottleneck = (110 – 8.90)/1.5 = 67.40

TPAR Return per hour/cost per hour = 67.40/42.56 = 1.58 (to 2 decimal places)

18 A, C, F

The factors that are included in the TPAR are selling price, material costs, operating expenses and bottleneck time. Increasing the selling price and reducing costs will improve the TPAR.

Increasing the time each service takes on the bottleneck (the senior stylists time) will only reduce the number of services they can provide, so this will not improve throughput.

Throughput accounting does not advocate the building of inventory as it is often used in a just-in-time environment and there no point increasing the activity prior to the bottleneck as it will just create a build-up of work-in-progress. Neither of these will improve the rate of throughput through the process.

19 B

Existing capacity:

	Cut	**Treatment**
Assistants	48,000	16,000
Senior stylists	7,200	4,800
Junior stylists	8,000	9,600

If another senior stylist is employed, this will mean that their available hours will be (4 × 2,400) = 9,600.

This will give them capacity to now do 9,600 cuts (9,600 hours/1 hour per cut) and 6,400 treatments (9,600 hours/1.5 hours per treatment).

As a result, the senior stylists will still be the bottleneck activity for treatments but for cuts the bottleneck will now be the junior stylists as they can only do 8,000 cuts compared to the senior stylists of 9,600.

20 A

The theory of constraints is focused on identifying restrictions in a process and how to manage that restriction (commonly termed a bottleneck).

It is based on the concept of managing throughput, operating expenses and inventory.

It does use a series of focusing steps but is not complete once the bottleneck has been overcome. In fact, it is an ongoing process of improvement, as once the bottleneck has been elevated it is probable that another bottleneck will appear and the process will continue.

It cannot be applied to all limiting factors as some, particularly those external to the organisation, may be out the organisations control.

21 A

Learning curve formula = $y = ax^b$

Cumulative average time per unit for 8 units: $Y = 12 \times 8^{-0.415}$ = 5.0628948 hours.

Therefore cumulative total time for 8 units = 40.503158 hours.

Cumulative average time per unit for 7 units: $Y = 12 \times 7^{-0.415}$ = 5.3513771 hours.

Therefore cumulative total time for 7 units = 37.45964 hours.

Incremental time for 8th unit = 40.503158 hours – 37.45964 hours = 3.043518 hours.

Total labour cost for 8th unit = 3.043518 × S15 = $45.65 (to 2.d.p.)

22 70.00%

$Y = ar^n$ where r = 3 as output has doubled 3 times from the first unit to the 8th.

Y = cumulative average time per unit after 8 units = 34.3/8 = 4.2875

So $4.2875 = 12.5 \times r^3$

$r^3 = 0.343$

r = 0.7 = 70.00%

23 A, C, E

An 80% learning rate means that the learning was faster than expected.

Factors which are present for a learning curve to take effect are a highly manual and repetitive process (so staff can become quicker the more they perform the same series of tasks), no stoppages to production (so the learning rate will not be lost whilst staff are idle) and a stable workforce (so the learning does not have to keep restarting).

It there is high staff turnover, stoppages in production and continual design changes, then the learning rate will not be effective and should be slower.

24 $362,600

As the variable cost per unit is changing depending on the production level, contribution for each level needs to be calculated and then the probabilities applied to the outcomes.

Demand (units)	Contribution per unit	Total Contribution	Probability	Expected budgeted contribution
10,000	17.00	170,000	0.3	51,000
22,000	17.00	374,000	0.5	187,000
35,000	17.80	623,000	0.2	124,600
				362,600

25 TRUE, TRUE, FALSE, FALSE

As marginal costing is based on variable costs it is easier when a readily identifiable variable cost has been established.

The budgeted volume of output does need to be determined for full cost-plus pricing as it would be used to calculate the overhead absorption rate tor the calculation of the full cost per unit.

Cost-plus pricing is internally focused, and a drawback of the technique is that it fails to consider influences, like competitor pricing strategies.

The mark-up percentage does not have to be fixed, it can vary and be adjusted to reflect market conditions.

26 Fabric: $3,500

Wood: $419

Fabric is in regular use, so the replacement cost is the relevant cost

(200m^2 × $17.50) = $3,500

30m^2 of wood will have to be ordered in from the alternative supplier but the remaining 20m^2 which is in inventory and not needed for other work can used and then replaced by an order from the usual suppler.

(30m^2 × $8.50) + (20m^2 × $8.20) = $419

27 Skilled: $1,200

Semi-skilled: $4,200

Skilled labour:

There is no cost for the first 150 hours as there is spare capacity The remaining 50 hours required will paid at time and a half, which is $16 × 1.5 = $24.

50 hours × $24 = $1,200

Skilled labour:

There is no spare capacity so the company will either need to pay overtime or hire in additional staff. The cost of paying overtime would be $18 per hour so it would be cheaper to hire in the additional Staff for $14 per hour.

300 hours × $14 = $4,200

28 $1,050

The electricity costs are incremental as the machine will be used more to produce the new order (500 hours × $1.50) = $750.

The supervisor's salary is not relevant as it is paid anyway. However, the overtime is relevant (20 hours × $15) = $300

Total = $750 + $300 = $1,050

29 B

The general fixed overheads should be excluded as they are not incremental, i.e. they are not arising specifically as a result of this order.

They are not sunk as they are not past costs. This is a common misconception.

30 C, D, F, G

An opportunity cost does represent the cost of the best alternative forgone. However, if it is historic (past) cost it would not be relevant.

Fixed costs can be incremental a decision and in those circumstances would be relevant.

Committed costs ate costs the organisation has already agreed to and can no longer influence and so are not relevant.

Notional costs are used to make cost estimates more realistic. However, they are not real cash flows and are not considered to be relevant.

Avoidable costs are saved if an activity is not undertaken and if this occurs as a result of the decision, then they are relevant.

Common costs are relevant if the whole process is being evaluated. However, they aren't relevant to a further processing decision.

Differential costs relevant in a make or buy decision as the organisation is trying to choose between two options.

SECTION C

31 CARAD CO

(a) (i) Sales price variance and sales volume variance

	Actual price	Standard price	Difference	Actual volume	Sales price variance
	$	$	$		$
Plasma TVs	330	350	–20	750	15,000 A
LCD TVs	290	300	–10	650	6,500 A
					21,500 A

Sales volume contribution variance = (actual sales volume – budgeted sales volume) × standard margin

	Actual sales volume	Budgeted sales volume	Difference	Standard margin	Sales price variance
	$	$	$		$
Plasma TVs	750	590	160	190	30,400 F
LCD TVs	650	590	60	180	10,800 F
	1,400	1,180			41,200 F

(ii) Material price planning and purchasing operational variances

Material planning variance = (original target price – general market price at time of purchase) × quantity purchased

($60 – $85) × 1,400 = $35,000 A

Material price operational variance = (general market price at time of purchase – actual price paid) × quantity purchased

($85 – $80) × 1,400 = $7,000 F

(iii) Labour rate and labour efficiency variances

Labour rate variance = (standard labour rate per hour – actual labour rate per hour) × actual hours worked

Actual hours worked by temporary workers:

Total hours needed if staff were fully efficient = (750 × 2) + (650 × 1.5) = 2,475. Permanent staff provide 2,200 hours, therefore excess = 2,475 – 2,200 = 275. However, temporary workers take twice as long, therefore hours worked = 275 × 2 = 550.

Labour rate variance relates solely to temporary workers; therefore ignore permanent staff in the calculation.

Labour rate variance = ($14 – $18) × 550 = $2,200 A

Labour efficiency variance = (standard labour hours for actual production – actual labour hours worked) × standard rate

(275 – 550) × $14 = $3,850 A

(b) Explanation of planning and operational variances

Before the material price planning and operational variances were calculated, the only information available as regards material purchasing was that there was an adverse material price variance of $28,000. The purchasing department will be assessed on the basis of this variance, yet, on its own, it is not a reliable indicator of the purchasing department's efficiency. The reason it is not a reliable indicator is because market conditions can change, leading to an increase in price, and this change in market conditions is not within the control of the purchasing department.

By analysing the materials price variance further and breaking it down into its two components – planning and operational – the variance actually becomes a more useful assessment tool. The planning variance represents the uncontrollable element and the operational variance represents the controllable element.

The planning variance is really useful for providing feedback on just how skilled management is in estimating future prices. This can be very easy in some businesses and very difficult in others. Giving this detail could help to improve planning and standard setting in the future, as management will be increasingly aware of factors which could create volatility in their forecasts.

The operational variance is more meaningful in that it measures the purchasing department's efficiency given the market conditions which prevailed at the time. As can be seen in Carad, the material price operational variance is favourable which demonstrates that the purchasing department managed to acquire the component which was in short supply at a better price than expected. Without this breakdown in the variance, the purchasing department could have been held accountable for the overall adverse variance which was not indicative of their actual performance. This is then a fairer method of assessing performance and will, in turn, stop staff from becoming demotivated.

Marking scheme

			Marks
(a)	**(i)**	Sales price variance – Plasma	1
		Sales price variance – LCD	1
		Sales volume variance – Plasma	1
		Sales volume variance – LCD	1
	(ii)	Material price planning variance	1
		Material price operating variance	1
	(iii)	Actual hours worked	3
		Labour rate variance	1
		Labour efficiency variance	1
			11
(b)	Controllability		2
	Material price planning		3
	Material price operating		3
	Other – planning/operational		1
			9
Total			**20**

32 THATCHER INTERNATIONAL PARK (TIP)

(a) TIP's financial performance can be assessed in a number of ways:

Sales growth

Sales are up about 1.3% (W1) which is a little above the rate of inflation and therefore a move in the right direction. However, with average admission prices jumping about 8.6% (W2) and numbers of visitors falling, there are clearly problems. Large increases in admission prices reduce the value proposition for the customer, it is unlikely that the rate of increase is sustainable or even justifiable. Indeed with volumes falling (down by 6.7% (W6)), it appears that some customers are being put off and price could be one of the reasons.

Maintenance and repairs

There appears to be a continuing drift away from routine maintenance with management preferring to repair equipment as required. This does not appear to be saving any money as the combined cost of maintenance and repair is higher in 20X5 than in 20X4 (possible risks are dealt with in part (b)).

Directors' pay

Absolute salary levels are up 6.7% (W3), well above the modest inflation rate. It appears that the shareholders are happy with the financial performance of the business and are prepared to reward the directors accordingly. Bonus levels are also well up. It may be that the directors have some form of profit related pay scheme and are being rewarded for the improved profit performance. The directors are likely to be very pleased with the increases to pay.

Wages

Wages are down by 12% (W5). This may partly reflect the loss of customers (down by 6.7% (W6)) if it is assumed that at least part of the wages cost is variable. It could also be that the directors are reducing staff levels beyond the fall in the level of customers to enhance short-term profit and personal bonus. Customer service and indeed safety could be compromised here.

Operating profit

Operating profit is up a huge 31.3% (W7) and most shareholders would be pleased with that. Operating profit is a very traditional measure of performance and most would say this was a sign of good performance.

Return on assets

The profitability can be measured relative to the asset base which is being used to generate it. This is sometimes referred to as ROI or return on investment. The return on assets is up considerably to 11.4% from 8% (W8). This is partly due to the significant rise in profit and partly due to the fall in asset value. We are told that TIP has cut back on new development, so the fall in asset value is probably due to depreciation being charged with little being spent during the year on assets. In this regard it is inevitable that return on assets is up but it is more questionable whether this is a good performance. A theme park (and thrill rides in particular) must be updated to keep customers coming back. The directors of TIP are risking the future of the park.

Workings

(W1) Sales growth is $5,320,000/$5,250,000 = 1.01333 or 1.3%.

(W2) Average admission prices were: 20X4: $5,250,000/150,000 = $35 per person.

20X5: $5,320,000/140,000 = $38 per person An increase of $38/$35 = 1.0857 or 8.57%.

(W3) Directors' pay up by $160,000/$150,000 = 1.0667 or 6.7%.

(W4) Directors' bonuses levels up from $15,000/$150,000 or 10% to $18,000/ $160,000 or 12.5% of turnover. This is an increase of 3/15 or 20%.

(W5) Wages are down by (1 – $2,200,000/$2,500,000) or 12%.

(W6) Loss of customers is (1 – 140,000/150,000) or 6.7%.

(W7) Profits up by $1,372,000/$1,045,000 = 1.3129 or 31.3%.

(W8) Return on assets:

20X4: $1,045,000/$13,000,000 = 1.0803 or 8.03%

20X5: $1,372,000/$12,000,000 = 1.114 or 11.4%

(b) Quality provision

Reliability of the rides

The hours lost has increased significantly. Equally the percentage of capacity lost due to breakdowns is now approaching 17.8% (W9). This would appear to be a very high number of hours lost. This would surely increase the risk that customers are disappointed being unable to ride. Given the fixed admission price system, this is bound to irritate some customers as they have effectively already paid to ride.

Average queuing time

Queuing will be seen by customers as dead time. They may see some waiting as inevitable and hence acceptable. However, TIP should be careful to maintain waiting times at a minimum. An increase of 10 minutes (or 50%) is likely to be noticeable by customers and is unlikely to enhance the quality of the TIP experience for them. The increase in waiting times is probably due to the high number of hours lost due to breakdown with customers being forced to queue for a fewer number of ride options.

Safety

The clear reduction in maintenance could easily damage the safety record of the park and is an obvious quality issue.

Risks

If TIP continues with current policies, then they will expose themselves to the following risks:

- The lack of routine maintenance could easily lead to an accident or injury to a customer. This could lead to compensation being paid or reputational damage.
- Increased competition. The continuous raising of admission prices increases the likelihood of a new competitor entering the market (although there are significant barriers to entry in this market, e.g. capital cost, land and so on).

- Loss of customers. The value for money which customers see when coming to TIP is clearly reducing (higher prices, less reliability of rides and longer queues). Regardless of the existence of competition, customers could simply choose not to come, substituting another leisure activity instead.

- Profit fall. In the end if customers' numbers fall, then so will profit. The shareholders, although well rewarded at the moment, could suffer a loss of dividend. Directors' job security could then be threatened.

Workings:

(W9) Capacity of rides in hours is 360 days × 50 rides × 10 hours per day = 180,000. 20X4 lost capacity is 9,000/180,000 = 0.05 or 5%.

20X5 lost capacity is 32,000/180,000 = 0.177 or 17.8%.

Marking scheme

		Marks
(a)	Sales growth	3
	Maintenance	3
	Directors' pay	2
	Wages	2
	Operating profit	2
	Return on assets	2
		14
(b)	Reliability of rides	2
	Average queuing time	2
	Risks	2
		6
Total		**20**